MW01484766

Palgrave Studies in Economic History is designed to illuminate and enrich our understanding of economies and economic phenomena of the past. The series covers a vast range of topics including financial history, labour history, development economics, commercialisation, urbanisation, industrialisation, modernisation, globalisation, and changes in world economic orders.

Palgrave Studies in Economic History

Series Editor
Kent Deng, London School of Economics, London, UK

Nicola Rossi

Reframing Italian Economic History, 1861–2021

Creative Destruction and the Italian Society

palgrave macmillan

Nicola Rossi ⓘ
Istituto Bruno Leoni
Milan, Italy

ISSN 2662-6497   ISSN 2662-6500 (electronic)
Palgrave Studies in Economic History
ISBN 978-3-031-67270-5   ISBN 978-3-031-67271-2 (eBook)
https://doi.org/10.1007/978-3-031-67271-2

This Palgrave Macmillan imprint is published by the registered company Springer Nature
Switzerland AG
The registered company address is: Gewerbestrasse 11, 6330 Cham, Switzerland

If disposing of this product, please recycle the paper.

As with all miracles that active
and creative freedom lasted very little,
but then it was real,
and you could touch it with your hand,
and see it written on men's faces.

Carlo Levi, L'orologio, *(1950)*

Foreword to Nicola Rossi's Reframing Italian Economic History, 1861–2021

Nicola Rossi's lucid and persuasive book will change the way we tell the economic history of Italy, and of many other places, too. It shows, with solid statistics and a range of cultural and political evidence that Italy broke out of the pack of modern economies only once, in the liberal years of 1947–1964. It was, Rossi shows, neither Keynesian investments nor neo-institutionalist incentives laid on by the state that allowed the Italians to break out. It was liberty.

It was not, however, "freedom" in the strange definition the word has recently acquired in English. Unlike Italian or German, English has for many centuries had of course two words for what has meant since ancient times "not being a slave"—liberty, *libertà*, from Romance and freedom, *Freiheit*, from Germanic. President Lincoln used both words in his Gettysburg Address in 1863, both in the ancient sense of no masters or slaves. By 1941, however, President Roosevelt could speak of "four freedoms." His first was the liberal freedom of speech, which is to say the new liberty of a free person to speak against the master or the government or anybody else. It is Isaih Berlin's "negative" liberty, classical liberalism, the non-slave's autonomy against his master or his state. Its statist opposite is Mussolini's declaration in October 1925, "Everything in the State, nothing outside the State, nothing against the State." The masters are to rule. In keeping with such modern statism, Roosevelt plugged also his third "freedom," "freedom from *want*." It expressed his, often contradictory, attempts during the crisis of the 1930s, largely failed even by

1941, to achieve higher income by public expenditure and regulations and transfers—in parallel with many of Mussolini's policies at the time. In most eras after 1861, in both Italy and the United States, and for that matter in every other modern nation, a masterful state has had the ambition to eliminate want and to achieve prosperity by the top-down policies of *lo Stato*. The result of such state action, largely ineffectual compared with the individual efforts of Italians and Americans, and Italian Americans, was supposed to be Berlin's other, "*positive* liberty," which is to say the income or wealth allowing you to do things. Buying a cappuccino. Driving a Vespa. Getting a state pension. Sending a son to university. The state's apologists claim that, to achieve such positive liberty *directly*, the modern state takes upwards of 50 per cent of the nation's product and spends it on its dear friends. "I'm from the government, and I'm here to help you to positive freedom/liberty."

On English tongues over the past century and a half, in other words, Berlin's two definitions of liberty—the classical liberal one of other humans *not* having physically coercive power over you, and the "new-liberal" one of you achieving a high income, either by liberty or, more and more, by the state—have merged. The merger makes a meaningless tautology out of the classical liberal hypothesis that negative liberty *leads* to positive liberty, to that high income. The hypothesis was in fact confirmed spectacularly after 1776, implementing slowly the liberal promise of a liberty of permission—the unalienable rights to life, liberty and the pursuit of happiness. Modern statism, though, posits that *direct* way to achieve "freedom": take from Peter to pay Paul, tax Milan to subsidise the autostrada to Palermo. Rossi observes that the only time that the Italian state stopped coercing top-down, stopped trying directly to achieve positive freedom, and instead permitted negative liberty to flourish, was precisely the decade and a half of the Italian Miracle. Negative liberty then did lead, indirectly, to the pursuit of happiness—that cappuccino, Vespa and income for education and old age, not to speak of a cultural explosion in film, novel and song, from *Ciao, ciao, bambina, un bacio ancora* to *Via del Campo, c'è una graziosa*.

The economic history of Italy, that "geographical expression," is narrated by Rossi in a manner similar to the standard narrative of the North of Italy compared with the Mezzogiorno, the former Kingdom of Piedmont compared with the former Kingdom of the Two Sicilies Rossi notes of Italian economic growth that it "has moved, at best, at the same pace as its main partners without ever catching up with them or, rather, without ever permanently decreasing the distance that sepa-rated and still separates it from them." If you look at GDP per capita in Italy since 1861 it runs parallel to, say, the UK's for all periods except the years of the Miracle. But with that one exception it never permanently gains ground. Among the modern thoroughbreds in the race of economic growth, Italy seldom gets out of its historical rank. Likewise, the regional GDP of the South of Italy compared with the North is seen as a horserace, inspiring a large literature telling a tragic story of the South. From Carlo Levi's beautifully told memoir in *Christ Stopped in Eboli* (1945) through Edward Banfield's dismal theory in his *The Moral Basis of a Backward Society* (1958) of the South's ineradicable "amoral familism" down to Robert Putnam's *Making Democracy Work: Civic Traditions in Modern Italy* (1993), the claim has been made over and over that the South is hopeless. In aid of such a claim the doubly racist calumny by northern Italians is that "Africa begins south of Rome."

Yet the same has been said of Italy as a whole by Europeans north of the Alps. I was in 1967-68 a research student in London, shortly after the Miracle, and remember vividly the shock to the British ego when at some exchange rates Italian per capita income came to equal the British. The British had long viewed Italy the way the northerners view the Mezzo-giorno, as a nice place to holiday, but pretty hopeless at any serious business.

Yet it is worth noting that running parallel to Britain, or to Piedmont, even if never quite catching up, is a big, big enrichment, part indeed of the Great Enrichment in the world after liberalism. World real income per head has risen during the past two centuries from, well under $5 a day in present-day prices to $50 a day. It has risen, that is, from the present income of South Sudan to that of Brazil. And Italy is much higher. Among the truly big, diverse economies—which leaves out, say, Norway and Monaco—it is in fact now sixth among the 190 nations of the world, at $144 a day per person, slightly below the UK and well above Spain. It seems tasteless, even unethical, to whine and worry about remaining decade after decade in sixth place among the thoroughbreds racing forward when the real problem in the world is the appalling lag of the donkeys, such as South Sudan at $4.40 a day.

Yet the modest gap remains and was definitely closing 1947-1964. In explaining it, Rossi is both wise and original in focusing on attitudes, ethics, ideologies, customs, what in Tocqueville is *moeurs*, his "habits of the mind and heart"—and I would add the habits of the tongue, how we talk to and about each other in the *passeggiata*, at the kitchen table, in our fictions. It's not in the institutions. Institutions matter for the good if the adult and sensible *moeurs* and habits and speech are at work. The big mistake in economic science is to walk by the attitudes and the language, stopping with merely material accounting. It's committed nowadays by all the neo-institutionalists, such as Douglass North, John Wallis, Barry Weingast, Avner Greif, Daron Acemoglu, James Robinson and most economists at the World Bank. The three Soviet constitutions since 1917 were beautiful documents, guaranteeing, for example, the fullest freedom of speech. Lovely. But when a constitution is run by bloodthirsty thugs, you know the outcome. The properly lined-up incentives, the natural advantages, the investments in machines, the good education, the rule of law might some of them, though with substitutions, be necessary for enrichment, and especially for maintaining it once it is achieved. But such quasi-necessary routines were present in many places for millennia. The English king's law of property and contract was pretty much fully developed before the time of Edward I, which is to say 1272, and Roman law was proverbially excellent. The *sufficient* cause of the Great Enrichment after 1776 was the release by liberalism of human creative from its former slavery. It came, that is, from innovation, whether what Rossi calls the "passive innovation" of imitating the frontier or what he especially praises as the "really genuine" innovation of expanding the frontier. Every sentient Italian knows that the nation has an idiotic *governo ladro*, "thief government"—though they keep on voting to give it more powers. Yet Italy nonetheless manages in its cracks of liberty to be creative. Tocqueville wrote in 1835, "Looking at the turn given to the human spirit in England by political life; seeing the Englishman... inspired by the sense that he can do anything... I am in no hurry to inquire whether nature has scooped out ports for him, or given him coal or iron."

Rossi notes that the frantic institutional changes after Unification and then in the past few decades did not result in Italy streaking ahead. Yes, they made Italians uniform in pressure from the state, such as forcing standard Italian on everybody. Yes, they added another layer to governance. But no catching up occurred: Long periods of continuity of institutions led to great variation in results, such as in 1947–1964. Institutions are not where the action is. As Rossi puts it, "Last but not least, the standpoint taken in these pages suggests that rather than the material aspects (the

resorces) or the intangible but formal ones (the structure of the incentives, the nature of the institutions, the configuration of the rules in play)
the aspects that counted in defining the process of the unified nation's
growth were the intangible and mostly informal ones (the values, the
habits, the customs). This, in turn, allows us to believe that the more
strictly economic perspective, though necessary, may be insufficient."

Rossi speaks of internal migration, the young men from Calabria
moving to Turin to work making autos. The economic historian the late
Gianni Toniolo, a native Venetian who taught for a long time in his
hometown, told me that if he went to the train station he would often
be accosted by the guard—who knew him well, of course, from school,
Venice being a small town. "*Ciao*, Gianni. Come here. I can't understand
her at all. I think she's speaking Sicilian." The *mamma* had come up
from Catania to visit her son working in Mestre. Or Germany and other
points north. The Italians, unlike the French, have always been vigorous
migrants.

I first lived in Italy for six months 1959-1960, in the closing years of
the economic miracle. I was 17 years old, monolingual in English—as I
still am, to my shame—and so in Florence my friends a teenager needs so
urgently were the young, English-fluent smugglers of cigarettes gathering
in the coffee shop in the Piazza della República. They all wanted to find
and marry an American woman, which I was not, to transport them to
the United States, where the streets were paved with gold. They were
I believe southerners. That's the internal migration to the North, with
frequent trips back to Sicily to pick up smuggled and untaxed cartons of
Marlboros—heavily taxed when legal to protect the wretched cigarettes
made by the *governo ladro*.

But of course, the even larger migration from the South was seven
or eight decades earlier, to the States and Argentina and everywhere.
They came flooding out from Naples and Messina, Puglia and Abruzzo—
Settembre, andiamo. È tempo di migrare. They were mostly poor and
unskilled, with no English or Spanish, and illiterate in their dialect, not to
speak of standard Italian. And yet they were mad for education and took
full advantage of the liberty of permission they found in the United States,
the UK, Australia, Argentina and even France. They prospered mightily.
People whose last names end in a vowel populate the ruling classes of
their new nations.

The fact strongly supports Rossi's theme that the *moeurs* of which
people talk determine largely what they can accomplish by way of passive

or active innovation. But it tells against the theory my dear friend Joel Mokyr's, following many other economic historians, such as my friendly enemy the late David Landes—that Italians were "growth-averse," as though the aversion was not in their talk but in their blood. As Rossi summarises Mokyr's claim, they were, "unwilling with respect to the relentless effort to improve one's living conditions, to the consequent risk-taking, and to the associated positive predisposition to change." Yet Italians outside Italy dug ditches in the first generation, graduated from secondary school in the next, and from university in the third, meanwhile opening innovative businesses and making innovative art, everywhere.

No, as in many other nations in the modern world of statism, it is not in the blood but in *lo Stato* where one finds "the desire on the part of the ruling classes to make up for the cultural weaknesses of Italians by taking all important decisions off their hands, in a paternalistic attempt to protect them from themselves. The unsurprising result of this was that it further entrenched the Italians' desire for protection and engrained their reluctance to face modernity even more."

The English proverb, doubtless with an Italian parallel, is that when you find yourself in a deep hole the first thing to do is to stop digging. Another is that the definition of insanity is to keep doing a stupid thing and yet believing it will now have a different result. Both proverbs apply to Italy outside its miracle decade and a half and to many other countries, including my own. Industrial policy, for example, the bureaucrats and politicians in Rome or Washington or Brussels choosing winners and subsidising them, as advocated by the Italian-American economist Mariana Mazzucato, is nowadays strongly favoured by the US senators Mario Rizzo from the right and Elizabeth Warren from the left. Both the Maga Republicans and the standard Democrats now favor protective tariffs. Rossi speaks of the Italian habit, which is only a little less strong in the United States, of giving bailouts to failing companies instead of letting creative destruction do its good work. Trial and error creates, as in natural evolution. Every year in the United States fully **30,000** new "consumer packaged goods" are introduced into stores, a small percentage surviving to become standard items in the grocery or hardware store. Most genetic mutations are not adaptive, but without the trial and error, no evolution occurs. Central planning, laying own the future by the exercise of reason, sounds nice and rational, but doesn't in practice make a lot of sense.

A warning, though, about the words. As Pope John Paul II used to say: *La libertà* does not "consist in doing what we like, but in having the right to do what we must." Uh oh. In Italian, as in other Romance languages, the word *dovere* that the Pope deployed is ambiguous among English "must," "have to," and "ought to." German and John Paul's native Polish, like English, do not exhibit this ambiguity. John Paul's Italian was the old theological ruse for resolving the apparent conflict between human liberty and God's omnipotence—Leibnitz' theodicy. In the past few centuries, God has been replaced in many minds by the state. By many on the left and right and centre along the conventional spectrum. The statist, anti-liberty ruse emerged in political thinking in Rousseau's notion that your individual will and la *volonté générale* can magically cohere. French *devoir* and Spanish *deber* also meld the two Germanic words should/must, *sollen/müssen*. Your *libertà*, say the secular authoritarians such as the economist Daron Acemoglu and the religious authoritarians such as the political theorist Patrick Deneen, is to obey—to be coerced into what you must do (*dovere*) by Father State as by Mother Church, in economic or religious policy. Such, they say, is true liberty.

And a warning about the numbers. Would we know about the alleged stagnation if we didn't have the statistics? And are the statistics correct? You hear again and again the claim, for example, that real wages in the United States have not risen since, say, 1974, which is obviously and experientially wrong. The quality of goods and services, among other biases, have risen, making the official deflators for inflation biased against showing progress. People believe all manner of such wrong histories, as Rossi points out repeatedly. His careful use of the statistics is to be admired. But watch out.

In short, Rossi's is a brilliant, pathbreaking book. Whether you are an Italian still voting for bigger government, or merely someone puzzled by the league tables of GDP, read it.

August 2024

Deirdre Nansen McCloskey
Distinguished Scholar, Isaiah
Berlin Chair in Liberal Thought
Cato Institute
Washington, DC, USA

ACKNOWLEDGEMENTS

A great many intellectual debts are contracted when writing of arguments such as the one in these pages, and in most cases, they are so high and long-term as to make repayment highly uncertain. In my case, the greatest intellectual debt has without doubt been matured over the years to Gianni Toniolo—a dear friend more than a colleague and one to whom I owed (and owe) my taste for reading economic events through the lens of history. Over the years this taste has transformed itself into the conviction that without wearing such spectacles an economist's life is much more complicated as well as much less fun. These pages—for which only I am responsible of course—were largely completed before his sudden death and benefited from his first comments and observations. They—and I personally—will miss the content and outcome of the in-depth discussions that we had promised to ourselves that we would soon carry out. I also owe particular thanks to Giovanni Vecchi—much more a dear friend than a capable student—who, not by chance I believe—decided to become an economic historian. Many of the topics discussed below are also the outcome of countless economic-gastronomic appointments (pandemic permitting, obviously) and many of the passages that follow benefited from his comments, and not marginally. Thanks, are also due to those who had the patience to read, comment on—sometimes even twice!—and indisputably improve these pages at various moments as they were being drafted: Carlo Bellavite Pellegrini, Michele Boldrin, Francesca Cassano, Sabino Cassese, Natale D'Amico, Michele Grillo, Deirdre McCloskey,

Alberto Mingardi, Luigi Paganetto, Serena Sileoni, Carlo Stagnaro, Vito Tanzi, Ignazio Visco. Last but not least, I would like to thank the Istituto Bruno Leoni—which, once again, revealed itself to be an ideal intellectual location for anyone who wishes to carry out research, freely (and how could it be otherwise?)—and, in particular, its President, Franco Debenedetti, its Director, Alberto Mingardi, and all those who animate it daily, from Serena Sileoni to Carlo Stagnaro, from Carlo Amenta to Carlo Lottieri, from Filippo Cavazzoni to Vera Costantino, from Sara Scordari to David Perazzoni, from Veronica Cancelliere to Francesco Catalfamo.

I would also like to thank Claire Giordano and Francesco Zollino for providing me with access to the data on the total factor productivity referred to in their work; Federico Barbiellini Amidei, Corrado Bonifazi and Frank Heins for having done the same, respectively, with reference to the data on patents and to the quantitative information on internal migration. Their collaboration went well beyond the access to the data and also extended to quite a few exchanges relating to the quantitative information referred to above and to updates of them in more recent years. I am grateful for this too just as I am grateful to Luca Alzona, Piero Bini, Michela Cimatoribus and Carlo Stagnaro for useful information on the subject of business bailouts, as well as to Angelo Pace and Silvana Bartoletto for precious information on the evolution of Italian public debt and, more in general, on Italian public finances, and to Antonio Gibelli for some valuable information about the attitude of Italian emigrants. I would furthermore like to thank the staff of Biblioteca Baffi of the Bank of Italy and of the Central Legal Library of the Ministry of Justice as well as the staff of the Historical Archives of the Assonime (the Association of Italian Joint Stock Companies), of Barilla, of the Bank of Italy, of ENI and of Unicredit for their kind availability and competent collaboration. Thanks are due, in particular, to Roberto Pagliari (Barilla Historical Archive) for providing the cover image.

The exhausting research into businesses births and deaths—begun in far-off 2017—availed in the first place of the knowledge and competence of Stefano Chianese to whom I am grateful for his crucial collaboration both in the archival research phase and, later, in the subsequent processing of the elementary information; thanks also for their effective collaboration to the staff of the Chambers of Commerce of Milan-Brianza (Gianfranco Vanzelli), of Rome (Barbara Cavalli) and of Turin (Claudio Savio) and, in particular, to the personnel in charge of managing the Historical Archives of the same Chambers. In Milan Cristina Trudu, in Rome Silvana Forte, Luca Vallocchia and Marco Esposito, in Turin Giuseppe Galliano. The collaboration of Donato Iacobucci was essential in establishing a very positive relationship with the Ancona Chamber of Commerce. Thanks to all of these for their much-appreciated collaboration and great helpfulness. Over the years, the digitalisation and transcription of the basic information drawn from to the historical archives of the four Chambers of Commerce also involved a large group of young people at different times and ways and, in particular, Claudio Bianchi, Claudio Braghiroli, Francesco Brunetti, Maria Giulia Cassinis, Andrea Celico, Alessandro Costa, Francesco Diana, Michela Di Santo, Alessandro Fratarcangeli, Cristiano Giordano, Davide Giovannetti, Valeria Giuliani, Mariantonietta Iannella, Roberto Leoni, Alessandro Lombardi, Davide Lombardi, Alessio Loretucci, Ludovic Marchionni, Lorenzo Matta, Michela Mauloni, Iacopo Monterosa, Francesca Ocello, John Paton, Roberto Petrucci, Valerio Podrini, Zakhar Podvirnyy, Matteo Quattrini, Elena Stella, Sonia Vecchi, Alberto Volpiani and Sara Zippari. My thanks to all of these, thanks that are also extended to Adriano Guzzi for his assistance when drafting the paragraph on internal mobility.

The research described in these pages, promoted and supported by the Istituto Bruno Leoni, would not have been possible without the generous personal contribution of Gianfelice Rocca and without the financial support of the Cariplo Foundation, the Compagnia di San Paolo Foundation, the Aristide Merloni Foundation, the Pirelli Foundation, the Atlas Network, the General Federation of Italian Commerce and Tourism (Confcommercio), the General Federation of Italian Artisans and Craftsmen (Confartigianato), Net Insurance SpA. To all of them go the most grateful thanks of the Istituto Bruno Leoni and mine personally.

Furthermore, I would like to give thanks to the participants in the "Eternal City Economic History Workshop «Stefano Fenoaltea»" (ECEHW) seminar and to the 8th ASE Annual Meeting and in particular to Federico Barbiellini Amidei, Giacomo Gabbuti and Fabio Lavista as well as to the participants in the RSE/IREH Fast Track Meeting and, in particular, to Andrea Colli, Alessandro Nuvolari and Michelangelo Vasta. Their comments turned out to be accurate and useful.

Of course, there can be no book without its editor. At Palgrave Macmillan, Ellie Duncan guided the book through the editorial process while Aishwarya Balachandar coordinated the project. Their collaboration was very much appreciated.

The responsibility for what follows obviously lies with the author and not with the individuals or institutions mentioned above nor does it involve the Institution to which the author belongs.

Finally, no amount of thanks could repay those who are closest to me for the time I took from them. I hope that my being conscious of it may be deemed to mitigate. The addressees of these pages can only be Benedetto and Ottaviano.

Praise for *Reframing Italian Economic History, 1861–2021*

"A book that combines economic and social history, bringing together indicators of various kinds, literary, linguistic and cultural into a comparative design, to arrive at a diachronic synthesis. This book captures the essence of the Italian history since unification, evaluates successes and failures of Italian economy, will likely influence public debate on Italian politics and deserves a place of honour in the discourse on the role of Italy in the European Union."

—Sabino Cassese, *Justice Emeritus of the Italian Constitutional Court and former Minister for Public Administration*

"In this hugely important study, Nicola Rossi describes the contrast between the behaviour of the Italian economy and society in the epoch of the 'economic miracle,' the years which came before and those which followed. A must read."

—Edmund Phelps, *2006 Nobel Laureate*

"Nicola Rossi rereads the history of Italian economic development on the basis of an unusually rich set of elementary data on business demographics and innovative activity. However controversial his findings may be, this attempt to identify the deep-seated factors that have limited innovation and creative destruction leads to a must-read for economic historians (not only Italian) and policy makers."

—Ignazio Visco, *Governor Emeritus of the Bank of Italy*

CONTENTS

About the Author

Nicola Rossi holds a Ph.D. in Economics from the London School of Economics and is a former full professor of Economics at the University of Rome "Tor Vergata". Throughout his career he has been moving back and forth from the academic world (University of Venice "Ca' Foscari" from 1988 to 1990, University of Modena from 1990 to 1993) to the world of economic institutions (the Bank of Italy from 1977 to 1980 and the International Monetary Fund from 1986 to 1987) and the realm of politics (as economic advisor to the Italian prime Minister from 1998 to 2000, as Member of Parliament from 2001 to 2008 and, finally, as member of the Italian Senate from 2008 to 2013). A past President of the Istituto Bruno Leoni, he is now a member of its board. His keen appreciation of the importance of ideas in shaping political decision-making lies behind his decades-long contribution to the Italian public debate. He has published extensively in Italy and abroad on econometric modelling, theory and measurement of consumer behaviour, design and evaluation of social policies, Italian economic history. The last topic is his main current research interest.

Abbreviations

ASBI	Archivio Storico Banca d'Italia
Assonime	Associazione fra le Società Italiane per Azioni
CCIAA	Camere di Commercio, Industria, Artigianato e Agricoltura
CDP	Cassa Depositi e Prestiti
CSVI	Consorzio Sovvenzioni Valori Industriali
EAGAT	Ente Autonomo Gestione Aziende Termali
EFIM	Ente Partecipazioni e Finanziamenti Industria Manifatturiera
EGAM	Ente Gestione Attività Mineraria
ENEL	Ente Nazionale Energia Elettrica
ENI	Ente Nazionale Idrocarburi
EPO	European Patent Office
FIM	Fondo per il Finanziamento dell'Industria Meccanica
FinTecna	Finanziaria per i Settori Industriale e dei Servizi
GePI	Gestione Partecipazioni Industriali
IL	Istituto di Liquidazioni
IMI	Istituto Mobiliare Italiano
Invimit	Investimenti Immobiliari Italiani
IRI	Istituto per la Ricostruzione Industriale
ISA	Istituto Sviluppo Agroalimentare
ISAP	Istituto per lo Sviluppo delle Attività Produttive
ItaInvest	Italia Investimenti
Lanerossi	Lanifici Rossi
OECD	Organization for Economic Co-operation and Development
REL	Ristrutturazione Elettronica
SACE	Servizi Assicurativi del Commercio Estero

SME   Società Meridionale Finanziaria (formerly Società Meridionale di Elettricità)
SPI   Promozione e Sviluppo Industriale
STM   SGS-Thomson Microelectronics
Terni   Società degli altiforni, fonderie e acciaierie di Terni
UIBM   Ufficio Italiano Brevetti e Marchi
USPTO   United States Patent and Trademark Office

LIST OF FIGURES

LIST OF TABLES

CHAPTER 1

Introduction

Italy is going, once again, through a delicate phase in its life. The disappointing decades-old trend in productivity and the fragile condition of public finances are squeezing the Italian economy in a vice, forcing it along a path marked by a disappointing growth rate, enduring instability and creeping economic and social backwardness. Nor, from this standpoint, should the ephemeral jolts of vitality that occasionally occur mislead us. At the time these pages were being written, Italy's per capita product in real terms—uniquely among the large European economies—was still below the level of the years preceding the Great Recession.

These discouraging trends should come as no surprise. Contrary to what is often imagined, since the beginning of its unified history Italy has moved, at best, at the same pace as its main partners without ever catching up with them or, rather, without ever permanently decreasing the distance that separated and still separates it from them. With one exception: the fifteen-to-twenty years immediately following the Second World War. Not coincidentally this period is known as "the economic miracle" and unified Italy's entire catch-up experience is concentrated in it.

The argument advanced in these pages is that the contrast between the behaviour of the Italian economy and society in the years of the "economic miracle" on the one hand and, on the other hand, the performance recorded both during the preceding eighty years and in the sixty years that

© The Author(s), under exclusive license to Springer Nature
Switzerland AG 2024
N. Rossi, *Reframing Italian Economic History, 1861–2021*, Palgrave
Studies in Economic History,
https://doi.org/10.1007/978-3-031-67271-2_1

followed contains valuable information for arriving at a different reading of the development of the Italian economy after unification. In turn, we suggest that this evolution—with the significant exception of the years 1947–1964—can better be understood as the outcome of the combination of two factors. First of all, a culture, often widespread among large parts of the public, that—to paraphrase Joel Mokyr (2016)—we could define as growth-averse: unwilling with respect to the relentless effort to improve one's living conditions, to the consequent risk-taking, and to the associated positive predisposition to change. And, secondly, the desire on the part of the ruling classes to make up for the cultural weaknesses of Italians by taking all important decisions off their hands, in a paternalistic attempt to protect them from themselves. The unsurprising result of this was that it further entrenched the Italians' desire for protection and engrained their reluctance to face modernity even more. Conversely, the years between 1947 and 1964 are the only ones in the course of Italy's economic history as a unified nation in which—thanks in part to contemporary events—the ruling classes were driven by the conviction that Italy could only rise again from the rubble into which fascism and the war had plunged it by leveraging the entrepreneurial spirit of the Italians and their determination to redeem themselves. And an essential ingredient of this recipe was the need to restore to the Italian people their full freedom to express themselves, to try and to succeed or fail. Freedom that most Italians did not hesitate to make their own. Hence began a brief season of "innovism" à la McCloskey (2016) or grassroots innovation à la Phelps (2013) that allowed Italy to become, temporarily, a leading Western economy.

Although we would refrain from suggesting that the proposition put forward in these pages will be "proven" beyond reasonable doubt, the rationale of this work is to gather as much evidence as possible from different sources so as to offer a reasonably straightforward reading and to enable a specific re-enactment of the events. The evidence collected here is different from the material, mainly macroeconomic in nature, that has mostly accompanied the narrative of Italian economic history up to now (see Toniolo [2013], for example) and can offer insights into the configuration of hitherto more or less unexplored terrains. We will therefore proceed in steps backwards, starting from the usual international comparison of the trends of the most immediate indicator of well-being—i.e., the per capita gross domestic product—to point out how, contrary to what is often thought, the Italian run up with respect to the main Western countries was concentrated in the two decades immediately following the Second World War, without extending very much to the preceding decades as to the following decades. Taking a first step back, we will see this trend in the component that is often considered the most enigmatic of the dynamics of gross domestic product, namely total factor productivity. From the international comparison of trends in total factor productivity—and building on the work of Aghion et al. (2014)—we will try, firstly, to extract information about the relative weight, as regards Italy and at different points in time, of both imitation (or passive innovation) and really genuine innovation. A further step back will allow us to try to look inside the black box of total factor productivity by bringing together this last piece of information and the data for patenting activity. Here we will find further confirmation of the well-known contention that innovative activity was low throughout the entire history of unified Italy—with the sole exception of the immediate post-Second World War period.

Taking a further logical step backwards, we will seek further confirmation of our working hypothesis by reconstructing, starting from the 1920s, the trend of the degree of "creative destruction" present in the Italian society. This is the first century-long reconstruction of the phenomenon to date, and not only Italian. It is the result of several years of "digging" into the evidence contained in the historical archives of the most relevant Italian Chambers of Commerce and of analysing an impressive mass of elementary information on business demography. We will observe the neat correlation of these indicators with the already mentioned indicators of the evolution of patenting activity and of total factor productivity: as well as—it is hardly necessary to underline it—with the demographic trends which, in the last thirty years, although global, appear to be more pronounced in Italy than elsewhere. With this—in addition to contributing to enriching the broad framework of knowledge recently summarised in Aghion et al. (2021)—we will establish a link between the processes of growth and the opening of society—to various degrees at different moments—towards the ceaseless process which in modern market economies leads to the arrival of new goods, to the identification of new production processes, to the opening of new markets and to the appearance of new firms and the disappearance of others.

At this point, a further step backwards will seem inevitable, aimed at indirectly identifying the contours of the determinants of the social attitudes prevailing from time to time beyond the usual reference to institutional architectures and their evolutions. We will, in other words, try to describe and possibly quantify a few economic-social phenomena that can provide evidence of the circumspect and cautious—if not reluctant—attitude of Italians with respect to the nature of market economies, namely the ever-present process of "reshuffling" from which winners and losers, opportunities and failures, emerge seamlessly. First of all, we will focus our attention on the processes of internal mobility experienced in the country's unified history and the reasons for them, and in order to underline the specific nature, scale and quality of the large flows of internal migration recorded in the period after the Second World War. We will then closely examine the frequency and extent of the bailouts of financial and non-financial firms that have regularly (or almost regularly) peppered Italy's history, offering the first reconstruction to date of the phenomenon over the entire span of the last one hundred and sixty years. Finally, the trends in public finances from Unification on will provide further and significant information on the evolution of the relationship between citizens and the State.

Furnished with this corpus of information, which is brand new to some extent, as we have seen, we will then be able to reconsider the economic aspects of the Italian history since unification and strive, for example, to provide answers to a number of unresolved questions. Why was it that the institutional reform effort during the years following Unification—unprecedented in its intensity—did not translate into sustained rates of growth? And why has the same phenomenon seemed to have occurred in the last three decades? How is it possible that—as was the case in post-unification Italy—disappointing economic performances were associated with significant improvements in the dimensions of well-being that were not strictly economic? How is it possible that the often-remembered relative institutional continuity between the years before and after the Second World War was associated with such radically different economic performances? What lies behind Italy's persistent territorial dualism?

Reviewing Italy's post-1861 economic history will allow us, finally, to suggest and emphasise the fruitfulness of a different standpoint, allowing a consistent reading of Italian economic history and helping us to understand not only the past but, if possible, the present too (and perhaps even the near future), so that we do not trek again along the paths already beaten in the past (as is quite likely and perhaps already happening) with consistently disappointing results.

These are paths that have repeatedly led us to look outside ourselves—to ascertain the lack of raw materials or physical capital, to complain about the quantitative and qualitative insufficiency of human capital, to denounce the inadequacy of our institutions. Factual elements largely irrefutable but—this is the message of these pages—probably not decisive. Indeed, it is inside and not outside us that we should look. In the course of their life since Unification—and, in all probability, even before it—the Italians have maintained an attitude mainly of caution if not outright distrust towards economic freedoms. The belief was that the dangers implicit in "being or not being chosen" and, therefore, in surviving (or not) the assessments of the market were largely greater than the risks deriving from a limited freedom to "choose", i.e., from restrained or manipulated functioning of the markets themselves. This attitude was comforted, indeed strengthened, by the complementary attitude of the Italian ruling classes who have translated their deep-rooted negative judgement of the Italians into the daily tendency to replace them and to do so by restraining, limiting or in any case controlling the functioning of the markets. Obviously there has been no lack of calls for greater economic freedom in every phase of Italian unitary economic history, nor within the ranks of the ruling class has there been an absence of warnings relating to the implications of significant limitations of the same, but these—for various reasons—have never or almost never been strong enough to impose themselves and to become a rooted, persistent and shared feature of the national culture. At various times the fundamental nature of political freedoms has imposed itself in the collective imagination and, more recently, civil liberties have been making headway. But never—with the only partial exception of the twenty years immediately following the second postwar period—have Italians looked at economic freedoms as a determining element of their identity.

All of this—although obviously not exclusively—has had significant consequences for the ability of the Italian economy to move the frontier of its production possibilities forward, more than and differently from what others had done or were doing. The result is that today's Italy—as it also was yesterday's—is a copybook example of an economy whose growth capacity was and still is closely linked to whatever the economic freedoms elsewhere in the world are able to express. The postwar twenty years reveal that the fate of the follower is not written in stone but for this to be the case, the starting point must be clear to all of us.

Last but not least, the standpoint taken in these pages suggests that rather than the material aspects (the resources) or the intangible but formal ones (the structure of the incentives, the nature of the institutions, the configuration of the rules in play) the aspects that counted in defining the process of the unified nation's growth were the intangible and mostly informal ones (the values, the habits, the customs). This, in turn, allows us to believe that the more strictly economic perspective, though necessary, may be insufficient. The hope is that these pages will not only trigger further investigation and completion but also integration in various directions, and that jurists, historians of political thought and historians of Italian culture find the stimulus in these pages for future research.

A word of caution: in an attempt to render the pages that follow more readable even to a public that is not composed exclusively of "insiders", the more technical aspects have been confined to the appendices as far as possible. We cannot say that the attempt has been successful but, if it is even partly so and whatever the degree of agreement with the arguments put forward in them, these pages will have achieved their main aim: contribute, even if only minimally, towards making us all aware of the nature and scale of the challenges that the country is facing.

REFERENCES

Aghion, P., Akcigit, U., & Howitt, P. (2014). What Do We Learn from Schumpeterian Growth Theory? In P. Aghion & S. Durlauf (Eds.), *Handbook of Economic Growth* (Vol. 2, pp. 515–563). Elsevier.

Aghion, P., Antonin, C., & Bunel, S. (2021). *The Power of Creative Destruction*. Harvard University Press.

McCloskey, D. (2016). *Bourgeois Equality*. The University of Chicago Press.

Mokyr, J. (2016). *A Culture of Growth*. Princeton University Press.

Phelps, E. (2013). *Mass Flourishing. How Grassroots Innovation Created Jobs, Challenge and Change*. Princeton University Press.

Toniolo, G. (2013). An Overview of Italy's Economic Growth. In G. Toniolo (Ed.), *The Oxford Handbook of the Italian Economy Since Unification* (pp. 3–36). Oxford University Press.

PART I

Italian Business Dynamism

CHAPTER 2

A Different Perspective

THE *SOUFFLÉ*

It was more than legitimate to expect that the celebration of the 150th anniversary—now over a decade ago—would have provided us with an unambiguous reading of the economic vicissitudes of unified Italy. Aside from the significance of the event, such an expectation was suggested by the wide-ranging preparatory work that the institutions (above all the Bank of Italy and ISTAT, the Italian statistical office) had dedicated to it. At a distance of more than ten years from that anniversary it would seem that things did not turn out quite like that and, far from converging, opinions on the evolution of the Italian economy from Unity onwards have apparently moved apart over time.

On the one hand, in fact, a reading has been made of the first hundred and fifty years of the history of unified Italy that is not without elements of concern but is nevertheless fundamentally positive, and the most authoritative and reasoned expression of this is undoubtedly the one attributed to Gianni Toniolo (2013, p. 5): "framed in a standard convergence narrative, Italy's economic history from 1861 to 2011 is characterised by a central period of about a century (mid-1890s to early 1990s) of robust catch-up, framed between two «tails» of sluggish growth (1861–1896 and 1992–2011) when the country lost ground to the productivity leaders".

N. Rossi, *Reframing Italian Economic History, 1861–2021*, Palgrave Studies in Economic History,
https://doi.org/10.1007/978-3-031-67271-2_2

On the other hand, Emanuele Felice (2017, pp. 25 and 32) did not hesitate to define the growth process of unified Italy as a "suboptimal trajectory", and underlined that "in relative terms in one hundred and fifty years Italy had underperformed all its main European competitors" so that, as Paolo Di Martino and Michelangelo Vasta (2017a, p. 10) add— "by continuing to follow suboptimal paths, Italy risks distancing itself definitively from the condition of prosperity that had been achieved with such fatigue". A decisively gloomier description than the previous one.

If a little humour is allowed, downstream from the 2011 appointment, the depiction of Italy's economic performance from Unification to the present day somewhat recalls a soufflé: turgid and swollen when it emerges from the oven and then sometimes collapsing on itself until it deflates completely in just a few minutes (or years in our case). The metaphor apart, over time the success story—enclosed in two periods of time marked by challenges and hardships but, at the same time, far from devoid of glory days allowing those difficulties to be overcome[1]—ended up being flanked if not replaced by an essentially deluding history in which Italy would never have been able to fully express its growth potential (if there was one). Two images that, obviously, could never be more different, but which can basically be traced back to the same *primum movens*: the institutions (however defined). Without with this wanting to underestimate the importance of their work, Emanuele Felice (2015) or also Paolo Di Martino and Michelangelo Vasta (2017b) in fact, put Daron Acemoglu and James Robinson in the places of Douglas North and Mancur Olson who had been evoked in Gianni Toniolo's account, and replaced the "distributive coalitions" with the "extractive institutions",[2] focussing attention anyway on different representations of the rent extraction process.

There is no shortage of elements that support the thesis which we shall refer to as "convergence and two tails". The very pages of Toniolo's aforementioned work—and the entire research activity of which Toniolo (2013) constitutes the premise and the synthesis—are full of references that would appear to back it beyond any reasonable doubt. During the thirty-five years following historic 1861, the positive impact of unification

---

[1] "Italy, however, is not unable to change particularly when cornered by serious crises" (Toniolo, 2013, p. 35).

[2] The former are explicitly recalled, for example, in Rossi and Toniolo (1994, p. 43).

on the growth potential of the newborn unified state did not materialise as a result of the inevitable delays that had occurred both in the creation of a unified market and in the realisation of the necessary institutional infrastructure. Instead, during the twenty years straddling the twentieth and twenty-first centuries the country's reduced capacity for growth was induced by the definitive obsolescence of what was already in itself the country's insufficient institutional architecture. Between these two periods came the season of the convergence: the pursuit crowned by success of the most advanced economies. A rare combination of growth and distributive fairness.

The great merit of the "convergence and two tails" narrative is that it supersedes the traditional reading "in periods" of the Italian story since Unification and places its individual aspects into a coherent framework. No longer, therefore, liberal Italy or fascist Italy, the boom years and subsequent stagnation, but rather a difficult start, a long march towards convergence and the subsequent "institutional fatigue". Within this, furthermore, it is easy to place interpretative hypotheses that, while highlighting different causal links from time to time, are only apparently far apart. For example, if appropriate account is taken of the time intervals considered by the individual authors, the decisively optimistic depictions by Vera Zamagni (1993) and by Jon Cohen and Giovanni Federico (2001)—the former that describes the Italian economy's convergence process as a "passage from the periphery to the centre" and the latter that explicitly speaks of "a considerable success"—are not in the end so distant from that of Gianni Toniolo. Just as Pierluigi Ciocca's unquestionably more doubtful reconstruction (2020) is not either.[3] And, finally, as explicitly admitted by the authors, the narrative from Lorenzo Codogno and Giampaolo Galli (2022), though limited to the period after the Second World War, is also similar to that of Gianni Toniolo from many points of view.[4]

---

[3] In Vera Zamagni's case, the analysis covers the period 1861–1990, while Jon Cohen and Giovanni Federico stop in 1960. Pierluigi Ciocca on the other hand also properly covers the pre-unity decades (starting from 1796).

[4] This is not the case of Rolf Petri's narrative (2002). While agreeing with the idea that for Italy it is necessary to "speak of outright success", he sees in the period that runs from the 1920s to the 1960s "a national project of economic development [...] shared from time to time, and with different accents and formulations, by all the political regimes seen at work during the period of observation and, probably, by a majority part of the Italians" (Petri, 2002, p. 357). In many ways this is a very different thesis compared to

It should be recognised, though, that the wealth of arguments under-lying the "convergence and two tails" narrative is not sufficient for dissipating all remaining doubts. A perusal of the quantitative informa-tion made available following the research activity carried out on the occasion of the 150th anniversary does not always and in any case seem compatible with the "convergence and two tails" tale. It is no coincidence that rather than talking about a success story book-ended between two difficult moments in his *Ascesa e declino* ("Rise and fall", 2015) Emanuele Felice talks about an initially gradual growth process that then became impetuous after the Second World War, followed by a period of increasingly evident (relative) decline.[5] This parabola, more-over, as we have seen, gradually flattens in Emanuele Felice (2017) until it completely stops being one altogether and becomes a horizontal straight line interrupted in at least a couple of periods by sporadic and random positive episodes. Isolated growth periods that, according to Paolo Di Martino and Michelangelo Vasta (2017a, pp. 15–16) can be attributed to "fortuitous and limited circumstances" (implying that the Italians only became "rich by chance") and "scarred", always and in any case, by widespread institutional shortcomings that would "reduce the coun-try's ability to consolidate its growth processes, align with the frontier of global technology and converge with the leading countries". An evolution dominated, essentially, by an inescapable persistent factor:

> from unification Italy was never really a leader nor had it really worked at the technological cutting edge; instead, during the course of its history it was constantly having to adapt to international trends and exogenous shocks.

the literature just referred to and also to the reading that we will be proposing—of which further on.

[5] "After a tough start, the new state nevertheless launched a process of industrialisation and modernisation that was able to achieve notable successes and which in the span of a century, made it into one of the major capitalist powers in the world ... But for about twenty years this virtuous mechanism has jammed ... It is this, in short, that is the story that we are about to trace" (Felice, 2015, pp. 53–54). This chronicle is not so different from the one explicitly prefigured by Emanuele Felice and Giovanni Vecchi (2015, p. 508): "... after an impressive revival, which took place mostly during the second half of the twentieth century, Italy managed to reach the «centre» of the world economy ... In the recent past, however, Italy's economic performance has been disappointing, by any standards ... most socioeconomic indicators reveal the country to be sliding down the charts".

And adapt badly, they add, for an underlying reason already seen: the Italian economy was the victim of extremely inertial institutions that were refractory to change. In essence, therefore, apparently very different readings of the Italian economic history have been starting from the same point even if they arrive at rather different conclusions: leveraging on persistence much more than on discontinuities and, even less, on the differential information contained in the latter with respect to the former.

The continuity—or, rather, the repeated overlapping of institutional architectures—and, conversely, the essentially epidermic (but not for this reason less eloquent) nature of the institutional breaks are now widely recognised as bearing elements of the history of the Italian state.[6] With great clarity and from the standpoint of a jurist Sabino Cassese (2014, pp. 37–38) has traced the role of the persistent factors and of the discontinuities on the history of unified Italy:

> The main institutions of the present state almost all date back to the years of its foundation if not even earlier [...]. The same can be said of many laws [...] The story is the same for the legislative and administrative conventions, traditions, customs and practices. However, this continuity is not absolute, but relative. It regards some of the "layers" the state is composed of. Indeed, it can be said that the layers almost have a life of their own, with different cycles, and therefore are overlaid in a disordered manner leading to a weak legality. Liberal-authoritarian institutions continued during the fascist era [...], fascist regulations lasted at length in the Republican age [...]. Therefore, there are no real breaks. Where there are, we have the reappearance after decades of original features in accordance with the atavistic model.

All of which makes it possible to imagine that it is when we are looking at the breaks that we can also correctly read the continuities. That the question is not an idle one—that the persistence in the Italian case can at least partly be as enlightening as the discontinuities and that the latter help to understand the former—is also suggested by some historians, one for all being Roberto Vivarelli (2013). According to him, in another reading, Italian history since Unification would seem rather to be characterised by

---

[6] For all, see Cassese (2014) but also Tedoldi (2018) and the extensive literature listed in them. Similarly, the persistence of the "administrative question" still puzzles historians of the Italian public administration (Melis, 2020). It is interesting to note that the topic attracts much less attention from economic historians.

a relative uniformity of behaviour during the entire century and a half analysed with the sole "exception" of the twenty years after the Second World War, the period that is not without reason called the "economic miracle". In Vivarelli's reading, the foundations of this fundamentally homogeneous reading of the Italian economic history can be traced to the prevalent decisions taken only one decade after Unity. Decisions that would have created an environment hostile to growth, an environment that would only be attacked by the "economic miracle" and whose characteristics were destined to re-emerge domineeringly from the 1970s right up to the present day. As popular wisdom would have it, "one miracle does not make a saint" and the twenty years after the Second World War would remain an exceptional event in Italy's economic history. An event, moreover, that the necessarily limited nature of human memory would transform into something permanent (or, at least, potentially such). This is a thesis to which we will return a few lines further on.

The need to take persistence properly into account as well as the discontinuity is implicit in Toniolo's narrative too, where the nature— deep-rooted over time—of the deficiencies in the Italian institutional architecture cannot be but recognised but, at the same time, it becomes impossible to avoid asking how and why age-old institutional shortcomings only manifested themselves in negative terms at the end of the twentieth century. The transformed international context and the success of the convergence process itself thereby become factors that highlight an institutional environment that is inadequate per se. It is an argument that is suggestive and probably not groundless (exemplary is Toniolo's reference to the case of education) but is it enough? Does it let us understand the evolution of north-south dualism, just to pick one example? Evolution that all things considered was relatively constant over the years with the single important exception, of course, of the period after the Second World War.[7]

At the same time, referring to the institutions (in the broadest sense of the term) in order to interpret every stage and every aspect of Italy's economic development—whatever these may be—gives rise to a compelling narrative at times but which sometimes appears to be hard for its own proponents to sustain. For example, Emanuele Felice (2017,

---

[7] Which is perhaps a reason, in one way, for the more nuanced reading of the events to be found in Rossi et al. (2011) or the even less marked reading found in Toniolo (2022, pp. 100–101).

p. 25) underlines how the far from positive assessment implicit in the "suboptimal trajectory" hypothesis "is in large part fruit of the decline experienced by the last generation: twenty-five years ago, the assessment would have been much more favourable". Which, as we can understand, it is a bit puzzling: Did the prevalently "extractive" profile of the Italian institutions that are supposed to have been present right from Unification emerge only in the last quarter of a century? More in general, what leaves us perplexed—and which leaves us with the feeling of being faced with an "unfalsifiable" interpretative hypothesis—is not so much the unavoidable amplitude of the concept of "socio-institutional arrangement" (which would include [Felice 2017, p. 60] the social structure, the political, economic and the social institutions as well as the formal and informal rules that permit its operation and that inevitably end up mixed in with the values, the social norms and the cultural traditions of a community) but rather the tendency to throw light case by case on different aspects of the same rather than instead fully exploiting the informative content contained specifically in the divergence which manifests itself from time to time between the rules of the game and the customs of a community.

One example can help to clarify the point. That the Second World War did not constitute the sharp break that, according to some, it would have been legitimate to expect, is—as we have seen—something that is well-known and noted by Emanuele Felice (2017, p. 41) in a few, meaningful words: "at the time [during the years between the two wars] significant changes were produced on the institutional side that would accompany the years of the economic miracle". These institutions were similar in many ways, therefore, if not in some cases identical before and after the Second World War, but—quite clearly—profoundly different turned out to be the results. Which, in turn, end up being accommodated by adapting the socio-institutional structures to them. So that in Emanuele Felice's reading (2017, p. 62) socio-institutional structures passed from being "extractive" to becoming "inclusive" while having remained, in essence, the same to a far from negligible extent, as has been said. In the interpretation of Paolo Di Martino and Michelangelo Vasta (2017b, pp. 241–242) on the other hand, the operation of relatively unchanged socio-institutional structures became, before the Second World War, distorted by the "cognitive deficit of the rulers" and, afterwards, by the "burden of established interests". It is certainly possible that things actually went that way and that as Pierluigi Ciocca and Gianni

Toniolo (1998, p. XV) have said, the issue of the "decline of the economic institutions, of their life cycle, and of the reasons that allowed them to outlive themselves" is a subject that is still open and worthy of investigation, but it is also possible—as we will attempt to suggest and as seems not to be so easy to exclude—that instead there are other important persistent elements in the Italian case, elements that can be illuminated specifically by the events after the Second World War.

If the hypothesis of the "suboptimal trajectory" is then put face to face with the data, it reveals some unquestionable signs of fragility. If we consider the hundred and sixty years as a whole (Table 2.1, column [a]),[8] the growth rate of the Italian gross domestic product per capita is seen to equal that of the European countries that we summarised in the Europe "of 4" aggregate (EUR-4, i.e. France, Germany, Belgium and the Netherlands) and of Europe "of 7" (EUR-7, i.e. Greece, Spain and Portugal in addition to the four countries just mentioned). But also, somewhat higher than the growth rate of the gross domestic product per capita of the UK and lower, on the other hand—as perhaps we might expect—than that of the corresponding figure for the United States.[9] In what sense therefore can we talk about a "suboptimal trajectory"? Do we want to maintain that the only optimal trajectory would be the one coinciding with the dynamics observed in the case of the twentieth century's technological leader, the United States? Do we really think that Italy's productive potential would have allowed it to achieve a similar result if fully utilised?

Some trouble in facing the evidence contained in the data emerges, moreover, in the reading of the "convergence and two tails" hypothesis. If the "suboptimal trajectory" thesis does not necessarily appear to be in line with the facts (to the extent that the data represent them), the

---

[8] Table 2.1 is based on Bergeaud et al. (2016) which, in turn, refer to Baffigi (2015) and update the Maddison Project Database information (Bolt e Van Zanden, 2020) on which Table 1.3 in Toniolo (2013, p. 9) is based. It is appropriate to point out that the 2020 version of the Maddison Project Database is not limited to updating the previous one but also adopts a different methodology. Still, the picture provided in Table 2.1 is fully consistent with Toniolo's one or Felice (2017, p. 32).

[9] Comparisons such as those conducted in Table 2.1 (and subsequent ones)—typical among economists but much less among economic historians—inevitably raise many questions as one can legitimately doubt whether the necessary level playing field is there. It is no coincidence, therefore, that Table 2.1 (and subsequent ones) adopt different reference points in order to hopefully alleviate similar doubts.

Table 2.1 Growth rate of the real gross domestic product per capita ($ 2010; 1862–2021, selected subperiods)

Differentials in average per capita GDP growth rates	1862–2021 (a)	The tale of convergence and two tails			A miracle. And that's all		
		1862–1896 (b)	1897–1992 (c)	1993–2021 (d)	1862–1946 (e)	1947–1964 (f)	1965–2021 (g)
Italy–EUR-4	0.0	−0.4	0.3	−0.7	−0.1	0.4	0.0
Italy–EUR-7	0.0	−0.3	0.4	−0.6	0.0	0.8	−0.1
Italy–UK	0.3	−0.3	0.9	−0.9	−0.3	4.0	0.1
Italy–USA	−0.3	−0.9	0.2	−1.1	−1.5	4.6	0.0

Notes EUR-4 = France, Germany, the Netherlands, Belgium; EUR-7 = EUR-4, Spain, Portugal, Greece

Source Bergeaud et al. (2016; Retrieved March 18, 2024, http://www.longtermproductivity.com/index.html [v. 2.6]) for per capita GDP and Maddison Project Database, Retrieved March 18, 2024, (https://www.rug.nl/ggdc/historicaldevelopment/maddison/releases/maddison-project-database-2020?lan g=en) for population data

"convergence and two tails" narrative does not in fact seem to be the only one that is consistent with the information available to us. Table 2.1 attempts to illustrate the point.

Columns (b)–(d) clearly tell a story that overall is one of success, even if contained between two episodes that are "awkward", in some sense, but limited in terms of time, and traceable to difficulty in adapting to a new and different context: the reality of the unified state, in the second half of the nineteenth century, and the reality of globalisation and of a new technological paradigm in the years straddling the twentieth and the twenty-first centuries. It is, nevertheless, a story charged with optimism (as was proper for the 2011 celebrations): If in the twentieth century Italy was able to climb to higher and higher positions in every ranking until it became one of the leading economic powers on the planet what is it that is preventing it from being able once again to resume that path already from tomorrow? What is it that lets us suppose that Italy, pushed into a corner, will not once again show that it can change and catch up with the more dynamic countries?

Columns (e)–(g) instead tell a profoundly different story, one that is similar to the one described by Roberto VIvarelli[10]: that of a country that for almost the totality of its history since Unification has been unable to do more, when things were going well, than maintain, with a great effort, the distance between itself and its main partners and competitors that was already present at the moment of Unification without ever catching up with them or, more simply, getting close to them. A "follower" country,[11] which "does what someone else does or suggests doing" as the Cambridge Dictionary would put it. Full stop. In one word: mediocre (in the literal sense of the term).[12] Having emerged from mediocrity (and rapidly returned to it moreover) thanks to an episode—summed up in column (e)—which unsurprisingly the Italians consider to be a miracle: to quote most dictionaries a "miracle" is an event that is contrary to the

---

[10] For what it's worth, also hinted at in Rossi (2012).

[11] The term "follower" should not be understood—as many would imagine—with reference to Italy's place in the international arena but rather with reference to Italy's inability to do more and better than what had been done by the technological leaders between the second half of the nineteenth century and the early decades of the twenty-first century. With the sole significant exception, as we have said, of the fifteen years or so following the Second World War.

[12] "Just acceptable, but not good" according to Cambridge Dictionary.

established laws of nature and attributed to a supernatural cause. A very amazing and extremely unusual occurrence thought to be almost impossible. An episode—as we will attempt to suggest—that was not the fruit of chance (as Paolo Di Martino and Michelangelo Vasta [2017a] seem to think) but, on the contrary, the expression perhaps of clearly identifiable factors and ones that were in large part absent both in the previous eighty years as well as in the sixty that followed; an episode that is not so far back as to have faded from the collective memory but not so near as to allow its specifics, or rather its exceptionalism, to be objectively recalled. In this sense, the economic miracle during the years 1947–1964[13] is and

---

[13] Establishing the beginning or the end of a specific sub-period is often—except in very particular cases—an operation that cannot be defined as anything more than arbitrary. In the case here, the possibility was imagined of framing the economic miracle between (a) the year in which, also from a political point of view, it is possible to consider to be closed the emergency phase that followed the end of the Second World War and the economic policy decisions that would mark the decades to follow took off, and (b) the middle year of the 1963–1965 period that, far from configuring a simple economic downturn, corresponds in reality with a point at which there is a longer-lasting reversal of the trend. Let us remember: 1947 is the year of Alcide De Gasperi's trip to Washington, the signature of the peace treaty in Paris, the massacre at Portella delle Ginestre, the fourth De Gasperi government (a single-party one supported by centrist forces), the establishment in Milan of the Piccolo Teatro and, in Rome, of the Premio Strega literary award, the launch by the Constituent Assembly of the Republican Constitution, and the stabilisation of the lira. And also to jog our memory: 1964 was then the year in which the distance between Italy and Switzerland was shortened by the Great St. Bernard Tunnel, the leader of the Communist Party, Palmiro Togliatti, died and the inauguration took place of the Autostrada del Sole; and, just as in 1947, monetary policy was called upon to stabilise the lira while fiscal policy was concerned with cooling the economic situation. This having been said, it should be emphasised that the choice of the start year and end year is relatively unimportant for the purposes of the story we are telling here. Indeed, selecting 1947 as the starting point of the "miraculous" fifteen-year period considerably undervalues the impact of the tumultuous growth process during those years in relation, in particular, to the performance of the other European countries and, as a consequence, renders the disappointing performance of the previous eighty years less evident. Conversely, choosing 1964 as the point of arrival has a precise meaning. In 1964 Aldo Moro succeeded himself as Prime Minister after a government crisis that apparently matured on a minor issue of funding for private schools but essentially on the issue of the overall definition of economic policy and the consequent definitive change of direction with respect to the choices of the previous fifteen years. And one should not be deceived by the few more years of growth observed in the second half of the 1960s: economic events and inertia often go hand in hand.

remains a great collective anaesthetic, the exception that relieves us from the thankless task of seeing the norm.[14]

Let it be clear: there is no doubt that in the one hundred and sixty years since unification, while not starting off among the leaders and despite the disappointing last twenty-five years, Italy ended up enjoying and today still enjoys levels of well-being close to those of its main European partners and, if not exactly close, at least not so abysmally distant from those of the twentieth century's technological leader, namely the United States. The ratio between Italian income per capita at constant prices and the corresponding figure referred to selected nations (UK and United States) or groups of nations (Europe "of 4", i.e. France, Germany, Belgium and the Netherlands and Europe "of 7", namely the above plus Spain, Portugal and Greece) reaches in the early decades of the twenty-first century higher values than those recorded on the day after the meeting in Turin of the first national Parliament. And whatever term of comparison is used. Certainly, events did not unfold monotonically. However, compared to their great-great grandparents the Italians heading into the twenty-first century seem to have certainly gained ground compared to Great Britain and, even to a lesser extent, to the heart of the European continent as well as to Europe enlarged to include the periphery.

The point, though, is that—as Table 2.1 makes it clear—the entirety of the Italian catch-up experience is restrained in the immediate postwar period. Nothing more (and nothing less). That is, if the "miracle" had never actually been a "miracle", then, the hint of convergence manifested by Italy with respect to the main Western economies would have transformed itself, in the best hypothesis, into a pure and simple crystallisation of the relative position while, in the worst, Italy—during its history as a unified nation—would have lost position rather than gained. In any

---

[14] Actually, there are two fortuitous and lucky events in the readings of Emanuele Felice (2017), of Paolo Di Martino and Michelangelo Vasta (2017a) and of Pierluigi Ciocca (2020). The years after the Second World War and the so-called "Giolitti decade" (1903–1913). Without wishing by this to undervalue the interest of the Giolitti era, if in this case too we use the criterion that we have adopted so far (i.e. the gap between the growth rate of the Italian gross domestic product per capita in real terms and that of other comparable situations) it is difficult to consider the "Giolitti decade" as "the real Italian miracle" (the expression comes from Giorgio Mori [1992]). The average of the growth rates of per capita GDP was below the corresponding figure observed for the aggregates, Europe "of 4" and the Europe "of 7", by 0.3% and 0.1%, respectively, and above the UK and US growth rate by 1.0% and 0.2%, respectively. This is not exactly a miraculous performance (and perhaps not even a particularly exciting one).

case, it would be frankly difficult to think of Italy's achievements as a success story. Just as it would be difficult to make a success story out of the performance of a wingman, of someone who sweats and pedals in the pack, ready to hand over his bicycle to the team leader if he needs it or to smooth the way for him—without ambitions to win, well aware of the fact that only some exceptional circumstance will ever let him win a stage. And never more than just one stage. In the history of cycling, as in economic history, cases of wingmen who become leaders do occur, however rarely.[15] This is clearly not the Italian case.

It would be possible to object that by many other metrics, Italy's story was one of great success, even in relative terms. From nutrition to health, from distribution of resources to protection from risks (and with the sole exception of education—significant as we shall see), the living conditions of the Italians in the last one hundred and sixty years have undergone an extraordinary improvement and every reading of this period not only must take this into account but should also attempt to suggest valid reasons for the visible divergence between economic trends in well-being, on the one hand, and the non-economic ones, on the other. Which is what we will make an attempt to do below.

---

[15] For cycling enthusiasts: it seems that Chris Froome (four times winner of the Tour de France and once of the Giro d'Italia) and Jan Ullrich (world champion, Olympic champion, and winner of a Tour de France) are the most significant examples.

A Growth-Averse Culture[16]

As we can see, what we are going to propose is a reading that does not deny that a tendency towards convergence did occur—even if only for a very brief time—nor deny that the Italian economic history of the last hundred and fifty years or so was dominated by persistent elements that were able to significantly limit the country's growth but attempts, instead, to exploit the differential information contained in that very brief "miraculous" period compared with the performance in the preceding and following periods in order to highlight a different view of the economic history of unified Italy. To this end it is not possible, obviously, to base ourselves on the columns of a table, however evocative. Nor we can limit ourselves to referring exclusively to a benchmark—gross domestic product per capita—the limits of which are known and whose reliability is subjected daily to verification. And it is no accident, in fact, that the pages that follow will have recourse to other and different indicators. But this is obviously not enough. To be minimally feasible, a reading of the facts that diverges significantly from the prevailing opinion needs a visual angle, a perspective that can illuminate the entire century and a half that we have behind us, giving us back an image, possibly, that does not differ much from the snapshot seen in the columns (e)–(g) in Table 2.1. And this must be done without pretending to want to explain everything and the opposite of everything, but on the contrary levering on that little great natural experiment that was the economic "miracle" in order to throw light on some of the long-term features of the Italian economy.

---

[16] The term "culture" should be considered with caution. Deirdre McCloskey (2021b, p. 19) rightly observes that "«culture» is merely the vague way which economists talk when they have not actually taken on board the exact and gigantic literature about ideas, myths, stories, rhetoric, ideology, metaphors, ceremonies, and the like". As much as possible, we will attempt to be more specific in the following pages. For the time being, it is appropriate to remember that by culture we mean the set of information ("beliefs, values and preferences", would specify Mokyr [2016, p. 8]) that is capable of influencing human behaviour, acquired through teaching, imitation, more generally, and any social channel that transmits the information itself (and is shared by at least one significant subset of society). In short—forgetting about the far from minor differences between beliefs, values and preferences—what a given community believes and what it thinks it knows. This implies that in the following pages we will refer to the definition of culture adopted—as noted by Alberto Alesina and Paola Giuliano (2015, p. 900)— in almost all of the empirical analyses on the subject (neglecting the distinctions, although present, between beliefs, values and preferences and their interactions).

Mutatis mutandis this is somewhat the work method adopted by Alan Greenspan and Adrian Wooldridge in "Capitalism in America. A History" (2018) in which the perspective is the Schumpeterian one of "creative destruction" and the cultural attitude of the United States towards it. Greenspan and Wooldridge do not pretend to cover every aspect of US economic history in the last two centuries but, instead, try to read it in a unitary manner from a specific point of view: that of the "perennial «gale» that uproots businesses – and lives – but that, in the process, creates a more productive economy" (2018, p. 14), and of the resistance that usually accompanies it. If you like, a version in a historical-economic key of Gary Cooper's 1949 memorable monologue in "The fountainhead".[17]

Well, the working hypothesis in the pages that follow is that in the Italian case this visual angle cannot be other than the negative of the perspective proposed by Greenspan and Wooldridge and therefore the difficulty with which—in the decades following Unification just as today (and perhaps just as before) with the sole brief (and, literally, miraculous) exception of the fifteen years, or little more, following the Second World War—the Italians and Italy managed to come to terms culturally with the forces implicit in a market economy. Those were fifteen or twenty years in which—in virtue of a series of circumstances and contrary to what happened before and afterwards—the "growth culture" became dominant and informed the country of itself. It was certainly an exception—given the fact that in the previous eighty years and in the sixty afterwards that same "growth culture" invariably ended up being a minority one if not marginal altogether—but, as we will make an effort to suggest, it was an exception that is not perhaps incomprehensible if observed from this point of view and indeed, just for a change, it is one that is capable of confirming the norm.

The terms "minority" and "dominant" are not accidental. As we will try to suggest in what follows, a culture open to the market has always been present, as has its opposite. But the latter was certainly (and almost always) been more capable than the former of becoming the prevailing culture. Able to set the agenda and impose itself in the public debate, to become, if you like, a common opinion that was accepted—Joel Mokyr (2016, p. 8) would say—by a decisive subset of society. For the former to prevail, the shock of the Second World War and the memory of the

---

[17] Retrieved March 18, 2024, https://www.dailymotion.com/video/xtymi7.

years of the regime were necessary. And in order for it to succumb after only fifteen years more or less, and then be marginalised until the end of the century if not right up to the present day, it was sufficient for the extraordinary growth of the 1950s and early 1960s to be disassociated from the set of values that had promoted and supported it—unlike what happened elsewhere—but on the contrary for the imbalances that had inevitably accompanied that same extraordinary growth to be linked to those values.

Which, by the way, helps perhaps to understand the meaning of the debate about the prevalence, in the Italian case, of the "animal spirits" of capitalism or, on the contrary, about the decisive role of large companies and mixed banks for which reference should be made, for example, to Giovanni Federico (1996, pp. 779–780) who, not surprisingly, speaks in favour of the former precisely because, otherwise, "one should assume an epochal change in the 1950s and the 1960s". As has been observed, the epochal change or, better, the exception of the 1950s and 1960s could not be found so much in the affirmation of one development model over another as in the temporary capacity of capitalism's "animal spirits" to inspire the country, leading it intellectually and morally, something that never happened before and afterwards.

Going back to Schumpeterian creative destruction, we better be careful not to ask Joseph Alois Schumpeter himself about it: in fact, he took care not to provide a precise definition of it and between his *Theorie der wirtschaftlichen Entwicklung*, from 1911, and the later (1942) "Capitalism, Socialism and Democracy"[18] he changed his viewpoint more than marginally.[19] The difficulty is reflected in the pages of Alan Greenspan and Adrian Wooldridge (2018) themselves where the drive towards the efficient input allocation in which the creative destruction is substantiated is initially identified in technological innovation and then progressively broadened to coincide with a more generic "growth" culture. The desire to "take unusual risks in pursuit of a better life" (2018, p. 389) which, in turn, translates into something "rather more subtle than invention: making innovations more user friendly; producing companies that

---

[18] Here we will refer, in the former case, to the third edition, dated 1949, of the 1934 English version entitled *"The Theory of Economic Development"* (Schumpeter, 1949) and, in the latter, to the second edition, dated 1947 (Schumpeter, 1947).

[19] Going from the economic growth driven by the *deus ex machina* of the scientific discoveries to the economic growth that springs from and is nourished by enterprise.

can commercialize these innovations; and developing techniques for the running of these companies successfully" (2018, p. 104). Not simply, therefore, the ability to produce brilliant ideas on a regular basis but also, if not above all, the desire and the capacity to drop those ideas into the reality of the market, the ceaseless interior impulse to give complete form daily to what is still formless.

What Edmund Phelps describes in even more general terms in "Mass Flourishing" (2013), calling it "grassroots innovation"[20]—and identifies with "engagement, meeting challenges, self-expression, and personal growth" (2013, p. vii). In other words, involvement in the broad sense in every stage of the innovation process. An involvement that implies an aptitude for change and for comparison, uninterrupted pursuit of originality and discovery, a desire to make a difference. Involvement, Phelps emphasises, that "may be narrowed or weakened by institutions arising from imperfect understanding or competing objectives" (2013, p. vii) but that cannot be created by them as it is nourished by the fundamental values of a society even more than from its regulations.

In Phelps's reading this involvement only becomes possible with the arrival of modern market economies. Because it is only in these that we come again to find the constituent elements of that which we might define the "dynamism" of an economy: the openness towards that which is new, the aptitude for change and the ability to interpret it, in an institutional context that permits it. A sum of circumstances that precedes innovation and which cannot, therefore, be confused with (and which goes beyond) the "vivacity", with the capacity, that is, to grasp opportunities the moment they present themselves.[21] And this clarifies the main theme that is the subject of these pages: it is perfectly possible for an economy to grow if it is vivacious, able, that is, to grasp the opportunities that spring from the opening towards dynamic economies. And therefore, grow on a par with and, sometimes temporarily, even more than its main partners.

---

[20] "Indigenous innovation" and therefore neither cultivated nor imported but actually coming from the base, from below.

[21] "We must also understand the concept of an economy's dynamism. It is a compound of deep-set forces and facilities behind innovation: the drive to change things, the talent for it, and the receptivity to new things, as well as the enabling institutions. Thus dynamism, …, is the willingness and capacity to innovate, leaving aside current conditions and obstacles. This contrast with what is usually called vibrancy: an alertness to opportunities, a readiness to act, and the zeal to «get it done» (as Schumpeter puts it)" (Phelps, 2013, p. 20).

Getting close to them without, moreover, reaching them not to mention bypassing them. But vivacity is not sufficient on its own for generating autonomous growth: if the dynamism around us loses vigour our ability to grow will fade away with it.

Therefore, the dynamic economies of our time are not built only with incentives but also—if not above all—from an economic and not only economic culture that is capable of giving free rein to the creativity of individuals and to their intuition. Creativity and intuition will run into limits but will also discover channels in the institutional structures, in the entrepreneurial judgements, in the considerations of the financial system and, lastly, in the choices of users.

At this point shrewd readers will have understood that this writer has been accumulating, line and after line, page after page, significant intellectual debts—not only to a Nobel laureate such as Edmund Phelps but also to a renowned economic historian, Joel Mokyr (2016), and to such a polyhedric personality as Deirdre McCloskey (2006, 2010, 2016),[22] a rare example of "general purpose intellectual".[23,24] Towards the first and to his "A Culture of Growth" that contains an erudite but nevertheless fascinating reconstruction of the cultural processes that made some sixteenth-century "cultural entrepreneurs" into agents of a profound cultural change, in particular as regards the attitude of human beings towards the surrounding world and their propensity and capacity for guiding it and controlling it for their benefit. A cultural change leading— according to Mokyr—to the tumultuous technical progress observed in modern times and the consequent, and unprecedented, economic growth. The "great enrichment", to use Deirdre McCloskey's expression, was that extraordinary event, unprecedented in human history, that brought a significant number of our kind—after hundreds and thousands of years scraping the bottom of the barrel—to find themselves all things considered to be generally well off. This was an event which, in the pages

---

[22] The reference here is to the three volumes of the extraordinary work of Deirdre McCloskey on the bourgeoisie, recently summarised in McCloskey and Carden (2020).

[23] The paternity of the quote belongs to Joel Mokyr (2016, p. IX).

[24] As well, of course, as from the debate between them, an example being the one hosted by Liberty Fund (retrieved March 18, 2024, oll.libertyfund.org/page/liberty-matters-donald-boudreaux-deirdre-mccloskey-economists-ideas-bourgeois-era). Or, more recently, the one implicit in the exchange contained in McCloskey (2021a, 2021b) and Mokyr (2022).

of her monumental trilogy "Bourgeois Era", Deirdre McCloskey links to the gradual but profound change recorded in the political and social culture of North-western Europe between the fourteenth and seventeenth centuries: a change that was able to attribute full dignity to the common people, whose artisan and merchant activities were given levels of social appreciation that had never been recorded before; a change capable of sweeping away the "tax of the dishonour"—Don Boudreaux called it[25]— that society had imposed on those activities until that time, deeming profit and the accumulation of wealth to be dishonourable and as a consequence discouraging them or limiting their diffusion. Those common people were finally allowed to attempt to innovate freely and anywhere, timidly at first and in an increasingly tumultuous manner later. And to find, or not find, confirmation of their intuition in the market. "Free to choose and free to be chosen", as Alberto Mingardi would say.[26]

Ideas, therefore, much before than—attention: "much before than" and not "rather than"—institutions, regulations, natural resources, capital or, more in general, material conditions,[27] ideas that are free to be born and take form, ideas that are free to challenge clichés, conventions, habits, the commonly accepted arguments. Even the pre-established order. Ideas, even against the stream—free to translate themselves into change ("dissent with modification", to use the words of Deirdre McCloskey once again), change that is also profound, that is often disruptive and destructive for the lives of individuals and for the destinies of entire communities. But nevertheless, change that is capable of producing an extraordinary overall improvement in the living conditions—in the broad sense and not simply in strictly material terms—of many if not exactly everyone.[28]

---

[25] The reference is to the aforesaid debate organised by Liberty Fund.

[26] Retrieved March 18, 2024, https://fee.org/articles/reviewing-deirdre-mccloskeys-bourgeois-trilogy/.

[27] Which does not exclude, of course, the presence of interactions, including significant ones, among the terms mentioned (and between ideas and institutions in particular) nor does it allow us to set aside the unavoidable questions relating to the ways in which some ideas prevail in the "marketplace of ideas". For a review of these themes, see the lively debate on neo-institutionalism, the essential terms of which are provided in the debate in the *Journal of Institutional Economics* (2016) as well as the summary by Alberto Alesina and Paola Giuliano (2015).

[28] It is right to point out that the sequence that leads to freedom of thought and expression ("no effective restriction – either prohibition or complete lack of support – on the curiosity-motivated explorations of the mind") to innovation in the broad sense ("the

From the methodological point of view these pages follow Schumpeter's (1949, p. 58) advice stressing the need for a historical perspective in the analysis of the growth process.[29] From this point of view, as we do not yet have or only partially have a picture of the geographical variability which would be of great interest in the case of Italy (and which we hope might be a field of future research), the underlying hypothesis is that the years of the economic boom were to some degree (and with all the appropriate caution) the crucial source of variability if compared to the preceding and subsequent decades. To say it in statistical terms (and with all the appropriate precautions), the "treated" sample.

This then is the perspective and also the key for reading the events of over a century and a half of Italian economic history that we wish to propose in the following pages. Let it be clear, there is no shortage of precedents for this perspective[30] and they may all be represented by the sentence with which Pierluigi Ciocca and Gianni Toniolo (1998, p. XV)—recalling the words of Carlo Cipolla—conclude their introduction to their *Storia economica d'Italia* ("Economic History of Italy"): "«culture is required» for continuing to produce «things that the world likes»". But the aim of the additional effort in the pages that follow is to get over the limit that they themselves pointed out (1998, pp. XIII–XIV):

> the economist looks for the generalisation, the «model» applicable to numerous circumstances if not to all of them; historians tend to underline the uniqueness, the originality of the events. [...] Both approaches are useful depending on the investigative goals proposed. [... But] as the analysis gradually moves from the principle macro-variables to researching the most significant details, from the mechanical causes of growth [...] to

search for new theories, new data, and new applications") and from these to the dynamic of productivity ("the rate of addition to the stock of useful knowledge") and then to real growth was already present, in terms only hinted at, if you like, but absolutely topical, in Kuznets (1968, pp. 82–122).

[29] In the same perspective, see Paul Romer (1993) and Ufuk Akcigit and Tom Nicholas (2019) as well as Philippe Aghion, whose thirty years of work is summed up by Aghion et al. (2021).

[30] The reference here is not to the very extensive literature on the relationship between culture (as variously defined) and growth—for which reference should be made, for example, to Spolaore (2014)—but is limited to the different interpretations of the economic events of Italy after unification.

the profiles that more closely regard attitudes of the animal spirits, the entrepreneurship, it is always less easy to formulate generalisations.

As we will see, the centre of the stage will not be occupied by the macro-variables, and the "mechanical causes of growth" will remain in the background, but this will not prevent us from trying to offer an overall key to reading the history of the unified state: a key to reading potentially able to help us to understand how this country is readying itself to tackle a period that could turn out to be extraordinarily demanding (granted for the sake of argument that it is preparing to do so); a key that differs from the common view in several points. A case of dissent—of which this writer is well aware—that may not necessarily reveal itself "with modification".[31]

References

Aghion, P., Antonin, C., & Bunel, S. (2021). *The Power of Creative Destruction.* Harvard University Press.

Akcigit, U., & Nicholas, T. (2019). History, Microdata and Endogenous Growth. *Annual Review of Economics, 11,* 615–633.

Alesina, A., & Giuliano, P. (2015). Culture and Institutions. *Journal of Economic Literature, 53*(4), 898–944.

Baffigi, A. (2015). *Il PIL per la storia d'Italia. Istruzioni per l'uso.* Marsilio.

Bergeaud, A., Cette, G., & Lecat, R. (2016). Productivity Trends in Advanced Countries Between 1890 and 2012. *Review of Income and Wealth, 62*(3), 420–444.

Bolt, J., & van Zanden, J. L. (2020). Maddison Style Estimates of the Evolution of the World Economy. A New 2020 Update. *Maddison Project Working Paper 15.* Retrieved March 18, 2024, https://www.rug.nl/ggdc/historicaldevelopm ent/maddison/publications/wp15.pdf

Cassese, S. (2014). *Governare gli italiani. Storia dello Stato.* Il Mulino.

Ciocca, P. (2020). *Ricchi per sempre? Una storia economica d'Italia (1796–2020).* Bollati Boringhieri.

Ciocca, P., & Toniolo, G. (1998). Introduzione. In P. Ciocca & G. Toniolo (Eds.), *Storia economica d'Italia* (Vol. I, pp. V–XIX). Laterza.

Codogno, L., & Galli, G. (2022). *Meritocracy, Growth, and Lessons from Italy's Economic Decline: Lobbies (and Ideologies) Against Competition and Talent.* Oxford University Press.

---

[31] The perspective adopted in these pages is, finally, one that the few lines above and the associated quotations obviously do not cover in their entirety (so that interested readers are strongly advised to read the texts mentioned above).

Cohen, J., & Federico, G. (2001). *Lo sviluppo economico italiano 1820–1960*. Il Mulino.

Di Martino, P., & Vasta, M. (2017a). Introduzione. In P. Di Martino & M. Vasta (Eds.), *Ricchi per caso. La parabola dello sviluppo economico italiano* (pp. 9–21). Il Mulino.

Di Martino, P., & Vasta, M. (2017b). Istituzioni e performance economica in Italia: un'analisi di lungo periodo. In P. Di Martino & M. Vasta (Eds.), *Ricchi per caso. La parabola dello sviluppo economico italiano* (pp. 231–264). Il Mulino.

Federico, G. (1996). Italy, 1860–1940: A Little-Known Success Story. *Economic History Review, 49*(4), 764–786.

Felice, E. (2015). *Ascesa e declino, Storia economica d'Italia*. Il Mulino.

Felice, E. (2017). Dalla convergenza al declino: l'economia italiana dall'Unità ad oggi. In P. Di Martino & M. Vasta (Eds.), *Ricchi per caso* (pp. 23–73). Il Mulino.

Felice, E., & Vecchi, G. (2015). Italy's Growth and Decline, 1861–2011. *Journal of Interdisciplinary History, 45*(4), 507–548.

Greenspan, A., & Wooldridge, A. (2018). *Capitalism in America*. Penguin Press.

Kuznets, S. (1968). *Toward a Theory of Economic Growth with «Reflections on the Economic Growth of Modern Nations»*. Norton & Co.

McCloskey, D. N. (2006). *The Bourgeois Virtues. Ethics for an Age of Commerce*. The University of Chicago Press.

McCloskey, D. N. (2010). *Bourgeois Dignity. Why Economics Can't Explain the Modern World*. The University of Chicago Press.

McCloskey, D. (2016). *Bourgeois Equality. How Ideas, Not Capital or Institutions, Enriched the World*. The University of Chicago Press.

McCloskey, D. N. (2021a). *How Growth Happens: Liberalism, Innovism, and the Great Enrichment*. Retrieved March 18, 2024, www.deirdremccloskey.com/docs/pdf/McCloskey_HowGrowthHappens.pdf

McCloskey, D. N. (2021b). *Institutions Matter, But Not Much as Neo-institutionalists Believe*. Retrieved March 18, 2024, www.deirdremccloskey.com/docs/pdf/McCloskey_InstitutionsMatter2021.pdf

McCloskey, D. N., & Carden, A. (2020). *Leave Me Alone and I'll Make You Rich. How the Bourgeois Deal Enriched the World*. The University of Chicago Press.

Melis, G. (2020). *Storia dell'amministrazione italiana*. Il Mulino.

Mokyr, J. (2016). *A Culture of Growth. The Origins of the Modern Economy*. Princeton University Press.

Mokyr, J. (2022). Incentives, Institutions and Industrialization: A Prelude to Modern Economic Growth. *Rivista di Storia Economica/Italian Review of Economic History, 38*(2), 127–146.

Mori, G. (1992). L'economia italiana dagli anni Ottanta alla Prima guerra mondiale. In G. Mori (Ed.), *Storia dell'industria elettrica in Italia. Le origini, 1882–1914* (pp. 1–106). Laterza.

Petri, R. (2002). *Storia economica d'Italia. Dalla Grande Guerra al miracolo economico (1918–1963)*. Il Mulino.

Phelps, E. (2013). *Mass Flourishing. How Grassroots Innovation Created Jobs, Challenge and Change*. Princeton University Press.

Romer, P. (1993). Idea Gaps and Object Gaps in Economic Development. *Journal of Monetary Economics, 32*(3), 543–573.

Rossi, N. (2012). Introduzione. In N. Rossi (Ed.), *Sudditi. Un programma per i prossimi 50 anni* (pp. 11–32). IBL Libri.

Rossi, N., & Toniolo, G. (1994). Un secolo di sviluppo economico. In P. Ciocca (Ed.), *Il progresso economico dell'Italia* (pp. 15–46). Il Mulino.

Rossi, N., Toniolo, G., & Vecchi, G. (2011). Introduzione. In G. Vecchi, *In ricchezza e in povertà. Il benessere degli italiani dall'Unità a oggi* (pp. XI–XXVII). Il Mulino.

Schumpeter, J. A. (1947). *Capitalism, Socialism and Democracy*. Harper and Brothers.

Schumpeter, J. A. (1949). *The Theory of Economic Development*. Harvard University Press.

Spolaore, E. (Ed.). (2014). *Culture and Economic Growth*. Edward Elgar.

Tedoldi, L. (2018). *Storia dello Stato italiano. Dall'Unità al XXI secolo*. Laterza.

Toniolo, G. (2013). An Overview of Italy's Economic Growth. In G. Toniolo (Ed.), *The Oxford Handbook of the Italian Economy Since Unification* (pp. 3–36). Oxford University Press.

Toniolo, G. (2022). *Storia della Banca d'Italia* (Vol. I). Il Mulino.

Vivarelli, R. (2013). *Italia 1861*. Il Mulino.

Zamagni, V. (1993). *Dalla periferia al centro. La seconda rinascita economica dell'Italia 1861–1990* (II ed.). Il Mulino.

CHAPTER 3

Innovation and Growth

Total Factor Productivity

Whether it is the "grassroots innovation" of Edmund Phelps or the "innovism" of Deirdre McCloskey, for the first one (2013, p. 21) there would seem to be no doubts. Referring to the decades straddling the nineteenth and twentieth centuries, and while recognising the Italian economy's ability to grow in productivity terms his conclusion is quite clear: "no economic historian would suggest that Italy's economy had much dynamism at all, let alone the American level". And, with the complicity of the corporatist turning point and the permanence of corporatist features after the Second World War, the same judgement is given by Phelps for the period between the two wars and for the more recent decades.

More nuanced is the assessment of Deirdre McCloskey who—with Art Carden (2020)—suggests that in a way the Italians have a certain tendency towards—how shall we put it?—the strongman and, as consequence, towards a context that is not really favourable to the "dissent with modification" which is at the root of innovation (2020, p. 7) while,

© The Author(s), under exclusive license to Springer Nature
Switzerland AG 2024
N. Rossi, *Reframing Italian Economic History, 1861–2021*, Palgrave
Studies in Economic History,
https://doi.org/10.1007/978-3-031-67271-2_3

at the same time, underscoring their creative capacity and, therefore, to say it with Phelps, their dynamism.[1]

A little supplementary analysis can therefore be useful and appropriate if not indeed, necessary. And, with all its limits, the starting point cannot but be total factor productivity (TFP), i.e., the part of output whose evolution cannot be explained by the corresponding evolution of the inputs used in the production process (capital and labour, for example). The so-called Solow residual conveniently—it must be said[2]—attributed by economists to innovation, considered—in the words of Moses Abramowitz—to be a "measure of our ignorance" but, at the same time accounting for a substantial proportion of the evolution of economic growth indicators. In Peter Howitt's (2005, p. 1611) words "it seems that almost everything to be explained by the theory lies in the Solow's residual" (i.e. in TFP growth).

Thanks to the Banque de France and, in particular, to the work of Antonin Bergeaud et al. (2016) annual estimates of total factor productivity are freely accessible today for 23 countries and for the time interval between 1890 and 2021. As long as we are ready to accept the rather strict conditions under which the "Solow residual" may be deemed a good indicator of the impact of the innovation[3] activity, this will allow us to analyse the evolution over time of the TPF but also to attempt to

---

[1] This later aspect is quite evident in Deirdre McCloskey's interview in the financial daily, *Sole 24 ore* on 24 October 2015. Retrieved March 18, 2024, https://st.ilsole24ore.com/art/cultura/2015-10-24/lo-strano-caso-deirdre-mccloskey-101220.shtml?%20uuid%20=ACFaCfMB.

[2] If the shares out of the total output from capital and labour are constant over time, total factor productivity is nothing if not the ratio between the output level and the aggregate that measures the contributions of the capital and labour factors (weighted with the respective shares on total output). Stated in other terms, total factor productivity represents the shifts over time of the production function and, as a consequence, in terms of growth rates, measures the growth of output per unit of a composite productivity factor. Being a residual term, it incorporates among other things errors of measurement and of specification (and suffers from distortions of the markets, from the presence of externalities and non-constant returns to scale).

[3] The TFP limits are to a large extent (but not exclusively) attributable to the heterogeneity of factor inputs that are usually grouped under two main headings: capital and labour. In the first case between capital goods belonging to the same "vintage" or belonging to different "vintages". In the latter case between workers with different characteristics. To the matter of the heterogeneity of factor inputs one should add the problem of their degree of use as well, in discrete terms, as that regarding the estimate of the shares of the same and, on the product side, the theme of the change in the quality of

read the interactions between different countries in terms of the same magnitude.

Barry Bosworth and Susan Collins (2003), among many others, have pointed out that technical progress plays a significant role in explaining growth progresses as well as in determining the differentiated performance of different countries.[4] These conclusions are also referable to a considerable extent to the case of Italy (Fig. 3.1).[5] Claire Giordano and Francesco Zollino (2020, p. 20) assess that for the whole period considered (1861–2017) the contribution of the TFP to GDP growth was about 40% and summarise the Italian situations as follows (2020, pp. 20–21): TFP in moderate growth in the first thirty years of life of the unified state, accelerating in the first decade of the twentieth century and, above all in the 1920s in correspondence with a significant wave of technological innovation; sharply decelerating during the great depression. Afterwards, the great leap forward in the golden postwar era linked to the transfer of technology from the leaders of the moment (the United States) but also to organisational improvements and to economies of scale. Finally, in the early 1970s, the start of a progressive reduction of TFP growth rates culminating in the negative values observed during the double crisis of 2008–2011 and followed by a modest recovery in the second half of the twenty-tens of the current century.

The relative TFP trend (in relation, therefore, to the TFP trend in other countries or groups of countries) is already evident right from the lines above and seems to be in line with the interpretative hypothesis

---

the same. Solutions are possible in all the cases cited and in different degrees. Moreover, at the aggregate level, calculating the TFP rests on the possibility of legitimately defining an aggregate known as "added value". Finally, it is likely that there is something in the TFP that goes beyond technical progress: the same technology, transplanted into the context of individual countries may give rise to different levels of efficiency that reflect the incentive structure prevalent in the countries themselves (Acemoglu, 2009, p. 149).

[4] To give an example, Bosworth and Collins (2003, p. 123), with reference to the last forty years of the last century, estimate that at global level (84 countries) the TFP explains about one quarter of the average growth rate observed. This proportion rises to roughly 30% in the case of the industrial countries and even drops below zero in the case of African countries.

[5] As regards Italy, the information on total factor productivity is taken from Giordano and Zollino (2020) which should be referred to for the details. It is appropriate here to emphasise that—although not immune from criticism (Fenoaltea, 2020, p. 106) with reference to the first decades of the period considered—their estimates take account as far as possible of the heterogeneity of the production factors.

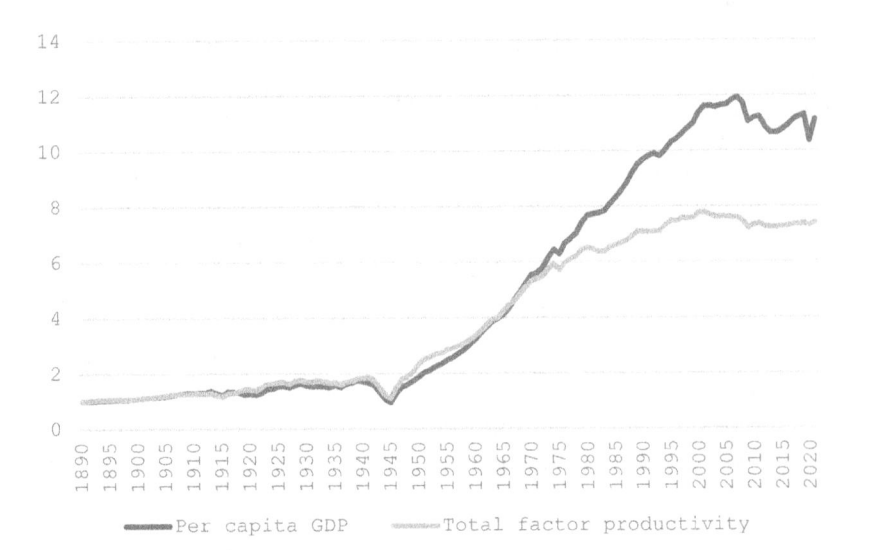

■■■■Per capita GDP   ■■■■Total factor productivity

Fig. 3.1 Per capita gross domestic product (GDP) and total factor productivity in Italy (cumulated growth, 1890–2021; 1890 = 1) (*Source* Bergeaud et al. [2016]. Retrieved March 18, 2024, http://www.longtermproductivity. com/index.html [v. 2.6])

formulated in the previous chapter. For greater clarity, Table 3.1 reproposes it for sub-periods, along the lines of Table 2.1, with an important but unfortunately inevitable difference. As the data for the TFP are available for the 1890–2021 period it was deemed appropriate—in the case of the "convergence and two tails" hypothesis—to suppress the first tail rather than limit it to the years 1891–1896 only.

The first obvious observation is that, in the certainly more appropriate terms of the total factor productivity, the hypothesis of the "suboptimal trajectory" (if taken at face value) frankly appears difficult to support. Over the more than 150 years, the growth rate of the Italian TFP does not differ to a significant extent from that of the aggregates labelled as Europe "of 4" and Europe "of 7", or even for that of the United States, and is significantly higher than the growth rate of the TFP in the UK. To reiterate a concept already expressed, even if we make a great effort, it is truly difficult to maintain that the economic performance of unified Italy was less positive than that of its main competitors.

Table 3.1 Growth rate of the total factor productivity (%; 1891–2021, selected subperiods)

		Convergence and two tails		A miracle And that's all		
Differential in the average TFP growth rate	1890–2021 (a)	1891–1992 (b–c)	1993–2021 (d)	1891–1946 (e)	1947–1964 (f)	1965–2021 (g)
Italy–EUR-4	–0.1	0.1	–0.5	0.1	0.2	–0.4
Italy–EUR-7	0.1	0.2	–0.4	0.3	0.7	–0.3
Italy–UK	0.5	0.8	–0.5	0.1	4.0	–0.1
Italy–USA	0.0	0.2	–1.0	–1.1	3.5	–0.1

Notes EUR-4 = France, Germany, the Netherlands, Belgium; EUR-7 = EUR-4, Spain, Portugal, Greece; population weighted average of the corresponding TFP growth rates
Source As in Fig. 3.1 for TFP and Maddison Project Database, Retrieved March 18, 2024, (https://www.rug.nl/ggdc/historicaldevelopment/maddison/releases/maddison-project-database-2020?lang=en) for population data

At the same time, the passage from per capita GDP to total factor productivity does not change—indeed perhaps makes even more explicit—the basic message implicit in the previous pages. No great dash during the twentieth century, apparently crowned by success, to catch up with the world's technological leaders, but really a not particularly brilliant trudge over the whole period considered with the sole "miraculous" exception of the fifteen-to-twenty year postwar period.[6] This was a fifteen-to-twenty-year period in which Italy—far from contenting itself with pushing the frontier of productive possibilities forward within the limits in which the dynamism of others permitted it—seems to release all its potential and even push itself beyond what was permitted by merely replicating the performance of others.[7] At first sight, therefore, from the

---

[6] What has been said above is valid as regards the "Giolitti decade" in which, in terms of TFP growth, the Italian performance was less satisfying than that of the European countries (even if appreciable with respect to the United Kingdom and to a lesser extent with respect to the United States).

[7] As has already been observed, all periodisation contains a margin of arbitrariness. In this case too moreover, as in the case of the per capita GDP, moving the initial or

viewpoint of technical progress, Italy did nothing more when all was well—over a lifetime of little more than a century and half (save the fifteen-to-twenty-year postwar period)—than place itself in the wake of the more dynamic economies, be that Great Britain, the United States or even those of continental Europe. Such behaviour—let it be clear—is anything but obvious and is certainly not without merits, but it is not exactly what could be defined as a success story.

Let us repeat, acquiring the technological know-how from abroad (directly or indirectly thanks to joint ventures with multinational enterprises) and adapting it to the prevalent domestic conditions goes well beyond pure and simple "imitation". It requires technical skills that are far from ordinary, abilities that are often rare, and adaptation capacities that are anything but widespread. But—it is useless to beat about the bush—it is quite different from innovative activity in the true sense as this implies an invention or even a new and different combination of factor inputs at some point or other of the production process.[8] And it is even possible to grow when this is absent but not to be masters of one's own destiny, at least to any great extent.[9]

It could be objected, all things considered, that the life of the follower is really not so miserable. In the words of Gianni Toniolo (2013, p. 5), on the date of birth of the Kingdom of Italy, "the gross domestic product per capita was more or less equal to the current average of Africa's forty-two «richest» states today... Life expectation at birth was about thirty years, a lot lower than that today in the less developed countries ...". And so on. But this is exactly the point. Things may not go so badly as long as there is someone there at the front from whom you can "suck the wheel" (if

---

final periods backwards or forward by a few years does not change the substance of the argument.

[8] The binary distinction between passive innovation and innovation in the true sense is quite probably sufficient for our purposes but notably unsuitable for grasping the many nuances of the reality. Where do we place, for example, the so-called incremental innovation, the improvement at the margins (rather than simple adaptation) of the existing knowledge that notoriously constitutes one of the strengths of Italian enterprises and, in particular of the small ones (Colli, 2002)?

[9] Comprehensibly, the literature on this point is quite vast. Renato Giannetti (1998) among others, and to whom the title of the next paragraph is due, has written illuminating pages. More recently, see the works of Cristiano Antonelli and Federico Barbiellini Amidei (2007), of Barbiellini Amidei et al. (2013) and of Alessandro Nuvolari and Michelangelo Vasta (2017).

for the sake of the argument we accept that you know how to do so). But when this does not happen, simply staying in the group without slipping to a position in the rear can turn out to be very difficult. We will see further below how this is the problem that the country could find itself tackling today and in the span of a few years. But before worrying about the future, it is necessary to dig further down into the past. We must ask ourselves, for example, if and to what extent the evolution of the TFP in the fifteen years of the "miracle" had something to do with the country's ability to advance its knowledge of how and what to produce autonomously: counting not only on its entrepreneurship but also on its ingenuity; leveraging on its willingness to experiment and take risks and exploiting the social recognition of the value of experimentation and risk (Phelps, 2013). And if it were so, we could ask ourselves why a quality that is usually attributed to the Italians only manifested itself for a brief time lapse and disappeared or, rather, remained dormant for nine tenths of the Italian economic experience since Unification.

This, in turn, is the equivalent of asking ourselves if and to what extent it is possible to describe the dynamics of technical progress. This topic was tackled over half a century ago by Richard Nelson and Edmund Phelps (1966) and examined again more recently in particular by Philippe Aghion and his co-authors from time to time[10] as well as, empirically, not so long ago by Raicho Bojilov (2020). The latter, starting from a previous version of the dataset on which Table 3.1 is based, set himself the target of distinguishing between imported innovation (implicit in the attempt to reproduce processes and products that correspond to the best practice available from time to time) and spontaneous innovation (that originates in the local enterprise of a specific country and contributes to shifting the frontier of the productive possibilities both of the country in question and of its competitors). His results, referred to a group of 13 countries, can be summarised as follows in general terms (Bojilov, 2020, p. 49): in the years before the First World War, innovative activity originated above all in the UK, in the United States, in France and, to a lesser extent, in Germany; in the period between the two wars the spontaneous dynamism *à la* Phelps would have revealed itself in particular in the United States and in France; in the decades following the Second World War the United States and, to a lesser extent, the UK returned to being the technological

---

[10] Among others, Peter Howitt (1992), Daron Acemoglu and Fabrizio Zilibotti (2006), Peter Howitt and Fabrice Murtin (2011), Ufuk Akcigit and Peter Howitt (2014).

leaders, accompanied in this case by the Scandinavian countries. Within this framework, Italy's role would be clear: after the Second World War and up to the early 1970s, over 80% of the technological innovation originated externally; thereafter, the spontaneous innovation component would grow until it neared 50% but in the context of TFP growth rates that were continuing to shrink to the point of becoming negligible. To put it bluntly: a nation of saints, poets, navigators but above all—and in the best of cases—copycats.[11]

Nothing new under the sun. Already at the end of the 1990s, Renato Giannetti (1998, p. 201) concluded his *Tecnologia e sviluppo economico italiano 1870–1990* ("Technology and Italian Economic Development 1870–1990") with a few clear words: "… the invention of technology had a quite limited role in Italian economic development. From the aggregate standpoint, for example, the comparison with some European countries highlights the greater role … of imitative skills over innovative ones". And agreeing with him, at a distance of ten years, or just less, Giovanni Federico and Pier Angelo Toninelli (2003, pp. 210–214) reproposed "the image of Italian industry that is rarely positioned at the technological frontier and prevalently dependent on importing technology from abroad". More recently, Federico Barbiellini Amidei et al. (2013, pp. 574–575) reiterated the "modesty" of Italian innovation activity and, conversely, the importance of imported foreign technology for Italian enterprises right from Unification. And after them, Alessandro Nuvolari and Michelangelo Vasta (2017, p. 153): "… Italy's innovative performance in the long term, …, was very weak in general and well behind that of countries with similar income levels". In short, with his analysis Roicho Bojilov (2020) was knocking down a door that was already pretty open (at least as far as we are concerned). And, whereas imitation in a technological context is an activity that is anything but banal, there would be no reason to return to the subject except, of course, to discuss the policy implications—not always convergent—deriving from conclusions that, as we have seen, are similar to a great extent. Except that—as we

---

[11] There is an interesting parallel to this lapidary conclusion—to be treated with all due care—in the institutional field: Sabino Cassese (2014, pp. 362–368) observes that over the course of its unification Italy was a net importer of institutional structures. This is understandable, moreover, given that Italy was a latecomer as a nation state. The few cases in which the Italian experience was the subject of attention beyond its borders can be counted on the fingers of one hand and regard—Cassese also observes—aspects that are administrative in nature rather than institutional.

have already said—the underlying theme of these pages is not so much to retrace the persistent elements in Italy's economic history that have already been widely signposted, but to attempt to exploit the coexistence of persistent elements (along the entire arc, at this point, of the 160 years) and discontinuities (in the fifteen-to-twenty postwar years) in order to suggest the possibility of adopting a different point of view in reading the story of unified Italy: so that, in other words, it would not simply be a waste of time to ask ourselves what it was that only allowed "Italian genius" to show tangible signs of life in the period immediately after the Second World War.

INNOVATION AND IMITATION

The exercise carried out by Roicho Bojilov (2020) does not sweep all the doubts from the field. Technically the role of imported innovation and spontaneous innovation emerges in his case from an application of factor analysis, i.e. of that branch of statistics that attempts to measure the existence of non-measurable "factors" (e.g. "spontaneous" innovation) starting from a set of variables (TFP growth rates) that can be observed directly and that are supposed to be linked in some way to the non-measurable factors. The limits of factor analysis are known and to a great extent traceable to the difficulty in correctly selecting the latent factors that are the primary goal of the analysis. Superimposed on these in Bojilov's case is the search for structural breaks inside the sample which—though not without statistical backing—adds a further element of arbitrariness. Finally, as has already been observed, to the extent that is consistent with evidence from other sources, Bojilov's conclusions do not permit a precise analysis of the role of the immediate postwar period vis-*à*-*vis* the decades before and after it.

It can therefore be useful to attempt to respond to the questions raised by Roicho Bojilov by starting from a body of information that is largely the same but selecting a different starting point and following a different research strategy in order, among other things, to verify the robustness of his conclusions in this way.

Inspired by the cited works by Richard Nelson and Edmund Phelps (1966) (and, more recently by Daron Acemoglu et al. [2006]), Philippe Aghion et al. (2014) depict the dynamics of the average productivity in an economy as the weighted average of the productivity levels of the innovating sectors (which will see their productivity increase γ times following the innovation activity) and of the imitating sectors (which, instead, will be content to raise their productivity levels closer and closer to the frontier), the weights being given—at time t and in country i— by the fractions of innovating (δ_{it}^{IN}) and imitating (δ_{it}^{IM}) sectors out of the total. However extremely stylised it may be, it is a description of the dynamics of productivity that highlights the question at the core of these lines, namely Italy's ability—in the course of its history as a unified country and notably in the post-Second World War period—to produce innovation autonomously and not simply limit itself to importing the technological skills and imitating the behaviour of the rest of the world. The body of information on which Table 3.1 is based lends itself, quite naturally, to testing such a hypothesis, possibly providing estimates of the values assumed by the two parameters at the centre of our attention at this moment which summarily represent the propensity for spontaneous innovation *à la* Phelps and the propensity for innovation that we could define as passive and that translates into merely imitative behaviour.

Referring to Appendix A for the details and assuming—for the time being—that the parameters of interest can vary in space but not in time, here we can limit ourselves to examining the main results. From the estimates listed in detail in Appendix A, we can deduce—for different countries and with reference to the whole 1891–2021 period—the estimated value of two distinct magnitudes:

- $\delta_i^{IN}(\gamma - 1)$: the product of the share of innovating sectors (δ_i^{IN}) and the productivity growth factor resulting from the innovation activity (γ); under the simplifying hypothesis that γ is—in addition to constant in time and space—positive and greater than one (that is, the innovation activity increases the productivity level γ times) and that the share of front runner sectors is in turn positive but less than one, we expect the term $\delta_i^{IN}(\gamma - 1)$ to be positive and less than one, therefore falling between zero and $(\gamma - 1)$, i.e. the long-term productivity growth rate; if the term $\delta_i^{IN}(\gamma - 1)$ turns out not to be significantly different from zero we are forced to conclude that the propensity for spontaneous innovation—the dynamism—of the country i can be deemed to be negligible if not actually non-existent;
- δ_i^{IM}: the fraction of imitating sectors.

Estimation results, summarised in Fig. 3.2, allow some immediate considerations to be made. In the case of the United States—as we would naturally expect for the technological leader—the fraction of imitating sectors is on average zero over the period 1891–2021. This is not so for all the other countries and passive innovation appears significant in particular in continental Europe and notably in Italy (even more than in other countries of Mediterranean Europe). Instead, as regards the fraction of innovating sectors—given the presence of the term $(\gamma - 1)$ that, as has been said, we can consider to be positive and presumably common to the different countries considered—we could in principle limit ourselves exclusively to consider the relative role of the individual countries in terms of dynamism. Given that in the cases in which the term $\delta_i^{IN}(\gamma-1)$ is negative (Greece, Italy, Portugal and Japan) it is not significantly different from zero, it is immediate to conclude (also in the light of the results given in detail in Appendix A) that of the Euro-area countries considered in this analysis, only Germany and the Netherlands—as well as Spain, marked however by obvious institutional peculiarities up to 1975—reveal significant symptoms of spontaneous innovation activity that are not far off those found in the UK and United States. In all the other cases it is easy to conclude that the attitude to spontaneous innovation was, on average, at best extremely low. Should we wish to go further (Fig. 3.2) and letting 3%—approximately the average TFP growth rate in the United States in the period considered—be a reasonable approximation for $(\gamma - 1$ (i.e. for the productivity growth factor resulting from the innovation activity), the share of innovating sectors would fall between 50 and 80% in the highly dynamic countries (the United States, Germany, the Netherlands),[12] would touch about 40% in the UK and in Spain, would not exceed 20% in Belgium and France.

Appendix A leaves no doubt that in some cases (including Italy, but also Belgium, Germany and the Netherlands) the composite parameter $\delta_{it}^{IN}(\gamma - 1)$, unlike the parameter δ_{it}^{IM}, cannot be considered not to vary with time. As such, it would be inappropriate to conclude that the Italian share of innovating enterprises has been nil throughout the

---

[12] The presence of the Netherlands should not surprise and not simply because of its historical merits (McCloskey & Corden, 2020, pp. 171–175) or contemporary ones (for years the Netherlands has constantly been in the top group of the Global Innovation Index) but also because of the innovative performance of the country over the course of the whole twentieth century (Verspagen, 2008).

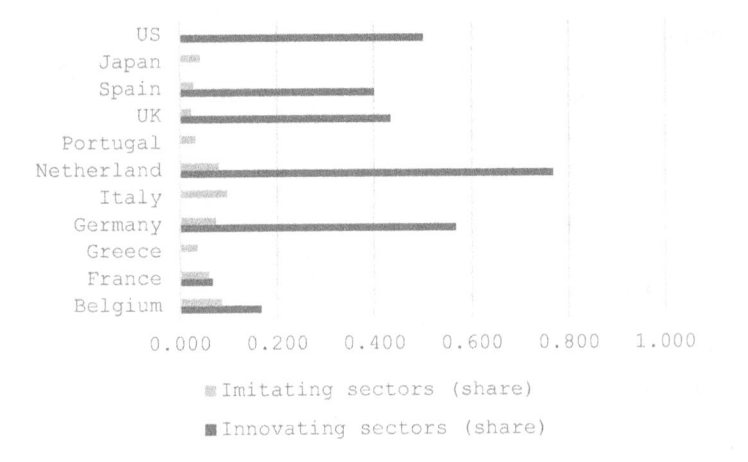

Fig. 3.2 Innovation vs imitation activity (1891–2021) (*Note* The negative and not significantly different from zero estimates of the share of innovating enterprises in Greece, Italy, Portugal and Japan have been set to zero. *Source* See Appendix A)

more than a century-long time span. If appropriate account is taken of this aspect—and Appendix A summarises the associated results—the working hypothesis formulated in the preceding paragraph is confirmed even further.

For example, the use of the Kalman filter—a recursive algorithm providing estimates of unknown variables given the evolution of measured quantities over time (Appendix A)—for estimating the share of innovating sectors (or, to be more precise, for estimating the parameter $\delta_{it}^{IN}(\gamma - 1)$) leads to the estimates in Fig. 3.3 where the graph shows the value of the quantity of interest—i.e. the share of innovating sectors times the productivity growth factor—expected for year t conditioned on the information set available up to year $t - 1$. The message of Fig. 3.3 is quite clear. The Italian economy's capacity for spontaneous innovation shows some signs of vitality (although not significantly different from zero) between the end of the nineteenth century and the start of the twentieth. In the second half of the 1920s the dynamism of the Italian economy falls considerably: from this standpoint the 1930s and 1940s appear to be the most asphyxiated of the entire 130 years under consideration.[13]

Innovators begin to reappear on the scene in the early 1950s: the weight of innovating sectors out of the total grows in a tumultuous manner until the end of the 1960s when touches about two thirds (if we assume, as before, the productivity growth rate to be constant and presumably close to the long-term growth rate of the United States TFP, and therefore equal to 3%). From that moment on—a little at a time as the memory of the economic miracle fades—stasis intervenes initially and is then followed by a decline starting from the middle of the nineties. The Italy of the early decades of the twenty-first century, from this viewpoint, has nothing for the Italy of Zanardelli, Sonnino, Giolitti or Luzzati to

---

[13] It is interesting to ask oneself what could ever be hidden behind the marginally (in statistical terms) negative values of the $\delta_{it}^{IN}(\gamma - 1)$ quantity observed for Italy in the 1930s and 1940s. The most convincing hypothesis is related to the increasing segmentation of the world economy and closure of the Italian economy starting right then from the 1930s. Gianni Toniolo (1980, pp. 277–287) observed that, though we make the aforesaid autarky date from 1934, many roads had been travelled in that direction during the years immediately beforehand. Conversely, the first loan from the US Export Import Bank, also to be usable for purchasing American machinery and technology, was granted in January 1947 during the visit of the Italian Prime Minister Alcide De Gasperi to the United States. Now, as recalled in Appendix A, the interpretative hypothesis suggested by Philippe Aghion et al. (2014) assumes that the technology diffusion process meets no obstacles which, instead, during the 1930s and 1940s and beyond, were unquestionably present given what was envisaged by the sanctions imposed on Italy by the League of Nations. The presence of constraints of this kind does not of course eliminate the presence of technology importing sectors but partly or totally prevents these from filling the gap that separates them from the frontier. At the same time, it cannot be excluded that the presence of obstacles to the diffusion of technology translates into incentives for non-imitative innovation process. The former of the two phenomena leads to imagining that the term $\delta_{it}^{IN}(\gamma - 1)$—in the depiction of the productivity growth process of Philippe Aghion et al. (2014)—could also incorporate a further negative component equals to the amount of the productivity growth lost following the limited activity of passive innovation. The latter would obviously go in the opposite direction. That the first of the two phenomena prevailed is exactly what can be inferred from the introduction of a *dummy* variable referred to the 1930s. It can be noted how the phenomenon also tends to manifest itself in France, though in less clear terms. With Belgium and Switzerland, Italy and France—in those fateful years of the 1930s—were part of the so-called golden block which, more than the sterling area or that of the mark, bore the consequences of the global "fragmentation" in those years (Feinstein et al., 1997, pp. 146–165).

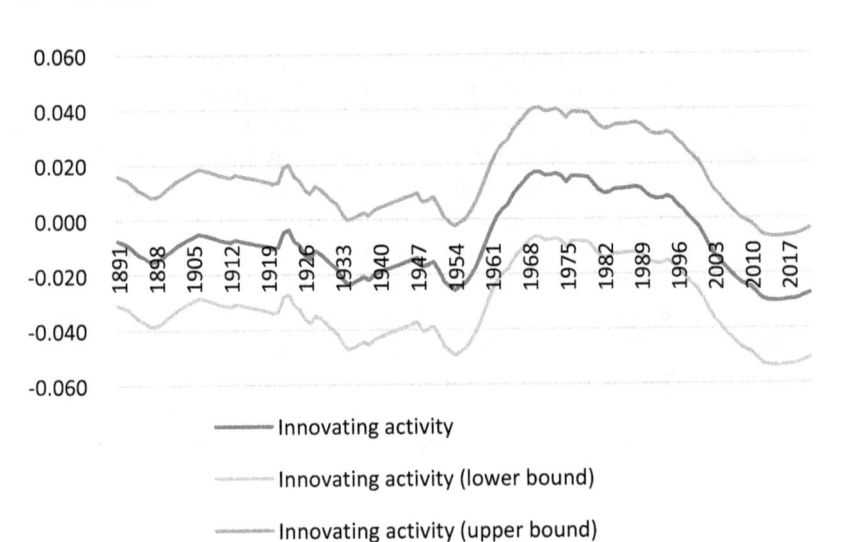

Fig. 3.3 Innovating activity (1891–2021; Italy, estimate of the parameter $\delta_{it}^{IN}(\gamma - 1)$ deriving from application of the Kalman filter along with estimated upper and lower bounds) (*Source* See Appendix A)

envy—if we can put it this way—and behaves even marginally worse than the Italy of Mussolini, Volpi di Misurata or Jung.[14]

A detailed analysis of the evolution of spontaneous innovation in the main European countries clearly exceeds the objectives of this work. From a comparative point of view, it is interesting though to underline one striking regularity. Figure 3.4 reports the distance recorded, over time, between the estimate of the parameter $\delta_{it}^{IN}(\gamma - 1)$ based on the Italian data and the corresponding estimates referring to some of the countries already mentioned in Fig. 3.2. The first thing that catches the eye is that, apart from a blip in the years between the nineteenth and twentieth centuries, the role of innovative sectors appears in Italy always and in any case lower than that recorded elsewhere in Europe up to the "miracle" years. A significant recovery—in particular compared to what is observed in Europe—is recorded starting from the early 1950s and up to the second half of the 1960s when the role of innovative activity in

---

[14] Similar indications are given—*mutatis mutandis*—by the rolling estimates of the parameters of interest, referred to in Appendix A.

Italy exceeds that recorded elsewhere. This is followed by about thirty years of stagnation with respect to UK and United States and decline with respect to the main European countries followed, starting from the second half of the 1990s, by a continuous and increasingly worrisome backsliding of Italy in relative terms. Compared to the main European powers (France, Germany and the UK) and to Spain, the innovation performance in Italy seems to be subdued for most of the 130 years, with the sole exception—as has already been observed—of the 1950s and 1960s where a momentous upturn is evident. In this respect, it may prove instructive to associate the information underlying Fig. 3.4 with the accurate reviews reported, at a national level, in Foreman-Peck and Federico (1999) and cantered, in particular, on the relationship between the State and the market. The relative stability of the distance between the weight of innovative activity observed in Italy and that recorded elsewhere in continental Europe can be then traced back—as far as Belgium is concerned—to the widespread anti-competitive practices recorded in the latter country in the 1930s, 1940s and 1950s and then again in the 1970s and 1980s (Hens & Solar, 1999). These practices then laid the foundations for the slowdown in the dynamism of the Belgian economy observed starting from the 1990s. The dynamism of the French economy experiences a positive trend starting from the early years of the twentieth century and then abruptly reverses course towards the end of the 1920s in correspondence with the proliferation of dirigiste initiatives aimed at placing limits on the market economy after the Great Depression. Only in the 1950s—and with the launch of the Fifth Republic—does France recover the dynamism that had completely disappeared in the 1930s and 1940s. In this case, too, the process was to be interrupted in the 1970s but, unlike what happened in Italy, in France the activity of spontaneous innovation, significantly other than zero up to the present day, only experiences a contained decline entirely consistent with the defensive strategies put in place in recent decades—strategies that are essentially indifferent to the theme of economic dynamism (Dormois, 1999, p. 92). A long-term decreasing trend, followed by substantial stability, characterises German innovative activity until the 1950s and 1960s, even though it remains, before and after that date, at levels well above those observed in France or Italy. In the German case, starting from the mid-1930s the consequences of the policies of rearmament and preparation for the war events of the first part of the 1940s become evident. Just as the reversal trend recorded on the occasion of the return to a market economy (even if "social") starting from the 1950s appears equally evident (Feldenkirchen, 1999). Finally, in the Spanish case, any assessment cannot disregard the political context which—more than elsewhere and in particular in terms of closure towards the rest of the world—characterised it between the mid-1930s and the mid-1970s (Fraile Balbin, 1999) making it a special case from many points of view.[15]

As regards the estimates of δ_{it}^{IM} on the other hand, the evidence—analysed in detail in Appendix A—is by and large one of relative stability in all the countries considered, followed in the last two decades by a sudden fall. In general, the weight of the imitating sectors oscillates between 5

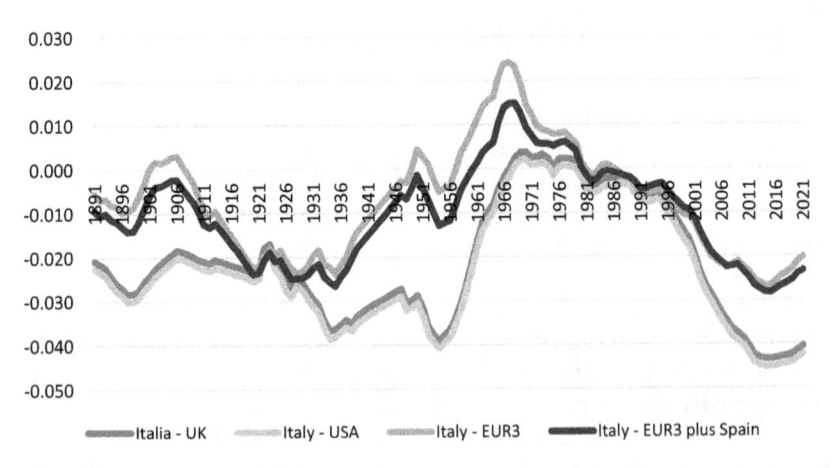

Fig. 3.4 Innovating activity (1891–2021; differences between Italy and selected countries in the estimates of the parameter $\delta_{it}^{IN}(\gamma - 1)$ deriving from application of the Kalman filter) (*Note* EUR-3: Belgium, France, Germany; it was deemed appropriate to neglect the case of the Netherlands in the light of the unreasonably large estimates of the innovating activity implied by the Kalman filter estimates. *Source* See Appendix A)

---

[15] The unreasonably large estimates of the Dutch economic activity implied by the Kalman filter estimates suggested to disregard the Netherlands. It should be mentioned, though, that the significant negative distance between Italy and the Netherlands, evident throughout the observed period, may have a lot to do with the deep-rooted adherence of Dutch society to the principles of market economies, with the attention paid to the independent management of companies belonging to the public sector and with the respect for the autonomy of private enterprise (van Zanden, 1999).

and 15% and appears to be significantly greater than zero up until the early years of the current century. In fact, starting from the years marked by the global financial crisis a vertical collapse is recorded in innovation activity, even if passive: a collapse whose origin could be traced, among other things, to the impact of the twin 2008 financial crisis and 2011 crisis of sovereign debts (OECD, 2012, Chap. 1; 2015).

Children of the "Miracle"

The Italian performance—as depicted in Fig. 3.3—appears to be consistent with many of the conclusions that historians and economic historians have reached in the attempt to understand technology's role in Italian economic history,[16] and it is relatively easy to place many of the events that have marked the relationship between technology and growth during the 160 years since Unification in it. For example, it is possible to place Italy's entry into the Second Industrial Revolution (mainly through direct investments from abroad as well imports of machinery and equipment and licensing agreements) especially in the chemical and iron and steel sectors in the decades before the First World War (Giannetti, 1998, pp. 99–115; Vasta, 1999). It is not surprising therefore that the estimate of the attitude towards adopting and diffusing foreign technologies is placed at historically high levels up until the mid-1930s.

During the fascist *Ventennio*, as much as the import of technology from abroad remained significant because of licensing agreements, joint ventures and patents lodged in Italy by foreign companies, the role of direct foreign investment was significantly scaled back. The shrinking weight of imitation activity up until the middle of the 1940s was affected by the overall climate at the time as well as by the domestic decisions of the period and in particular the autarky. Having overcome the Second World War, the attitude towards acquiring technological capacity from others reached the peak for the 160-year period: these were the years

[16] Renato Giannetti (1998, pp. 41–45), for example, uses investment data in machinery and equipment and patenting information in Italy and in the United States to assess the relative weight of the capacity for autonomous innovation. Based on this indicator, Italy's autonomous innovation capacity is lower for a large part of the period considered (1893–1980) than that of the other countries analysed (Germany, the United Kingdom, France and Spain). If compared to the adoption and diffusion of technology developed elsewhere, Italy's aptitude for spontaneous innovation tends to increase starting from the post-Second World War period (as is also implicit in Fig. 3.3).

of the transfer of American technology towards Italy via the European Recovery Program and of the importance of technological standards in engineering, in chemicals, in iron and steel and in the more traditional sectors (Giannetti, 1998, pp. 138–150). There would then be a relative decline in the share of imitators before growing once again gradually as the country began to catch up with, and then take part fully in, the globalisation era. In more recent times, as we have already said, the sharp downsizing of the tendency to acquire foreign technologies seems to have felt the impact of the events of the four-year 2008–2011 period.

In the same way, the pattern over time of the country's attitude towards creating innovation autonomously (rather than simply absorbing it) seems to be consistent with the evidence relating to specific periods. As we have seen, though not significantly different from zero, the values of the share of innovators experiences two important distinct moments in the decades preceding the Second World War. The first phase (between the end of the nineteenth century and the start of the twentieth in Fig. 3.3) in which we can spot a few timid signs of a capacity for creating innovation autonomously (the estimate still being close to zero) and a second phase in which the same capacity seems to be completely absent (Giannetti, 1998, p. 50). Having gotten through the tragic pages of the Second World War, innovative performances of some prominence—concentrated in the major companies but often also short-lived—were recorded in chemicals, in engineering and in rubber (Giannetti, 1998, pp. 50–51) and, by no coincidence the attitude towards the production of innovation tends to rise in Fig. 3.3 in the period immediately after the Second World War. It was this period, according to Franco Amatori (1980) that saw the emergence of the few entrepreneurial figures who can be likened in some way to the profile of the Schumpeterian entrepreneur. When the boom years began to become an increasingly distant memory over time the country seemed to return to its old habits and the few innovative episodes of some importance—the biotechnologies of the 1980s, for example (Giannetti, 1998, p. 64)—were not such as to reverse an initially flat trend that later clearly became a downward one. In this the Italian economy reveals itself to be significantly different from economies like the German or the French that seem in the last few decades to have maintained an ability to innovate that was attained (in the French case) or already been experienced (in the German one). On the whole, the common opinion is apparently that if there has been innovation during the century and a half and more that separates us from 1861, this was concentrated in the major companies (Giannetti, 1998, p. 74). This conclusion however contributes towards clarifying the point.

What seems to be completely missing in the Italian case—and perhaps, as we shall see, with the sole exception of the two decades following the Second World War—is what Edmund Phelps calls "grassroots innovation": the widespread aptitude and the frequent capacity for creating innovation and the willingness of society to grasp it and make it its own. This aptitude and this capacity could and can be found elsewhere in the world in the small innovative enterprises, but not only in them, and these were absent in Italy or, when this was not the case, they were short-lived (Giannetti, 1998, p. 75) and they certainly could not be replaced by the activities aimed at adapting existing technologies typical of the Italian industrial districts more than at innovating in the narrow sense of the word. An aptitude and a capacity of which, as has been noted, however, the signs are not lacking in the immediate post-Second World War period in which "a small-medium enterprise [...] which records unsuspected dynamism" (Colli, 2002, p. 85) takes shape. The first motorway refreshment point (dated 1947) due to the ingenuity of Mario Pavesi—from which the current world leader in the sector, Autogrill, would later be born—is an excellent example.[17] Just as was the birth, in 1946, of the first motorcycle with a load-bearing body—the legendary Vespa—designed by Corradino D'Ascanio and produced by Piaggio[18] or the entry, in 1958, on the market of childcare products by Pietro Catelli's Artsana

---

[17] In the 1940s Mario Pavesi was a young industrialist from Novara, son of a baker. In 1947 he opened a small biscuit outlet (serving the *Biscottini di Novara*, later renamed *Pavesini*) on the Milan–Turin motorway, close to the Novara exit and not far from the nearby family factory: a simple bar with tables and chairs surrounded by a pergola. Not long afterwards, the refreshment point would be transformed to include a restaurant serving the motorists who were beginning to travel around the country. Starting from 1959, the Autogrills—designed by the architect Angelo Bianchetti—became one of the icons of the economic miracle.

[18] Founded in 1884, the Rinaldo Piaggio Company had gradually dealt with naval and railway furnishings and, with the arrival of the First World War, with aeronautical and military production. After having experienced a corporate downsizing linked to the events of the owner family and the destruction of some factories during the early 1940s due to war events, Piaggio passed, in 1965, under the control of the Agnelli family and, starting from 2003 of Roberto Colaninno, becoming the leader of a group focused on the production of motorcycles (which also includes Aprilia, Moto Guzzi and Moto Laverda). Since 1946, Vespa production has known no interruptions: 16 million units have been produced to date.

with the "Chicco" brand.[19] Just as is the "invention" by Pietro Ferrero, in 1946, of Nutella—the result of the postwar cocoa shortage, born as Giandujot and then becoming Nutella in 1964—[20] or even the container for powdered coffee (dated 1949) due to the creativity of Beppe Lavazza (in which, in 1955, the legendary "Lavazza blend" will find its place, fruit of the intuitions of his son Emilio).[21] Just like the metal absorbent (getter, dated 1957)—a widely used component in televisions and household appliances—by Paolo Della Porta which will contribute to making SAES company (today SAES Getters) a world-class company[22] or even—in a completely different sector—the introduction in 1948 by Valerio Gilli and Clara Calissano of a completely new payroll system (the so-called slip).[23] Just like, again, in 1964 the first brake discs intended for the spare parts market and introduced by Brembo, a name still spoken of today[24] or the machines for processing and packaging introduced by IMA (the current world leader for tea bagging) in the 1960s.[25] Just like, finally, the armchairs and the sofas designed by Marco Zanuso and produced by

[19] The son of a worker from Como, Pietro Catelli founded in 1946, at the age of twenty-six, a syringe distribution company called Artsana, now operating in 150 countries and with production units in Italy and Europe.

[20] In the early 1940s, Piera and Pietro Ferrero transformed a pastry shop into a confectionery factory. In 1956 Ferrero opened a first production plant abroad, in Germany. France followed shortly after. The Ferrero group is today a multinational which is responsible for a very significant part of Italian agri-food exports. Just under 400,000 tons of Nutella are produced annually.

[21] Drogheria Lavazza, opened in Turin in 1895 by Luigi Lavazza, was transformed into the company, Luigi Lavazza Spa, in 1927. At the end of the 1950s, it established itself as the leading Italian company in the coffee sector and among the leaders in Europe.

[22] The company Società Apparecchi Elettrici e Scientifici (SAES) was founded in Florence in 1940. Paolo Della Porta took over the leadership in 1952. Saes Getters is today a multinational listed in Milan and New York.

[23] The company Innovazione Aziendale (InAz) was founded in 1948 focusing its attention on the management of human resources. A few years after its conception, Valerio Gilli's "slip" would become the "pay slip"—mandatory for companies—pursuant to law no. 4 of 1953. Led by the third generation, today the InAz group is an example of the so-called Italian "fourth capitalism" (Zamagni, 2021).

[24] Founded in 1961 by Emilio, Sergio, Alberto Bombassei and Italo Breda, Brembo started as a small mechanical workshop and followed immediately after a decade-long path marked by technological innovation and research to become a leader in Italy and worldwide and to eventually see its very company name becoming a synonym for "brake".

[25] IMA (Industria Macchine Automatiche) was established in 1961 in Bologna and since 1963 owned by the Vacchi family.

Arflex in Milan since 1947 thanks to the innovative use of foam rubber and elastic tapes,[26] the first Italian supermarket opened in Milan in 1957 on the initiative of an Italian-American joint venture headed by Nelson Rockefeller and, on the Italian side, by Bernardo and Guido Caprotti,[27] or the current Italian pet food leader born in 1963 from an intuition of Baldassarre Monge.[28] The Prato wool district—recalls Andrea Colli (2002, p. 164)—took its cue from product innovation (the use of regenerated wool) and from process innovation (the so-called fancy fabrics) to establish itself steadily over time. The "many small workshops, scattered in the pre-Alpine valleys"—Andrea Colli points out again (2002, p. 167)—are, in the immediate postwar period, the cradle of product and process innovations in which the current iron and steel industry in Brescia has its roots.

And it is impossible not to remember how in those years between the second half of the 1940s and the first half of the 1960s we also find the roots of an important slice of what we presently call the Italy of luxury. Enzo Ferrari produced the first car with his own brand in Maranello in 1947: a brand that seventy years later would be recognised as the most influential in the world. Fifty kilometres away—in Cento—Ferruccio Lamborghini returned from the front and founded Lamborghini Trattori in 1948 innovating the operating mode of its tractors (petrol starting and oil operating). It was joined by Lamborghini Auto in 1963: the Lamborghini Miura, presented in 1965, was considered a work of art, so much so that it was exhibited at the MOMA in New York. In a different field, in 1953, Ottavio Missoni and his wife Rosita Jelmini opened a small workshop in their home, not far from Milan: with them, "made in Italy knitwear" was born, i.e. knitwear items unique for their combinations of patterns and colours. In 1954, Mariuccia Mandelli from Bergamo began producing women's clothes in Milan under the Krizia brand: her "black and white" style would mark the 1960s. Not unlike

---

[26] Founded in 1947 by Carlo Barassi, Renato Teani (both coming from the Pirelli tyre company), Pio Reggiani and Aldo Bai, Arflex is—after more than seventy years—still releasing its classic, timeless pieces. A rare combination of technology and aesthetics, of craftmanship, creativity and iconic design.

[27] The Caprotti brothers acquired 51% of Supermercati Italiani in 1961 and it was then the Italians who transformed the initial Supermarket Italiani brand into Esselunga.

[28] In 1963 Baldassarre Monge understood that the transformations of the Italian family would lead pets—and with them their diet—to become an integral part of family units.

what the geometries of the Valentino fashion house founded in 1960 in Rome by Valentino Garavani and Giancarlo Giammetti will do. Innovations certainly different from the previous ones but equally disruptive and long-lasting and certainly capable of influencing the country's growth prospects.

In short, whatever analytical method is used the indication of the data seems to be unequivocal. Some have recognised in these trends the adaptability and capacity of the Italian economy and society for overcoming their shortcomings—limited natural resources and a relative availability of unskilled labour—and give rise to Italian economic development "against every prognosis" while making a virtue out of necessity as the saying goes (Cohen & Federico, 2001, p. 8). The dear, old Italian art of "making do". Others, on the other hand, have maintained that these same trends are, first of all, the fruit of the absence of a systematic tradition of technological innovation (Giannetti, 1998, p. 198) or, mainly, of the presence of widespread vested interests and of human capital that was poor in quality and quantity, and these would constitute a powerful barrier to growth (Toniolo, 2013, p. 46). Still others have opted for the idea according to which the trends described derive from a "structurally weak [national] system of innovation" (Nuvolari & Vasta, 2017, p. 137),[29] while the inadequacy and lack altogether of adaptability and the "extractive" nature of the institutions would have prevented the country from expressing its full potential for growth (Di Martino & Vasta, 2017, p. 18). The point made in these pages is that even when Italy had already had more "inclusive" institutions—and in some phases in its history it quite probably did—these, though necessary, would not have been sufficient (as, in effect, they were not sufficient) for overcoming the fundamental obstacle: a deep-rooted (and mostly dominant) culture that was averse to growth. It is no coincidence that when Italy, for a very short period, opened itself to a different reading of the world (and of itself), and briefly regained the liberty and the possibility and the desire to exercise it, it also managed to overcome the formidable obstacle of institutions that in other historical

---

[29] On the concept—or better on the concepts—of "national innovation system" see the review contained in Nuvolari and Vasta (2017, pp. 133–137). Here it is sufficient to underline how, whatever definition of it is given, a national innovation system would appear to be unable to take shape unless there is a network or a body of institutions (comprising, among other things, the scientific and technological policies and the training of the human capital) capable of determining its performance.

moments and in a quite different cultural context had produced radically different results. And vice versa.[30]

It would be very interesting to be able to repeat the exercise carried out in the above lines, while making a distinction between the southern and insular Italy macro-region and the centre-north one. There are, in fact, many reasons for thinking that rather than being an economic one, the distance between the two Italys belongs to the cultural sphere, to the shared system of "beliefs, values and preferences" capable, according to Joel Mokyr, of influencing human behaviour. Unfortunately, the information available does not make it possible to replicate at the macro-region level the growth accounting exercise carried out by Claire Giordano and Francesco Zollino (2020) for the country in its entirety[31] and for the whole time interval of the unification experience. Such information covers, and with quite a few difficulties, no more than the seventy years following the Second World War (if not less).[32] The theme therefore remains open for future research.

This having been said, it is appropriate, however, to suspend judgement for the moment and put it back to the closing pages of the following chapter. Before drawing conclusions, even preliminary ones, it is in fact necessary to remember the non-negligible limits of total factor productivity on which we have based our assessments up to this point. It is appropriate not to exaggerate the scale of the econometric exercises such as the one described in the preceding lines. These are useful bases for reasoning, indispensable modalities for distilling the information available, and are therefore necessary but not enough on their own for allowing us

[30] It is very interesting to note that the specificity of the 1950s and of the early 1960s also emerges in the context of readings of Italian economic history that are quite far from the one implicit in these pages. For example, the following are the words of Giulio Sapelli (1989, p. 628): "After the second postwar period [...] an entrepreneurial culture widespread among the subaltern working and peasant classes [...] was liberated [...]. After 1951 a «new industrial bourgeoisie» was born in Italy that was to an initially unusual extent wrapped up in the small and medium enterprises: concentrated initially in the traditional sectors [...], it then developed in innovative sectors [...] and, I want to underline, with a growing ability to introduce technological innovation".

[31] An exercise which—as far as Italy is concerned—is at the basis of the information collected by Antonin Bergeaud et al. (2016).

[32] It is not by chance, in fact, that the subject has been analysed recently, but with reference to company data and only for recent decades (e.g. by Emanuele Ciani et al. [2019] who found TFP levels in southern Italy that were roughly below from 13 to 33% compared to north-west Italy and lower than those prevalent in other geographical areas).

to consider the thesis we have been proposing to be fully reliable. In short, in addition to the TFP trends, it is necessary to add other sources of information that are capable of throwing light on the question that we are posing: has there ever been dynamism in the Italian economy? If yes, was it confined to the miraculous years after the Second World War? And, finally, if yes again, why?

References

Acemoglu, D. (2009). *Introduction to Modern Economic Growth*. Princeton University Press.

Acemoglu, D., Aghion, P., & Zilibotti, F. (2006). Distance to Frontier, Selection, and Economic Growth. *Journal of the European Economic Association, 4*(1), 37–74.

Aghion, P., Akcigit, U., & Howitt, P. (2014). What Do We Learn from Schumpeterian Growth Theory? In P. Aghion & S. Durlauf (Eds.), *Handbook of Economic Growth* (Vol. 2, pp. 515–563). Elsevier.

Aghion, P., Antonin, C., & Bunel, S. (2021). *The Power of Creative Destruction*. Harvard University Press.

Aghion, P., & Howitt, P. (1992). A Model of Growth Through Creative Destruction. *Econometrica, 60*(2), 323–351.

Aghion, P., Howitt, P., & Murtin, F. (2011). The Relationship Between Health and Growth: When Lucas Meets Nelson-Phelps. *Review of Economics and Institutions, 2*(1), 1–24.

Amatori, F. (1980). Entrepreneurial Typologies in the History of Industrial Italy 1880–1960. *Business History Review, 54*(3), 359–386.

Antonelli, C., & Barbiellini Amidei, F. (2007). Innovazione tecnologica e mutamento strutturale dell'industria italiana nel secondo dopoguerra. In C. Antonelli, F. Barbiellini Amidei, R. Giannetti, M. Gomellini, S. Pastorelli, & M. Pianta, *Innovazione tecnologica e sviluppo industriale nel secondo dopoguerra* (pp. 3–358). Laterza.

Barbiellini Amidei, F., Cantwell, J., & Spadavecchia, A. (2013). Innovation and Foreign Technology. In G. Toniolo (Ed.), *The Oxford Handbook of the Italian Economy Since Unification* (pp. 378–416). Oxford University Press.

Bergeaud, A., Cette, G., & Lecat, R. (2016). Productivity Trends in Advanced Countries Between 1890 and 2012. *Review of Income and Wealth, 62*(3), 420–444.

Bojilov, R. (2020). Sources of Indigenous Innovation and Channels of Its Transmission Across Countries. In E. Phelps, R. Bojilov, H. Teck Hoon, & G. Zoega, *Dynamism* (pp. 48–67). Harvard University Press.

Bosworth, B., & Collins, S. (2003). The Empirics of Growth: An Update. *Brookings Papers on Economic Activity, 34*(2), 113–206.

Cassese, S. (2014). *Governare gli italiani. Storia dello Stato.* Il Mulino.

Ciani, E., Locatelli, A., & Pagnini, M. (2019). TFP Differentials Across Italian Macro-regions: An Analysis of Manufacturing Corporations Between 1995 and 2015. *Politica Economica, 35*(2), 209–242.

Cohen, J., & Federico, G. (2001). *Lo sviluppo economico italiano 1820–1960.* Il Mulino.

Colli, A. (2002). *I volti di Proteo: storia della piccola impresa in Italia nel Novecento.* Bollati Boringhieri.

Di Martino, P., & Vasta, M. (2017). Introduzione. In P. Di Martino & M. Vasta (Eds.), *Ricchi per caso. La parabola dello sviluppo economico italiano* (pp. 9–21). Il Mulino.

Dormois, J. P. (1999). France: The Idiosyncrasies of «Volontarisme». In J. Foreman-Peck & G. Federico (Eds.), *European Industrial Policy. The Twentieth-Century Experience* (pp. 58–97). Oxford University Press.

Federico, G., & Toninelli, P. A. (2003). Business Strategies from Unification Up to the 1970s. In R. Giannetti & M. Vasta (Eds.), *Evolution of Italian Enterprises in the 20th Century* (pp. 191–238). Il Mulino.

Feinstein, C. H., Temin, P., & Toniolo, G. (1997). *The European Economy Between the Wars.* Oxford University Press.

Feldkirchen, W. (1999). Germany: The Invention of Interventionism. In J. Foreman-Peck & G. Federico (Eds.), *European Industrial Policy. The Twentieth-Century Experience* (pp. 98–123). Oxford University Press.

Fenoaltea, S. (2020). The Fruits of Disaggregation: The Engineering Industry, Tariff Protection, and the Industrial Investment Cycle in Italy, 1861–1913. *PSL Quarterly Review, 73*(292), 77–110.

Foreman-Peck, J., & Federico, G. (1999). *European Industrial Policy.* Oxford University Press.

Fraile Balbin, P. (1999). Spain: Industrial Policy Under Authoritarian Politics. In J. Foreman-Peck & G. Federico (Eds.), *European Industrial Policy. The Twentieth-Century Experience* (pp. 233–267). Oxford University Press.

Giannetti, R. (1998). *Tecnologia e sviluppo economico italiano 1870–1990.* Il Mulino.

Giordano, C., & Zollino, F. (2020). Long-Run Factor Accumulation and Productivity Trends in Italy. *Journal of Economic Surveys, 35*(3), 741–803.

Hens, L., & Solar, P. (1999). Belgium: Liberalism by Default. In J. Foreman-Peck & G. Federico (Eds.), *European Industrial Policy. The Twentieth-Century Experience* (pp. 194–214). Oxford University Press.

Howitt, P. (2005). Coordination Issues in Long-Run Growth. In L. Tesfatsion & K. Judd (Eds.), *Handbook of Computational Economics* (Vol. II, pp. 1605–1624). Elsevier.

McCloskey, D. N., & Carden, A. (2020). *Leave Me Alone and I'll Make You Rich*. The University of Chicago Press.

Nelson, R., & Phelps, E. (1966). Investment in Humans, Technological Diffusion and Economic Growth. *American Economic Review, 56*(1), 69–75.

Nuvolari, A., & Vasta, M. (2017). Un fantasma in soffitta? Il sistema innovativo italiano in prospettiva storica. In P. Di Martino & M. Vasta (Eds.), *Ricchi per caso. La parabola dello sviluppo economico italiano* (pp. 129–182). Il Mulino.

OECD. (2012). *Science, Technology and Industry Outlook 2012*. OECD.

OECD. (2015). *The future of productivity*. OECD.

Phelps, E. (2013). *Mass Flourishing*. Princeton University Press.

Sapelli, G. (1989). Modelli della crescita e progresso tecnico Riflessioni dall'italia. *Società e Storia, 12*(45), 619–659.

Toniolo, G. (1980). *L'economia dell'Italia fascista*. Laterza.

Toniolo, G. (2013). An Overview of Italy's Economic Growth. In G. Toniolo (Ed.), *The Oxford Handbook of the Italian Economy since Unification* (pp. 3–36). Oxford University Press.

van Zanden, J. L. (1999). The Netherlands: The History of an Empty Box? In J. Foreman-Peck & G. Federico (Eds.), *European Industrial Policy. The Twentieth-Century Experience* (pp. 177–193). Oxford University Press.

Vasta, M. (1999). *Innovazione tecnologica e capitale umano in Italia 1880–1914. Le traiettorie tecnologiche della seconda rivoluzione industriale*. Il Mulino.

Verspagen, B. (2008). Challenged Leadership or Renewed Vitality? The Netherlands. In C. Edquist & L. Hommen (Eds.), *Small Countries Innovation Systems* (pp. 319–354). Edwar Elgar.

Zamagni, V. (2021). *INAZ Innovazione aziendale. Una azienda di persone per le persone*. Il Mulino.

CHAPTER 4

Patents and Business Demography

PATENTS

Going beyond the limits of total factor productivity necessarily implies looking for alternative quantitative indicators of innovation activity. From many viewpoints patents are—or should be—the most reliable indicator of the innovation activity carried out in a given country in a given unit of time. In reality it is not so in the sense that in this case too, as in the case of total factor productivity, there are quite a few limits that characterise this indicator and that must be taken into account accurately at the moment in which its informative content is assessed.

From our point of view, the main one is certainly linked to the representativeness of the indicator. Patents represent a subset of innovative activity: generally, the activity carried out inside bigger companies. Not all activity necessarily produces a patent datum. This can be because of its nature, or because of the existence of a different or more convenient way of protecting an innovative activity. More in general, Phelps' spontaneous innovation is quite a much broader concept of innovative activity that as we have said does not always translate into a patent. Innovative activity often and deliberately springs from the kind of knowledge that Hayek would call "dispersed", whose protection is implicit in the very nature of

© The Author(s), under exclusive license to Springer Nature Switzerland AG 2024
N. Rossi, *Reframing Italian Economic History, 1861–2021*, Palgrave Studies in Economic History,
https://doi.org/10.1007/978-3-031-67271-2_4

that knowledge.[1] Patents are, we might say, the echo, a returning refrain like in music that can end up by reproducing the initial sound, often in a dampened and less intense tone. Conversely, alongside the theme of representativeness is a problem of decipherability. The rules (formal and informal) that govern the examination of patent applications and subsequent registration of the same are not homogeneous from country to country and over time, and this obviously constitutes a significant limit in all the cases in which comparability is an important part of the analysis. This has often led to analysing the patents registered by different countries in one country alone (the technological leader) in order to guarantee reasonable comparability of the data.

Having said this, the relationship between patenting activity and the dynamics of productivity is something that emerges from the data with a certain clarity. In Fig. 4.1 each point corresponds, for any given country, to the configuration of TFP growth rate and per capita patenting activity (as proxied by the ratio between the number of patents granted in the same time interval by the United States Patent and Trademark Office to residents in each individual country and the population of the latter) observed on average between 1890 and 2020 (the grey dot representing the average configuration observed for Italy in the cited time frame). The slope of the interpolating line (the dotted line)—if positive, as in this case—denotes the existence of a positive correlation between the two quantities of interest: for the 23 countries considered by Antonin Bergeaud et al. (2016), average TFP growth rates go roughly hand in hand with levels of patent activity per capita.[2]

Given the above, in what follows we will simply summarise—with a few minor adjustments—the evidence provided in the works of Renato Giannetti (1998), of Alessandro Nuvolari and Michelangelo Vasta (2017) and of Federico Barbiellini Amidei et al. (2013) who, among others, have analysed the innovative activity in unified Italy in quite different

---

[1] See, for example, the testimony by Pietro Gnutti, a skilled mechanic in Sarezzo (a small town near Brescia), reported by Andrea Colli (2002, p. 167): "Immediately after the war we built a first rotary shear which, like a sort of rolling mill with knives, penetrated the red-hot rail and cut it in one fell swoop into three pieces [...] we were the first in an absolute sense, it was an innovation that I didn't even think of patenting, and so it turned up everywhere".

[2] A similar relationship seems—in the work of Ufuk Akcigit et al. (2017)—to link the growth rate of the GDP per capita with the logarithm of the patents granted state by state during the course of the twentieth century in the United States.

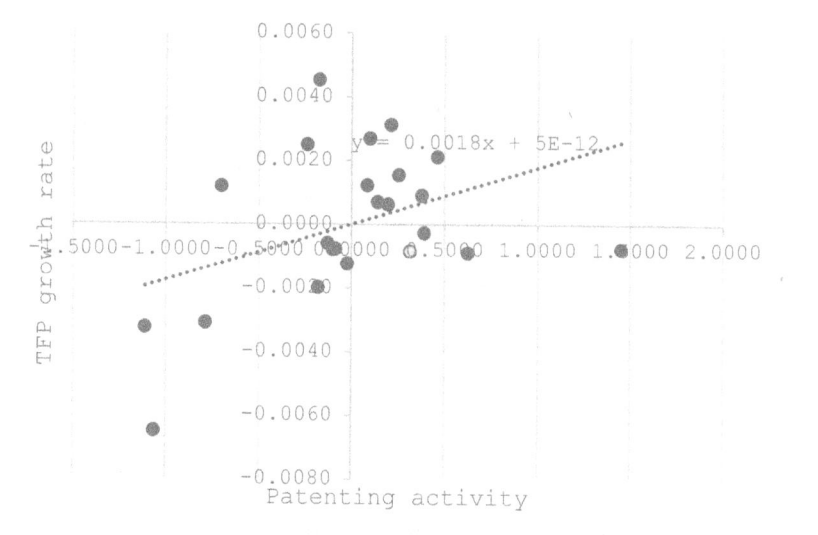

Fig. 4.1 Total factor productivity (TFP) growth rate and per capita patenting activity (1890–2020) (*Note* In order to prevent spurious correlations and to take account of effects of scale, both the average of TFP growth rates and the average patenting activity have been stripped of the impact of the initial conditions of the single countries [the logarithm of the total factor productivity and logarithm of the patenting activity indicator in the first year]. Also note that the starting date is 1963 for one of the 23 countries to which the data base of Antonin Bergeaud et al. [2016] refers—i.e. Finland. *Sources* For patents data, for the years 1883–1962, USPTO, *Technology Assessment & Forecast. Seventh Report*, March 1977. Retrieved March 18, 2024, https://www.uspto.gov/web/offices/ac/ido/oeip/taf/taf7_tbla3_fo.pdf; for the years 1963–2021, USPTO, *Extended Year Set. Patent Counts by Country, State and Year*. Retrieved March 18, 2024, https://www.uspto.gov/web/offices/ac/ido/oeip/taf/cst_utlh.htm and successive updates; for population and TFP data, as in Fig. 3.1 and Table 3.1)

detail through the lens of patenting activity. Compared to their work, the evidence discussed in the lines that follow manages to cover the entirety of the 2010s. Figure 4.2 depicts the per capita patenting activity of Italy, of its main European partners and of the UK in the United States between 1883 and 2020 and requires a few words of comment.

Overall, Italy's performance would not actually seem to be so distant from that of its terms of reference but, unfortunately, in the Italian case the scale is the one shown on the right in the graph whereas the scale

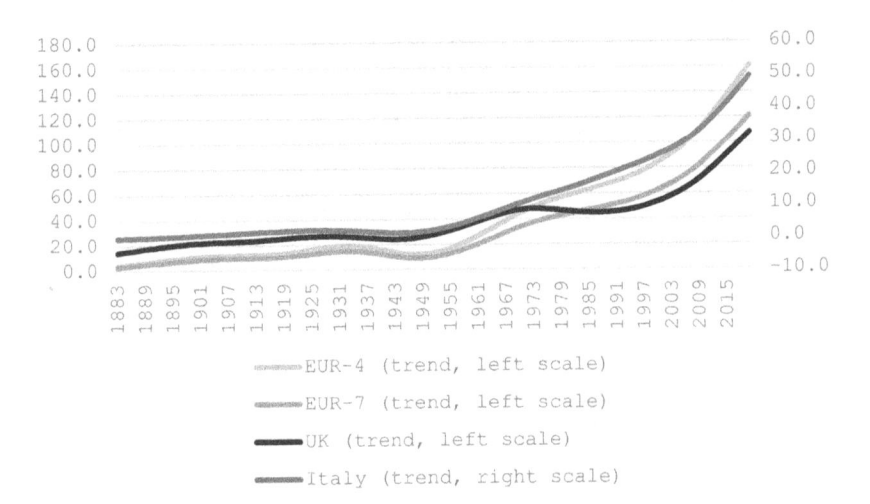

Fig. 4.2 Patenting activity of specific countries or groups of countries in the United States (trend components, 1883–2020) (*Note* [i] EUR-4: France, Germany, The Netherlands and Belgium; EUR-7: EUR-4 plus Greece, Spain and Portugal; [ii] the trend components are those that result from the application of a Hodrick and Prescott filter to the original series [to identify the value of λ in this and subsequent application of the Hodrick and Prescott's filter see Martin O. Ravn and Harald Uhlig (2002)]. *Sources* As in Fig. 4.1)

applicable to the Europe "of 4" and "of 7" and the UK is the one on the left. An initial significant conclusion can also be drawn and is evident from Fig. 4.2: during the whole (or almost) 160-year epoch, Italy—understood as an innovator country—can be seen for what it is: a dwarf. At over a century and a half from the first sitting of the Italian Parliament—18 February 1861 in Turin—Italy's relative per capita patenting activity does not exceed 30% of the corresponding activity of its main continental European partners (France, Germany, the Netherlands and Belgium) or 40% of the same amount when referred to an aggregate enlarged to include the peripheral countries (Greece, Spain and Portugal, in addition to the four countries already mentioned).

The per capita patenting activity indicator as so defined appears to be preferable compared, for example, to the share of patenting activity that can be attributed to an individual country out of the total for the same activity as registered in the United States which, evidently, does not take proper account of the size of the country of origin. Moreover, the information underlying Fig. 4.2, allows to focus on the Italian relative patenting performance by simply comparing the evolution over time of the Italian indicator of per capita patenting activity (in the United States) *vis-à-vis* that of individual countries (the UK) or groups of countries (EUR-4 or EUR-7) in the same country, as in Table 4.1 where the standard format we have been using for per capita GDP and TFP comes up again.

In browsing through Table 4.1, the reader should bear in mind that the data are affected, more than anything, by the starting point (particularly low in the case of Italy). As a result, the Italian relative patenting performance in the first decades of the twentieth century is largely illusory. Nevertheless, the data record timid patenting activity growth during the Giolitti era but the "great leap forward" obviously seems to start in the 1950s. In the Giolitti era (1903–1913) the relative increase in Italian patenting activity is visible but all things considered it is relatively limited. Italy's per capita patenting activity compared to the Europe "of 4" aggregate actually goes from 7 to 12% in that time span, for example. This is a significant increase but, all things considered, it is not really so far from the one observed during the previous twenty years compared to the same

Table 4.1 Growth rate of the per capita patenting activity (%; 1891–2020, selected subperiods)

Differential in the average per capita patenting activity growth rate	1890–2020 (a)	Convergence and two tails		A miracle And that's all		
		1891–1992 (b–c)	1993–2020 (d)	1891–1946 (e)	1947–1964 (f)	1965–2020 (g)
Italy–EUR-4	5.6	7.1	0.2	8.5	11.8	0.8
Italy–EUR-7	5.7	7.2	0.2	8.5	12.1	0.8
Italy–UK	8.1	10.4	−0.3	7.6	28.6	1.9
Italy–USA	9.4	12.0	0.1	9.5	30.8	2.5

Notes EUR-4 = France, Germany, the Netherlands, Belgium; EUR-7 = EUR-4, Spain, Portugal, Greece
Sources As in Fig. 4.1

aggregate. Notice that at the end of the First World War (in 1919) the indicator touches 38%. This evolution can be entirely attributed not so much to the renewed dynamism of the Italian economy rather than to the impact of the First World War on the German economy and consequent reduction of about 90% of German patenting activity in United States (which dropped from over 22 patents per 100,000 inhabitants in 1914 to little more than 2 patents per 100,000 inhabitants in 1919).

Perhaps the same can also be said of the years marked by the Second World War, but at the end of the 1940s the recovery of Italian patenting activity is substantial and only starts to wane at the beginning of the 1970s before then stopping completely with the arrival of the 1990s. It is difficult not to conclude that overall—and with the usual exception of the "miraculous" fifteen-to-twenty years—the performance is rather disappointing especially if compared to other European Union founder states. For those who would like "an easy win", the only thing remaining is to refer to the comparison with the technological leaders of the nineteenth century (the UK)—just as we have seen in other circumstances—but we are still well below 50% in terms of patenting activity too.

In any case, the anecdotes about Italian patenting activity (Giannetti, 1998, pp. 55–60, just to give one example) are not exclusively but are unquestionably linked to the name of Giulio Natta and his polypropylene in the middle of the 1950s, to the Lepetit pharmaceutical industry and chloramphenicol or rifampicin and (between the end of the 1940s and the early 1950s), and to Olivetti Programma 101 (the so-called "Perottina"), the first known personal computer that Pier Giorgio Perotto developed in the first half of the 1970s, just to give a few examples. And from the same anecdotes we learn that—unlike what happened in the cited cases of grassroots innovation (Pavesi, Lavazza, Artsana, Ferrero, SEAS, IMA, InAz, Brembo, Arflex, Esselunga, just to quote some of them)—in 1963 Olivetti transferred its activities in the electronic field to General Electric, while in 1964 Dow Chemical took over Lepetit, and in the period straddling the 1960s and 1970s Istituto Donegani—an integral part of Montecatini first and later Montedison—abandoned its research into new materials. Naturally, there was no shortage of sporadic innovative initiatives both before and after the Second World War but unfortunately these are the known exceptions that confirm the rule.

The disappointing time profile of the relative Italian per capita patenting activity that emerges from the US information sources is precisely confirmed by the data from the Ufficio Italiano Brevetti e

Marchi (UIBM) (the Italian Patents and Trademarks Office). Figure 4.3 shows the quota of patents granted by the UIBM to residents and, for comparison purposes, the quota of patents granted by the USPTO to US residents. If we take away the wartime periods—in which patents of a domestic origin grew clearly in Italy and less in the United States for evident reasons that have little or nothing to do with the country's innovative capacity—the data sourced from the UIBM are much more explicit. The quota of patents issued to domestic residents sails along between 35 and 40% without significant deviations (except for the wartime events) until the years immediately before the Second World War. It grows significantly, exceeding 50% right up to the 1950s but then declines depressingly and actually drops below the prewar average in the 1970s. In the same time span, the corresponding quantity for the United States oscillates between 90 and 70% along a downward trend.[3] The whole distance between leader and follower can be seen from the space between the two curves.

When looking at the figure for Italy the information contained in USPTO publications obviously does not make it possible to identify the region of residence of the natural or legal person to whom the patent application refers. In other words, here again it is unfortunately impossible—at the present state of knowledge—to assess the different patenting performance at the level, for example, of the single Italian macro-regions.[4] In this case too it is to be hoped that future research will want and be able to fill this gap.

The few lines above do not do justice to the wealth of information contained in the patent data—of which full account is given in the works mentioned above, among others—nor do they give due space to Italy's patenting activity in countries other than the United States and, especially, in Europe in the last thirty years (through the European Patent Organization or EPO). For additional information reference should be made to the

---

[3] Notice that during the decade 2011–2021, the share of patents granted by European Patent Office to its 38 member states averaged around 44%.

[4] Once again, the operation is feasible only with reference to more recent decades and in particular beginning with the launch of the European Patent Office. For what it is worth, on average for the period 1997–2012, the patents issued by the EPO to residents of the Italian Centre-North regions amounted to little more than 10 per one hundred thousand inhabitants and only a little more than 1 per one hundred thousand inhabitants of the Southern and Island Regions (https://www.istat.it/it/archivio/16777, Retrieved March 18, 2024). Any comment would be superfluous.

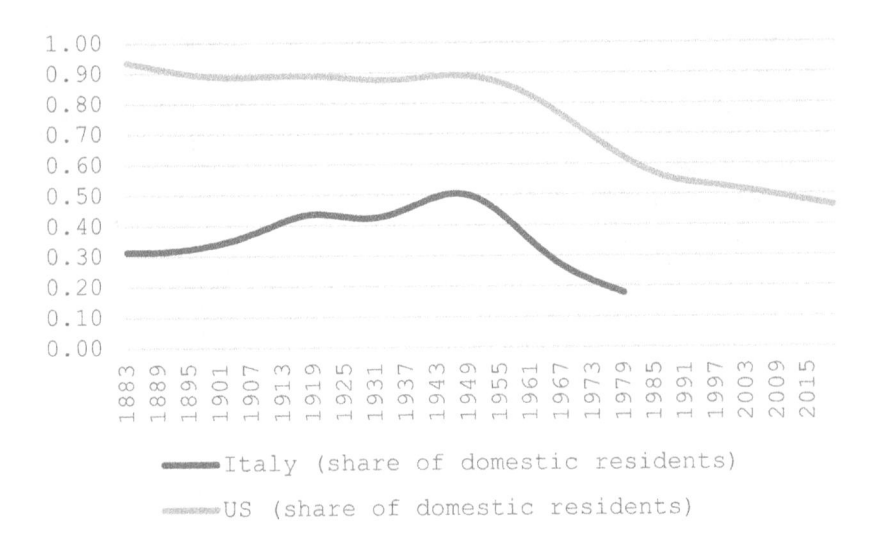

Fig. 4.3 Italy' and United States' patenting share in Italy and in the United States, respectively (numbers of patents granted to residents, trends, 1883–2020) (*Note* The UIBM data—directly or from the World Intellectual Property Organization [WIPO]—are missing for the years 1965–1967, 1969, 1975–1978 and 1980–1986; starting from 1997, Italian patents have only been granted by the European Patent Office [EPO]; the breaks in the series make the extraction of the trend component less reliable. *Sources* For the United States data, as in Fig. 4.1; for the Italian data, ISTAT, Annuario Statistico Italiano, Retrieved March 18, 2024, https://ebiblio.istat.it/digibib/Annuario%20Statistico%20Italiano/ and WIPO, Historical Dataset, Retrieved March 18, 2024, https://www.wipo.int/ipstats/en/)

already-mentioned works, but the substance remains unchanged: whatever viewing angle is taken, Italy's relative performance appears modest and a few, significant, attempts to catch up with our main partners can only be seen in the years of the economic boom and in the upsurge generated by it (and completely exhausted for some time today).

BUSINESS DEMOGRAPHY

In a study like the one we are carrying out no other proofs are available other than "circumstantial" ones: no direct proofs, therefore, but demonstrable facts that taken together are useful for giving substance to a specific reconstruction of the events. Among these circumstantial proofs a crucial position is held by business demography—the process of birth, growth, decline and death of companies.

The theories of growth that build on the Schumpeterian concept of "creative destruction"—already recalled in this chapter—underline the perpetual motion that characterises market economies: new enterprises tackle the open sea and others abandon the field in more or less orderly fashion, new products see the light while others sit on the shelves before ending up in oblivion, new production processes come into being to replace others that are deemed inefficient, new markets open almost daily in an economic scenario whose features mutate ceaselessly, sometimes gradually and sometimes without warning.[5] Naturally not all companies (already active or only potential)—and, just as naturally, not all the workers—have the abilities and the willingness necessary for tackling the change. To be fair, some companies and some workers are themselves agents of change, but others can do nothing else but bear the consequences or at least attempt to kick the can down the road and push them further into the future. Increases in the productivity of the system are linked to the former enterprises and to the former workers, to their willingness to accompany—if not indeed urge—the creative destruction processes, and to the presence of policies that can facilitate them (or at least not discourage them). And vice versa.[6]

More particularly, in the experience of many countries, the main channel—although not exclusive one—for introducing innovations into

---

[5] The recent work by Philippe Aghion et al. (2021), entitled *The Power of Creative Destruction*, constitutes a complete review of the research, both theoretical and empirical, carried out on the matter in the last thirty years. *Openness to Creative Destruction* by Arthur Diamond (2019) completes it worthily from the point of view of historical perspective. Finally, the recent *The Economics of Creative Destruction* edited by Ufuk Akcigit and John van Reenen (2023) best illustrates the usefulness of the concept of "creative destruction" in addressing the central issues of our time: from inequality to climate change.

[6] The reference here is to the impact of creative destruction processes on medium to long-term growth. Ricardo Caballero, among others, examined the cyclical implications. See Caballero (2008) for a concise review.

the system and for generating new jobs would actually seem to be new enterprises. Even though they experience higher market exit rates than average they would be the ones that, if and when they manage to survive, would present the best prospects for growth. Conversely, the market exit of marginal companies (and therefore the ones characterised by lower productivity levels than the market leaders) would contribute, in turn, towards increases being recorded in the system's average productivity.[7] We would expect, then, to find quite a close link between the processes of birth and death of enterprises and the dynamism of an economy, on the presumption that it is new enterprises—facing an existential alternative between growth and disappearance ("up or out")—that are the main driver of productivity.

Figure 4.4—based on information on the early decades of the current century—offers some evidence in this respect by examining the relationship between the most common index of creative destruction (i.e. the sum of the enterprise entry and exit rates, also known as the gross turnover rate or also the churn rate), to which we will return in the lines that follow, and the growth rate of the TFP as well as the per capita patenting activity (in the United States) indicator for each individual country.[8] As before, each point in the graph corresponds to the configuration of the quantities of interest observed for a given country in the cited time span (Italy being, again, represented in grey). The trend—as given, again, by the interpolating (dotted) line—is positive in both cases, much more clearly though in the first case. This is an interesting indication (also as regards the informative content of the patenting activity) to be taken though with more than a pinch of salt since it concerns a narrow time interval dominated by events of the greatest magnitude such as the 2008 financial crisis, the 2011 sovereign debt crisis and the 2020 pandemics. What emerges from Fig. 4.4 is a confirmation however: business demography is an important

---

[7] For a review of the evidence on these aspects reference can be made, among others, to the preparatory works for the collection at the OECD of a homogeneous set of information on business demography (later transferred to the EuroStat environment) and therefore, for example, to the works by Stefano Scarpetta et al. (2002) and Nicola Brandt (2004).

[8] The evidence contained in Fig. 4.4 should be considered with caution as the reliability and homogeneity of the underlying information are not always completely clear. For example, OECD sources do not necessarily match EuroStat ones and national sources do not necessarily match OECD or EuroStat ones (Ireland is a good case at hand). Notice, however, that the positive relationship depicted in Fig. 4.4, right panel, survives if the patenting activity indicator is replaced by other indicators of the same activity (such as the share of individual countries patenting activity in the United States).

source of information that is, in turn, able to summarise the impact of variables that are usually relevant for the purpose of the efficient allocation of resources (from costs associated with starting up a business to the availability of credit, the structure of the labour market, the institutional architecture and so on).

Of course, proposing to give some indication—however approximate—on business demography, not just in the course of the last two decades but

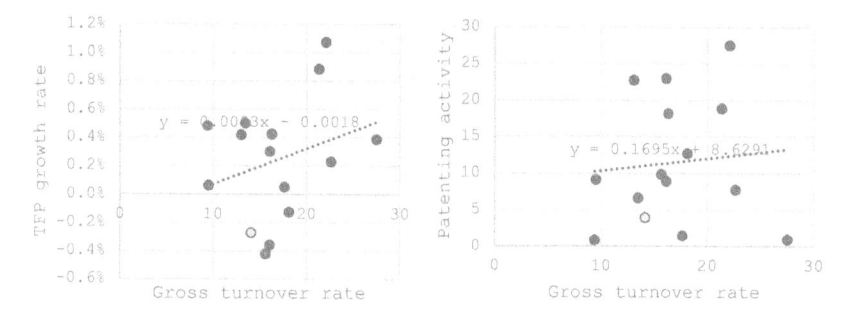

Fig. 4.4 Gross turnover rate, total factor productivity (TFP) growth rate and per capita patenting activity index (first and second decade of the twenty-first century; averages for the specific periods as in the note) (*Note* The graph uses the information available—mostly from EuroStat—and relating to the subset of countries considered by Antonin Bergeaud et al. [2016] namely: Austria [for the years 2004–2020], Belgium [2008–2019], Germany [2009–2020], Denmark [2013–2020], Spain [2008–2020], Finland [2008–2020], France [2009–2020], United Kingdom [2002–2020], Greece [2015–2019], Italy [2008–2020], Netherlands [2007–2020], Norway [2008–2020], Portugal [2004–2020], Sweden [2008–2019] and the USA [1978–2020]; the information refers to the aggregate labelled as "business economy". *Sources* For the gross turnover rate EuroStat, *Data Explorer.* Retrieved January 27, 2022, http://appsso.eurostat.ec.europa. eu/nui/show.do?dataset=bd_9ac_l_form_r2&lang=en for most European countries[9]; Office for National Statistics, *Business Demography UK.* Retrieved March 18, 2024, https://www.ons.gov.uk/businessindustryandtrade/business/activitys izeandlocation/bulletins/businessdemography/2021 for the UK; for the United States as in Fig. 4.1; for the TFP and the patenting activity of the individual countries in the United States: as in Fig. 4.1)

---

[9] Recent updates refer to 2021 only, which underlines the need to look at Fig. 4.4 with some skepticism.

over the last century and a half, might seem like a prohibitive task. The comparable information from the OECD and Eurostat sources on the businesses births and deaths does not make it possible—as we have just seen—to go back more than twenty years at best. In the United States the Census Bureau's Longitudinal Business Database starts in 1976. The CERVED records in Italy are limited to joint stock companies starting from 1993 and the ones from Assonime (the Association of Italian Joint Stock Companies), while covering a highly significant part of the 160 years since Unification, refer to too small a subset of the population to be somehow representative of the business population. The only option then is to have recourse to the information in the records (or more recently made public by the system) of the Italian Chambers of Commerce, Industry, Crafts and Agriculture (*CCIAA*) and, in particular, to the contents of the so-called register of businesses (or of enterprises since 1942) which, starting from 1910, collects information on the legal form, sector of economic activity, and registered address in Italy as well as all the records concerning the business activity. This is sooner said than done as can be seen in detail in Appendix B which should be referred to for an indication of the quite significant difficulties it is necessary to face in order to utilise the information source and for a precise description of the procedures followed for the reconstruction, as homogeneously as possible, of the information regarding the 1983–2021 period and for an initial and still partial rediscovery of the information present in the historical records of the Chambers of Commerce and relating to the 1910–1982 period. It is worth underlying that while from 1983 onwards these records are public knowledge and cover—with a few shortcomings here and there—the entire country, from 1983 backwards they are a hitherto unexplored source of information.

Some warnings are essential. First of all, in order to guarantee as far as possible some possibility of comparison with the information available for other countries (or groups of countries) we will refer below only to enterprises other than sole proprietorships (and therefore to joint stock companies and partnerships or, for example, to enterprises in cooperative form). The aggregate defined in this way seems to be the closest to the so-called employer enterprises (i.e., to businesses with at least one employee) to which the statistics available in other countries usually refer. Secondly, again for comparative purposes, the decision to overlook sole proprietorships implies essentially limiting our attention only to non-agricultural sectors (and in fact, once this decision is taken, the distance between indicators extended or otherwise to the agricultural sector is virtually negligible). Thirdly, we will exclude from the field of analysis the so-called unclassified activities, namely registered businesses for which at the moment of registration it was not possible to define a specific sector of activity. This category is anything but residual: it represents on average about 6% of the businesses registered to which an effective activity often does not correspond (only little more than one business out of ten in this category is found to be active) but potentially capable of distorting the results significantly (see Appendix B for the details).

Furthermore, we will analyse the phenomenon from different viewpoints. As an initial approximation, from the viewpoint of entrepreneurial attitude (and in particular of the number of new undertakings for a given number of inhabitants), and afterwards from the viewpoint of the dynamics of the business population making reference therefore to the entry and exit rates of businesses and to the net turnover, i.e. to the combined impact of the companies' entry and exit decisions, and gross turnover, and therefore to an indicator, however indirect, of the scale of the creative destruction phenomena in the system.

Figure 4.5 shows the evolution of the number of newborn enterprises (other than sole proprietorships) per 100,000 inhabitants of working age (aged 15–64) during the course of the last four decades (or so). The downward trend that characterises not only Italy as a whole but also, in relatively homogeneous terms, the four macro-regions is clear. Unfortunately, the Eurostat information does not permit the reconstruction of a similar indicator for a timespan greater than a decade (or almost) while in the case of the UK the information is only available starting from 2001. This is not true for the United States, however.

Figure 4.5 (left panel) therefore also gives the number of new plants (and note, not of newborn enterprises) observed in the United States since 1978 per 100,000 inhabitants of working age (as above). Bearing in mind that in the period considered the number of plants exceeds the number of businesses by about 20–25%, it is rather easy to conclude that, notwithstanding the downward trend of proportions similar to those observed in Italy, the Italian propensity for entrepreneurship fluctuates overall between 65 and 50% of the corresponding American figure (with lower values likely prevailing in more recent years).[10] With reference

---

[10] It should be noted that the definition of employer enterprise implies that a business with no employees at the moment of birth is however deemed to be like an additional

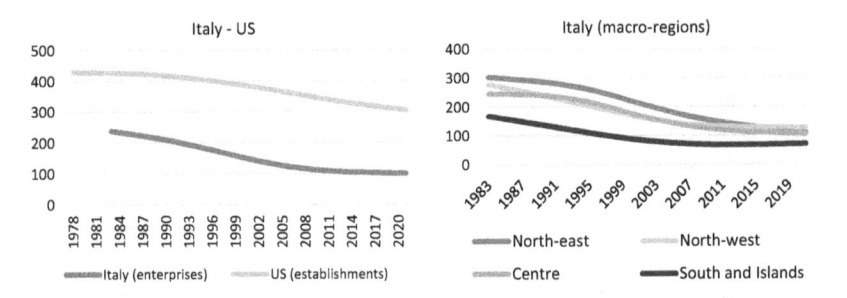

Fig. 4.5 New enterprises per 100,000 inhabitants (left panel Italy and United States, 1978–2021; right panel Italy, macro-regions; 1983–2021; trends components) (*Note* The trend components are those that result from the application of a Hodrick and Prescott filter to the original series. *Source* For Italy see Appendix B; for the United States as in Fig. 4.1)

to the last two decades, the distance from the UK seems even more pronounced as the propensity for entrepreneurship in that country is about four times higher than Italy's[11] (and rising during the brief period for which the data are available).[12] If we limit ourselves to the last decade or little more (and therefore with all the appropriate precautions) both the Europe "of 4" aggregate and the Europe "of 6" (the latter including—besides France, Germany, Belgium and the Netherlands— Spain and Portugal, but not Greece due to lack of relevant information) settle at entrepreneurship propensity levels that are not dissimilar from those of the United States and therefore significantly higher than the Italian ones.

plant at the moment in which it takes on the first employee. Conversely, the exclusion of sole proprietorships from the aggregate under observation implies that the same continue not to be considered even at the moment in which they take on an employee (as long as their legal form is not changed at the same time).

[11] Source for the United Kingdom as in Fig. 4.4.

[12] As proof of the potential distortion induced by the "unclassified activities" it should be noted that whenever they are treated in the same way as other sectors and therefore included in the number of new businesses (despite their paltry level of activity), the downward trend evident in Fig. 4.5 would weaken considerably starting from the early years of the current century. The gap between the Italian datum and the American one would diminish in the same way.

Just as in the United States (Hathaway & Litan, 2014), in Italy too, the clear downward propensity for entrepreneurship is a widespread phenomenon distributed virtually homogeneously throughout the nation (Fig. 4.5 right panel), although noteworthy is the gap between Italy's south and islands and the rest of the country. This gap contributes to a significant extent towards explaining the difference in entrepreneurship terms between Italy and the other Western countries mentioned. This distance is less pronounced today than it was in the 1980s in absolute but not in relative terms, and only on account of the particularly pronounced negative trend in the other macro-regions and certainly not because the south of Italy revealed some kind of trend inversion.

It is interesting to note that the downward trend in the propensity for entrepreneurship triggered a broad debate in the United States around the hypothesis of a secular decline in American dynamism and its capacity to be a bearer of innovation. The debate was echoed in international organisations and led to the isolation of some factors potentially able to explain the trend evident in Fig. 4.5. In first place, demography. James Liang et al. (2018) among others have noted that two forces seem to be at work from this viewpoint: on the one hand creativity—a necessity for a business activity—and the attitude towards risk which can legitimately be presumed to decline on average with age and, on the other hand, specific entrepreneurial skills which require some work experience to have been matured, preferably in positions with managerial and decision-making content. The combination put in place by the two factors means on one hand that the propensity for entrepreneurship grows with age up towards "middle age" and then declines gradually as the "age advantages" weaken; and, on the other hand, that in an ageing society the less youthful generations constitute an obstacle that is increasingly more difficult to overcome for those young people who want to acquire the experience necessary for doing business. But while wanting and being able, those young people might not find—according to Robert Gordon (2016)—opportunities worth taking at hand's reach and, as a consequence, could abandon the idea of doing business. And though wanting and being able, those young people could instead be dissuaded by the legal and regulatory context in which the business would have found itself. And furthermore, dissuading potential entrepreneurs could be a byproduct of an increasing degree of concentration of the markets linked, say, to the introduction of ICT technologies. Finally, Ufuk Akcigit and Sina T. Ates (2021) are to be thanked for the attempt to put the greater or lesser intensity of the diffusion of knowledge at the centre of the debate on the decline of American entrepreneurial dynamism.

This is certainly not the place to give opinions on the outcomes of the debate. What is worth emphasising in these lines is that there is no trace in Italy of such a broad debate on a theme that is likely to be central for the future of Italy's national economy. The same worthy research activity carried out by the Bank of Italy on the subject was limited to evoking some of the structural limits of the Italian economy when it was not concentrated prevalently on the current economic situation.[13] It is legitimate to presume that this is the consequence of the narrow time window that characterises business data—whose use is of course crucial for the analysis of business demography—but perhaps it is equally legitimate to observe that the virtual disinterest for the theme is in reality nothing if not the projection of the role played by business in the culture of many Italians. How else to explain the different attention paid by the institutions to the issue of the plunge in birth rates compared to the evident drop in the country's aptitude for doing business despite the clear impact of both phenomena on the country's long-term growth profile and despite the obvious link between the two phenomena?

A simple econometric exercise discussed in detail in Appendix B confirms the impact of ageing processes on entrepreneurial propensity trends and suggests that increases equal to one percentage point of the share of the over-64-year-old population may correspond in the long run to reductions in the entrepreneurial propensity (defined, as has been said, as the number of new businesses per 100,000 inhabitants aged between 15 and 64)[14] more than proportional with respect to the initial impulse. In the face of demographic forecasts that assume an increase in the share of over-64-year-olds of around 10 percentage points over the next thirty years (starting from the 23% share observed in 2021), this implies that we should expect a decline in the propensity for entrepreneurship over the

---

[13] And the attention has been concentrated on "the usual suspects": the legal system, Italian business's dependence on the banks, and the "relational" nature of the Italian economic system. As well, of course, on the difficulties encountered by the country in adopting the reforms necessary for overcoming the obstacles mentioned (Rossi, 2018).

[14] The impact would be significantly diversified among macro-regions. Greater in north-western and central Italy, lower in north-eastern Italy and around the national average in southern and insular Italy.

next few decades that will not be all that different, in relative terms, from that which occurred in the last forty years which led from 200 to 250 new businesses per hundred thousand inhabitants in the second half of the 1980s to just over 100 new businesses per hundred thousand inhabitants on the eve of the 2020s. Nonetheless, the country's highest offices often refer to the subject of the decline in births, and with heartfelt tones. There are no such things as far as entrepreneurial trends are concerned (without adjectives like "youthful" or "feminine").

Associating the data in Fig. 4.5 with some quantitative representation of the demographic trends which have been visible for decades now in Italy to conclude that "it's the demography, stupid" would be, however, too easy. As we have seen, it is certainly true that the reasons for the main and most recent trends in business demography must be sought in demography in the strict sense, but it's not just demographics that matter. Given that the share of the over-64-year-old population out of the total is changing in southern Italy and the islands as in the other districts (with an increase close to ten percentage points in the most recent forty years) albeit at slightly lower levels (about two or three percentage points) and with an impact not that different from the national average on the propensity for entrepreneurship, the significantly lower propensity for entrepreneurship in southern and insular Italy cannot be attributed to the demographic trend. Just as it is not, nor is not only, to demographic trends that the previously observed gap in the propensity for entrepreneurship between Italy, the United States, the UK and the main countries of continental Europe can be attributed. This recalls the more general reasons repeatedly referred to in the text with the important consequence that, if in the case of demographic trends, the future is written in the present, the same is not necessarily true for the underlying motivation that leads some of us to start a business.

The decline in the entrepreneurial attitude in the last forty years is reflected—understandably but not obviously—in a downward trend in the enterprise entry rates (defined as the ratio between the number of new enterprises in a given period and the stock of existing enterprises at the beginning of the same; Fig. 4.6). This passed in fact from 6 to 10% in the mid-1980s to less than 3% in the early years of the century before then settling stably between 1 and 2% in the last ten years. And this in all the macro-regions, and in broadly comparable terms: the correlation rates between the entry rates in the various macro-regions swing between 80 and 95%, though a certain "decoupling" between Southern/Insular

Italy and the rest of the country is apparent. And the same can be said as regards production sectors.

Moreover, if we also consider the company exit rates (defined as the ratio between the number of businesses that close in a given period and those in existence at the beginning of the same; Fig. 4.6) the net birth rate (or net *turnover*) has been stubbornly below zero for twenty years by now (Fig. 4.7). Put in other terms, when things go well as many firms are born as die every year. And they have not been going well at all for two decades.

If the subject were cradles, we would be talking about zero growth and "empty cradles". But perhaps we should talk, without reticence, about shrinkage and "empty sheds": in many of the production sectors, there has been a significant shrinking of the productive base since 2008. In the last thirty years the number of manufacturing companies has been dropping over 1.5% per year, almost 2.5% starting from 2008 (and without any significant reversal of the trend in recent years). The trends have been less pronounced in the building industry or commerce. And even the services sector, which seemed to be growing in the nineties, reversed direction in

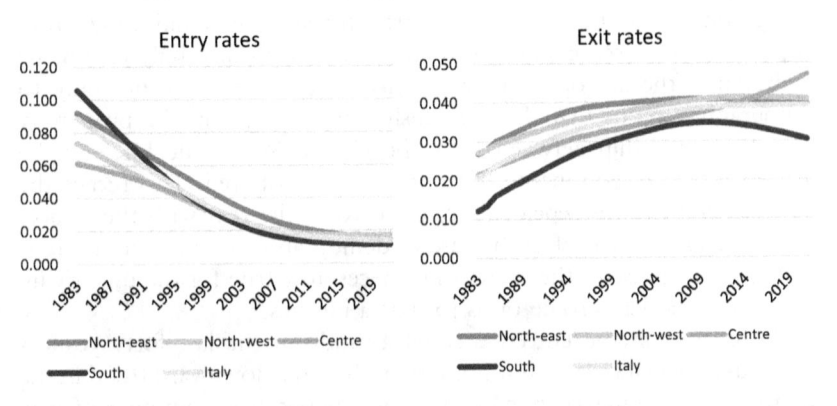

Fig. 4.6 Business entry and exit rates (%, Italy and Italy's macro-regions), trend components 1983–2021) (*Note* [a] ratio of new businesses other than sole proprietorship to the beginning-of-period stock of enterprises, net of the "unclassified activities", for the entry rate; [b] ratio of ceased businesses other than sole proprietorship to the beginning-of-period stock of enterprises, net of the "unclassified activities", for the exit rate; [c] the trend components are those that result from the application of a Hodrick and Prescott filter to the original series. *Source* For Italy see Appendix B)

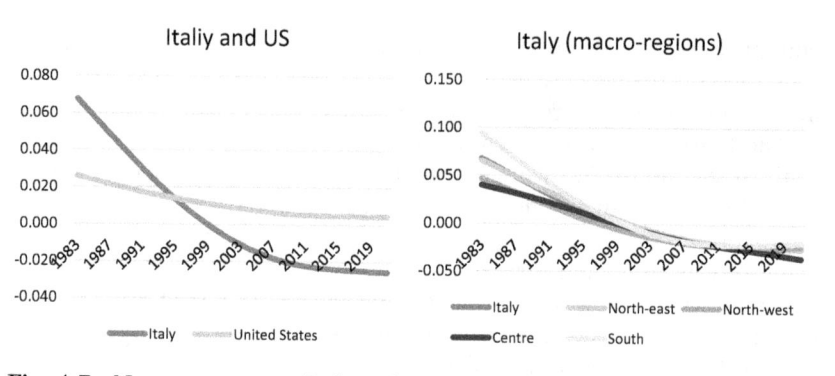

Fig. 4.7 Net turnover rate (Italy and the US, and Italy's macro-regions, trend components 1983–2021) (*Notes* For Italy: [a] ratio of new businesses other than sole proprietorships to the stock of enterprises in existence, net of the "unclassified activities", for the entry rate; [b] ratio of business closures other than sole proprietorships to the stock of enterprises in existence, net of the "unclassified activities", for the exit rate; [a]–[b] for the net turnover rate; for the United States: [c] new plants [excl. farms] with at least one employee compared to the stock of plants in existence for the entry rate; [d] closed plants [excl. farms] with at least one employee compared to the stock of plants in existence for the exit rate; [c]–[d] for the net turnover rate; the trend components are those that result from the application of a Hodrick and Prescott filter to the original series. *Source* As in Fig. 4.5)

the last decade without appreciable second thoughts. And our shrinkage seems to be a relatively solitary one. The net birth rates in other European countries (as calculated by Eurostat) have been affected without question by the crises but in recent years they have become positive again. To be precise, on average for the period 2009–2019 the turnouts for the Europe "of 4" aggregate (France, Germany, Belgium and the Netherlands) and Europe "of 6" (Europe "of 4" plus Spain and Portugal) show net turnover rates of 3.4% and 2.5%, respectively. The net turnover rate for the UK was a little below 2%.

Unlike what happens with population trends, it is not necessarily said that the zero or negative net business birth rates foreshadow fewer job opportunities in the future or that, above all, they imply that the channels of innovation are drying up thereby affecting future productivity growth rates. And this is simply because a zero or even negative net business birth rate may conceal significant levels of dynamism in an economy: many enterprises being born and taking the place of many that die—what we have called "creative destruction". Or vice versa they can hide the stasis, immobility. From this profile the international comparison is illuminating.

The Italian case would seem to belong more to the second type than to the first. And to a growing extent. The gross turnover rate (or the sum of the business birth and death rates) not only reveals lower values in the international comparison (Fig. 4.8) but ones that decrease over time in many sectors. Both industry and services pass from over 7% during the previous twenty years to about 5–6% during the decade afterwards. On the other hand, in the case of the United States, a net turnover rate not so far-off zero in the course of the last thirty years conceals a degree of business turnover that is actually decreasing, if you like, but is still much greater than in Italy. It is hardly necessary to recall that the average TFP growth rate in the United States during the same period was more than double Italy's (1.2% compared to 0.5%).

And the distance is significant when compared to our European partners too. The gross turnover rate for the Europe "of 4" aggregate is 16.5% on average for the period 2009–2019, it is 17.4% for the Europe "of 6" aggregate and about 24% for the UK. Three if not four times the corresponding figure for Italy. At territorial level it is once again the South that sets itself apart with the greatest fall than elsewhere in the gross turnover rate: a datum that asks us to assess domestic (and European) regional policies of the last quarter century from this standpoint too.

Having a picture for the last forty years is certainly a step forward but it is still a very partial result. Long-term trends such as the ones we are evoking can hardly be tackled on the basis of four decades. And it is no coincidence that the basic objective of these pages is precisely that of throwing some light on trends that go well beyond forty years to trace back, if possible, to the decades immediately following Unification.

As highlighted in Appendix B, the idea of reconstructing the company birth-deaths profile starting from the early twentieth century and digging into the records of the Chambers of Commerce is a partly prohibitive exploit because of the mountain of search activities implicit in reconstructing the elementary information in the Business registers first of all, and then in the Company registers kept in over 100 of the country's Chambers of Commerce, up to just a few years ago, and in a little more than 70 of them today. Furthermore, it would simply be impossible given the fact that in quite a few cases events (from wars, weather,

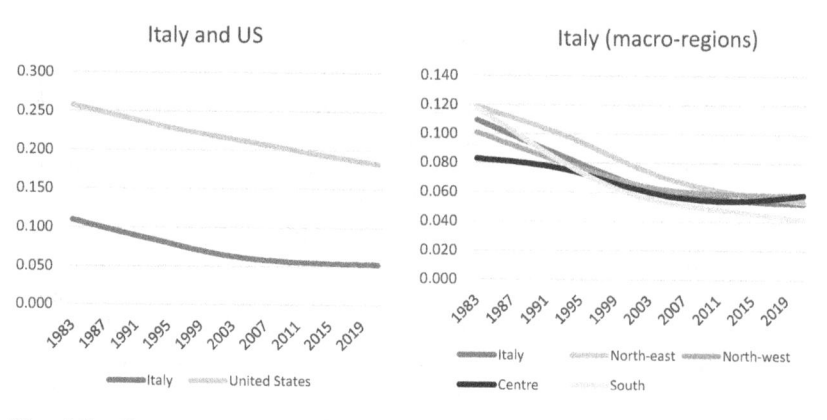

Fig. 4.8 Gross turnover rate (Italy and the US, 1983–2020) (*Notes* For Italy: [a] ratio of new businesses other than sole proprietorships to the stock of enterprises in existence, net of the "unclassified activities", for the entry rate; [b] ratio of business closures other than sole proprietorships to the stock of enterprises in existence, net of the "unclassified activities", for the exit rate; [a]+[b] for the gross turnover rate; for the United States: [c] new plants [excl. farms] with at least one employee compared to the stock of plants in existence for the entry rate; [c] closed plants [excl. farms] with at least one employee compared to the stock of plants in existence for the exit rate; [c]+[d] for the gross turnover rate; the trend components are those that result from the application of a Hodrick and Prescott filter to the original series. *Source* As in Fig. 4.5)

earthquakes and so on) or human neglect have simply cancelled all traces of such elementary information. In what follows we therefore decided to concentrate on a few—significant—provinces (Ancona, Milan, Rome and Turin) with the presumption that such a sample would reflect the country's main characteristics (Milan and Turin the industrial base and Rome the services' one in the large urban centres, and Ancona the economy of the periphery) and be largely representative of the country's most general trends.[15]

The sample (limited to businesses other than sole proprietorships in order to be fully comparable with the current international information

---

[15] Unfortunately, it was not possible to broaden the sample to take in at least one of the main cities of the south (Naples, Palermo or Bari) because of the condition of the historical records in the some of the relevant Chambers of Commerce.

on the topic) ignores the data, even when available, for the period 1911–1927 as they are irremediably contaminated by the regulatory changes introduced between 1924 and 1926 (discussed in detail in Appendix B). It is based on approximately 2 million elementary records and corresponds—in the post-1983 period for which both provincial and national information are available—to over 17% of the national population and over to 24% of the total number of registered businesses. The degree of correlation between the main indicators of the sample and the corresponding indicator at national level fluctuates between 0.71 (exit rates) and 0.91 (entry rates). It should be underlined that excluding sole proprietorship amounts to excluding small, family-owned, independent businesses which cannot easily be regarded as agent of creative destruction. On the contrary, focusing on specific sectors such as manufacturing (more than on the legal status) would run the risk of overlooking innovations in the services sector (which—as we saw in the previous chapter—may be far from negligible).

Figure 4.9 therefore proposes the evolution of the net and gross turnover rates for the sample discussed above. Appendix B details the problems tackled in the course of the reconstruction and—when found to be possible—the ways to overcome them. It is worth noting that such issues mostly concerned the recording of enterprise deaths and were linked to regulatory innovations in the period considered or to specific events that drained informative content from single observations. What has been said above regarding the sample remains valid though, and it is useful once more to underline that as far as we know this is the first reconstruction on a scale of about a century of the net and gross turnover indices (and therefore in this latter case of the index of creative destruction).

Given this (and allowing for the short-term obvious variability that trend components do not highlight), the main trends are evident once again. In the first place, however moderate, the net business birth rate has never been as consistently negative as it has been in the last twenty years. Certainly, exits exceeded entries at the time of the great 1929 crash (something that obviously does not emerge from the trend figures but can be deduced from the information discussed in Appendix B) but during the years afterwards the stock of enterprises started growing again by 3–5% per year. This is nothing similar to what has been observed starting from the 1990s (with the significant exception of 1997—not visible here

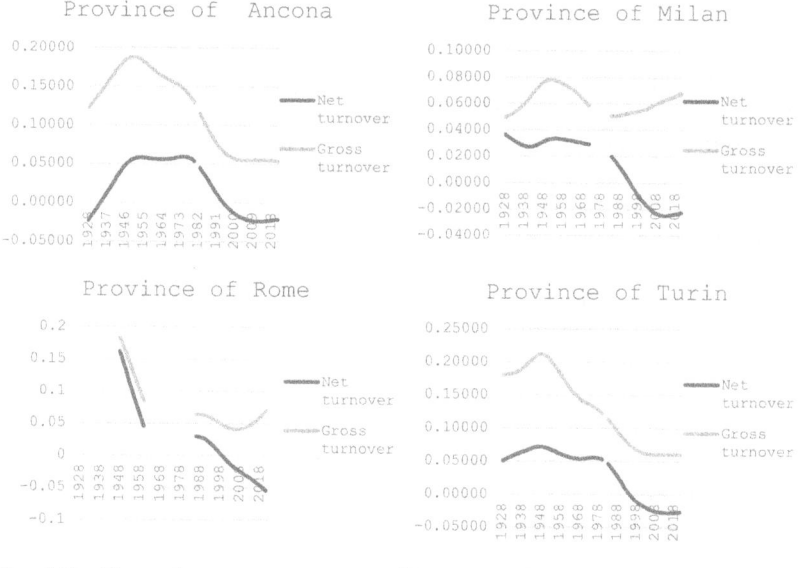

Fig. 4.9 Net and gross turnover rates (Provinces of Ancona, Milan, Rome and Turin, 1928–2021; trend components) (*Note* The trend components are those that result from the application of a Hodrick and Prescott filter to the original series. *Source* See Appendix B)

either in the trend components—attributable very probably to a regulatory innovation). Passing to gross turnover (i.e., the sum of the entry rates and exit rates) and therefore to "creative destruction", the pattern already observed more than once repeats itself, perhaps with even greater clarity. Any "creative destruction"—if Italy has ever experienced an example of it—is concentrated in the years between 1947 and 1964, years in which Italy touched levels comparable to those experienced in the United States in the nineteen-1980s when Ronald Reagan greeted the Americans with the words "It's morning again in America". Before and afterwards (and perhaps especially afterwards) very little "creative destruction" was ever seen. As a consequence—as we have already noted—innovative capacity languished and total factor productivity went into hiding. And we should not be deceived by the apparent rise in the gross turnover rate recorded in Milan in recent years: this rise is unfortunately due to the combination of a significant annihilation of companies associated with stasis in the birth of new ones. To make sure, go back to Fig. 4.8 to observe how in the last forty years the Italian gross turnover has experienced a progressive and unequivocal tendency towards reduction. At a sectoral level, the pattern described by Fig. 4.8 occurs in largely homogeneous terms. The gross turnover rate for the manufacturing sector for the years 1947–1964 turns out to be almost triple with respect to the 1928–1939 period (as for services) and almost double with respect to the following 1965–1972 period (less than double for services).

Figures 4.10, 4.11, and 4.12 close the circle showing the positive relationships—as given by the positively sloped dotted lines—during the last one hundred years, or so, between the provincial indices of "creative destruction" (or gross turnover) and the growth rates of the per capita gross domestic product, of the total factor productivity and the patenting activity (all at national level),[16] i.e., the welfare indicator and the technological progress indicators from which our analysis started.

Notice that establishing a relationship between aggregate growth indicators and provincial indexes of creative destruction is far from being devoid of content. The similar pattern of the creative destruction index among provinces is quite striking and clearly points out towards a nation-wide "common feeling" whose long-run impact on nation-wide outcomes clearly goes beyond the strictly local dimension.[17] Moreover, it is hardly necessary to underline—to answer the comprehensible doubts and the legitimate reservations of sceptical readers—that the relationship would remain unchanged (if not indeed strengthened) if we were to eliminate the extreme observations linked to wartime events of the years 1940–1946.

Several observations are appropriate. The information content of the three sets of graphs is clearly different. As long as patenting activity refers to a subset of innovative activities, as already pointed out, and if on the other hand the index of creative destruction expresses in some way the economic "effervescence" which comes before, and in some way accompanies, innovation at all levels and in all forms, we would expect to

---

[16] Unfortunately, no information is available at annual level as regards the evolution of the per capita gross domestic product at regional level. However, as underlined in the following lines, there are compelling reasons to believe that regional growth indicators would not be the appropriate match in this case.

[17] Rossi (2024) makes use of the provincial information to estimate the country-wide evolution of creative destruction phenomena for the 1928–1981 years. His results are largely comparable if not outright equivalent to the ones referred to in this Section.

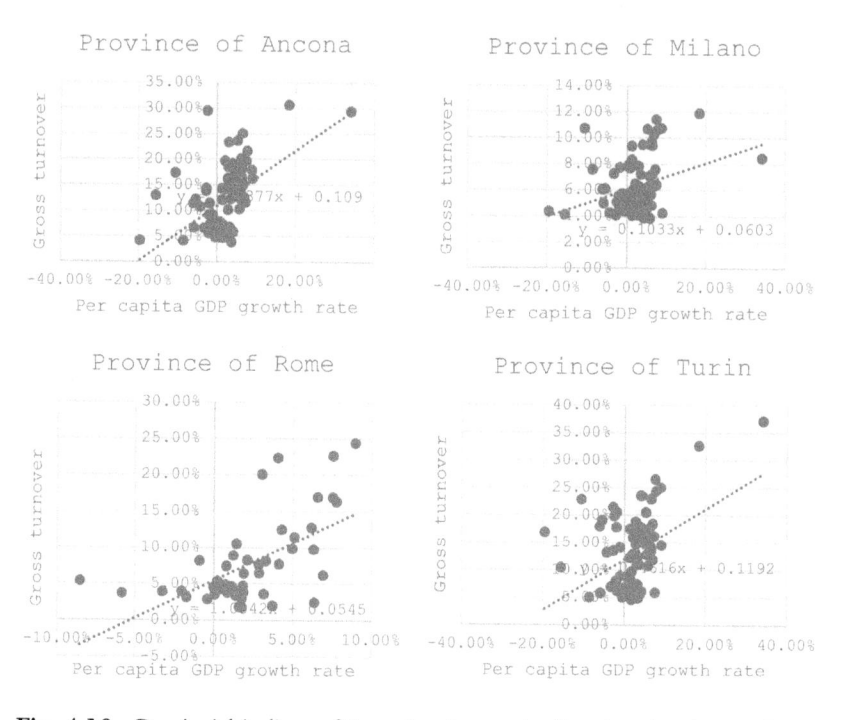

Fig. 4.10 Provincial indices of "creative destruction" and national growth rate of the GDP per capita (1928–2021) (*Source* See Appendix B for the gross turnover rate; for real per capita GDP as in Table 2.1)

record higher rates of correlation between indices of creative destruction and TFP growth rates than between the former and the growth rates of patenting activity. And we would expect this to be evident in the provinces much more than in large urban centres. Furthermore, as long as per capita GDP growth is affected by factors other than technological progress, we would expect to observe higher rates of correlation between indices of creative destruction and TFP growth rates than between the former and the per capita GDP growth rates. And, in effect, things would seem to have remained just in these terms (Table 4.2) while this by the way, suggests that of the two readings that Schumpeter himself wanted to give to the creative destruction processes (that, to be clear Arthur Diamond [2006, p. 121] labelled as "big is better" and "small is better")

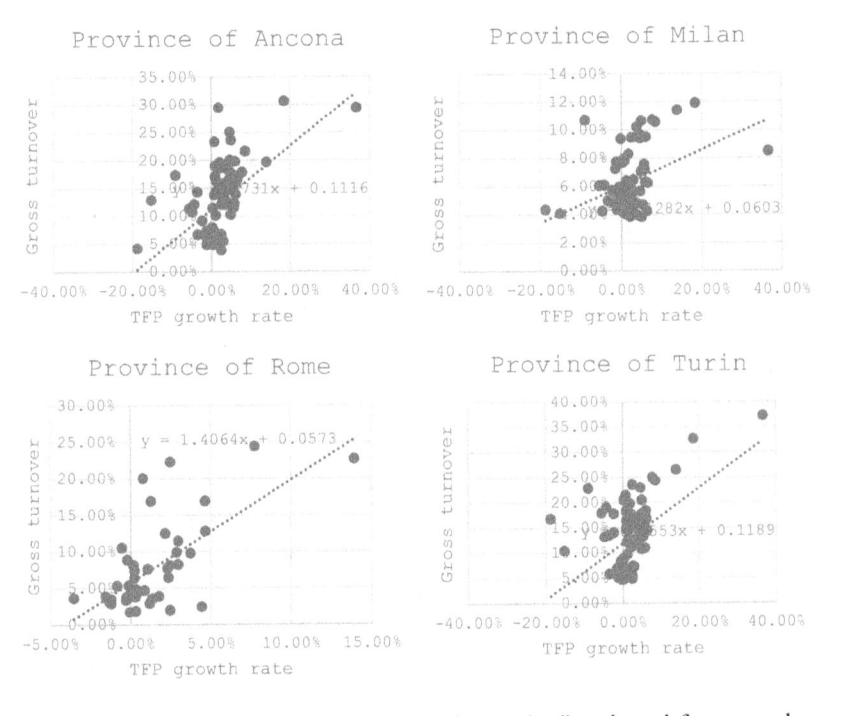

Fig. 4.11 Provincial indices of "creative destruction" and total factor productivity growth at national level (1928–2020) (*Source* See Appendix B for the gross turnover rate; for real per capita GDP as in Table 3.1)

it is the second, in our case anyway, that reveals itself to be more useful for interpreting the facts.

In other words, without prejudice to the role of technological progress as a source of growth and economic well-being, the ability to promote innovations in the broad sense seems to reside more inside firms—often and willingly in small ones if not indeed in start-ups or in wannabe-firms—rather than in the universities or in the laboratories of large companies equipped with significant market power. And this, in turn, would direct us more towards an element that is *lato* sensu cultural rather than to questions that are more closely connected to the different institutional architectures.

Naturally, it is hardly necessary to observe that noting the existence of an association between an index of creative destruction and different

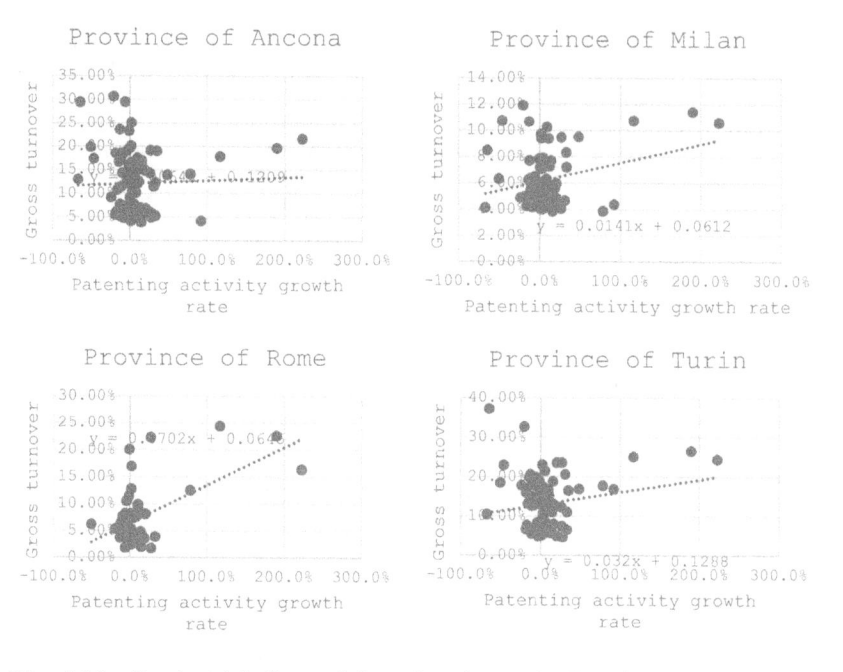

Fig. 4.12 Provincial indices of "creative destruction" and patenting activity growth rates at national level (1928–2020) (*Source* See Appendix B for the gross turnover rate; for real per capita GDP as in Table 4.1)

representations of the growth process does not at all establish that there is a relationship of cause and effect between the quantities mentioned. Nor does it tell us anything about the mono-directional or—why not?—bidirectional nature of some relationship between processes of creative destruction and the dynamics of the system.

The theme, obviously, is not a new one. Among others, Paul Reynolds (1999, pp. 97–136)—analysing the local US labour markets between the middle of the 1970s and the early 1990s—reached the conclusion that though few doubts seemed to exist regarding the common dynamics between the indices of creative destruction and economic growth, the

Table 4.2 Correlations between provincial indicators of creative destruction and the per capita GDP growth rates, TFP growth rates and growth rates of the patenting capacity at national level

	Growth rate of the per capita GDP		Growth rate of the TFP		Growth rate of patenting activity	
	(a)	(b)	(a)	(b)	(a)	(b)
Creative destruction indicator:						
– Province of Ancona	0.49	0.62	0.52	0.63	0.04	0.18
– Province of Milan	0.32	0.38	0.39	0.53	0.28	0.39
– Province of Rome	0.58	n.a	0.67	n.a	0.57	n.a
– Province of Turin	0.42	0.55	0.49	0.61	0.19	0.34

Notes (a) including the years characterised by wartime events (1940–1946), (b) excluding the years characterised by wartime events (1940–1946)
Sources See Appendix B for the gross turnover rate; for real per capita GDP as in Table 2.1; for TFP as in Table 3.1, for patenting activity as in Table 4.1

conclusions regarding any causality relationship between the magnitudes mentioned would have to be quite more nuanced.[18]

There is no shortage of reasons for considering the conclusions of Paul Reynolds preliminary, to say the least—the methodology adopted for assessing the causality links being on top of the list[19]—and these reasons call for further investigations to be carried out. In particular, the nature of the quantitative information collected so far suggests that a further exploration can be carried out by making reference to Granger's causality concept, that is by asking ourselves if and up to what point indices of creative destruction can play a role in forecasting the future evolution of different depictions of the process of economic growth or vice versa or if, finally, both things are true or false. Appendix B provides the results of the econometric investigation aimed at ascertaining the existence of causal links *à la* Granger between the growth rate of the TFP (at national level)

[18] "… higher levels of business volatility, or creative destruction, appear to have a strong association with economic growth. On the other hand, creative destruction does not, by itself, appear to be a source of economic growth. Without creative destruction, there is no growth; creative destruction does not seem to cause growth" (Reynolds, 1999, p. 98).

[19] It is notoriously quite hard to infer the existence or otherwise of a causal relationship starting from the explanatory capacity of regressions that may or may not comprise indices of creative destruction, and therefore on the basis of commonly used information criteria.

and indicators of creative destruction at provincial level and clarifies the limits—anything but minor—of the exercise. However, it does suggest that—with reference to the sample that covers the years 1951–1960 and 1988–2019—a causality link in the sense already indicated would seem to exist between indicators of creative destruction and the TFP growth rate, the evidence relating to a causality link in the opposite sense apparently being quite weaker (but not therefore non-existent).

The basic message contained in the previous pages is that going beyond the pure and simple static contrast between large and small and medium enterprises—around which the Italian debate almost always takes place—and questioning the dynamics of the system considerably enriches the discussion (Giannetti & Velucchi, 2006, for example) and points out how, in addition to asking ourselves questions about what appears to be an Italian specificity (the proportion of small and medium-sized enterprises out of the total), we should above all ask ourselves why so few enterprises are born, why small ones do not become medium and medium-large companies, and why in the process they leave the market less than elsewhere; and what might be the consequences of this "slow motion" that always seems to have interested the Italian economy, with the usual exception of the postwar fifteen to twenty years. A "slow motion" which—as international comparisons clearly point out—goes far beyond the impact of demographic trends which, it could be argued, affect the entire Western world.

It is hardly the case to say it again: all that these lines are able to offer is an alternative hypothesis for reading the economic vicissitudes of unified Italy. The intention is not so much to demonstrate but to suggest to curious and expert readers that perhaps a different visual angle is possible and, with it, a reconsideration of the choices that we should be making to return the country to a path that is not a dead end like the one Italy has been treading in recent times.

References

Aghion, P., Antonin, C., & Bunel, S. (2021). *The Power of Creative Destruction*. Harvard University Press.

Akcigit, U., & Ates, S. T. (2021). Ten Facts on Declining Business Dynamism and Lessons from Endogenous Growth Theory. *American Economic Journal: Macroeconomics, 13*(1), 257–298.

Akcigit, U., Grigsby, J., & Nicholas, T. (2017). *The Rise of American Ingenuity: Innovation and Inventors of the Golden Age* (NBER Working Paper 23047). Retrieved March 18, 2024, https://www.nber.org/system/files/working_papers/w23047/w23047.pdf

Akcigit, U., & van Reenen, J. (Eds.). (2023). *The Economics of Creative Destruction.* Harvard University Press.

Bergeaud, A., Cette, G., & Lecat, R. (2016). Productivity Trends in Advanced Countries Between 1890 and 2012. *Review of Income and Wealth, 62*(3), 420–444.

Barbiellini Amidei, F., Cantwell, J., & Spadavecchia, A. (2013). Innovation and Foreign Technology. In G. Toniolo (Ed.), *The Oxford Handbook of the Italian Economy Since Unification* (pp. 378–416). Oxford University Press.

Brandt, N. (2004). Business Dynamics and Policies. *OECD Economic Studies 38.* OECD.

Caballero, R. (2008). Creative Destruction. In S. N. Durlauf & L. E. Blume (Eds.), *The New Palgrave Dictionary of Economics* (pp. 2429–2434). Palgrave Macmillan.

Colli, A. (2002). *I volti di Proteo: storia della piccola impresa in Italia nel Novecento.* Bollati Boringhieri.

Diamond, A. (2006). Schumpeter's Creative Destruction: A Review of the Evidence. *The Journal of Private Enterprise, 22*(1), 120–146.

Diamond, A. (2019). *Openness to Creative Destruction.* Oxford University Press.

Giannetti, R. (1998). *Tecnologia e sviluppo economico italiano 1870–1990.* Il Mulino.

Giannetti, R., & Velucchi, M. (2006). The Demography of Manufacturing Firms. In R. Giannetti & M. Vasta (Eds.), *Evolution of Italian Enterprises in the 20th Century* (pp. 63–86). Il Mulino.

Gordon, R. (2016). *The Rise and Fall of American Growth.* Princeton University Press.

Hathaway, I., & Litan, R. E. (2014). What's Driving the Decline in the Firm Formation Rate? A Partial Explanation. *Economic Studies at Brooking.* The Brooking Institution.

Liang, J., Wang, H., & Lazear, E. P. (2018). Demographics and Entrepreneurship. *Journal of Political Economy, 126*, 140–196.

Nuvolari, A., & Vasta, M. (2017). Un fantasma in soffitta? Il sistema innovativo italiano in prospettiva storica. In P. Di Martino & M. Vasta (Eds.), *Ricchi per caso. La parabola dello sviluppo economico italiano* (pp. 129–182). Il Mulino.

Ravn, M. O., & Uhlig, H. (2002). On Adjusting the Hodrick-Prescott Filter for the Frequency of Observations. *Review of Economics and Statistics, 84*(2), 371–380.

Reynolds, P. (1999). Creative Destruction: Source or Symptom of Economic Growth. In Z. Acs, B. Carlsson, & C. Karlsson (Eds.), *Entrepreneurship, Small and Medium-Sized Firms and the Macroeconomy* (pp. 97–136). Cambridge University Press.

Rossi, N. (2024). *The «miracle» of creative destruction*. Mimeo.

Rossi, S. (2018). *Firm Dynamics and Economic Growth*. Retrieved March 18, 2024, https://www.bis.org/review/r181219c.pdf

Scarpetta, S., Hemmings, P., Tressel, T., & Woo, J. (2002). The Role of Policy and Institutions for Productivity and Firm Dynamics: Evidence from Micro and Industry Data, *OECD Economics Department Working Paper 329*. OECD.

PART II

Beliefs, Values, and Preferences

CHAPTER 5

Mobility

BEYOND CREATIVE DESTRUCTION

If we assume for the sake of the argument that the reconstruction of the events appears so far to be worthy of interest at the very least, if not indeed potentially reliable, then a final crucial step remains to be undertaken. What happened in the twenty years following the Second World War that did not happen before or after it? What made those fifteen-to-twenty years unique in the history of the unified nation? What is there behind the "creative destruction"?

It is not a new question, of course, and to a large extent is contained in the reflection of William J. Baumol (1968)—over fifty years ago by now—on the role of entrepreneurship in economic theory and on its determinants. A reflection that can be considered at the basis of the belief—apparently widely shared—about the decisive weight of institutional arrangements and incentive structures implicit in public policies, not only on the propensity for entrepreneurship[1] but also on its underlying nature: "productive, unproductive and destructive" (Baumol,

---

[1] Which, in Baumol's viewpoint, belongs to worlds distinct from the economic world: "… these issues [the supply of entrepreneurship] are to a very considerable extent matters of social psychology, of social arrangements, of cultural development, and the like" (Baumol, 1968, p. 69).

© The Author(s), under exclusive license to Springer Nature Switzerland AG 2024
N. Rossi, *Reframing Italian Economic History, 1861–2021*, Palgrave Studies in Economic History,
https://doi.org/10.1007/978-3-031-67271-2_5

1990). From Baumol's point of view, intervening on society's cultural traits to stimulate its propensity for entrepreneurship or to change its characters is much slower, uncertain and more tiring than changing the rules of the game and, with them, the cost-effectiveness of the entrepreneurs' choices themselves.[2] Hence the choice—in summaries such as those of Philippe Aghion et al. (2021) or Arthur J. Diamond (2019), which cover decades-long research activity on the theme of creative destruction[3]—to focus the attention on the rules of the game, completely neglecting the system of values that should constitute its underlying.

But, as has been observed several times with reference to the Italian experience (and as we will see even better in the next chapters), it is by no means certain that different rules of the game correspond to different behaviours or that constant rules of the game give rise to unchanged behaviours. The point is that the economic dynamism *à la* Phelps or the "innovism" of Deirdre McCloskey do not lend themselves easily to being locked up inside the walls of a research laboratory or within a company's boundary fence. To use the words of Edmund Phelps (2013, p. vii), a dynamic economy rests on the "broad involvement of people in the process of innovation" and, in turn, the foundations of this "mass flourishing" can be found in individual attitudes and experience, in openness to involvement, in positive exposure to challenges, in the desire to express oneself and in the firm commitment to pursue personal growth. Much more, then, than patenting activity or the attitude towards entrepreneurship referred to in the previous paragraphs, but a broader concept not limited to the individual as inventor or entrepreneur but rather to the individual as such—every single person be it a woman or a man—even if still a student, job seeker or employee, or even a pensioner.

And there's more. The cultural categories we refer to in these pages are not easily assimilable or superimposable to those usually used in the literature on the subject (Alesina & Giuliano, 2015, pp. 905–915). The economic dynamism à la Phelps or the "innovativeness" of Deirdre

---

[2] A "… designer of policy [...] does not have centuries at his or her disposal and [...] is notoriously ineffective in engendering profound changes in cultural influences or in the structure of preferences… It is for this reason that I have chosen to take entrepreneurial goals as given and to emphasize modification in the structure of the rewards to different activities as the more promising line of investigation" (Baumol, 1990, p. 916).

[3] One could also cite the entry "creative destruction" in the New Palgrave Dictionary of Economics (Caballero, 2008).

McCloskey, the "active and creative freedom [which, when it exists, can be seen] written on the faces of men" of which Carlo Levi wrote (1950, p. 41) in the years immediately after the war, it can also involve a high degree of trust in interpersonal relationships but it does not end there.[4] It can imply and indeed usually implies a predisposition towards personal affirmation and individual rights (compared to collective interests) but it is not limited to it. It can coexist with very different interpretations of family ties and with a wide range of more or less cooperative behaviours and, although it requires a full awareness of the importance of work, it goes beyond this aspect too. And—Max Weber will excuse us—it is not so easily attributable to religious choices or ethnic affiliations. For example, the propensity to accept or not accept risk, the predisposition to take positions that are different and distant from common opinion or to accept that others do so, and the taste for challenge escape this list.

With Baumol (1968, p. 71) one could observe that we are referring to aspects of little interest from the point of view of economic policy, capable of evolving only very gradually. The most recent literature on the subject not only does not fail to underline this aspect but rather leverages it to analyse the relationship between culture, institution and economy (Guiso et al., 2006). Could "the slow and undependable process of change in social and psychological climate" ever be reconcilable with what happened in Italy between the late 1940s and the mid-1960s? This is, in reality, a less stringent observation than it might appear, consequent—if one may say so—to the "representative individual syndrome" which is often very difficult to free oneself from. In every historical phase and in any society, different sets of "values, beliefs and preferences" coexist but, for the most part, only one of them—and not always the same one—stands out for its ability to guide the community's journey. And the transition from one reference culture to another is, at times, extraordinarily gradual and at other times, instead, the result of equally extraordinary events that can change the points of reference of a community. There is certainly no

---

[4] Luigi Guiso et al. (2006, pp. 35–36) observe a positive relationship between the level of trust (in turn connected to a specific religious choice or to a specific ethnic origin) and the choice to start an entrepreneurial activity. However, they do not fail to point out the possibility that the impact of the cultural background on entrepreneurial choices follows other channels: "perhaps cultural background affects attitudes towards risk, which in turn affects the choice to become entrepreneur".

shortage of cases of societies capable of reaching a high degree of homogeneity, just as the opposite cases are not unusual, but what we want to underline here are the limits of exercises that consider cultural changes implausible while referring not to individuals or more or less well-defined social groups but also to the aggregate of the same.

From an empirical point of view, the path of resorting to opinion polls—often followed by the recent literature that investigates the relationships between culture, institutions and economic performance, for which reference is made to the review by Alberto Alesina and Paola Giuliano (2015, pp. 903–905)—is, from a historical perspective, visibly as impractical as that which uses evidence deriving from experimental investigations. Hence the choice of these pages: to try to identify "cultural markers" from which to extract information about the system of "values, beliefs and preferences" prevalent in different moments of Italian unified history. The use of "cultural markers"—and the consequent choice to replace statistical analysis with historical narrative—is an attempt to identify uniformity in cultural attitudes despite significant changes, for example, in the institutional environment. Or vice versa to isolate differences in the behaviour of individuals visible in, for example, largely comparable institutional contexts.[5] And to build a bridge between the economic evidence discussed in the previous chapter and the rereading of the events referred to in the next chapter.

As a general rule, the presence (or absence) of competition in the economy would seem to be an obvious candidate,[6] also because of the documented reluctance of the Italians to look on it positively (Gigliobianco & Giorgiantonio, 2017) at least until the 1990s. Except that the relationship between competition and innovation and therefore between competition and growth is less immediate than might appear at first sight. Philippe Aghion et al. (2021, pp. 54–74) have summarised what is known about the subject and underlined that the response to an intensification of

---

[5] As such, the analysis of "cultural markers" conducted in these pages has some points of contact with the exercise discussed in Guiso et al. (2003) in which the implications for the reference culture of the Catholics are examined in the light of the changes brought about by the Second Vatican Council (1962).

[6] Alfredo Gigliobianco and Gianni Toniolo (2017) and Pierluigi Ciocca (2020, pp. 43–47) consider the competitive conditions (and their evolutions over time) to have significantly influenced Italian growth, under the hypothesis that competition contributes positively to determining the growth path. The same can be said, though indirectly and limited to the last seventy years, for Lorenzo Codogno and Giampaolo Galli (2022).

competitive conditions is not homogeneous across incumbent firms (for new entrants, innovation being the highway for conquering a space, as has been seen in the preceding pages). As regards firms already operating in the market and near the technological frontier, tighter competitive conditions constitute an incentive to innovate, innovation being the way for them to avoid feeling the breath of their competitors on their necks or feel it less. On the other hand, as regards firms already in existence and distant from the technological frontier (and therefore characterised by a significantly lower productivity level than that of firms at the frontier) intensification of competitive conditions constitutes a disincentive for innovation since the greater competitive pressure leads to reduced profits. As a consequence, the net effect of an intensification of the competitive conditions is not independent from the relative weight of the two groups mentioned, and greater competitive "tension" will have different impacts depending on the initial competitive conditions.[7] The relationship between competition and growth is, in other words, less linear than might be imagined. In addition to this is the fact that it is not completely obvious if the most common metrics of the degree of competition of an economy are effectively able to measure what they promise. This is true, for example, for the measurements of concentration just as it is true for the average mark-ups (Aghion et al., 2021, pp. 63–67).[8] In short, if there

---

[7] If the initial competitive conditions are not particularly "tense", businesses will have an incentive to innovate by locating themselves close to the technological frontier and will react to an intensification of the competitive conditions with increasing doses of innovation (to get away, as we have seen, from the growing competition). A positive relationship between the evolution of the competitive conditions and growth will therefore prevail. If, instead, the initial competitive conditions are already quite "tense", the innovative efforts by the frontier firms will end up by driving the straggling businesses further away from the technological frontier, discouraging them further—if the competition conditions intensify—from taking the innovation route. In this case a negative relationship could prevail between the trend of the competitive conditions and growth.

[8] We should not therefore be surprised by the relatively indeterminate conclusion reached by Alfredo Gigliobianco and Gianni Toniolo (2017, pp. 29–30) when reviewing the events since Italian unification: "a picture emerges which, even because of its scale, cannot be attributed easily to a single concise result". Also contributing to this conclusion are the indications—not always unequivocal—implicit in the trends of different indicators, as well as the performance of identical indicators deriving from different sources. For example, the mark-up trend at the aggregate level would seem to indicate a lack of competition for the manufacturing sector (Giordano & Zollino, 2017) in the decades following the Second World War while concentration indices would suggest an increase in the level of competition during the same period (Barbiellini Amidei & Gomellini, 2017).

are many reasons for thinking that anti-competitive elements have been, and probably still are, part of the culture of the Italians, it is possible but, at least as a general rule, it is not automatic to deduce that this has constituted—in every phase of the history since unification—an obstacle to growth and measuring it is not easy at all even when this occurred.

A second, in many ways already explored possibility, would seem to be given by the detached if not exactly distorted relationship—if we can put it this way—between the Italians (and their ruling classes) and the theme of the formation of human capital.[9] Tullio De Mauro (2011) wrote about it in great detail, and, more recently, the theme has been underlined among others by Brian A'Hearn and Giovanni Vecchi (2017, pp. 206–211) and Gianni Toniolo (2013, pp. 32–33) and reproposed by Ignazio Visco (2014). And there would be no reason, therefore, for returning to the subject except to observe that the thing of importance here is not just the relative poverty of the human capital documented by the data on school attendance or by the information on the quality of Italian education (A'Hearn & Vecchi, 2017; Bertola & Sestito, 2013) but also—if not above all—by its composition over time. Jerome Vandenbussche et al. (2006) have underlined that the adoption of technologies already tried out elsewhere—the imitation game—requires skills that are different from those of importance for the purposes of innovative activity in the proper sense. So that, for a given level of human capital, the presence of an efficient system of higher education becomes crucial at the moment in which a country approaches the technological frontier (and must, therefore, rely to a growing extent on its own innovative skills). In this same phase, the contribution of primary and secondary education becomes less relevant but is nevertheless decisive when the catching-up potential is significant. Important from this standpoint are the procedures for implementing the primary education obligation—documented, for example, by A'Hearn and Vecchi (2017)—in the first half century of the life of the unified State and, during the decades thereafter, the whole of obligatory education. Conversely, during the years immediately after

---

An intensification of competitive conditions was already present, moreover, in the mark-up estimates for the immediate postwar in Rossi and Toniolo (1993) and their divergence from those of Giordano and Zollino (2017) just quoted would merit further exploration.

[9] Distorted because it was focused, more than on the users of the public education and training system (and therefore on the fallout from the system itself on growth), on the operators of the same, on the teachers at every level and on the non-teaching staff.

the economic boom when the technological frontier was only one step away, or almost so, Italy would have needed a higher education system unquestionably different in terms of autonomy, governance and resources but, at the same time, radically distant from the one that started shaping up from the end of the 1960s, thanks to legislative interventions that were the fruit of a cultural climate that was to cripple the Italian university for decades to come.[10] It is highly likely—as observed by Carlo Bastasin and Gianni Toniolo (2023, p. 31)—that the low sensitivity of Italian society (of its public opinion no less than of its ruling classes) can be traced to the "often unavoidable but also near-sighted decisions taken as regards the management of public finances". But it is difficult not to see the echo of important cultural traditions in that reduced awareness: "the hostility of Catholics towards obligatory state education" (Bastasin & Toniolo, 2023, p. 31) typical of the decades after unification, the fear that the State might abdicate from its role of funder of higher education and that, as a consequence a "commercialisation of culture" would take place (Perotti, 2008), an idea that was widespread among the public in different forms and ways since the 1960s.[11]

Therefore, setting competition and education aside, we must look elsewhere to find reliable and even measurable expressions of the "social and psychological climate" to which Baumol referred.

---

[10] A cultural climate that did not limit itself to affecting higher education but affected the entire scholastic system, with the results recalled briefly in Bertola and Sestito (2013, pp. 352–355). It is interesting to note how the relationship between the level of human capital (as approximated by the average number of years of education of the active population) and the per capita gross domestic product—shown in Fig. 9.4 in Bertola and Sestito (2013, pp. 367–368)—would seem to suggest that the Italian economy was "more productive in general that what it should have been suggested on the basis of its resources of human capital". This conclusion, fairly evident up until the Second World War, has been increasingly less true as little by little the country left the years of the economic miracle behind, as confirmation of the enduring damage inflicted on it by what Lorenzo Codogno and Giampaolo Galli (2022, p. 29) called the "egalitarian, anti-meritocratic culture of the Italian «68»" protest movement.

[11] Among the most coherent expressions of this cultural position, it is possible to mention, with regard to the higher education, the pages written by Gianfranco Viesti (2018).

Migrations

Finding an indicator (quantitative even) of this "feeling" of individuals is, as you can imagine, quite arduous. But perhaps it is not completely impossible. To start with, if the vitality (or more correctly "flourishing", in the vocabulary of Edmund Phelps [2013, p. vii]) is above all "experience of the new: new situations, new problems, new insights, and new ideas to develop and share" then, perhaps, some indication of the changing "feeling" of the Italians in the course of the century and a half plus of unification can be extracted—with all the appropriate precautions—from their willingness to change and, therefore, move. To leave one's place of origin or of residence to experiment new situations, to tackle new problems, to follow new intuitions, to give form to new ideas; to seek different ways to escape from economic and social conditions that cease to become sustainable for some reason, and to search for solutions that become, or appear to be, practicable for different reasons. With this in mind, perhaps, the available information on internal mobility may be of some help. Far from being simple flows that can be observed in an unchanged and unchangeable context, the internal migrations have contributed, in the word of historians, sociologists and demographers,

> to redesigning the human geography of the country, through the displacement of huge volumes of people from the countryside to the city, from the interiors to the coasts, from the hills and mountains and from the deprived areas to the more dynamic ones. [...] they were a constructive part of the main processes of transformation that interested Italian society from Unification to the present day. (Bonifazi & Heins 2011)

As such, therefore, they were among the most powerful expressions of the "feeling" of the country and of its inhabitants.[12]

The idea of looking at the country's internal mobility as a different key to reading the features of a society is anything but new and is due, among

---

[12] The focus primarily on internal migrations, rather than migrations *tout court* (for which reference should be made, for example, to Gomellini et al. [2017]), derives from the consequences that the former can have on the equilibrium of the domestic labour market and, as a result, on the efficiency levels of the system. The above lines, though, ought to suggest that there is very probably more than this. Such as the historians—Guido Crainz (2005, pp. 108–117), for example, or Paul Ginsborg (1989, pp. 293–309)—have guessed.

others, to two historians—Angiolina Arru and Franco Ramella (2003)—who make it the starting point of their analysis of internal migrations. Anna Badino (2008) and Stefano Gallo (2012) then developed specific aspects. As Michele Colucci (2012, p. 24) affirms, an important aspect of historical and sociological research is actually the reassessment of the picture of migrants: no longer "remissive, passive and submissive"; no longer "victims of choices made over [their] heads, of exploitation, of the distortions of development". But instead, masters of their own destiny, capable of making "considered decisions and of [...] initiatives that can break with the respective social contexts of reference". But let us let the figures speak first.

Figure 5.1—which updates the information contained in the reconstruction by Corrado Bonifazi and Frank Heins (2011)—displays the internal migration rate starting from 1902 and rests on different sets of information. The annual demographic balances (and associated Registry Office registrations and cancellations as a result of internal migration) and, only starting from 1955, Registry Office registrations and cancellations because of transfers of residence.[13] With the exception of the year 1962 and of the contiguous ones to which we will return shortly, the two information sources, as was foreseeable, tell a story that largely coincides and two significant moments stand out in them. The 1930s and then the fifteen years between the mid-1950s and the end of the 1960s (the recovery of internal migrations in the last decades being still far from the levels on those occasions): these are two moments to whose importance relative magnitudes like those shown in Fig. 5.1 to not do full justice, as we will see.

Let us proceed in an orderly manner. The 1861 population census reports that little more than 15% of the Italians lived at the time in a different municipality from the one of their births. The figure included 31% or little more for the department of Parma and Piacenza and about 5% for Sicily. Immediately after Unification, therefore, the country was relatively immobile for reasons that were largely objective: the frontiers that used to furrow (and partly continued to furrow) the land, and the infrastructures for mobility that were scant if not often completely absent.

---

[13] Note that the demographic balances make reference to the country's boundaries of the time. Furthermore, until the year 1929—the year in which the "register of the population" was introduced—not all the municipalities recorded the associated information (Di Rienzo, 1965, p. 671). The two sets of information diverge because of several regulatory interventions as well as the post-census adjustments.

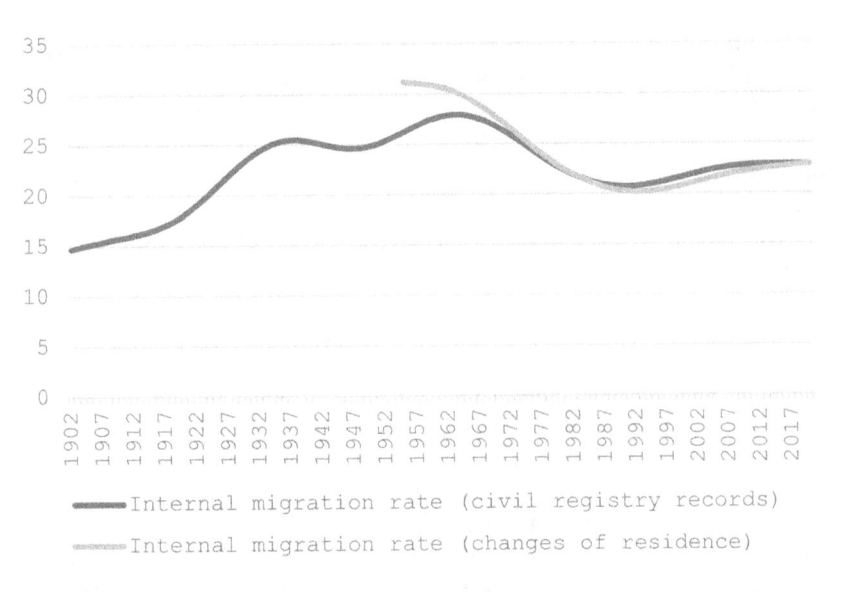

Internal migration rate (civil registry records)

Internal migration rate (changes of residence)

Fig. 5.1 Internal migration rate (civil registry records, 1902–2020, and transfers of residence, 1955–2020; per thousand inhabitants, trend components) (*Note* The trend components are those that result from the application of a Hodrick and Prescott filter to the original series. *Source* Bonifazi and Heins [2011, p. 53] and, for the updates, Istat, Iscrizioni e cancellazioni anagrafiche [civil registry registrations and cancellations]. Retrieved March 18, 2024, http://www.istat.it/it/files//2016/06/Bilancio-demografico-2015-1.pdf and later ones)

Things had not changed significantly forty years later in 1901. Only 8% of those surveyed lived in a province other than the one they were born in and that was particularly true for Southern Italy.

The picture changes in the first decades of the twentieth century. The first significant wave of internal mobility was observed right from the first half of the 1920s and reached a peak in the second half of the 1930s, in strict, or almost, correspondence with the measures of containment enacted between 1928 and 1939 by the regime and which became progressively more and more restrictive. These measures culminated in the famous 1939 provision that envisaged that those who wanted to transfer their residence to the larger municipalities should have an occupation for which the employment laws in force established that it was only possible to be employed if resident—an ante litteram Catch 22 that Luigi

Einaudi branded as a return to fiefdom (Einaudi, 1956, p. 578). In net terms (and therefore in terms of net migration turnover) between 1934 and 1940, on average, just less than 13 thousand southerners Italians left their place of residence every year. And that's not all. The same was the case with about 30 thousand northerners (natives of Veneto, Trentino, Friuli and Emilia). The regions receiving most of them were Piedmont, Lombardy and Lazio.

Twenty years afterwards the scale would have been completely different, and the parts reversed, but those who would move most would still be them, the southerners (about 120 thousand per year between 1955 and 1964) and the northerners closest to the Adriatic (a little more than 20 thousand). Initially they largely moved in clandestine ways and then, after the abolition in 1961 of the 1939 norm, they moved out into the open (after, obviously, regularising their position, as can be deduced from the peak observed in 1962 in residence transfers but which were clearly referable to movements that had occurred previously).[14]

Migration rates in the 1930s and between the 1950s and 1960s are not, as we can see, really all that different but, as we have said, in this case relative magnitudes conceal the quite different scales of the two phenomena (Fig. 5.2) that are immediately evident in the trends of the migratory balances for the macro-regions. It is not by chance that the second internal migratory wave would remain impressed in the memory of the Italians for many reasons. By saying this we obviously do not want to undervalue the significance of internal mobility during the fascist era, amply illustrated in the work of Anna Treves (1976), but simply take note—to use the words of Treves herself (1976, p. 32)—that, "the dimensions of the two problems [were unquestionably] different" and that, from this viewpoint, the internal mobility observed after the Second World War constitutes a *unicum* in the history since Unification that differs from what we have seen for other indicators of a strictly economic nature.

But it is not just a matter of order of magnitude. The migratory phenomena of the 1930s also differ from those of the 1950s and 1960s—above all—in their nature. In the 1930s, the regime's anti-urban rhetoric—culminating in Mussolini's famous Ascension Day speech (26

[14] On controlling migratory flows in the late 1940s and in the 1950s, see Gallo (2012, pp. 156–170). On the significance of the 1962 peak also see Gomellini et al. (2017, pp. 249–251) and Tortorici (2023).

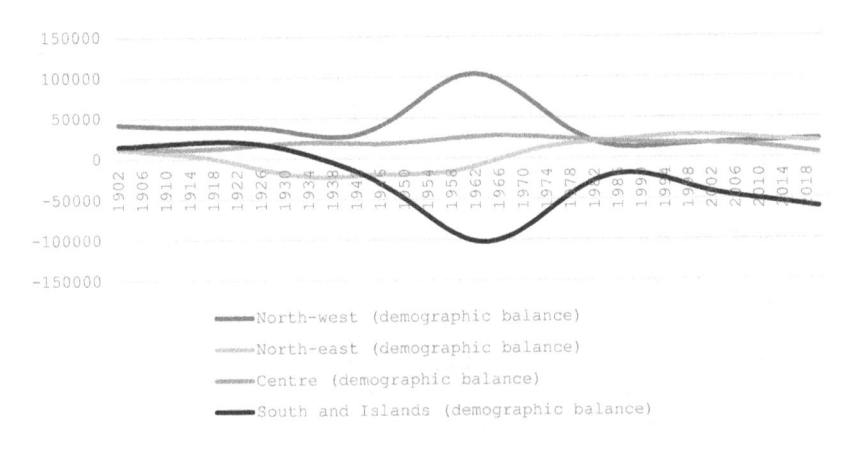

Fig. 5.2 Migratory balance by macro region (civil registry records, 1902–2020, units, trend components) (*Note* The trend components are those that result from the application of a Hodrick and Prescott filter to the original series. *Source* As in Fig. 5.1)

May 1927)[15]—was of course to a great extent almost exclusively rhetoric. To quote Anna Treves (1976, p. 101):

> an effectively restrictive regime against immigration in the cities was never implemented over the entire twenty-year fascist timespan … official anti-urbanism [reduced] itself to lots of propaganda, to marginal police provisions and failed efforts.

Indeed, in other ways fascism contributed significantly towards stimulating the flows of migrants that began to cross Italy to a growing extent starting from 1923, by urging and organising it, and promoting it through the Commissariat for migrations and internal colonisation towards areas where reclamations were in progress or in any case public works were planned. Between 1930 and 1949, Stefano Gallo (2012, p. 109) calculated that the internal migratory flows of a little less than 40

---

[15] "In order to count for something Italy must face the threshold of the second half of this century with a population of no less than seventy million inhabitants" (quoted in Treves, 1976, p. 69). In order to encourage birth, it was necessary as a consequence to blacklist the "tentacular metropolises" as they were evidently capable of discouraging them.

thousand units were linked to reclamation works and colonisation. This may be a small figure, but it is not negligible if related to the registry office registrations (or cancellations) during the period and is actually marginally higher than the demographic balance of the macro-regions in the red in terms of demographic balance. At the margins, therefore, the migrations were really planned and coordinated and had little to do with the initiative of individuals. When this was not the case, Anna Treves (1976, p. 159) underlined, they were "desperate and almost directionless, determined rather more by expulsion factors than by ones of attraction". At a distance of twenty years from those events, in 1955, Paolo Sylos Labini[16] summarised the sense of it as follows:

> Those who abandon the countryside attempt ... to pour into the towns. And this not so much because they are attracted by the prospects of getting work in the industries, as because they hope to have more possibilities of getting by, of obtaining subsidies or help of various kinds ... granted more easily in the towns than in the country.

The motivations for the internal migratory phenomena in the 1950s and 1960s were quite different: motivations that are better described by the pens of writers than by the arguments of historians or sociologists, Carlo Levi, for example, writes (1950, p. 285):

> ... some who fled from the ruins of the old house, some who wandered around searching for lost relatives and friends, some who returned after having been dragged here and there by unforeseeable events, some who came and went without any real need, driven by a longing for movement, by an exuberance of vitality by vague hopes of work and income. [...] But most of them bought, sold, dragged bundles, and bartered goods: everyone for themselves, ready to get around prohibitions, overcome obstacles and support fatigue. Italy's body, battered by bombs and by armies, started breathing again: a new and unexpected blood circulated in millions of corpuscles that drowned the required oxygen everywhere in the most underhand and unlawful manners. There had never been such travelling when everything was in peace and in order.

There had never been such travelling ... And in effect—as Stefano Gallo (2012, p. 137) observed—"the power to be able to move all over the

---

[16] Quoted in Treves (1976, p. 159).

country free from fear and from the horrors of war was, for many Italians, an event of enormous psychological and emotional impact". The simple act of moving became the way to leave behind the events of the first half of the 1940s: a concrete way of manifesting the desire to start off again from a new beginning.

"During the economic boom of the 1950s and 1960s, Italy was, literally, a country on the move" (Tortorici, 2023, p. 86). The unemployed and unskilled workers migrated, but the petite bourgeoisie migrated too, "agitated by the febrile mirage of evasion, going far away, of changing existence"—noted Guido Piovene (2017, p. 634). As recalled by Goffredo Fofi (1964, pp. 85–86)—"the most qualified, those who had the most culture, a level of knowledge and a superior ability to analyse, however instinctive it might be, migrated".

Young people migrated, and often for the joy of changing—observed Ugo Ascoli (1979)—of breaking every link with their place of origin. Women migrated—yes, women too, as suggested by Anna Badino (2008, p. 131)—determined to improve their living conditions but also to achieve "a condition of personal independence". As recalled again by Goffredo Fofi (1964, p. 85) "the best, the most active, the most restless, the most dissatisfied … those who felt the unsustainability and anguish of their situation with greater intensity".[17]

And not only did they migrate over long distances but over short and medium ones too: to move from the small rural centres towards ones that were only just a little bigger in the same province or adjacent provinces as well as towards the big cities; leaving the mountains and moving down to the foothills, the plain and the sea—in directions that did not just point from the south towards the north, but which also contemplated

---

[17] The diaries and memories of many migrants of the time are extraordinarily eloquent. In addition to Fofi (1964) and Badino (2008) quoted above, we should also mention Patrizia Gabrielli (2011) who examined the diaries regarding the postwar years conserved in the Archivio Diaristico Nazionale (*National Diary Archive*) at Pieve Santo Stefano, and summarised their content as follows: "… notwithstanding the differences between the authors of this story, of which the style and the forms preselected in the narrative in addition to the preferred themes, give account, the positive judgement on these years is striking. If some manifest their awareness of the imbalances and dysfunctions of the system and at times severe judgements of the ruling class are expressed, in most cases the accent is on the new affluence achieved, on the improvement of their homes and of the electrical appliances with which they are furnished, on the availability of leisure time, on the possibility of eating more and better compared to the previous decade" (2011, p. 13).

moves from the east towards the west. "Hooked by signs of material affluence that were conquering the imagination of the Italians" (Gallo, 2012,
p. 140).

The Italy of the economic boom was one without precedents (and,
if it can be said, without "succedents"). Italy was assailed by a process
of transformation that does not seem to have spared any aspect of daily
life: the family and leisure time, consumption and saving habits, language
and customs. A process of transformation in which the goal of improving
one's living conditions was pursued by means of decisions and strategies
of a purely individual nature, beyond the bounds of all collective architecture but with evident collective fallout. In this way—recapitulates Paul
Ginsborg (1989, pp. 326 and 339)—

> the miracle revealed itself to be an exquisitely private phenomenon [...] For
> millions of Italians the change in their material living conditions brought
> by the «economic miracle» represented above all an effective liberation
> from old constraints.[18]

---

[18] According to the historian, John Foot (2005), even the famous "*coree*"—the
apparently haphazard and disorderly urban settlements that sprang up in some of the
municipalities around Milan during the years of the Korean war—were not an expression
of misery but, on the contrary, of the initiative and dynamism of the migrants. They
were not haphazard and disorderly at all. Nothing comparable, in other words, to the
bidonville but, on the contrary "villages of houses constructed by immigrants who had
purchased land in the outskirts ... without a precise plan, often with additions made at
a later moment ... [encouraged by] the positive attitude of local politicians (in particular some mayors) and [by] their «flexible» application of laws and rules that regulated
immigration and rights of residence" (Foot, 2005, pp. 142–143). "One characteristic of
the *coree*"—observed Foot—"was their dynamism, the continuous change" (Foot, 2005,
p. 147). At an initial stage, the immigrants purchased the first plots of land and often
started the construction of their houses up against pre-existing rural buildings in which
the migrants lived until the construction work was complete. During this stage, there
were none of the infrastructures that usually make a town (roads, water and electricity
services ...) and it was often the case that the building work was halted because the financial resources ran out. In short, however, the *coree*—only minimally consisting of illegal
constructions it should be noted—constituted towns. The streets appeared and the municipalities provided the first infrastructures. The buildings were completed and often partly
rented by the migrant proprietors to immigrants—often of homogeneous provenance—as
soon as they arrived. Bustling activity could be seen around the *coree*. The buildings were
knocked up in the hours before and after work in the factories, but construction was only
one of the many activities generated by the *coree*: experts and middlemen took care of
the red tape, traders organised the supply of the materials required, bankers or less official
financiers procured the extra cash when the migrants' savings were no longer sufficient.
John Foot's conclusion exemplifies, in the specific field of urban history and perhaps as

Not that all this was not steeped in loneliness and nostalgia and did not entail fatigue and sweat, that it did not come without pain or tragedies or that there were no imbalances, including profound ones destined to leave their mark for decades to come, but—to use the words of Carlo Groppi[19]—"... they were fantastic years just as the twenties are for every single person: I felt an overwhelming interior force, I felt myself capable of being able to complete any exploit". At a distance of just less than a century the Italians discovered what Cavour meant to say by "sense of liberty". It would not last very long.

It was therefore enough that the freedom to move and do, try and change was given back to the Italians for many of them to seize it, thus transforming not only themselves but also the landscape around them. An interesting confirmation of what has just been said can be found on an apparently very distant side: that of the great external migrations which brought millions of Italians—between the end of the nineteenth century and the beginning of the twentieth, and then again during fascism and, still, in the immediate postwar period—to cross borders and seek fortune thousands of kilometres from the homeland. An in-depth analysis of external migrations is obviously beyond the scope of these pages, but some ideas present in the vast literature on the subject deserve at least to be mentioned. Just as the postwar twenty or so years helped us and will help us to read the characteristics of the Italian economy and society in the preceding and following decades, the experience of Italians in contexts that were radically different from those of origin can help to clarify the characteristics of the latter.

---

well as it is possible to do, the sense of these pages: that of the *coree* "is a story of sacrifices and of hard work, inscribed into the material culture of the house and in the frequent changes and additions that were made to it, an architecture of individualism and of success" (Foot, 2005, p. 155).

[19] The author of an autobiography that recalls childhood years and then the youth and political militancy up to 1963. The diary is conserved in the Archivio Diaristico Nazionale (*National Diary Archive*) at Pieve Santo Stefano and the piece quoted is reproduced in Gabrielli (2011, p. 22).

The first aspect that deserves to be underlined is the awareness—now acquired by historians[20] and economic historians alike[21]—of the difficulty of considering the migratory waves of contemporary Italy just as the result of poverty and overpopulation. In other words, the stereotyped image of a particularly southern exodus, driven by the miserable conditions of Southern Italy and comparable to a pure and simple demographic expulsion would not stand up to a careful evaluation of the data. At the same time, not all migratory flows from Italy and towards the rest of the world would seem to be attributable solely to wage differentials (however significant) or to so-called network effects. Quite a few contributing causes seem to emerge, often connected to the overall conditions in the areas of departure that could impede economic initiative and limit the spirit of enterprise. Andreina De Clementi (2014, pp. 24–25 and 60–67), referring in particular to the last decades of the nineteenth century, underlined, for example, the static and "impermeable" nature of the southern agricultural sector and highlighted the consequences of criteria of hereditary transmission which tended to distribute each individual property among all the heirs, thus giving rise to a fragmentation incompatible with the economic management of the properties themselves (as well as an expression of a visible and quite telling distrust of money as a store of value). Finally, she underlined the growing role of the public operator in the economy expressed by a significant progression of the tax burden capable of generating widespread situations of insolvency which, in turn, contributed to filling the steamers leaving for the United States or for the Latin America.

The passengers of those steamers were probably more gifted and motivated than those who had bade them farewell as they departed (Gomellini et al., 2017, pp. 226–232). Nonetheless, for many of them fate reserved low-skilled jobs, hardships, pains and humiliations, but more—and we're not just talking about the more well-known cases[22]—would have shown "great entrepreneurial initiative [becoming] self-employed, the bosses of

---

[20] The most immediate, but not exclusive, reference is to the monumental *Storia dell'Emigrazione Italiana* ("History of Italian Emigration") edited by Piero Bevilacqua et al. (2001) and, more recently, to the work of Matteo Pretelli (2011), Andreina De Clementi (2014), Amoreno Martellini (2018), and Emilio Franzina (2023).

[21] For all, see Gomellini et al. (2017).

[22] Among the many Gomellini et al. (2017, p. 244) cite, for example, Amedeo Obici (the "peanut king"), Filippo Mazzei (to whom the American Declaration of Independence

themselves" (Vecoli, 2001, p. 59). For the latter, the Americas would prove to be—in the words of Antonio Gibelli (1994, p. 596)—the "American resource", the place in which to seek "job opportunities, life prospects, opportunities to invest skills and competences" evidently elusive if not outright unattainable in the places of departure. Opportunities to be seized even leaving behind not poverty but working conditions that were sometimes far from insignificant, as in the case of many Ansaldo workers "who took leave to go to America" in the mid-nineteenth century (Gibelli, 1994, p. 602). Opportunities to be exploited by setting up a "bizness": barbers, tailors, builders, importers and local producers of Italian food products, restaurant managers. Showing a face, they hadn't wanted or been able to show at home. And which—and this is the data of great interest from our point of view—they could not or would not have shown once they returned home. Because sometimes it happened[23]—Francesco Paolo Cerase (2001, pp. 123–125) has well documented it—that, after experiencing success, one returned to the land of origin and here "except in rare cases, especially in the South of Italy, the crops, the cultivation systems, the agricultural investment prospects of the returned emigrants [would not have] differed much from the traditional ones". As if another option—even if tested and practised elsewhere—had not been available in Italy. And in cases where, on the other hand, the return had been interpreted as an opportunity to test the ideas and values that had been introjected into the land of destination,[24] the projects and efforts of the returned emigrants would have "clashed - particularly in the

owes something) and Lorenzo Da Ponte (the first professor of Italian literature at what would become Columbia University).

[23] Far from being a residual phenomenon, repatriations amounted—in the century that begins shortly after the Unification—to about a third of the total number of expatriations, with peaks of about 50% in years other than the first fifty years of life of the new century. In part they were nothing but the expression of a desire, present from the beginning of the migratory adventure, to conclude the life cycle in the places of birth and in part they were, undoubtedly, the result of a lack of integration and were followed by a return "to the conditions of life and work [...] from which [one had] tried in vain to escape" (Cerase, 2001, p. 118). But in significant part it was, instead, a realization of the initial project—a social promotion in the places of origin translated into the possession of the land—or rather a conscious decision to put to the test in the departure countries what was learned in the destination countries (Cerase, 2001, pp. 118–123).

[24] "To open your eyes, you have to walk the world, you have to suffer," wrote the Abruzzese farmer Francesco Cangini to his wife in 1915 (Martellini, 2018, p. 22).

Southern Italy – with misunderstandings, resistance, if not hostility at the local level", in an overall atmosphere of substantial indifference.

As if returning to Italy, the feeling of a newfound freedom present in the letters and diaries of Italian migrants abroad in the decades between the nineteenth and twentieth centuries and then in the twentieth century evaporated as soon as they set foot on their homeland again.[25] Giuseppe Previtali, who emigrated to the United States at the end of the nineteenth century to become the doctor of many immigrants over time, summarises the terms of the problem thus: "Oh America! What sweet freedom, I did not know in Italy!" Carmine Iannace, drawing on his own experience as an emigrant to the United States in the first decade of the twentieth century, thus describes the distance between his new world and the one he had left behind: "The most important element, the touchstone between the American and the non-American, is the idea of work as a dignified activity. In coming to America, one enters a new dimension if, consciously or unconsciously, he accepts the idea of work as a vital opportunity to express himself, as a hymn to life and the physical and mental possibilities of being productive, as a means of communicating with the others and with the new society".[26] Maria Rosaria Ostuni quotes excerpts from a diary of an Italian emigrant[27] travelling by train in 1912 between the United States and Canada in which the expression "treating us demogratically",[28] referring to the attitude of the train crew, describes at best the emotion for finally a full citizenship and summarises the gap, not only geographical, between the country of origin and that of destination. Ferdinando Fasce (1985, p. 17) recounts the factory life of Italian immigrants in the United States in the years between the First World War and recalls the words of a corporate training manager: "institutions become something real for them and are no longer source of

---

[25] And with it also evaporated the hope that Luigi Einaudi, among others, had placed in the capacity of international migratory flows to induce the transformations that Italy certainly needed (Manzotti, 1962).

[26] The autobiographies of Carmine Iannace and Giuseppe Previtali are cited in the interesting work by Ilaria Serra (2007, pp. 74–76 and 137–140) dedicated to the autobiographies of Italian emigrants to the United States.

[27] The diary is part of the documentary heritage of the *Fondazione Paolo Cresci per la Storia dell'Emigrazione Italiana* (Paolo Cresci Foundation for the History of Italian Emigration. Retrieved March 18, 2024, https://www.museoemigrazioneitaliana.org/app rofondimenti/in-viaggio-con-le-lettere/).

[28] I.e., "democratically". The grammatical error is present in the original text.

astonishment or fear". In perhaps more obvious terms, twenty years later, in 1931 and therefore in the middle of the *Ventennio*, Cesira Galassi—who emigrated to the United States with the aim of starting a family with her future husband Nazzareno—cannot avoid underlining that "here in America with regard to parties, it's a great thing that everyone can think whatever they want" (Salonna, 2012).[29] About a century after the cited testimonies, Vito Tanzi (2015, pp. 4–5)—a cultured and attentive connoisseur of both the US and the Italian reality for having left the latter in his early twenties without ever ceasing to frequent it—still describes in this way what the Atlantic separates: "the difference is in the proportion of people who, in the two countries [the United States and Italy] believe in [the] possibility … of improving their standard of living and their social position and occasionally even of making a fortune" counting on their own strength. Undoubtedly, personal considerations and impressions and, undeniably, drops in the sea of the epistolary and diary documentation that the Italian migrants have left us but capable of vividly representing the distance between the context of arrival and that of departure not differently from how the testimonies of those who moved around the interior of the peninsula immediately after the Second World War expressed the distance between the world that was and the one that had been (and which, in many ways, would return to being).

References

Aghion, P., Antonin, C., & Bunel, S. (2021). *The Power of Creative Destruction*. Harvard University Press.

A'Hearn, B., & Vecchi, G. (2017). Education. In G. Vecchi, *Measuring Wellbeing. A History of Italian Living Standards* (pp. 175–214). Oxford University Press.

Alesina, A., & Giuliano, P. (2015). Culture and Institutions. *Journal of Economic Literature, 53*(4), 898–944.

Arru, A., & Ramella, F. (2003). Introduzione. In A. Arru & F. Ramella (Eds.), *L'Italia delle migrazioni interne* (pp. ix–xxii). Donzelli Editore.

Ascoli, U. (1979). *Movimenti migratori in Italia*. Il Mulino.

Badino, A. (2008). *Tutte a casa?* Viella.

---

[29] In Italy where a large part of the Galassi family, recipient of the letter, still resided, the National Fascist Party was the only one admitted since 1926.

Barbiellini Amidei, F., & Gomellini, M. (2017). Concorrenza e crescita nell'industria. In A. Gigliobianco & G. Toniolo (Eds.), *Concorrenza mercato e crescita in Italia: il lungo periodo* (pp. 309–350). Marsilio.

Bastasin, C., & Toniolo, G. (2023). *The Rise and Fall of the Italian Economy*. Cambridge University Press.

Baumol, W. J. (1968). Entrepreneurship in Economic Theory. *American Economic Review, 58*(2), 64–71.

Baumol, W. J. (1990). Entrepreneurship: Productive, Unproductive, and Destructive. *Journal of Political Economy, 98*(5), 893–921.

Bertola, G., & Sestito, P. (2013). Human Capital. In G. Toniolo (Ed.), *The Oxford Handbook of the Italian Economy Since Unification* (pp. 343–374). Oxford University Press.

Bevilacqua, P., De Clementi, A., & Franzina, E. (Eds.). (2001). *Storia dell'emigrazione italiana*. Donzelli.

Bonifazi, C., & Heins, F. (2011). La mobilità interna nei 150 anni di storia unitaria. In S. Avveduto (Ed.), *Italia 150 anni. Popolazione, welfare, scienza e società* (pp. 51–55). Gangemi Editore.

Caballero, R. (2008). Creative Destruction. In S. N. Durlauf & L. E. Blume (Eds.), *The New Palgrave Dictionary of Economics* (pp. 2429–2434). Palgrave Macmillan.

Cerase, F. P. (2001). L'onda di ritorno: i rimpatri. In P. Bevilacqua, A. De Clementi, & E. Franzina (Eds.), *Storia dell'emigrazione italiana: Partenze* (pp. 113–126). Donzelli.

Ciocca, P. (2020). *Ricchi per sempre? Una storia economica d'Italia (1796–2020)*. Bollati Boringhieri.

Codogno, L., & Galli, G. (2022). *Meritocracy, Growth, and Lessons from Italy's Economic Decline: Lobbies (and Ideologies) Against Competition and Talent*. Oxford University Press.

Colucci, M. (2012). Così lontane, così vicine: le migrazioni interne ieri e oggi. *Meridiana, 75*, 9–25.

Crainz, G. (2005). *Storia del miracolo italiano*. Donzelli Editore.

De Clementi, A. (2014). *L'assalto al cielo. Donne e uomini nell'emigrazione italiana*. Donzelli.

De Mauro, T. (2011). *Storia linguistica dell'Italia unita*. Laterza.

Diamond, A. (2019). *Openness to Creative Destruction*. Oxford University Press.

Di Rienzo, P. (1965). Movimento migratorio interno in base alle iscrizioni e cancellazioni anagrafiche per trasferimento di residenza. *Annali di Statistica, 8*(17), 669–685.

Einaudi, L. (1956). *Lo scrittoio del presidente*. Einaudi.

Fasce, F. (1985). Immigrazione italiana e fabbrica USA: il caso Scovill (1915–1920). *Studi Storici, 26*(1), 5–27.

Fofi, G. (1964). *L'immigrazione meridionale a Torino*. Feltrinelli.

Foot, J. (2005). Dentro la città irregolare. Una rivisitazione delle coree milanesi 1950–2000. *Storia Urbana, 108,* 139–156.

Franzina, E. (2023). *Varcare i confini. Lettere e letture, scritture e canti dell'antica emigrazione italiana.* Il Mulino.

Gabrielli, P. (2011). *Anni di novità e di grandi cose. Il boom economico fra tradizione e cambiamento.* Il Mulino.

Gallo, S. (2012). *Senza attraversare le frontiere.* Laterza.

Gibelli, A. (1994). La risorsa America. In A. Gibelli & P. Rugafiori (Eds.), *La Liguria* (pp. 585–651). Einaudi.

Gigliobianco, A., & Giorgiantonio, C. (2017). Concorrenza e mercato nella cultura. In A. Gigliobianco & G. Toniolo (Eds.), *Concorrenza mercato e crescita in Italia: il lungo periodo* (pp. 151–198). Marsilio.

Gigliobianco, A., & Toniolo, G. (2017). Concorrenza e crescita in Italia. In A. Gigliobianco & G. Toniolo (Eds.), *Concorrenza mercato e crescita in Italia: il lungo periodo* (pp. 3–39). Marsilio.

Ginsborg, P. (1989). *Storia d'Italia dal dopoguerra a oggi.* Einaudi.

Giordano, C., & Zollino, F. (2017). Una stima del potere di mercato nel lungo periodo. In A. Gigliobianco & G. Toniolo (Eds.), *Concorrenza mercato e crescita in Italia: il lungo periodo* (pp. 199–234). Marsilio.

Gomellini, M., O Grada, C., & Vecchi, V. (2017). Migration. In G. Vecchi, *Measuring Wellbeing. A History of Italian Living Standards* (pp. 215–254). Oxford University Press.

Guiso, L., Sapienza, P., & Zingales, L. (2003). People's Opium? Religion and Economic Attitudes. *Journal of Monetary Economics, 50*(1), 225–282.

Guiso, L., Sapienza, P., & Zingales, L. (2006). Does Culture Affect Economic Outcomes? *Journal of Economic Perspectives, 20*(2), 23–48.

Levi, C. (1950). *L'orologio.* Einaudi.

Manzotti, F. (1962). *La polemica sull'emigrazione nell'Italia unita.* Società Dante Alighieri.

Martellini, A. (2018). *Abasso di un firmamento sconosciuto.* Il Mulino.

Perotti, R. (2008). *L'università truccata.* Einaudi.

Phelps, E. (2013). *Mass Flourishing. How Grassroots Innovation Created Jobs, Challenge and Change.* Princeton University Press.

Piovene, G. (2017). *Viaggio in Italia.* Mondadori.

Pretelli, M. (2011). *L'emigrazione italiana negli Stati Uniti.* Il Mulino.

Rossi, N., & Toniolo, G. (1993). Un secolo di sviluppo economico italiano: permanenze e discontinuità. *Rivista Di Storia Economica, 10*(2), 145–175.

Salonna, M. G. (2012). *Lettere dall'America. Una storia d'amore e d'emigrazione.* Affinità Elettive Edizioni.

Serra, I. (2007). *The Value of Worthless Lives. Writing Italian American Immigrant Autobiographies.* Fordham University Press.

Tanzi, V. (2015). *Dal miracolo economico al declino? Una diagnosi intima.* Jorge Pinto Books.

Toniolo, G. (2013). An Overview of Italy's Economic Growth. In G. Toniolo (Ed.), *The Oxford Handbook of the Italian Economy Since Unification* (pp. 3–36). Oxford University Press.

Tortorici, G. (2023). Irregular Citizens: Internal Migrations and Anti-urbanism in Italy (1955–1965). *Rivista di Storia Economica/Italian Review of Economic History, 39*(1), 63–88.

Treves, A. (1976). *Le migrazioni interne nell'Italia fascista.* Einaudi.

Vandenbussche, J., Aghion, P., & Meghir, C. (2006). Growth, Distance to Frontier and Composition of Human Capital. *Journal of Economic Growth, 11*(2), 97–127.

Vecoli, R. J. (2001). Negli Stati Uniti. In P. Bevilacqua, A. De Clementi, & E. Franzina (Eds.), *Storia dell'emigrazione italiana: Arrivi* (pp. 55–88). Donzelli.

Viesti, G. (2018). *La laurea negata. Le politiche contro l'istruzione universitaria.* Laterza.

Visco, I. (2014). *Investire in conoscenza. Crescita economica e competenze per il XXI secolo.* Il Mulino.

CHAPTER 6

Bailouts

Storing vs. Frittering Away

There should be very few doubts[1] at this point about the fact that
the fifteen-to-twenty-year period following the Second World War was
a unique one in the history of the unified country and there should be
equally few doubts about the fact that the characteristics of that period
coincided to a great extent with the constituent elements of Phelps-style
dynamism—to use one of the terms of reference already mentioned, "an
appetite and capacity, a desire and capability" (Phelps, 2020, p. 5)—that
were necessary for creating innovation and for facilitating its absorption
into the economy and society.

However, we cannot stop at just one indicator, however suggestive,
of the ability of Italians to seize the spaces of freedom that were open
to them at the end of the Second World War. To complete the picture
we would also like to have an indicator—as measurable as possible—of
the opposite phenomenon: of the country's willingness—in the previous
eighty years and in the following sixty—to do what was and is necessary to
avoid the continuous "reshuffling" that characterises market economies.
A recognisable and recognised "persistence" capable of expressing that
"culture refractory to growth" that only the economic boom would

---

[1] This chapter draws heavily from Rossi (2024).

N. Rossi, *Reframing Italian Economic History, 1861–2021*, Palgrave
Studies in Economic History,
https://doi.org/10.1007/978-3-031-67271-2_6

temporarily force into the corner, but which was (and is) always and otherwise present and capable of conditioning—as we have said—the economic outcomes of the last century and a half.

A seldom beaten path is the one that glimpses the basic elements of a "growth-averse" culture in the bailouts of businesses in difficulty (measurable to some extent and with some effort) and by the attitude of the Italians towards them. This, in many ways, being the other side of the coin compared to the openness to change implicit in the evidence relating to internal mobility discussed previously. Impeding the market exit of marginal companies or of ones expelled from the markets by the waves of technological innovation, the rescues constitute in fact a powerful factor that obstructs the "remixing" process which, as we have suggested, allows "spontaneous" innovation to manifest itself and, as a consequence, lays the foundations for a growth process sustained by the dynamics of total factor productivity. In Joel Mokyr's (1990, p. 153) words: "the stronger the aversion to the disruption of the existing economic order, the less likely it is that an economy would provide a climate favourable to technological progress".

The years after the 2008 financial crisis (and, even more so, the recent pandemic events) spurred individual researchers and international institutions to analyse the phenomenon of "zombie firms" as bankrupt enterprises are sometimes called, and the consequences of the economic policy interventions that were and still are intended to prevent or in any case delay their exit from the market.[2] Important from our point of view is the fact that the analyses have confirmed, without ambiguity, that the insolvent businesses tend to have productivity levels that are lower than average and tend to induce market congestion effects that first of all penalise potentially incoming firms and that, as a consequence, penalise once again the average productivity levels of the system.

On what bailouts are (or are not), the pages written at the end of the nineteenth century by Maffeo Pantaleoni remain the mandatory starting point.[3] In his words, bailouts are distinguished from normal business

---

[2] The subject understandably aroused the attention of the main international and domestic institutions from the Bank for International Settlements to the OECD, the European Central Bank and the Bank of Italy. See, for example, Banerjee and Hofmann (2021), Storz et al. (2017), Andrews et al. (2017), and Pelosi et al. (2021).

[3] The essay entitled *La caduta della Società Generale di Credito Mobiliare Italiano* ("The Fall of the Società Generale di Credito Mobiliare Italiano") was published in 1895

transactions because "extraordinarily risky operations [or because] operations dictated by an *animus* that is no longer the common one of
business, because they are carried out when they would not normally
be done, or to an extent that it's not the usual one" (Pantaleoni, 1998,
p. 108). Although they use legal guises commonly used in the business
world, bailouts are characterised by the spur to action of the bailed-out
entity which is led to ask help in order to avoid bankruptcy. A condition—
Pantaleoni remarks—which in bailout operations is always well-known to
the rescuer. Of course, it is not certain that the bailout will manage to
avoid the worst outcome, just as it is not at all certain that the interest that
drives the rescuer to come to the aid of an enterprise on the rocks has only
to do with the latter's destiny. On the contrary, bailouts are often motivated—at least in the intentions of the rescuer–by the protection of wider
interests than those of the specific bailed-out entity. That said–Pantaleoni continues–addressing the issue of bailouts essentially means asking
whether and to what extent the State should (directly or indirectly) solicit
them or take direct part in them. That is why in what follows, we shall
focus exclusively on those bailouts—of financial or industrial enterprises—
that were favoured or promoted, directly or indirectly, by the Authorities
(in the broad sense). We will not consider transactions between private
parties which, while being deemed to be bailouts in the strict sense, did
not or do not imply (directly or indirectly) a burden for the taxpayer.

Historians and economic historians have certainly not failed to discuss
specific cases of bank or industrial bailouts in Italy, setting them inside
analyses dedicated to this or that period in the history of the unified
country. Much more rarely—perhaps never—have they instead assessed
their evolution and scale in overall terms[4] and a survey as complete as
possible of the phenomenon of bailouts cannot fail to recognise that over
time bailouts have been carried out in ways which have been anything
but homogeneous. Before the First World War most of the operations
were on the spot but indirect. Mediated, that is, by this or that Issuing
Institution and related to specific shaky financial or industrial entities.

by *Il Giornale degli economisti* (in the May, April and November issues). Reference is
made here to the 1998 reprint (Pantaleoni, 1998, pp. 105–167).

[4] In fact, "there is no complete account of bailouts by the State of businesses in
difficulty" (Cohen & Federico, 2001, p. 81). And, admittedly, the brief notes dedicated
to the subject by Vera Zamagni, though insightful, are too brief to exhaust the argument
(Zamagni, 1994, pp. 153–155).

From 1915 with the birth of the Consorzio per le Sovvenzioni sui Valori Industriali and practically up to the present time the State has equipped itself with specific tools for tackling industrial or banking situations that were (or are) deemed to be particularly severe for various reasons or in any case deserving of intervention. Consequently, over time, rescue operations have increasingly become non-specific, consisting of the provision of resources in favour of the institutions in charge of the bailout policy and responsible for selecting the entities to be bailed-out. This implies that it is certainly simpler—and, indeed, it is perhaps the only way forward—to evaluate the costs of the bailout policy over time much more than to actually take a census of the bailout operations. Consequently, in the following lines we will refer not to "bailout operations" but rather to "bailout-related events", meaning by the latter term both individual bailout operations—in cases where they can clearly be identified—as well as the actions aimed at guaranteeing the availability of resources to institutions belonging to what may be termed as the "Italian bailout industry". Resources to be used in carrying out a plurality of bailout operations. For example, in the 1960s, ENI's takeover of the Lanificio Rossi (a textile company) was nothing but a well-defined bailout operation, while the endowment funds attributed to a public holding such as EFIM in the same decade (and later) constituted an event which was followed by an undefined number of rescue operations.

Moreover, focusing on "bailout-related events" allows us to consider situations which, while consisting of more than one "bailout operation", need in fact to be analysed together due to links between the entities involved in the bailout operations or to the nature of the difficulties experienced by the entities themselves. For example, in 1921 the intervention of an interbank consortium made it possible to face the difficulties of the Banca Italiana di Sconto deriving from the latter's close ties with the Ansaldo group. Although involving two distinct entities, the cited event had a clear unitary nature. To sum up, the bailout-related events that make up the sample on which this chapter is based correspond in all likelihood to a much higher number of specific bailout operations. In addition to what has already been said, it is very likely—indeed, it is certain—that our sample ignores a series of minor bailout operations. On the one hand—as Maffeo Pantaleoni reminds us—some bailouts of lesser magnitude tend to be carried out swiftly and discreetly and, therefore, they tend to remain unknown. On the other hand, some minor bailout operations are mentioned here and there in the literature or in the daily press but in totally generic terms, so that a reliable assessment proves impossible. This is conceivable for the first sixty years since the country's unification during which bailouts were prevalently carried out indirectly (that is, by means of this or that banking institution). But it is also possible for the later decades. To put it in other terms, in the light of the prudential criteria adopted throughout, it is legitimate to expect our sample to be affected more by under-estimation than by over-estimation. Last but not least, before First World War the working hypothesis—for which there is no shortage of evidence—is that the stranded costs were financed through money supply increases or additional tax revenues, being therefore absorbed, directly or indirectly, by the taxpayers. As of First World War—that is since tailor-made rescue institutions entered the scene—and except for specific and identifiable cases, the balance sheets of those institutions (if not the liquidation reports, when available) made it possible to assess the fallout from the bailout operations on the public purse relatively accurately.

As for the reasons for bailouts, Pantaleoni was in no doubt that there were very few. In his words "Government-imposed bailouts are bailouts which only by chance may not be disastrous, inasmuch as they are ordered without knowledge of the facts, and only occur by substituting an illegal, unjust and greater sacrifice of all taxpayers for the sacrifice limited and just of those who have played the market badly" (Pantaleoni, 1998, p. 115). With the passage of time and with the emergence of major crises, the interpretation of bailouts has gradually become more diversified. Jon Cohen and Giovanni Federico (2001, p. 82)—discussing the Italian economic events up to the "economic miracle"—have underlined that the rescue operations are usually accompanied by "non-quantifiable benefits such as the protection of technical knowledge and indirect costs associated with misallocation of resources". Conversely, Giovanni Federico (1999, pp. 315–316)—focusing on the "golden years" of the post-war period—has emphasised the "massive waste of resources, inspired by purely political interests" taking place since the late 1960s and up to the 1990s. Vera Zamagni (1994, p. 154)—in her bird's eye view of the role of the Italian State since Unification—has recalled "the wealth of company know-how and of specialisation" protected by the rescue operations. More prudently, Gianni Toniolo seemed instead to back away from a generalised valuation, preferring, instead, a more articulated analysis, referring to the individual seasons the rescue phenomenon went through. And so, if at the end of the nineteenth century, the rescues could be justified by their stabilising abilities (Toniolo, 1988, p. 145), in the early 1920s the results in terms of stability and protection of the national technological heritage were accompanied by an undesirable distancing of the main Issuing Institutions from their own mission (Toniolo, 1993, p. 39), and, finally, in the 1930s of the same century they made it possible "to safeguard Italy from a catastrophe of the German kind, with real implications, as well as financial ones, of enormous proportions" (Toniolo, 1993, p. 94), thereby, safeguarding "the continuity of a productive apparatus that would have collapsed and which would have scattered under the impact of the crisis" (Berta, 2016, p. 58). Even if it is again Giuseppe Berta (2016, pp. 131–132) who, in pages rich in insights, writes:

> … without IRI and the rescue policy, fascism at the very least would have had to relinquish its foolish imperialistic ambitions with the colonial adventures. (…) And without the armaments industry, fallen into public hands, not even Italy's late entry into the Second World War would have been possible. (… Italy's story …) would probably have been a lesser one in the twentieth Century, more gradual and without shocks, without the breadth and profundity of the change typical of the 1950s and 1960s (…) At the very end an Italy without miracles but also alien from interminable declines such as the one we are living through.

Counterfactual reasoning, intellectually challenging as it is, makes no difference and, in effect, it would seem difficult to make a judgement on the appropriateness of the individual bailout operations. "The difficulty,"—observed Gianni Toniolo (2022, p. 376) referring to the case of bank bailouts—"springs from the intrinsic questionability ex ante of the probability of contagion of the crisis of an intermediary, from the so-called moral hazard, from the inevitable polemics stoked by implicit or hidden political interests that always accompany the action of the lender of last resort". However, an attempt to place the individual interventions in the historical context in which they materialised is unavoidable and, if read from this standpoint and contrary to common opinion, the data—as we shall see—will forcefully suggest that focusing on specific major bailout operations may turn out to be misleading: bailout operations were and are often and willingly not necessarily attributable to micro- or macroeconomic events of some importance. Which will lead us to advance the hypothesis of bailouts as an expression of a deep-rooted and even today unchanged preference of the country for the status quo, more than as a way of tackling and overcoming specific moments of crisis. As a fondness for the absence of any kind of "churning": more than like "a" way, but "the" way—the simplest and most immediate, the most convenient, if not indeed the only practicable one—for tackling hardships, individual ones, as well as, and perhaps more than, collective ones.

Bailouts' Costs and Proceeds

That said, between 1861 and 2021 it has been possible to record slightly less than 260 distinct bailout-related events. The essential features of the sample reconstructed in this way are shown in Figs. 6.1 and 6.2 (and in Appendix C), while details on the individual events are provided in a separate Appendix to Rossi (2024). Before going any further, it is worth noting that underlying Fig. 6.2, the reader can find two distinct notions of "costs" connected to bailout-related events. There are costs that we define as "direct", namely the resources put in play in bailout operations directly or indirectly through the Authorities (corresponding to the overall height of the dark grey or light grey bars in Fig. 6.2). And then, within the limits of the available information, there are the costs that we will define as "stranded"; that is, the losses recorded on the occasion of the bailout operations defined, in turn, as direct costs less proceeds deriving in any way from the operations themselves (recorded in grey or white in Fig. 6.2) so that the "stranded costs" are given by the distance between the dark and light grey and the grey or white bars in Fig. 6.2.[5]

Figure 6.1 suggests that far from being the consequence of extremely serious and relatively rare events, bailouts are an integral part of the Italian landscape. On average, there is one—whether big or small—every seven months. One year every two or three is marked by one or more bailouts. And, except unless you think of the history of unified Italy as a virtually

---

[5] Figure 6.2 adopts, if we can say so, the accrual criterion. In other words the (direct) costs of the individual bailout operations are assigned to the year in which the bailout operation itself was formalised (even if the resources involved were effectively paid out in different years) and, in parallel, the proceeds deriving from the rescue operation (and consequent stranded costs) are assigned to the same year even if effectively realised in several years (as typically happens in disinvestment operations). The temporal allocation of the costs and the proceeds—when both the former and the latter refer to several financial years—has not always been easy. Nevertheless, it seemed reasonable to back-date both the disbursements and the reimbursements that referred to dates after that of approval of the specific bailout, making reference to the evolution over time of the GDP deflator.

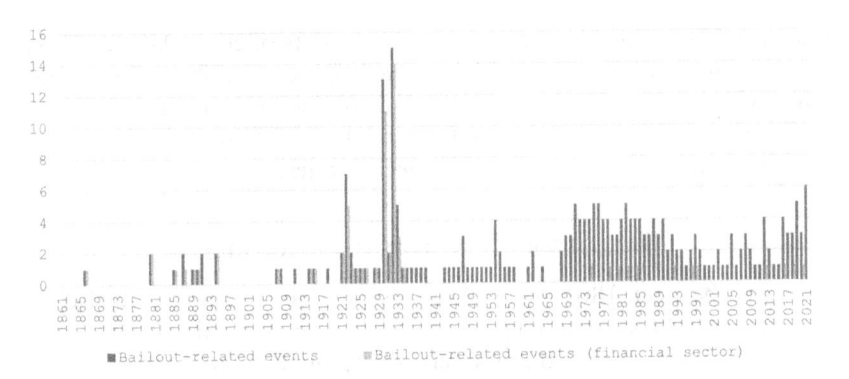

Fig. 6.1   No. of bailout-related event (*Source* Appendix C)

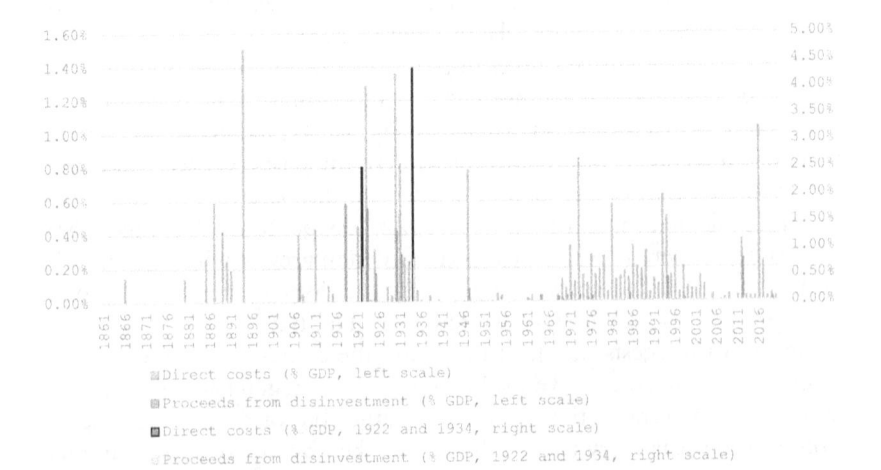

Fig. 6.2   Costs and proceeds associated with bailout interventions (% of GDP) (*Sources* Refer to Appendix C for the valuation of the costs; for the GDP, Baffigi [2015, pp. 178–184])

uninterrupted sequence of economic cataclysms, the matter cannot fail to make an impression.[6] In other words, over time, bailouts seem to be

---

[6] This did not escape the notice of Gianni Toniolo who, with reference to the decades before the Second World War, observed that "the «bailouts» were not invented for the

present in all the different phases into which Italy's economic history is usually divided, although not in a uniform manner. Bailout-related events are clearly more frequent between the wars and in the twenty-five years following the so-called economic "miracle". Moreover, to be fair, it is worth remembering how the under-estimation of the number of bailouts resulting from the presence of institutional intervention tools is certainly more present starting from the second half of the 1960s to which a share of rescues that is higher than that, already sizable (i.e. approximately 60%), observed in the sample should therefore be attributed.

That said, as in Fig. 6.1, bailouts in the financial sector should be obviously distinguished from bailouts in agriculture, manufacturing or non-financial services. Banks' role in maturity transformation exposes them to bank runs and, if confidence in the banking system is not maintained, the damage may be severe, widespread and long-lasting. The fact that one out of five bailout-related episodes can be traced back to the financial sector comes therefore as no surprise. Just as the presence of an explicit systemic motivation even in bank rescues of smaller size should not be surprising (and the examples of the Turin-based Banca Industriale Subalpina and Banca della Piccola Industria in 1880 or of a significant number of small Catholic banks in 1930–1932 are right on cue). Systemic motivation whose validity is, obviously, very difficult to establish. At the same time, the apparent concentration of bailouts of financial companies in the decades preceding the Second World War (while those of industrial or service companies proliferate in the following decades; Fig. 6.1) should be taken with care. It is, in fact, only an optical illusion to a large extent attributable to the different nature of the relationships between banks and businesses prevailing up to the 1930s and from then on. Up to the 1930s, in particular, bailing out the "big universal banks that over the years had turned themselves into something similar to industrial conglomerates holding majority stakes in the largest Italian firms" (Toniolo, 2013, p. 19) was tantamount to bailing out the firms themselves. All this changed with the 1936 banking law designed to avoid a close proximity between credit institutions and business entities. Not by chance, then, starting from the

occasion [Author's note: the 1930–1934 banking crisis] but were already part of that complex relationship between the State, the banks and industry that had characterised our country since the 1880s and that had reinforced itself and become entangled during World War One" (Toniolo, 1978, p. 386).

second half of the 1960s, direct intervention with regard to non-financial enterprises became the standard way of dealing with the problem.

From a geographical point of view, apart from cases in which the relevance or nature of the event is clearly a country-wide one, the message contained in the data is unambiguous and all in all understandable: the phenomenon of bailouts is almost exclusively a central-northern phenomenon, as to a large extent it was and is the productive base of the country (to an extent perhaps greater—it should be noted—than the geographical concentration of the taxpayers on which the ultimate burden of the bailouts fell and falls).

Figure 6.2 focuses, instead, on the financial impact of the bailout-related events and show—as percentages of the GDP of the time—the "costs" associated with the events that took place during the one hundred and sixty years we are focusing on. To facilitate reading, in Fig. 6.2 the scale on the right refers to the observations for the years 1922 and 1934, i.e. those of the great bank bailouts. The scale on the left, on the other hand, concerns the observations relating to years other than those just mentioned (which in a graph with a single scale would end up being difficult to read). On average for the period considered, we end up with stranded costs (as defined below) that were not far from 0.2% of the GDP on a yearly basis. If capitalised, the resources used for the bailout operations (after any reimbursements or proceeds deriving from disinvestments) would amount today to something like 550 billion euros (at 2020 prices): roughly 20% of our current public debt. Bailout-related events in the financial sector tend, on average, to imply a greater burden on taxpayer's pockets than similar events in the non-financial sector. However, after Second World War they tend to be rarer thereby implying a lesser weight per year on GDP.

Again, all Italian taxpayers—whether born in the nineteenth, twentieth or twenty-first century—appear to have borne the financial consequences of bailouts although, again, not uniformly. In particular, stranded costs hit a low in the twenty years following Unification as well as in the fifteen to twenty years following Second World War and reach a peak in the pre-First World War years as well as in the thirty years following the period known as the "economic boom".

The eye-catching feature of the sample, though, is its granularity. Without a doubt the list includes rescues of significant dimensions, and it is obviously these that have engaged historians and economic historians the most.[7] But—even before the 1970s burst onto the scene and a bailout "could not be denied to anyone"—there are also lots of small ones, and for the most disparate reasons. Right up to the 32 thousand lire given in 1937 to the Società Frigorifera Italia Centrale in order to "settle the economic situation of marquis Bufalini". Unsurprisingly, using a simple z-score (measuring the distance from the mean of a specific data point) to detect and set aside outliers,[8] we end up with a sample of some 254 observations with mean of 0.06% and not exceeding 0.5% in size. This picture—a large number of tiny day-by-day rescue operations forming the backdrop to very few large bailouts—repeats itself over time in different subsamples (with the average stranded cost reaching, once outliers are set aside, 0.18% in the 1861–1918 subsample, 0.05% in the 1919–1946 and 1965–1998 ones, 0.01% in the 1947–1964 subsample and, finally, 0.04% in the last subsample). This pattern turns out to be largely sector independent. Net of the five outliers, the average stranded costs per episode for the remaining 62 cases relating to the financial services sector equal 0.08% of the product. An amount very close to the overall sample average, excluding the outliers. In other words, as there were a lot of small and medium firms bailed out for each big business rescued, there were many tiny credit institutions for each credit behemoth.

Given all of the above, how can we value the burden implicit in Fig. 6.2? Is it, in some way, a heavy one? Is it not much? According to Ernesto Cianci—referring in particular to the period between the two wars—"the figures are considerable in both absolute and relative terms, but less dramatic in the end than painted to be ..." (Cianci, 1977, p. 298). Conversely—referring to the early 1920s—Luigi Einaudi had no hesitation in bluntly declaring that "the figure is huge" (Einaudi, 1923). More recently, Pierluigi Ciocca defines the scale of "the State's commitment to support and rescue operations" in the first half of the 1920s and then in the 1930s to be "enormous" (Ciocca, 2020, p. 198). For our purposes, it is not the absolute or relative scale that matters, nor Fig. 6.2

---

[7] There are obviously many references, but it is impossible not to mention, among others, the work of Antonio Confalonieri (1974 and 1975), that of Ernesto Cianci (1977) or even the pages dedicated to this topic by Gianni Toniolo (1988, 1993).

[8] I.e. Banca Romana (1894), Ansaldo-Banca Italiana di Sconto (1922), Banco di Roma (1923), Banca Commerciale Italiana (1931), Credito Italiano—Banca Commerciale Italiana—Banco di Santo Spirito—Credito Fondiario Sardo (1934), Gruppo Breda—Gruppo Caproni—Ducati—Gruppo Tosi—Gruppo Piaggio (1947), Cantieri Navali del Tirreno e Riuniti (1973), EFIM (1993).

is intended to offer a complete cost-benefits analysis of the bailout operations but rather to suggest—and the information underlying Fig. 6.2
visibly makes it possible to do so—a reading of the bailout operations that
do not necessarily coincide with some of those mentioned above. To start
with, cases of rescues that have turned out to be completely successful are
far from being easy to spot (assuming that a bailout can be considered
successful when the rescued firm is returned to the market, preferably with
no charges for the taxpayer).[9] Indeed, successful bailouts are apparently
quite rare, so rare as to merit explicit mention as in the case of Antonio
Confalonieri and his account of the rescue of the Società degli Altiforni,
Fonderie e Acciaierie di Terni, an iron and steel company (Confalonieri,
1974, pp. 209–221).[10] Or so rare as to clearly stand out from the available records as in the case of the silk industries whose difficulties were
solved in 1918 by the decision of the Bank of Italy to buy the industries'
production and to sell it at the right time (actually, with a little profit).
On the contrary it is anything but infrequent to find cases in which the
first bailout (a "definitive" one, obviously) is followed by a second one,
(also "definitive") and at times by a third intervention on behalf of the
same beneficiary.[11] Scrolling through the list of bailout-related episodes it
is easy to find quite a few repetitions confirming what has just been said.
Actually, out of around 120 bailout operations (and not events) recorded
in the sample, about 60 (that is, 50% or so) refer to entities appearing

[9] The definition of a successful rescue proposed in the text combines two elements (the
return of the company into the market orbit and the minimisation of the sacrifice for
taxpayers) clearly present in the establishing provisions of the main institutions that have
given shape, over time, to the politics of bailouts. An exception is the case of EFIM whose
founding provision did not place time limits on the public management of the acquired
companies. Needless to say, other—more subjective—definitions are certainly conceivable.

[10] Confalonieri himself observes that in the case in question the necessary favourable
conditions had materialised (a banking system capable of reacting, in close collaboration
with the government authorities and the Issuing Institution, and a positive economic
outlook for the company to be bailed out) (Confalonieri, 1974, p. 217). Conditions
which—and the reference is, in particular, to the "earning capacity of the assisted enterprises"—did not frequently materialise before and afterwards. The observation is obviously
unobjectionable but otherwise clearly partial: ingrained in bailout policy is in fact the
distortion arising out of the selection procedure. If a comparison with astronomy is legitimate (a field in which selection bias is at home), the celestial bodies (the businesses) that
are visible (or the ones that render themselves visible) to the bailout policy are only those
whose earning capacity is doubtful to say the least.

[11] The term "definitive" is not casual. It makes reference to its use in the context of
the bailout of Banca Commerciale Italiana in the 1930s (Toniolo, 1978, pp. 315–316).

more than once in the sample (Alitalia, in its different incarnations, being recorded 18 times since its birth some 75 years ago). Some cases are actually serial bailouts that started at the beginning of the twentieth century and continue to the present day. Apart from Alitalia—which runs the risk of celebrating in 2025, while wound up, its first fifty years from the first bailout—we have not heard ILVA (renamed Acciaierie d'Italia today)[12] spoken of in enthusiastic terms since the times of the war in Libya. Ansaldo—currently Ansaldo Energia—has been on the front pages of the dailies since 1921 and not always for strictly industrial reasons. Confirming the fact that bailouts, far from saving some economic entities allowed them—temporarily—to hold on to those structural characteristics that gave rise to their intrinsic weakness. In other words, far from saving the enterprises and their store of human and technical and indeed physical capital, the rescues may end up doing nothing more than postpone their departure from the market.

Moreover, the use of "go-betweens"—accompanied by a usually very convincing moral suasion for the realisation of bailout operations—far from solving the problem lays down the premises for it to be the go-between itself that will need to be rescued sooner or later (and the case of the Banca Nazionale del Regno in the second half of the nineteenth century is emblematic).[13] Even worse is if the patient still in intensive therapy is asked to look after the dying patient in the next room which is what we ended up doing.[14] Said in other terms and with specific reference to bank bailouts, it is difficult not to observe that the intervention

[12] In 1918, following the raid by the financier Massimo Bondi, the iron and steel group was rebranded as ILVA—Altiforni and Acciaierie d'Italia. As in the movies, in bailout policy too "sometimes they come back".

[13] Antonio Confalonieri is lapidary on this point: "most of Banca Nazionale's immobilised exposure was however closely linked to the bailout operations carried out on the request of government authorities" (Confalonieri, 1974, p. 143). But perhaps the most interesting example is the following: the bailout of Banca di Sconto e Sete, in 1907, was followed by the rescue of Società Bancaria Italiana—which had taken over the former—and, fifteen years later, in 1921, by the bailout of Banca Italiana di Sconto which itself had taken over Società Bancaria Italiana when it was being liquidated. And then again, in 1930 the first bailout of Credito Italiano that had taken over Banca Nazionale di Credito, the disinvestment body of Società Bancaria Italiana. Obviously in each of these cases there were also concurrent causes or greater or lesser importance but, notwithstanding this, the sequence of events is illuminating.

[14] In 2022 Banca Popolare di Bari—put into extraordinary administration in 2019, subject of a bailout in 2020 and then returning a balance sheet in red for the 2021 year

on the "proximate causes" of a bank crisis often makes it difficult to see—and therefore investigate—the "remote causes", with the result that the foundations are laid for the next bank crisis.[15]

Finally, as we have noticed, the idea that the monetary (direct or stranded) costs do not necessarily account for all the costs (and any benefits) deriving in some way from the bailouts is far from being an isolated one. In this respect, it is certainly true that bailouts are sometimes aimed at retaining a technical know-how which could, in principle, be lost or transferred elsewhere. But—apart from the major bailout-related events of the early 1920s or the mid-1930s—such bailout operations tend to be quite infrequent. Following Renato Giannetti and Margherita Velucchi's (2006, p. 72) classification of sectors according to technological intensity,[16] we can identify no more than 10 to 15 bailout operations in sectors that are classifiable, from a technological point of view, as "medium" or "high", out of slightly less than 60 non-financial bailout operations (and not events). And at times the consequences were unintended (as the sale of the Olivetti electronic business in 1965 following the 1964 bailout operation suggests). Much more frequent appears to be the case of bailouts—even of a smaller size—driven by an explicit employment support motivation. As in the case of the Raffineria Zuccheri in Ancona (1891) or the Raffineria Olii Minerali in Fiume (1922) or the Officine del Pignone in Florence (1954) or finally the Lanerossi in Schio (1962). Not

---

too—has taken over four branches of Banca del Sud, from Campania, under extraordinary administration since 2021.

[15] All of which usually leads to a multiplication of costs for the community. Given for the sake of argument that the bank-industry relationship was the exclusive cause, the bank crises between the end of the nineteenth century and the first half of the twentieth—up until the "definitive arrangement" of 1936—are good evidence of this.

[16] In their reading, the high technology aggregate is made up, between the wars, of the following sectors: (i) chemicals and chemical products, (ii) office machinery and computers, (iii) electrical machinery and apparatus not elsewhere classified, (iv) radio, television and communications equipment, (v) medical, precision and optical instruments, (vi) motor vehicles, trailers and semi-trailers, (vii) other transport equipment, while from 1950 to 1971, items (v) and (vi) are dropped. The medium technology aggregate is, instead, made up of (i) coke and refined petroleum products, (ii) rubber and plastic products, (iii) non-metallic mineral products, (iv) basic metals, (v) fabricated metal products, (vi) machinery and equipment, (vii) furniture and manufacturing up to Second World War, while, from 1950 to 1971, one should add to the above two further items (medical, precision and optical instruments and motor vehicles, trailers and semi-trailers).

to mention, of course, the bailouts attributable to the activities of EFIM or GePi in the 1970s.

Which of course does not allow us to conclude that the cost-benefits ratio always and in all cases recommends that the bailout road not be followed but it certainly raises quite a few doubts about the effectiveness of bailouts and, indeed, underlines their potentially negative impact in the medium and long term. As well as the costs and benefits that the literature on the argument has often listed, it is necessary in fact to add the failed growth in the long-term resulting from stubborn protection of the status quo.

A Permanent Temporariness

This having been said, we can take up the thread of Italian history again, beginning with an observation that should not be surprising at this point: for seven tenths of its unified existence, Italy has provided itself with structured institutional instruments for managing crises. To put it another way, for seven tenths of its unified existence Italy has put institutional entities into play that were (and are) permanent in essence (even if not formally so) for the purposes of tackling phenomena which, as a general rule, are transitory in nature.[17] Appendix C describes this century-long story in some detail, summarising its main events. Here we will confine ourselves to observing that, far from winding down, what Benito Mussolini had called the "banking hospital"[18] has been growing over the years, spreading into new wards, refreshing without ever suppressing the existing ones and equipping itself with new and more sophisticated instruments with the passage of time.

Briefly recalling the evolution over time of what might be termed the "Italian bailout industry" will help us to clarify a point: bailouts were (and quite probably still are) an integral part—perhaps we should say a fundamental one—of the culture of the Italian ruling classes, to the point of inducing them—in the run-up to the First World War—to jump the ditch

---

[17] Thereby providing a good example of what Sabino Cassese (2014, pp. 147–160) calls the "breakout of the State", intending by this the "growth of organisational structures for flanking the ministries (companies and authorities), giving rise to the formation of a multi-pole organisation of public powers".

[18] The quote is from Ernesto Cianci (1977, p. 68).

and construct a dedicated institutional architecture that was temporary in appearance but permanent in substance.

One might argue that this attitude was (and still is) nothing but the consequence of the way Italians looked at the institution of bankruptcy. Paolo Di Martino and Michelangelo Vasta and their co-authors have studied in details bankruptcy procedures in Italy, placing them also in a comparative perspective (Di Martino & Vasta, 2010; Di Martino et al., 2020; Hautcoeur & Di Martino, 2013). They convincingly argue that the Italian legal institutions were—right from Unification—such as to lead business on the rocks towards liquidation rather than continuation, thereby failing in performing their primary function: selection, among firms in critical conditions, of those deserving a further chance. In such an institutional context, it would be legitimate to imagine bailouts to be a second-best substitute for pro-restarting bankruptcy procedures. Although interesting in itself and notwithstanding the number of cases of bailouts of clearly unviable situations,[19] this hypothesis does nothing but shift the level of the topic addressed—albeit in a preliminary and tentative way—in this Section. That is, what lies behind the inefficient nature of the institutions intended to deal with business crises? In this respect, the opinion of legal experts, summarised by Giuseppe Portonera, among others, runs as follows: even if in an open and competitive market economy the failure of an entrepreneurial operation should be a normal event, it is "possible to wonder if bankruptcy, in Italy, has ever completely emancipated from its being, at once and inseparably, a «stumbling block» and a «deceit»" (Portonera, 2021, p. 15). Consequently, bailouts would be nothing but a way of bypassing an odd bankruptcy discipline which, however, would be in turn deeply rooted in the country's reluctant attitude towards the ever-present process of "reshuffling" from which winners and losers, opportunities and failures, emerge seamlessly. An attitude that cannot but deny "a fresh start" to the unsuccessful entrepreneur and therefore takes the form of sanctioning instruments for the debtor who is considered the author of a deception or fraud, often without the possibility of defence. It is interesting to note how this approach also characterises the recent Business crisis code (2019)—inspired, note, by a magistrate—in which "behind the screen of the commendable intention

---

[19] As it was already noticed, the evolution of most bailout-related institutions (CSVI, IL, EFIM, GePi and the like) is scarred by references to "companies that cannot longer be restored to health" or "bankrupt companies" and so on.

of seeking a solution to the crisis we can glimpse the attempt to put the company under strict surveillance, to avoid not so much the outcome of bankruptcy, but rather feared fraud" (Portonera, 2021, p. 10). Perhaps it is no coincidence that the use of the tools provided by the Business crisis code is, as of today, still relatively limited.

Gianni Toniolo (1993, p. 17), instead, reconnects the above attitude to the consequences of instability phenomena in the real sector and observes that "the Italian ruling class, right up to quite recent times, assessed in essentially pessimistic terms the solidity of the social structure, the stability of the institutional order, and where appropriate democracy itself. It tended therefore to take positions that were defensive and enormously prudent when faced with the manifestation of situations that could have increased society's fragility when facing aversive thrusts". Hard facts, however, suggest that "fragility of society" was perceived as an everyday occurrence rather than a "rainy day" one.[20]

Notwithstanding this rather widespread attitude, dissenting voices were heard here and there but they were (and very probably still are today) regularly and invariably in the minority. The most emblematic cases can, or almost can, be counted on the fingers of one hand.[21] In 1867, Francesco Ferrara, when approving the Government's actions regarding legal tender, did not fail to underline that "in ordinary circumstances the government is required to remain impassive when faced with a banking crisis for which it is not the cause and for which it has no remedies to

---

[20] Marco Molteni's (2020) review of the bankruptcies of small banking companies that occurred between 1925 and 1936 (i.e. in the decade preceding the 1936 banking law) provides an interesting example. These bankruptcies involved 280 ordinary credit institutions, popular banks or banking firms with total assets approaching 6.5 billion lire. During the same period, there were about 30 bank bailouts of small-scale banking firms with a total volume of assets not far from that of the failing banks and just above 5 billion lire. Referring to the same period but limiting our attention to the specific case of the Catholic banks, Gianni Toniolo (2022, p. 500) observed that in that case too "only quite a small minority was allowed to fail or be liquidated". It is difficult not to believe that failure was the exception and not the rule at that time, just as it was to a great extent before and after.

[21] Obviously, in the lines that follow justice is not done to the numerous occasions in which there were many who expressed reservations about the bailout policy but only a few particularly significant cases are examined. For a complete overview refer in particular to the articles by Piero Barucci (1981), Piero Bini (1981) and Simonetta Bartolozzi Batignani (1981) and to the recent book by Piero Bini (2021).

propose that are not worse than the illness itself".[22] Maffeo Pantaleoni (1998, p. 161) in 1895 was again, if possible, even clearer: there was no public interest to protect in a banking crisis and the State "for every time that it knows the right thing to do does the wrong thing nine times". At the beginning of the 1920s, it was Luigi Einaudi (1923) who publicly invited the State to "wash its hands" as regards the crisis. A few years later, in 1928, it would be Giuseppe Volpi—the then finance minister— who would take pen and paper and ask the Head of the Government to clarify, black on white, to avoid "harmful and dangerous precedents", that "the government could not «be called to intervene with taxpayers' money»" (Cianci, 1977, p. 59). And, again, little more than twenty years later, it was to be Luigi Einaudi (1947), in the columns of *Corriere della Sera* of 9 December 1947 who would return to the topic: "rushing to save this or that shaky enterprise (...) may at certain times be a *political* necessity [Author's italics], but those who submit to the necessity must be fully aware that they are committing a deed: that is morally condemnable (...) socially iniquitous (...), and economically dangerous". Expressions that are not substantially different from those used in those same years (1951) by *Don* Luigi Sturzo (1957, pp. 40–49), a prominent Italian Catholic priest and politician: "Today we have arrived at the absurdity of wanting to eliminate risk in order to attenuate responsibilities to the point of cancelling them ... Where is the risk? Evaporated. And the responsibility? Vanished. And the economy? Compromised. In Italy today, only companies belonging to poor devils can fail; the others are worthy of rescue". And then, once again at a distance of little more than a quarter century, Paolo Baffi—at the time Governor of the Bank of Italy—would recall that "the extension of the sphere of action of public enterprises, as the result of rescue interventions that are not compliant with a consistent line of economic policy, leads to the degeneration of public and private entrepreneurship and contributes to closing the system to European integration" (Banca d'Italia, 1973, p. 22).

However, it was the caution of the politicians and the prudence of the managements of the Issuing banks that would prevail first and those of the central bankers afterwards. The former were invariably tormented by the consequences of the crises, whether industrial or banking, also from the public order viewpoint, but especially fearful of the unpopularity of

---

[22] Quoted in Luzzatto (1968, p. 68).

more radical options, whereas[23] the latter were understandably attentive to the systemic nature of some risks and therefore ready to prioritise—at times *ultra petita*—stability objectives over efficiency goals.[24] The former and the latter, moreover, were not always fully aware of the limits of their respective roles.[25] On the other side—in the best tradition of the insiders—there would also have been no shortage of circumspect employers and of workers who were explicitly opposed as regards hypotheses of "remixing" that were visibly capable to putting at risk the positions of both one side and the other.[26]

---

[23] Confalonieri (1974), Cianci (1977), Toniolo (1993) and, more in general, the rich documentation in the historical series of the Bank of Italy (Retrieved March 18, 2024, https://www.bancaditalia.it/pubblicazioni/collana-storica/#:~:text=La%20Collana%20Storica%20della%20Banca,e%20favorire%20ricerche%20e%20studi) are the most immediate references with regard both to the attitudes of politicians and to the conduct of the management of the Issuing Institutions during the decades before Second World War. As regards the former some of the conduct is very revealing. Such as, for example, the attitude of Francesco Crispi, faced with difficulties of Banca Tiberina (Cianci, 1977, p. 159). But also, to give a second example, the behaviour of Benito Mussolini himself who, in responding to the requests of Giuseppe Volpi, carefully avoided making his own the "decision of principle" that Volpi deemed to have been imposed by the circumstances (Cianci, 1977, pp. 59–60). After Second World War (and up until the nineteen-nineties) all political reticence was abandoned. The State Holdings Ministry was established in 1956 and the bailouts policy—which as we have seen had ceased to be simply episodic for some time—also acquired a fully-fledged institutional role.

[24] See the previous note for the references. It is worth recalling here how Gianni Toniolo (1993, p. 7) sums up the relationship between the Bank of Italy and the banking system in the period delimited by the two wars: a period dominated "by the desire to take a system that struggled to leave serious crises behind and lead it back stably to a situation of normality, with the exclusion of any more emergency interventions". A summation that is not very difficult to consider appropriate both to the previous decades and to those that followed. Carlo Bellavite Pellegrini provides a careful evaluation of the relative weight of the stability and efficiency goals of the decisions of the Central Bank starting from Unification (Bellavite Pellegrini, 1996).

[25] The former—the political world—able when faced with the hesitations of the banking system at the height of a crisis, to point out that "the Government will know that in financial crises it will not be possible to count on the big Credit Institutions and will take account of this lesson" (the quote comes again from Francesco Crispi, quoted in Confalonieri [1974, p. 159]). The latter—the top managements of the Issuing Institutions—ready, when looking at balance sheets of questionable reliability "to show the Government … that the Bank is always ready to take action to prevent disasters", as declared by Giacomo Grillo, then head of Banca Nazionale nel Regno, quoted in Confalonieri (1974, p. 189).

[26] Piero Bini (2021, p. 139) recalls the positions expressed in the pages of "L'Industria", in 1914, by its director, Carlo Tarlarini, president of the Circolo industriale di

This widespread attitude of the Italian ruling classes, moreover, was not fluctuating in a vacuum but rested solidly on the convictions of a large part of what we call civil society today.[27] Just for a change, Luigi Einaudi (1923) pointed this out with his usual precision following the events involving Banca Italiana di Sconto: "it would be unjust to accuse this minister or that one for the bank interventions. These were imposed by over-excited public opinion, persuaded that it was the state's duty to save bank depositors, prevent the destruction of credit, protect national institutions from foreign plots, etc." Twenty years later, in 1944, Donato Menichella[28] reiterated the point:

In a country that is relatively capital-poor and with a scant financial tradition the collapse of a bank and/or the threat of the collapse of a bank have never been considered as normal events in economic life in which, as in that of individuals, prosperity may be followed by poverty and health by illness and death, but as events of an extraordinary nature that are capable of moving large parts of public opinion and therefore of provoking noise and violent debates in the press, unrest in the country, collapses of ministries, and so on ....

Referring to the 1970s and the 1980s, Giovanni Federico (1999, p. 330) summed up the matter as follows: "... support for such interventions was

Milano. Positions that pushed towards "maintaining that the crisis of a large company no longer constituted a private matter, but a question of national importance ... The specific costs sustained by the consumer to keep alive companies that would otherwise be destined to disappear would be balanced by the greater needs of the «national economy as a whole»". Positions that completely match those of the entrepreneurs who are involved directly or indirectly in this or that rescue operation, both before and after the First World War. From the trade union standpoint, in addition to the considerations above from Ernesto Cianci, references should be made to the memoirs of Guido Carli (1996, p. 264), references summarised in a judgement referring to trade union action in the 1960s: "Their policy [...] aimed in reality at the extension [...] of an assisted and corrupt industry in which the creation of jobs was fake «because neither work nor productivity corresponded to them»".

[27] The theme of the cultural interactions between ruling classes and society at large is a fascinating topic on which see Bisin and Verdier (2024).

[28] At the time Director General of IRI and Governor-to-be of the Bank of Italy. The quotation comes from a report presented to Capt. Andrew Kamark, representative of the Finance Sub-commission of the Allied Control Commission at IRI (Cotula et al., 1997, pp. 153–185). The report begins, significantly, with the following words: "Italy has been defined by a writer on economic matters as the country for bank bailouts".

widespread from local communities, trade unions and the populace at large (opposition parties included). Bailouts were almost by default".

The powerful words of Luigi Einaudi or Donato Menichella, eighty years on, remain essentially intact. Anyone who needs to be convinced of it could do well to follow some of the well-known morning and evening talk shows that, virtually every day, dedicate particular attention to this or that industrial crisis, giving voice to its main characters and sustaining the need for public interventions that are capable of saving single businesses and associated jobs: a need that is generally accepted—with extremely rare exceptions—by the guests present.

From a retrospective viewpoint, if anything both Luigi Einaudi's and Donato Menichella —two leading protagonists of the matters that interest us—were distorted downwards: not only were the banks able, from the start of unification, to solicit a collective cry for protection—one that was even able to manifest itself through the "sorrowful soul of the Roman Pope"[29]—but so too were businesses. Large, medium and even small. As well as their employees and their trade union representatives. Along with local communities and their political spokespersons, regardless of their political views.

To reiterate the point: a thought-provoking working hypothesis might revolve around the idea of bailouts as one of the most interesting persistent features of unified Italy: a persistence rarely analysed as such. In this respect though, the information provided by Figs. 6.1 and 6.2 is clearly important but is certainly not sufficient. It has been useful, if not essential, to review the public debate on the matter in the way that it has been disentangling over time and remember its outcomes in order to fully realise if and to what extent the snapshot of Italy contained in Figs. 6.1 and 6.2 is the expression of it. And it has been useful to do so from different but complementary angles. But it is necessary too to

---

[29] The quote is taken from a letter sent in 1929 by Pietro Tacchi Venturi, then the authoritative intermediary between Palazzo Venezia (used by Mussolini as residence and seat of government) and the Vatican, to the Director General of the Bank of Italy, Bonaldo Stringher (Guarino & Toniolo, 1993, doc. 103). Attached to the letter is a letter from the Archbishop of Fermo which requests the Government's intervention to save Società Bancaria Marchigiana and with it "poor Marche" from an unspeakable disaster and it was anticipated that "God will repay you for the many tears that you cooperate in drying on the poor people ruined by their blind faith in the Bancaria, considered to be the «Bank of the priests»". It is hardly necessary to observe that this is only one of the many examples on the matter that it is possible to mention.

take account of the objection that rightly sceptical readers will not have failed to raise: is the bailout policy—intended as both a permanent feature of state action and of the culture shared with society as a whole—an exclusively Italian phenomenon? It is an objection that is not so easy to answer in the absence—to the best of our knowledge—of reconstructions that are directly comparable to the one summarised in Figs. 6.1 and 6.2 (and in Appendix C). It becomes necessary therefore to assemble different sources of information in an attempt to reach some conclusion that may, perhaps, be advanced in these terms: during the period under examination (1861–2021) the phenomenon of bailouts (financial and/or industrial) is common to every latitude even if the terms and procedures may differ from case to case, but there do not seem to be any conclusive reasons for imagining that elsewhere in the Western World (in the United States or the United Kingdom and, as far as we have been able to see, in continental Europe) it had the same penetration and diffusion and the same degree of acceptance as in Italy. There are elements for believing that, in effect, recourse to bailouts (financial and/or industrial) was systematic—here too, at every latitude—starting from the 1970s of the last century, but this observation actually seems to underscore the specificity of Italy: i.e. a tendency to get around market mechanisms right from the dawn of the unified State (associated with a distinct propensity for transforming situations that of their nature ought to be transitory into permanent ones). This is a conclusion that is clearer perhaps in the case of the English-speaking countries and less so in the case of the European nations closer to Italy, as we might have expected anyway, but—based on the available evidence—apparently reliable.

For example, in the case of the United States, the bailout phenomenon—scattered up until the early 1970s of the last century—acquired greater frequency after approval of the Emergency Loan Guarantee Act, in 1971, for industrial rescues and after the emergence of an extensive interpretation of the so-called essentialism theory in the case of bank bailouts.[30] These however always remained confined, or almost so,

---

[30] The reference here is to a 1951 amendment to the 1950 Federal Deposit Insurance Act that was intended to permit bailouts of banking institutions that were deemed to be "essential" as they were present in rural contexts that otherwise had no banking infrastructures. This was an amendment which, from an extensive perspective, gave rise then in the 1970s and 1980s to various bank bailouts, some of which were probably outside the perimeter originally imagined by lawmakers (Nurisso & Prescott, 2017). It should be underlined, though, that only some of the bank crises in the United States led

to the emergence of crises of significant dimensions, accompanied by vigilant and significant control by public opinion: control that was intended to ascertain the emergency nature of the interventions as well as attention to the use of the taxpayers' resources; a control that signals the suspicion with which American public opinion considers the bailouts and which is not without consequences.[31] Similar assessments could be made in the case of the main European countries.[32] In this case too, the 1970s seem to mark a watershed, even if there is no shortage of examples of industrial rescues already at the end of the 1950s in Great Britain and in Germany as well as in Belgium in the early 1960s (Foreman-Peck & Federico, 1999). In particular, as far as industrial rescues are concerned Enzo Pontarollo (1976) has carefully documented the increasing role of bailouts in industrial policy in the UK, France, Belgium and Germany at the beginning of the 1970s, driven by the macroeconomic events that marked the middle of that decade. Before then, Pontarollo (1976, p. 7) himself notes that the cases were only "sporadic" and it is interesting to observe how James Foreman-Peck (2017), when making a long-term review of industrial policies in Europe, points to Italy (and France) as examples of relatively more intense *dirigisme* in the decades prior to the First World War and cannot avoid citing Italy as the most significant example of public intervention in the years between the two wars.[33] And it is interesting to

---

to bailouts. See Bordo and Eichengreen (1999), Bordo et al. (2001), and Reinhart and Rogoff (2009) and the Congressional Research Service (2020) for industrial ones.

[31] For example, the site https://www.propublica.org/article/government-bailouts (retrieved March 18, 2024) publishes and regularly updates bailout cases, with precise identification of the beneficiaries (whatever their size) and indicating the associated costs borne by the taxpayer and, where present, any consequent proceeds. It needs scarcely be observed that in the case of bailouts following the 2008 financial crisis, the site indicates net proceeds for the State amounting to a little more than 100 billion dollars (testifying among other things to the tangible temporariness of those events).

[32] As regards the bank crises in Europe, again only some led to bailouts (Bordo & Eichengreen, 1999; Bordo et al., 2001; Reinhart & Rogoff, 2009). Gianni Toniolo is an obvious reference for a comparison of the bailout policies in Italy and in central Europe on the occasion of the crisis in the 1930s (Toniolo, 1980, pp. 219–227; 2022, pp. 569–570).

[33] From this perspective let us not be deceived by the relatively limited burden borne by Italian taxpayers after the financial crisis of 2008 and the following 2011 sovereign debt crisis. It is in fact the direct consequence of the extremely low margins of Italian public finances rather than a different attitude towards public intervention. On these "difficult years" for Italy's central bankers, see Visco (2018).

observe, again, how contrary to what happened in the English-speaking nations, in continental Europe there were no signs of precise and effective control of public opinion as regards the use of taxpayers' resources for bailing out industrial and/or financial businesses.[34]

The above lines, of course, do not do full justice to a phenomenon whose comparative evaluation would require a lot more space and, on the contrary, open up an interesting area for future research. But they reveal how the hypothesis of an entirely Italian "specialisation"—and a long-lasting one—in the bailouts industry is not completely without foundation.[35]

We have been suggesting that the bailouts of businesses in difficulty (measurable with some effort) and the attitude of the Italians towards them represent an interesting "persistence" in Italian economic history since Unification, a "persistence" with potentially relevant implications. In every market-based economic system an even-handed degree of "entrepreneurial dynamism" is able to balance the benefits linked to the growth in productivity arising out of the reallocation of the factors with the costs associated with the reallocation itself (among the sectors, the businesses and the individuals). If the dynamism fails for some reason (because, for example, it is discouraged, compressed or even combated)—thereby making the creation of new businesses less straightforward or even because of the adoption on a wide scale of the technique of therapeutic persistence with regard to productive structures that are at this

---

[34] In the United Kingdom the *National Audit Office* (retrieved March 18, 2024, https://www.nao.org.uk/taxpayer-support-for-uk-banks-faqs/) provides an up-to-date review of the costs borne by the taxpayer following the 2007 bank bailouts. In Italy, the Bank of Italy (retrieved March 18, 2024, https://www.bancaditalia.it/media/approf ondimenti/2015/salva-banche/index.html) felt that it had to answer the questions posed by the investors who suffered following the procedures for the resolution in 2016 of several medium-scale banks in northern and central Italy (in an operation that, for our purposes, moreover, cannot be depicted as a bailout). It is evident that in the first case the addressee were the taxpayers and in the second case the directly interested investors. There is no evidence that, in the cases of bailouts that took place in Italy, the Authorities deemed it necessary to inform the taxpayers (nor that the latter asked for this as such).

[35] Interestingly, in the international review of business-government relationship edited by Hideaki Miyajima, Takeo Kikkawa and Takashi Hikino the one and only reference to bailouts is out in the Italian chapter (Federico, 1999). The very same point is underlined by Giovanni Federico and Renato Giannetti (1999, p. 145): "the evolution of industrial policy in Italy did not differ very much from that of other European countries. There were indeed some differences in emphasis. For instance, since the nineteenth century, bailouts have been more widespread and frequent than elsewhere ...".

stage out of the market—it is the community as a whole that pays twice the consequences. Not just through taxes but, above all, thanks to growth levels lower than those that would have been possible otherwise.

REFERENCES

Andrews, D., McGowan, M. A., & Millot, V. (2017). Confronting the Zombies: Policies for Producivity Revival. *OECD Economic Policy Papers 21.*

Baffigi, A. (2015). *Il PIL per la storia d'Italia. Istruzioni per l'uso.* Marsilio.

Banca d'Italia. (1973). *Assemblea generale ordinaria dei partecipanti tenuta in Roma il giorno 30 maggio 1973. Considerazioni finali.* Banca d'Italia.

Banerjee, R., & Hofmann, B. (2021). *Corporate Zombies. Anatomy and Life Cycle* (BIS Working Papers No. 882). Bank for International Settlements.

Bartolozzi Batignani, S. (1981). Il contributo degli economisti in alcuni quotidiani. In *Banca e industria fra le due guerre* (Vol. I, pp. 299–358). Il Mulino.

Barucci, P. (1981). Il contributo degli economisti italiani (1921–1936). In *Banca e industria fra le due guerre* (Vol. I, pp. 179–244). Il Mulino.

Bellavite Pellegrini, C. (1996). *L'evoluzione istituzionale del sistema finanziario italiano. Un modello formale e una verifica quantitativa.* Università Cattolica di Milano: Doctoral thesis.

Berta, G. (2016). *Che fine ha fatto il capitalismo italiano?* Il Mulino.

Bini, P. (1981). Il dibattito attraverso le «riviste di regime». In *Banca e industria fra le due guerre* (Vol. I, pp. 245–298). Il Mulino.

Bini, P. (2021). *Scienza economica e potere. Gli economisti e la politica economica dall'Unità d'Italia alla crisi dell'euro.* Rubettino.

Bisin, A., & Verdier, T. (2024). On the Joint Evolution of Culture and Political Institutions: Elites and Civil Society. *Journal of Political Economy* (132, forthcoming).

Bordo, M., & Eichengreen, B. (1999). Is Our Current International Economic Environment Unusually Crisis Prone? In *Capital Flows and the International Financial System.* Reserve Bank of Australia. Retrieved March 18, 2024, https://www.rba.gov.au/publications/confs/1999/bordo-eichengreen.html

Bordo, M., Eichengreen, B., Klingebiel, D., & Martinez-Peria, M. S. (2001). Is the Crisis Problem Growing More Severe. *Economic Policy, 16*(32), 51–82.

Carli, G. (1996). *Cinquant'anni di vita italiana.* Laterza.

Cassese, S. (2014). *Governare gli italiani. Storia dello Stato.* Il Mulino.

Cianci, E. (1977). *Nascita dello Stato imprenditore in Italia.* Mursia.

Ciocca, P. (2020). *Ricchi per sempre? Una storia economica d'Italia (1796–2020).* Bollati Boringhieri.

Cohen, J., & Federico, G. (2001). *Lo sviluppo economico italiano 1820–1960.* Il Mulino.

Congressional Research Service. (2020). *Federal Assistance to Troubled Industries: Selected Examples*. US Congress.

Confalonieri, A. (1974). *Banca e industria in Italia 1894–1906* (Vol. I). Banca Commerciale Italiana.

Confalonieri, A. (1975). *Banca e industria in Italia 1894–1906* (Vol. II). Banca Commerciale Italia.

Cotula, F., Gelsomino, C., & Gigliobianco, A. (1997). *Donato Menichella. Stabilità e sviluppo dell'economia italiana, 1946–1960*. Laterza.

Di Martino, P., Latham, M., & Vasta, M. (2020). Bankruptcy and Insolvency Laws Around Europe, (1850–2015): Institutional Change and Institutional Features. *Enterprise and Society, 21*(4), 936–990.

Di Martino, P., & Vasta, M. (2010). Companies' Insolvency and 'the Nature of the Firm' in Italy, 1920s–1970s. *The Economic History Review, 63*(1), 137–164.

Einaudi, L. (1923, October 5). I limiti e il costo dei salvataggi bancari. *Corriere della Sera*.

Einaudi, L. (1947, December 9). Non Cantabit. *Corriere della Sera*.

Federico, G. (1999). Harmful or Irrelevant? Italian Industrial Policy, 1945–1973. In H. Miyajima, T. Kikkawa, & T. Hikino (Eds.), *Policies for Competitiveness* (pp. 309–335). Oxford University Press.

Federico, G., & Giannetti, R. (1999). Italy: Stalling and Surpassing. In J. Foreman-Peck & G. Federico (Eds.), *European Industrial Policy. The Twentieth-Century Experience* (pp. 124–151). Oxford University Press.

Foreman-Peck, J. (2017). Industrial Policy in Europe in the 20th Century. *European Investment Bank Papers, 11*, 36–62.

Foreman-Peck, J., & Federico, G. (Eds.). (1999). *European Industrial Policy. The Twentieth-Century Experience*. Oxford University Press.

Giannetti, R., & Velucchi, M. (2006). The Demography of Manufacturing Firms. In R. Giannetti e M. Vasta (Eds.), *Evolution of Italian Enterprises in the 20th Century* (pp. 63–86). Il Mulino.

Guarino, G., & Toniolo, G. (Eds.). (1993). *La Banca d'Italia e il sistema bancario, 1919–1936*. Laterza.

Hautcoeur, P., & Di Martino, P. (2013). The Functioning of Bankruptcy Law and Practices in European Perspective (ca. 1880—1913). *Enterprise & Society, 14*(3), 579–605.

Luzzatto, G. (1968). *L'economia italiana dal 1861 al 1914*. Einaudi.

Mokyr, J. (1990). *The Lever of Riches. Technological Creativity and Economic Progress*. Oxford University Press.

Molteni, M. (2020). Measuring Bank Failures in Interwar Italy: Sources and Mehods for a Comparative Account. *Rivista di Storia Economica/Italian Review of Economic History, 36*(3), 345–398.

Nurisso, G., & Prescott, E. (2017). The 1970s Origin of Too Big to Fail. *Federal Reserve Bank of Cleveland Economic Commentary 17.*

Pantaleoni, M. (1998). *La caduta della Società Generale di Credito Mobiliare Italiano.* UTET.

Pelosi, M., Rodano, G., & Sette, E. (2021). Zombie Firms and the Take-Up of Support Measures During Covid-19. *Banca d'Italia Questioni di Economia e Finanza 650.*

Phelps, E. (2020). Introduction. A Theory of Innovation, Flourishing and Growth. In E. Phelps, R. Bojilov, H. T. Hoon & G. Zoega, *Dynamism. The Values That Drive Innovation, Job Satisfaction and Economic Growth* (pp. 1–19). Harvard University Press.

Pontarollo, E. (1976). *Il salvataggio industriale nell'Europa della crisi.* Il Mulino.

Portonera, G. (2021). Dal «fallimento» alla «liquidazione giudiziale»: cos'è mai un nome? *Istituto Bruno Leoni Briefing Paper 190.*

Reinhart, C., & Rogoff, K. (2009). *This Time Is Different. Eight Centuries of Financial Folly.* Princeton University Press.

Rossi, N. (2024). Italian Bailouts, 1861–2021. *Rivista di Storia Economica/ Italian Review of Economic History, 40*(1), forthcoming.

Storz, M., Koetter, M., Setzer, R., & Westphal, A. (2017). Do We Want These Two to Tango? On Zombie Firms and Stressed Baks in Europe. *European Central Bank Working Paper Series 2104.*

Sturzo, L. (1957). Politica di questi anni (1950–1951). In L. Sturzo, *Opera omnia* (Vol. XI). Zanichelli.

Toniolo, G. (1978). Crisi economica e smobilizzo delle banche miste (1930–34). In G. Toniolo (Ed.), *Industria e banca nella grande crisi 1929–34* (pp. 284–352). Etas Libri.

Toniolo, G. (1980). *L'economia dell'Italia fascista.* Laterza.

Toniolo, G. (1988). *Storia economica dell'Italia liberale.* Il Mulino.

Toniolo, G. (1993). Il profilo economico. In G. Guarino & G. Toniolo (Eds.), *La Banca d'Italia e il sistema bancario, 1919–1936* (pp. 5–101). Laterza.

Toniolo, G. (2013). An Overview of Italy's Economic Growth. In G. Toniolo (Ed.), *The Oxford Handbook of the Italian Economy Since Unification* (pp. 3–36). Oxford University Press.

Toniolo, G. (2022). *Storia della Banca d'Italia* (Vol. I). Il Mulino.

Visco, I. (2018). *Anni difficili.* Il Mulino.

Zamagni, V. (1994). Alcune tesi sull' intervento dello Stato in una prospettiva di lungo periodo. In P. Ciocca (Ed.), *Il progresso economico dell'Italia. Permanenze, discontinuità, limiti* (pp. 151–160). Il Mulino.

CHAPTER 7

Public Finances

A Debt Prone Country

Last, but not least, public finances. In their stocks and flows, in their balances and in their structure, in the composition of revenues and expenditures, the relationship between the State and citizens takes shape and consequently the nature of that relationship, prevailing in a community from time to time, comes into view. In what follows, we will make repeated reference to the temporal evolution of the main indicators of the state of public finances: from the public debt to GDP ratio to the share of revenues and expenses on the product itself, and to the composition both of revenues and of expenditures. We will do so not just to highlight the fluctuating stance of macroeconomic policy in this or that phase of the Italian experience since Unification (a recurring theme which, obviously, would require another space and which is treated exhaustively in the bibliographical references) but to extract—needless to say, indirectly—from those accounting items information about the beliefs, values and preferences of both rulers and ruled, as they end up being expressed from time to time, say, in the volume of resources intermediated by the public sector and therefore in the latter's "grip" and presence in the Italian economy and society. Or conversely, as expressed, in the spaces left to the private sector (the public debt being, in this context, nothing but a claim on

N. Rossi, *Reframing Italian Economic History, 1861–2021*, Palgrave Studies in Economic History, https://doi.org/10.1007/978-3-031-67271-2_7

future resources), as well as in the incentives or disincentives embodied in the structure of the budget.[1]

Reading the underlying culture of a community in the structure and evolution of public finances is by no means accidental and, even less, unprecedented. *Si parva licet*, our mind turns obviously to Joseph A. Schumpeter (1991, p. 100)[2]—"an enormous influence on the fate of nations emanates from the economic bleeding which the needs of the state necessitates, and from the use to which its results are put"—or to Antonio De Viti De Marco (1953, p. 31)—the state budget "is a factor of the very greatest importance in a people's historical fortunes; without understanding and taking account of it, you can write the descriptive and dramatic history of wars and revolutions, but you cannot give them an explanation"—or, finally, to Rudolf Goldscheid's recap suggesting that the Government budget is "the skeleton of the state stripped of all misleading ideologies".[3]

In the Italian case, we are indebted to Carlo Bastasin et al. (2019), among others,[4] for a recent attempt to retrace the Italian history since Unification with the help of the Government budget, albeit always within an overall reading that it is still that of the "convergence and two tails". Bastasin et al. (2019, p. 4) highlight the role of the Italian high public debt and the consequent high uncertainty in discouraging the accumulation of fixed capital and, consequently, in turning the two tails into disappointing episodes in a story that all in all was one of success. Moreover, they see the persistence of a high public debt to product ratio as the way with which from time to time the ruling classes were (and would still be) able to maintain an adequate degree of social cohesion in a country that did not (and perhaps, in their view, still does not) have any.

Doubts about the "convergence and two tails" hypothesis have already been expressed previously along with the preference for a depiction of

---

[1] It is hardly necessary to observe that the expansion of the public operator does not necessarily imply its greater authoritativeness or, more simply, greater efficiency and efficacy in its action. On the contrary, Sabino Cassese (2014, p. 27) observes how in the Italian case the literature on "too much state" tends to run step by step with that of the state's weakness.

[2] The reference here is to the English translation of "Die Krise des Steuerstaats" (1918).

[3] Quoted in Schumpeter (1991, p. 100).

[4] For example, Brosio e Marchese (1986), Marongiu (1995, 2017, 2019, 2020), Pedone (1967), and Tanzi (2012).

the Italian vicissitudes after Unification as a not particularly brilliant 160-year period within which, instead, there was a fifteen-year period or so of innovism à la McCloskey or grassroot innovation à la Phelps that let Italy achieve relative performance levels that had never been recorded before and that would never be recorded afterwards. Nonetheless, the reading of Bastasin et al. (2019) presents some interesting points of contact with the interpretative key of these pages which—as we have already seen—associates the cultural limits of the Italians with the usually high dose of dirigisme with which the ruling classes responded and (still respond) to those limits, dirigisme which translated (and still translates) into a growing degree of intermediation of present and future resources and, subsequently, into a reduced dynamism of the economic system which prevented those limits from being exceeded. And it still prevents it today, given that—as is implicit in the narrative of Bastasin et al. (2019)—those limits are just as present now as they were one hundred or one hundred and fifty years ago.

Of course, from the perspective of these pages, in attributing the less than brilliant performance of the Italian economy in the periods cited to the impact of a high public debt, Bastasin et al. (2019) would be focusing attention on one of the symptoms rather than on the pathology itself. Nevertheless, whatever the overall reading, the shared message is that it is also in the public budget—as well as in macroeconomic variables, in productivity trends or its determinants—that we need to look for the interpretative keys of the events of our last one hundred and sixty years. At the same time, it seems debatable to look at political and financial instability—a factor only partially attributable to the theme of institutional shortcomings, also dear to Bastasin et al. (2019)—as the key element responsible for the cloud of uncertainty that was to engulf and envelop Italy and which, in particular, would be at the root of the stunted evolution of productivity observed in the first and last thirty years of the history of unification.

Whether and to what extent Italy has been a politically unstable country is not an obvious question. Just as the idea that it was financially unstable due to its high public debt is not evident (it being understood that in this case the present would seem to lead to greater prudence). Bastasin et al. (2019) themselves point out that in the course of its unitary history, the Italian public debt would appear to have positioned itself quite regularly on converging trajectories. Moreover, the size of the public debt to GDP ratio and its sustainability are not synonymous and it is legitimate to imagine that conditions of financial uncertainty are linked to the latter concept much more than to the former (and, more precisely, to the probability of debt unsustainability). Of course, debt sustainability may, indirectly, be affected by the level of debt but—for any given cost of debt and growth configuration—it has to do primarily with the size of primary surpluses that are needed to support certain volumes of debt. As regards the last decades, there was nothing to stop Italy from taking a different path, but even if this were the case—as is in fact still possible—it would not be easy to make financial instability the key to understanding unified Italy's economic vicissitudes.

Extending our gaze to include the evolution of the main fiscal indicators required additional work, which is described in detail in Appendix D, Figs. 7.1, 7.2, and 7.3 summarise the main results and offer (as far as possible) a comparative picture. In Figs. 7.1, 7.2, and 7.3, in addition to the trend component[5] of the main variables, dashes pinpoint the available information for the usual international terms of reference—EUR-4 (i.e. France, Germany, Belgium and the Netherlands), EUR-5 (i.e. Spain in addition to the previous aggregate) as well as the United Kingdom and the United States—as reported in Tanzi and Schuknecht (2008).[6]

We will refer repeatedly to Figs. 7.1, 7.2, and 7.3 in what follows. However, some considerations of a general nature are already possible. Since the birth of the unitary state, Italy has recorded levels of the public debt to gross domestic product ratio that are higher—and, at times, significantly higher—than those observed in other European countries. The comparisons with the United Kingdom in the years between the two wars and with the main European countries after the Second World War are exceptions. The presence of a high public debt makes it possible to understand the primary surpluses (the fiscal effort) observed at the beginning and at the end of the one hundred and sixty-year period, whereas the years immediately following the Second World War show a significant fiscal effort despite the presence of very low public debt to GDP ratios due to the macroeconomic events of the period. The consistently high levels of the debt-to-product ratio are, in turn, the direct consequence

---

[5] As before, we prefer to concentrate our attention on the medium-to-long run trends.

[6] The international comparison of fiscal indicators is tricky due to the frequent lack of homogeneity between the reference aggregates (that is Central or General Government). Along with Appendix D, the note to Figs. 7.1 and 7.2 attempts to clarify the issue.

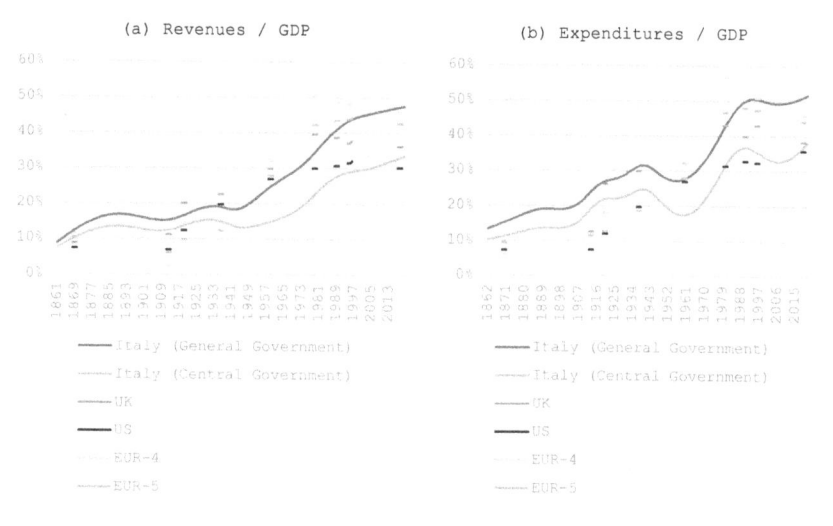

Fig. 7.1 Main fiscal indicators (revenues and expenditures, 1862–2021, %, trend components in the case of Italy) (*Notes* [i] EUR-4: France Germany, Belgium and the Netherlands; [ii] EUR-5: EUR-4, Spain; [iii] in Fig. 7.1a, data for France, UK and USA refer to the General Government aggregate while those relating to Belgium, Germany, the Netherlands and Spain refer to the Central Government aggregate; as a result, the information underlying the EUR-4 and EUR-5 aggregates is not entirely homogeneous; [iv] in Fig. 7.1b, data for France, Germany, UK and USA refer to the General Government aggregate while those relating to Belgium, the Netherlands and Spain refer to the Central Government aggregate; as a result, the information underlying the EUR-4 and EUR-5 aggregates is not entirely homogeneous; [v] in the case of the Italian data, the trend components are those that result from the application of a Hodrick and Prescott filter to the original series. *Sources* For the data for Italy, Appendix D; for the data relating to EUR-4, EUR-5, the UK and the USA, Tanzi e Schuknecht [2008, Tables I.1, III.1, III.5] up to 1997; The European Commission [retrieved March 18, 2024, https://economy-finance.ec.europa.eu/ economic-research-and-databases/economic-databases/ameco-database_en] and IMF [for the later information; for the construction of the EUR-4 and EUR-5, and therefore for defining the relative weights, the Maddison Project Database [retrieved March 18, 2024, https://www.rug.nl/ggdc/historicaldevelopment/ maddison/releases/maddison-project-database-2020?lang=en])

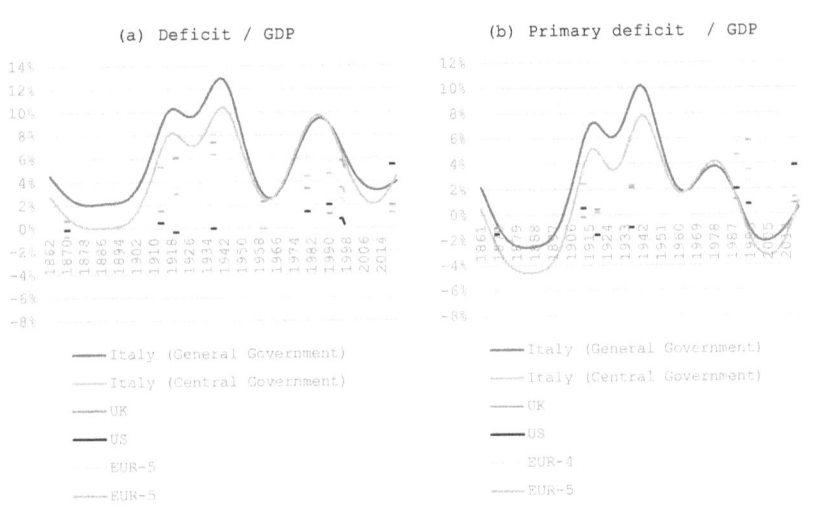

Fig. 7.2 Main fiscal indicators (deficits, 1862–2021, %, trend components in the case of Italy) (*Notes* [i] EUR-4: France Germany, Belgium and the Netherlands; [ii] EUR-5: EUR-4, Spain; (iii) Fig. 7.2a is derived from the information referred to in Figs. 7.1a and b; [iv] consequently the information relating to revenues and expenditures for the years 1937–1873 refers to non-homogeneous aggregates; [v] in Fig. 7.2b, data are obtained by adding the information referred to in Fig. 7.2a to the debt service burden of the Central Government; [vi] in the case of the Italian data, the trend components are those that result from the application of a Hodrick and Prescott filter to the original series. *Sources* As in Fig. 7.1)

of a trend in public expenditure that is often more sustained (for the same reference aggregate) than that observed elsewhere and, conversely and always for a given reference aggregate, a lower tax burden. In this context, it is interesting to observe right now how the containment of primary deficits (and therefore the fiscal effort) recorded in the immediate post-Second World War period was founded on a moderate increase in the tax burden associated with increased expenditure, net of interest on the debt, which was made feasible by the significant reduction of the latter.

Figure 7.3 (panel b) explores this specific aspect by reporting, in the usual long-term trend terms, the standard debt convergence indicator (i.e. the interest rate net of the growth rate or, if preferred, net of the "growth

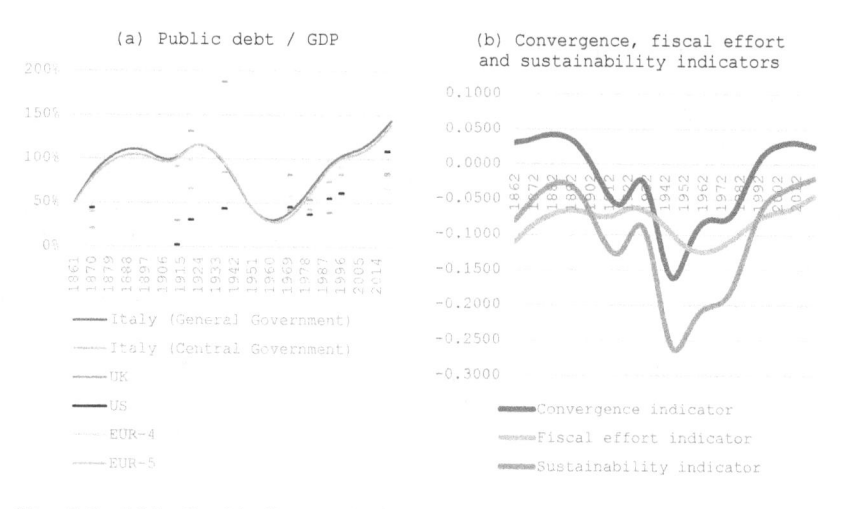

Fig. 7.3 Main fiscal indicators (public debt and convergence indicator, 1862–2021, %, trend components in the case of Italy) (*Notes* [i] In Fig. 7.3a, the data relating to France, Germany, Belgium, the Netherlands, Spain, the United Kingdom and the United States refer to the General Government aggregate starting from 1970 and to the Central Government aggregate previously; [ii] in Fig. 7.3b (based on the General Government aggregate), the "fiscal effort indicator" measures the extent of the long-term response, in terms of the primary surplus, to changes in the interest rate (net of the growth rate), a response which is not independent of the level of the ratio between public debt and gross domestic product in the sense that higher levels of the latter require, other things being equal, more restrictive budgetary policies which are not necessarily politically achievable (a phenomenon otherwise known as "fiscal fatigue"); in the same panel, a greater "fiscal effort" corresponds to more negative values; [iii] in Fig. 7.3b, (based on the General Government aggregate), the sustainability indicator combines the information deriving from the trend in interest rates (net of growth rates) and from the "fiscal effort" indicator to measure the distance between the state of public finances in a given year and its unsustainability (the latter corresponding to positive values of the indicator); to increasing interest rates (net of growth rates) must correspond—in order to guarantee debt sustainability—a fiscal policy response (a "fiscal effort") such as to offset or more than offset the impact on the levels of the ratio between public debt and gross domestic product; [iv] in the case of the Italian data, the trend components are those that result from the application of a Hodrick and Prescott filter to the original series. *Sources* As in Fig. 7.1)

dividend"). As is well-known, positive values of this magnitude imply—if the objective is that of stabilising the ratio between public debt and gross domestic product—the need for primary surpluses (i.e. surpluses of revenue over expenditure other than debt service expenses) which increases as the public debt-to-product ratio increases. As can be seen, the first forty years of the unified Italian economy were marked by positive and significant differences between the interest rate and the "growth dividend". Hence the need for a fiscal effort—for the measurement of which reference is made to Appendix D—which moreover tends to diminish with respect to what would have been necessary so as to bring the sustainability indicator (given, very simply, by the distance between the fiscal effort necessary to ensure debt sustainability and the effort actually put into practice) close to zero, i.e. very close to those positive values which coincide with the area of instability.

It is what, with reference to the mid-1880s, we will define as the "Magliani area" from the name of the person in charge of budget policies at the time. The phenomenon will repeat itself, over a century later, from the beginning of the second decade of the current century (and therefore regardless of the pandemic emergency). What is interesting to note, however, is how entry into the "Magliani area"—and therefore the emergence of a fiscal fatigue that becomes less and less bearable—follows and does not precede long periods of limited growth marked, among other things, by a significant activity of institutional reform.

INSIDE THE GOVERNMENT BUDGET

The relative evolution of some quantities within the revenue and expenditure aggregates deserves a brief comment. On the revenue front, the direct tax share of total tax revenues (Fig. 7.4, left panel) provides a very approximate and certainly rough indication of the overall progressivity of the tax system. Without wishing to summarise a body of literature that is as extensive as it is equivocal at times,[7] it is hardly necessary to recall how the hypothesis of a negative impact on the growth rate of increasing shares of direct taxation would seem to be largely shared (as would be that of a negative impact of the same magnitude on the volatility of growth

---

[7] See Martinez-Vasquez et al. (2009).

rates, given the automatic stabiliser nature of direct taxes) while the relationship between the same indicator and distributive indicators would be less clear-cut.[8]

Italy's closeness to the highest values observed in the international arena at the beginning and at the end of the 160-year period stands out, whereas in the immediate post-Second World War period the ratio settles

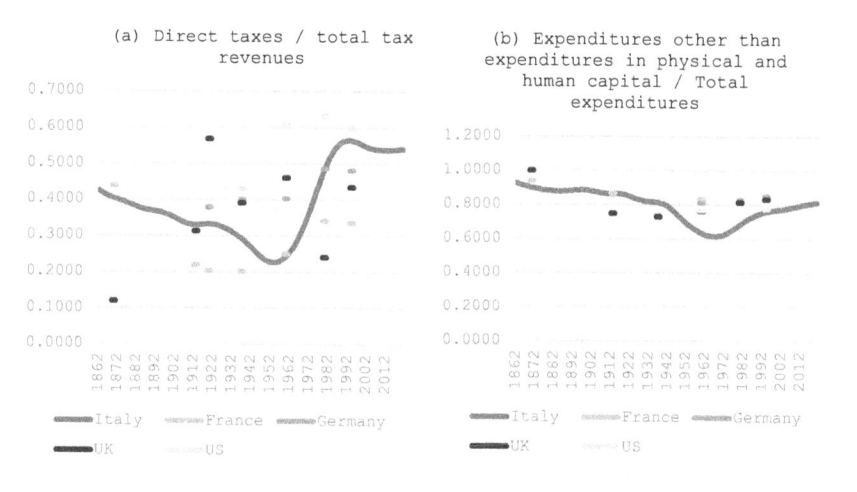

Fig. 7.4 Share of direct taxes on total tax revenues and share of public expenditures other than expenditures in physical and human capital on total expenditures (%; 1862–2021; trend components in the case of Italy) (*Note* [i] the available information prevents meaningful definition of the EUR-4 and EUR-5 aggregates as above; [ii] direct (income and wealth taxes) include inheritance and gift taxes; [iii] in the case of the Italian data, the trend components are those that result from the application of a Hodrick and Prescott filter to the original series. *Sources* For the data for Italy, Appendix D; for the data relating to France, Germany, UK and USA, Tanzi e Schuknecht [2007, Tables II.5, II.13, III.2] up to 1994)

---

[8] Aghion et al. (2021, pp. 96–103) summarise the recent research on the relationship between taxation and innovation by pointing out the negative impact of higher marginal personal tax rates on the propensity to innovate. In particular, in the case of the United States, a one percentage point increase in the top marginal personal tax rate would imply a discouragement of innovation activity and a 4% contraction in the number of inventors and patents. In the case of corporate tax, an increase of one percentage point in the rate would lead to a reduction of around 6% in the number of patents and around 5% in the number of "inventors".

around the corresponding minimum values. Furthermore, the clear and sudden trend reversal recorded from the second half of the 1960s cannot fail to strike: so sharp and sudden that it soon lifted Italy above some of its main European counterparts.

On the expenditure side and with all the necessary precautions,[9] the share of expenses not intended for increases in the stock of physical and human capital (Fig. 7.4, right-hand panel) may indicate the attention paid, in various historical phases, to the spending components that were presumably less capable of affecting the country's growth prospects. Also in this case, it is significant how Italy falls below the values observed internationally in the second half of the nineteenth century and then again in the decades immediately following the Second World War. In the mid-1960s, a sharp reversal of the trend is again recorded, leading Italy to reach the positions of other countries in the 1990s.

Both on the revenue side and on the expenditure side—and with all the necessary precautions—one can then imagine highlighting the items that directly or indirectly express a desire to preserve the status quo or to direct individual choices. The former case accounts for tax revenues that come to life whenever a significant "change of state" takes place. Taxes such as those on "use of goods" which, in theory, take the form of levies against which the state offers a service (e.g. the annotation in public registers confirming the legal existence and the date of an act) but which in practice have only an apparent link with the production costs of the service itself. For example, in the Italian tax system, registration, mortgage and cadastral taxes affect taxpayers when they change from being a tenant to a homeowner or even when they leave their original or previously established family nucleus to create a new one—getting married, for example, or getting divorced, or renting a house. Figure 7.5 (left panel) shows the evolution over time of such source of tax revenue in relation to gross domestic product.

Still on the revenue front, the latter case is given, for example, by revenues that define what is usually called the "nanny-state" and which in some sense betray a desire to protect citizens from themselves and

---

[9] The debate about the extent of the current nature of education expenditure is all too well-known to be mentioned here. It is a debate which in the Italian case moreover—for the reasons mentioned above regarding the real recipients of expenditure for education (i.e. the service providers much more than the users)—should be treated with an additional dose of skepticism.

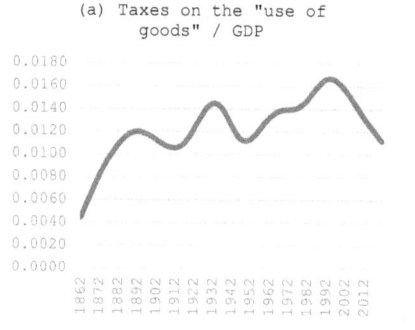
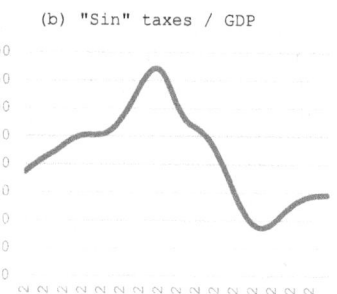
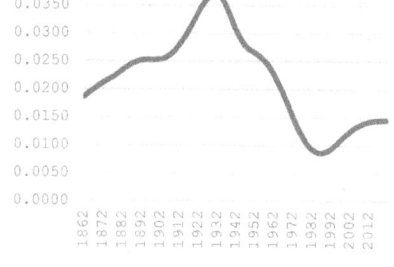

Fig. 7.5 Taxes on "use of goods" and "sin" taxes (% of GDP; 1862–2021; trend components) (*Note* [i] Fig. 7.5, panel [a], refer to "taxes on use of goods and on permission to use goods or perform activities" [IMF, Government Finance Statistics Manual, item no. 1145, https://www.imf.org/external/pubs/ft/gfs/manual/2014/gfsfinal.pdf, retrieved March 18, 2024]; [ii] in Fig. 7.5, panel [b], "sin" taxes include taxes on salt and tobacco, on sugar, coffee, cocoa, spirits and beer, and gambling activities. *Source* See Appendix D for the data regarding Italy)

to interfere with individual choices to keep them away from goods or activities deemed unworthy (Fig. 7.5, right panel). It is an aggregate that contains various items: from taxes on salt and tobacco to those on spirits and beer, from taxes on sugars, coffee and cocoa to those on the lotto and lotteries. Despite the fact that it was not possible to obtain reliable international terms of comparison in these cases, as had been done in others, the information reported in Fig. 7.5 confirms that the public budget is quite a reliable indicator of the basic choices of a community. As was perhaps reasonable to expect, the twenty years of fascism appear to be the period in which the paternalistic attitude of the ruling classes was most fully expressed (and the corresponding willingness of the Italians to follow its instructions), whereas the years immediately after the Second World War saw a clear retreat from that attitude, which is followed, at different moments over the years, by a resumption of old habits.

REFERENCES

Aghion, P., Antonin, C., & Bunel, S. (2021). *The Power of Creative Destruction*. Harvard University Press.

Bastasin, C., Mischitelli, M., & Toniolo, G. (2019). Living with High Public Debt, Italy 1861–2018. *LUISS School of European Political Economy WP 11*. Retrieved March 18, 2024, https://leap.luiss.it/wp-content/uploads/2022/09/WP11.19-Living-with-high-public-debt-Bastasin.Mischitelli.Toniolo-WP.pdf

Brosio, G., & Marchese, C. (1986). *Il potere di spendere*. Einaudi.

Cassese, S. (2014). *Governare gli italiani. Storia dello Stato*. Il Mulino.

De Viti De Marco, A. (1953). *I principi dell'economia finanziaria*. Einaudi.

Marongiu, G. (1995). *Storia del fisco in Italia. La politica fiscale della Destra storica (1861–1876)*. Einaudi.

Marongiu, G. (2017). *Una storia fiscale dell'Italia repubblicana*. Giappichelli.

Marongiu, G. (2019). *La politica fiscale dell'Italia liberale. (1861–1922)*. Giappichelli.

Marongiu, G. (2020). *Il fisco e il fascismo*. Giappichelli.

Martinez Vasquez, J., Vulovic, V., & Liu, Y. (2009). Direct versus Indirect Taxation: Trends, Theory and Economic Significance. *Andrew Young School WP 09–11*. Retrieved March 18, 2024, https://scholarworks.gsu.edu/cgi/viewcontent.cgi?article=1045&context=econ_facpub

Pedone, A. (1967). Il bilancio dello Stato e lo sviluppo economico italiano, 1861–1963. *Rassegna Economica, 31*(2), 285–341.

Schumpeter, J. A. (1991). The Crisis of the Tax State. In R. Swedberg (Ed.), *The Economics and Sociology of Capitalism* (pp. 99–140). Princeton University Press.

Tanzi, V. (2012). *Centocinquant'anni di finanza pubblica in Italia*. IBL Libri.

Tanzi, V., & Schuknecht, L. (2008). *Public Spending in the 20th Century: A Global Perspective*. Cambridge University Press.

PART III

Re-reading Italian Economic Events

CHAPTER 8

A "Cold Story"

THREE SONGS

Reviewing the previous pages, the logical sequence that we promised ourselves to use as our key for reading the economic history of unified Italy emerges with a certain clarity at the moment in which we exploit the variability implicit in the fifteen-to-twenty years following the Second World War to illuminate the entire century and a half and more since Unification. Sustained and lasting growth of total factor productivity presupposes among other things a significant innovative activity that is also capable of expressing itself through significant patenting capacity. In turn, a real predisposition towards innovation requires an attitude towards entrepreneurship that is similarly tangible and marches in step with continuous "turnover" of the economy: of its production and employment base and of the structure of markets. But an economy that is ceaselessly engaged in experimentation and innovation at all levels is only possible if the value system of society is such that it not only permits that transformation but also encourages it without interruption, and with the conviction that, notwithstanding the economic and social costs that

---

Cassese (2014, p. 327).

© The Author(s), under exclusive license to Springer Nature Switzerland AG 2024
N. Rossi, *Reframing Italian Economic History, 1861–2021*, Palgrave Studies in Economic History,
https://doi.org/10.1007/978-3-031-67271-2_8

inevitably arise out of such transformation, the final outcome can only be positive for the community as a whole.

Let it be clear, we are still well away from having demonstrated the basic thesis set out in the introduction—accepting that this is possible in any case (something that can be legitimately doubted in our field)— but the unbiased reader should agree that perhaps a reading that differs from the usual one is possible. A different reading—if we are allowed to make a digression that is only apparently unnecessary—that can best be photographed perhaps by three songs of great if not indeed enormous success which are part of the country's cultural history (Table 8.1).

The first is the very famous *Mille lire al mese* ("A thousand lire a month") by Carlo Innocenzi and Alessandro Sopranzi, dated 1938, a hit for Gilberto Mazzi and especially Natalino Otto and then rediscovered— note the date!—by Patty Pravo and Renzo Arbore in the mid-1980s and Fabio Concato in the last decade. It featured a simple and catchy motif that in 1939 was also to inspire a film (directed by Max Neufeld), a plastic representation—whether true or false—of everything that a dynamic society is not: the "modest job" as the main aspiration, the absence of "demands" as a programmatic declaration and "peace of mind" before anything else. A depiction that is not so different then from that of another piece of great success that is much closer to the present: *Una vita da mediano* ("A halfback's life") by Luciano Ligabue from 1999, in which the "modest job" is replaced by "precise tasks" to carry out inside "certain zones", and not beyond, because the fact of being "without good feet" means that we must be aware of our limits (and not even try to go beyond them). This hit passed into history when it became the anthem of a political movement in 2006 (which says a lot—much more than one might think—of Italy's so-called second republic and of its protagonists).

And then, between Natalino Otto and Luciano Ligabue, the flash of genius in 1958: *Nel blu dipinto di blu* ("In the blue painted blue"), better known as *Volare* by Franco Migliacci and Domenico Modugno. Twenty-two million copies sold, song of the year and record of the year in 1959, interpreted over the years—to name just a few of the many— by Dean Martin, David Bowie, Barry White and Paul McCartney. The

Table 8.1 Three songs, two Italies

1938	1958	1999
What desperation / What delusion	I think a dream like this will never come again	A halfback's life / Recovering balls Born without good feet/ Working on lungs
Trying to live / Always unlucky /Always penniless	I painted my hands and my face with blue	A halfback's life / With the precise task To cover certain zones / To play generously
But if a small job / Tomorrow dear, I'll find, / Of golden jewels / I'll cover you	Then suddenly I was whisked up by the wind	There/ Always there
If I could have / A thousand lire a month, Without exaggerating / I would be sure to find / Every happiness	And I began to fly in the endless sky	A halfback's life / of someone who rarely scores Who must pass the ball / To who finishes the game
A modest job / No great demands,	Flying oh, oh / Singing oh, oh / In the blue painted with blue/ Happy to stay up there	A halfback's life / That nature did not give you Nor the cue of the centre forward or of the striker, what a shame
I want to work / To be able to find / All my peace of mind	And I flew higher above the sun	There/ Always there
A little house / In the suburbs,	While the world slower and slower seemed distant down there	There in the middle / As long as you have it stay there
A little wife / Young and pretty / Just like you	Sweet music played only for me	There/ Always there
If I could have / A thousand lire a month, I'd do lots of shopping I'd buy lots of things / The nicest you'd want	Flying oh, oh / Singing oh, oh / In the blue painted with blue/ Happy to stay up there	There in the middle / As long as you have it stay there
I dreamt again / Tonight my love,	But all dreams vanish at dawn because	As long as you have it stay there
A inheritance / A distant uncle / American	When the moon goes it takes them away	A halfback's life / Of someone who burns out fast Because when you give too much / You must go and give way
But if this dream / Doesn't come true,	But I continue to dream in your beautiful eyes	A halfback's life / Working like Oriali Tears of exhaustion and blows and / Maybe you'll win the world cup
How will I do / I will sing again / The refrain	That are blue like a sky pierced with stars	There/ Always there
If I could have / A thousand lire a month, Without exaggerating / I would be sure to find / Every happiness	Flying oh, oh / Singing oh, oh / In the blue in the blue of your eyes/ Happy to stay ...	There in the middle / As long as you have it stay there
A modest job / No great demands,	Franco Migliacci e Domenico Modugno, Nel blu dipinto di blu (1958)	There/ Always there
I want to work / To be able to find / All my peace of mind		There in the middle / As long as you have it
A little house / In the suburbs,		As long as you have it / Stay there
A little wife / Young and pretty / Just like you		Luciano Ligabue, Una vita da mediano ("Life of a halfback") (1999)
If I could have / A thousand lire a month, I'd do lots of shopping I'd buy lots of things / The nicest you'd want		
A little house / In the suburbs,		
A little wife / Young and pretty / Just like you		
If I could have / A thousand lire a month, I'd do lots of shopping I'd buy lots of things / The nicest you'd want		
Ah, if I could have / A thousand lire a month!		
Carlo Innocenzi and Alessandro Sopranzi, Mille lire al mese (1938)		

plastic depiction of an Italy that does not hesitate to "think the unthinkable", whose ambitions have no limits. Paola Larese Gortigo writes in his diary[1]:

> in January 1958, after being at the Club to see S. Remo,[2] I came home with the sensation of having heard something that was absolutely new that moved me profoundly. The next day I said to Marina: there was a song that was so different, beautiful, and amazing. This was *Blu dipinto di blu*.

Just as the Italy of the economic miracle must have seemed different, beautiful and amazing.

It is probably true, as Jacopo Tomatis writes (2021, pp. 13–28), that the idea that the Italian song is a "mirror" of the country or even the "soundtrack of its time" is nothing more than a misconception. "A limiting and restrictive idea, accepting that it can help to explain the cultural context of a country …, certainly does not achieve the goal of making us understand the functioning of the song itself". But even with these limitations, it is difficult not to compare the parabola of Italian dynamism, as we have sought to depict it in economic terms in the preceding chapters, with the parabola sketched during the same years by the voices of Gilberto Mazzi, Domenico Modugno and Luciano Ligabue. To use the words of Tomatis again, "when we talk about music we are never talking «just about music»".

"See and Admire ... Do Not Do, Do Not Envy"

Having closed this musical parenthesis, we can return to the main thread of the story which should now be lowered into the economic events of unified Italy, providing a picture of it that will be necessarily concise (even if hopefully not too so), one that will not be intended to go over its salient events again (refer to the footnote references for these) but to illuminate some aspects of them, starting from the evidence discussed in the preceding pages and completing it. In other words, the lines that follow do not propose to add another economic history of Italy to the many more praiseworthy ones that already cover the subject but set themselves a much more limited goal: re-read its main episodes from the point of

[1] Quoted by Patrizia Gabrielli (2011, p. 15).

[2] A well-known yearly Italian song contest.

view described in the preceding chapters. The attempt will be to try to rediscover—with the help of the protagonists or of those who already told us the story—the thread that links the events of the period to the economic debate and to the culture, both of the ruling classes and of citizens at large, that was prevalent during the period itself. Assuming, of course that there is one such link and hoping to limit to the minimum possible the probability of adding to the queue of what Piero Barucci (1978, p. 7) called the "inextinguishable national industry composed of the second-hand quotations".[3]

But let us proceed in an orderly manner. Italy of the middle of the nineteenth century was—as recalled by Gianni Toniolo (2013, pp. 3–4) and Giovanni Vecchi (2017b, p. 2)—little more than a mere "geographical expression" furrowed by physical, legal, administrative and fiscal boundaries, by widespread illiteracy, by shorter life expectancy than elsewhere, and by transport and communications networks that were not so much deficient as completely absent. In this context, on the day after of that fateful 17 March 1861, the Piedmontese ruling class on whose shoulders rested the very heavy task of building the new unified country tackled the theme with pragmatism and practicality.[4] In five years from that date they tackled the infrastructure of the new Kingdom, passing the law on administrative unification first of all, and then following it with the law on administrative disputes. With the former the structure of municipalities and provinces was defined (in a strictly centralist key) while action was also taken with the latter to bring disputes regarding the public administration into the framework of the ordinary jurisdiction. During the same timeframe the premises were laid down for more effective control of the territory (through the law on public security) and complete form was

---

[3] Getting beyond the account, mediated to a lesser of greater extent, of what happened would imply making reference to sources such as, for example, the parliamentary acts or the daily newspapers. Such a task is certainly beyond the goals of this work but above all could certainly throw light on the behaviour and culture of the ruling classes but would not necessarily help us to understand the value system of the Italians.

[4] On the fortunes of what is usually defined as Liberal Italy, see, in particular, Toniolo (1988), Marongiu (1995, 2019), Banti (1996), Berselli (1997), Battilossi (1998), Cammarano (2011), Cassese (2014), Fenoaltea (2011), Tanzi (2012, 2018), Tedoldi (2018), and Melis (2020) as well, of course as the texts of Italian economic history already mentioned above. The debate relating to the nature of the process of unification, with particular reference to relationships between the north and south of the country, is obviously outside the scope of these pages (refer to Tanzi [2018] for a discussion).

given to the legislative and economic-financial unification of the nation. In 1866 in fact, the civil and civil procedure codes, and the code of commerce, among others, came into force. On the economic side, a few years earlier customs unification had been implemented without any hesitation, extending the protection already in force in the previous Kingdom over the whole new Kingdom (and by so doing giving life to a vast single market), the Italian lira was established as the accounting and legal currency of the new Kingdom, the public debt of the pre-unification states was unified, and the unification of taxation was launched,[5] thereby establishing the grounds for orderly and disciplined management of public finances that would culminate in balancing the state budget a few years later in 1876.[6] During the same period work also began on the material infrastructures: from the railway network (quadrupled in the fifteen years after unification) to the education system (informed right from the beginning by the principles of the 1859 Casati act and, in particular, the principle of obligatory and free primary education). Certainly, the institutional design of the new Kingdom deliberately replicated and in a far too evident manner by the Savoy institutional and administrative structures[7]—indeed, it would perhaps be necessary to say French rather than Savoy—but it is difficult to deny the extraordinary effort of state building—as we would say today—that was put in place in the span of a decade or little more by the Piedmontese ruling class to provide the country with many of the institutions required in order to ensure its take-off (and for guaranteeing control of the country). In order to guarantee—within the possible limits of the time, of the conditioning by the

---

[5] At the same time aligning the tax system to the most advanced examples to be found in Europe (Marongiu, 1995, p. XI).

[6] With which—observes Gianni Marongiu (1995, p. 416)—it was intended to "anchor fiscal policy to a principle: enshrine the existence, in a flexible constitutional system, of a material constitutional rule hierarchically above changeable and contingent choices. An even more appreciable attitude because no limits of expenditure were set in the Statute or in constitutional practice".

[7] Sabino Cassese (2014, pp. 42–46) recalls that it was the firm intention of Cavour "to make Italy and constitute it later" and, as a consequence, maintain the pre-unification administrative structures as far as possible as he was convinced that these were, in any case, a step forward compared to those prevalent elsewhere in the peninsula.

objecting realities of unification[8] and of the convictions of the protagonists—property rights, free enterprise, rule of law, balance between these and an adequate human capital. In the conviction, shared by many of the protagonists of those years that a new institutional architecture—borrowed from the Savoy experience and different in many aspects from that prevalent in many pre-unification states—would, along with a large domestic market, have guaranteed per se the civil and economic progress of the new Kingdom.

As is obvious, it was an effort that did not fail to have consequences, in particular, on the condition of the public finances. These were hoppled, on the one hand, by the fall in the revenues which was a consequence, in particular, of customs unification and also of the greater costs deriving from the commitment in the military and infrastructural field and, only subordinately, the education one. This meant that the trends in public finances—whose margins of freedom were compressed by the significant and growing burden of servicing the debt—soon revealed themselves to be one of the main problems for the new Kingdom. Spending by the public administrations passed from about 13% of the GDP in 1862 to about 18% in 1876 (Fig. 7.1, right panel),[9] reaching (at State level) three percentage points above the level recorded in the 1870s in Austria and Germany, four percentage points above the level for Great Britain, a little above the French figure and doubling of the figure for the United States (Tanzi & Schuknecht, 2008, pp. 3–8). Furthermore, the composition of the spending changed significantly, only partly as a result of the state building effort.[10] Conversely the tax burden passed from little more

---

[8] In the first place, the distance—however real or perceived (Tanzi, 2018) and not just in strictly economic terms—between the Mezzogiorno and the rest of the Kingdom, a distance that the ruling classes at the time were well aware of and to which the prudence of the same towards administrative decentralisation was traceable to a considerable extent.

[9] It is hardly necessary to point out that precise information regarding this or that state budget item in a given year, may not coincide exactly with the trend components indicated in Fig. 7.1–7.3.

[10] Between 1862 and 1876 the quota of spending absorbed by servicing public debt passed from just over 16% to a little more than 35% of the total State expenditure. During the same period, the capital account spending burden doubled, or almost so, from the initial 5%. Also, during the fifteen-year period, the spending for education and culture stabilised around a meagre 2% of total expenditure compared to spending on defence (less the outlay for keeping public order) that was firmly established close to 20% and even capable of touching 40% in specific years. And this immediately leads to the conclusion that in quite a few moments public spending other than for servicing the debt

than 7% of 1862 to a little less than 16% in 1876 (Fig. 7.1, left panel), only succeeding in counterbalancing (and in any case not entirely) the greater volume of expenditure in the second part of the same period. In more or less the same time frame, the tax burden in France and in the UK was between 9 and 15% without appreciable variations over time (Tanzi & Schuknecht, 2008, pp. 51–55). In this case too, the composition changed significantly, recording a significant decline in direct taxes compared to indirect ones over the whole fifteen years.[11] The dynamic of the flows—that visibly betrayed a presence of the public operator in Italian society that was much broader and above all growing more than elsewhere—did not take any time to have repercussions for stock trends: public debt, at the General Government level, climbed from about 40% of the GDP in 1861 to over 100% in 1876 (Fig. 7.3, left panel). This increase materialised to a great extent during the 1860s.[12]

In a context marked by significantly positive interest rates on public debt (net of the growth "dividend"),[13] only consistent primary surpluses could guarantee the sustainability of the public debt and reassure investors (Fig. 7.3, right panel). And this is exactly what happened, though with blander rhythms a little at a time as the debt grew and the fiscal effort required became heavier. This is the context—rather than a strictly ideological sphere—in which to place the aim of balancing the budget that

and for defence did not go far beyond one third of total expenditure. It is only proper, moreover, to recall that the 15-year period being discussed was marked by the struggle against brigandage in the south (a phenomenon with quite a few of the features of a civil war, concluded around 1865), by the Third War of Independence (1866) and by the capture of Rome (1870). Refer to Appendix D for the reconstruction of the main State Budget items.

[11] At the State level, income and property taxes (including inheritance taxes), amounting to over 50% of tax revenues in 1862, did not exceed 40% in 1876 (Appendix D).

[12] Here we will completely ignore (as being outside the scope of the analysis), the well-known theme of the origin of Italian public debt at the moment of Unification and, in particular, the theme of Unification as an implicit way of getting all the Italians to share a burden that related to the Savoy subjects to a prevalent extent (Tanzi, 2018, pp. 248–255) and broadly resulting from the first (1848–1849) and second (1859) wars of independence as well as from the Crimean war (1854–1855).

[13] That is net of the contribution to the reduction of the public debt/GDP ratio deriving from the growth process.

was set with clarity right from the launch of the new Kingdom,[14] then sought with determination to a very great extent mostly by means of additional tax revenues[15] and finally obtained—at the State level but not at the General Government one—in 1876.[16] In addition to the need to offer a guarantee of sustainability for a public debt held to a significant extent by non-residents,[17] the goal of a balanced budget—far from being a "myth" as has been written[18]—also responded to the need to contain the progression of public debt to leave more space for investments in the private sector (Marongiu, 1995, p. XII). In short, it was the "cornerstone" of a budget policy inspired by the need to protect "the youngest of the great European States" from the difficulty of economic dependency and consequent political subalternity.[19]

Institutions, reforms, infrastructures and financial discipline. Apparently, all the ingredients were there.[20] It is completely comprehensible

---

[14] Gianni Marongiu (1995, p. 27) recalls how already in February 1861, Cavour declared that: "if we do not start a path that leads to balancing revenue with spending, Italy will fall to bits". The theme of a balanced budget was already placed on the political agenda with the arrival, in 1862, of Quintino Sella in the Ministry of Finance.

[15] Also, of an extraordinary nature. An example for all was the taxation and expropriation of church property. Guido Melis (2020, p. 603) recalls that in the first fifteen years of life the Italian public administration did not record changes of any sort, neither in the personnel (reduced) nor functions (limited).

[16] In 1876 the General Government deficit equalled 2.2% of GDP (Appendix D).

[17] A result that—in the light of the evidence set out in Appendix D—may be deemed to have been achieved. The scale of the response of the primary surplus compared to public debt variations was in fact variable but in any case, was such as to place the debt/product ratio on a path towards sustainability, even in the presence of interest levels that, net of the growth rate, would not be recorded in the decades that followed.

[18] For example, Pedone (1967, p. 292).

[19] Gianni Marongiu (1995, p. 370) quotes the words used by Marco Minghetti in a public address in October 1874: "Imagine a mortal enemy of Italy's unity and liberty. I do not know what conduct could be more effective in its intent than pushing us towards increasing spending and restraining ourselves from increasing work and sacrifice, namely from taxes".

[20] This is testified, for example, by the work of Leandro Prados de la Escosura (2023) who summarised, also in quantitative terms, the progress made by 21 countries in some of the fields mentioned which can be traced back to the more general category of economic freedom. In our case, mention should be made of individual rights and property rights (as expressed by the independence of the judiciary, by the impartiality of the courts, by the transparency of the legal system and by the accessibility of the jurisdiction as well as by contract enforcement) in which Italy's progress is evident: the synthetic indicator of Italian

therefore for Gianni Toniolo (1988, p. 99), when summarising the early post-unification period, to pose a question that, in effect, is difficult to escape: "the income per inhabitant remains substantially stationary during the years of government by the *Destra* [Right]. This is the main phenomenon for economic historians of the period to explain". This question was answered little more than twenty years later by Gianni Toniolo himself (2013, p. 18) when he observed that "political unification was only a precondition for unifying the markets. Its effective implementation required time". Invoking, that is, times that were unavoidably long linked to the construction of the infrastructural architecture of the new Kingdom.[21] Delays to be combined (Bastasin & Toniolo, 2023) with the already mentioned impact of uncertainty affecting the private accumulation of capital.

But there is perhaps something more and more profound than the many mentioned and understandable delays and uncertainties generated by the state of public finances. There is—as Deirdre McCloskey would remind us, and as does not seem to have been completely clear to the Savoy ruling classes[22]—the fact that institutions, not to mention reforms

---

performance in these fields passes, in the first twenty years of the new Kingdom, from just over 60% to just under 70% of the corresponding indicator of the United Kingdom, an undoubted reference point for Cavour's Italy. The Italian performance seems to be to a large extent attributable in particular to the far from minor issue of contract enforcement whose temporal evolution is approximated by the role of the so-called contract-intensive money, i.e. by the fraction of money held in the form of deposits (Clague et al., 1999). As far as the other mentioned indicators are concerned—accounted for, it should be noted, *de jure* and not de facto—no relative changes of any significance have been found over time. It should also be noted that the work of Leandro Prados de la Escosura (2023) also includes the extent of market regulations (being it, credit, labour or goods) whose evolution during the first twenty years of life of the new Kingdom does not seem to show characteristics of any interest for our purposes.

[21] Moreover, the subject is anything but new, as Toniolo himself underlines, and is also well present in authors of the time. See Toniolo (2013, pp. 14–23) for a summary of the debate. With specific references to "implementation delays", Gianni Toniolo et al. (2003) offer an example of particular interest regarding the case of the integration of the financial markets. More recently, Vito Tanzi (2018, pp. 53–55) linked the disappointing performance of the new-born unified state to the "defective" nature of the unitary design, and to the shortcomings "in the ways and times for realising the unification project". This reading is certainly justified given the unplanned nature of the unitary process and not really so far from the hypotheses formulated in Toniolo (2013).

[22] It is again Gianni Toniolo (1988, p. 100) who recalled the "delusions felt by many after the hopes aroused, at least in a good part of the bourgeoisie by the political unification process". Alfredo Oriani (1939) summed up these delusions in 1892, underlining

and infrastructures, are necessary but not sufficient. Which is what Gianni Toniolo himself (1988, p. 86) points out, recalling the "widespread poverty of civil values and traditions, [the] existence of an asphyctic and short-sighted bourgeoisie, and [the] habit everywhere but deep-rooted in the Mezzogiorno – of relying on the paternalism of the prince residing in the capital but also on the protection systems and «personal clientele»" at local level. In other words, underlining the fact that the new institutions of the new Kingdom did not have the necessary value system behind them for making the prospect of growth a concrete reality. This observation is further supported significantly by the work, in particular, of Umberto Cerroni (1999) who can be referred to in order to recall the hiatus between the pre-unification intellectual world in Italy and the concrete, daily modernity that others in Europe had already experienced a few decades ahead of Italy and that Italy is probably still far from having fully experienced today.[23]

Count Cavour died only a few weeks after the fateful 17 March 1861. The only person who, saying of himself: "I am the son of liberty, and to her owe everything that I am",[24] would have been capable—perhaps, who knows?—of taking on the thankless task not just of "making the Italians" but of transmitting to them the sense of individual and collective opportunity that Unification offered them.[25] Not one of his successors knew how to transmit a similar message to the Italians whom, moreover, they themselves perceived as distant if not indeed hostile. And none of

that the Piedmontese ruling class had not proved capable of placing the new Kingdom at a level of modernity similar to that prevailing in France or Great Britain.

[23] Vito Tanzi (2018, pp. 208–237) attributes the difficulties of the new Kingdom to the centralist decision made at the moment of unification and, as a consequence, to the value system prevalent in the Savoy ruling class. This approach grasps one of the two aspects of the problem but underplays the characteristics of the specific value system of the Italians—and perhaps especially of the southerners—that is widely confirmed in the assessments of the protagonists of the time and in the analyses of historians and economic historians.

[24] Liberty was, notoriously, the ideal reference of Cavour's entire action: "the premise of his action, in politics as in economics, was represented by liberty: liberty inside the state and from the outside world, along with the spaces of administrative functionality that a unified state could occupy" (Ciocca, 2020, p. 82).

[25] In the same vein, see Marongiu (1995, p. 53). It is hardly necessary to observe that repeated reference will be made in the text to the "State building" during those years, emphasising in this way the distance with respect to "nation building" that neither occurred then nor afterwards (Cassese, 2014, pp. 61–64).

them probably actually wanted to do it. On the one hand the problems—those linked to public finances among other—were hanging over them. There was a widespread sensation that the new Kingdom could prematurely succumb to its domestic and foreign difficulties. On the other hand, with Cavour gone, the idea rapidly took hold—with the likes of Silvio Spaventa and of Francesco De Sanctis or of Quintino Sella if not also the likes of Marco Minghetti—that modernisation of Italian society was possible only thanks to significant doses of interventionism (Cammarano, 2011, pp. 10–11).[26] And the discovery during those years by the Italians of Samuel Smiles[27] and his call to rely on your own strength could not have been sufficient to overthrow a reality that Francesco Ferrara[28] described thus in 1866:

> the nation remains immobile in the niche of its past, the spark of progress never touched it; it cultivates as it already cultivated; it exercises its ancient trades, it does not feel the need for great enterprises and does not find a way to carry them out; the spirit of association does not enliven it; still barely sensitive to the notion of beauty, it is not attracted by the good and the useful; a distracted and inept generation follows one that was servile and indolent. The surrounding world proceeds at an excited pace; the inventions, the new methods, the needs of social life rise every day to regenerate all the branches of industry, but Italy sees and admires as much as it can, but it does not do, it does not envy. Italy does not even feel the need for economic emancipation. The person of its government is always at its side to regulate its actions, to guide the businesses, to dispense ideas, to grant credit. Italy accepts the protection and remains silent.

For unification and the state building that followed also to be growth enhancing it was necessary for the Italians to give a different reading of themselves and of their ambitions. Of their desires and of their role in the world. And that in this activity the governments should not propose to substitute themselves for the Italians. Something that did not

---

[26] Raffaele Romanelli (1991, p. 716) observes moreover that the interventionism was for the most part on paper leading to a Unification that "at the same time was so weak as to be largely ineffective and so vigorous as to multiply the adverse reaction of the country and reinforce centuries-old particularistic sentiments".

[27] See the pages of Silvana Patriarca (2010, pp. 49–55) for more on Samuel Smiles —the "English self-help guru" and on his Italian disciples.

[28] Quoted in Luzzatto (1968, p. 13).

happen. And which was frankly difficult to happen in a country in which "economic-social backwardness [...] was deemed [by the ruling class of the time] to be synonymous with limited autonomy of political judgement [and] civil society continued, therefore, for the right, to be an object to be moulded" (Cammarano, 2011, p. 49). As a result the great legislative, administrative and financial work of the Savoy ruling classes—if you like managerial more than political in the strict sense of the term—ended up resting on fragile and diversified foundations.[29] And this appeared evident, furthermore, at the moment in which, in 1876, with the historic left the "less modern elements, i.e. [the] typical and most widespread elements of a bourgeoisie such as the Italian one prevailed" (Carocci, 1975, p. 49) and the institutional infrastructure of the first decade of unification began to be hollowed out from the inside: an example that can stand for all is the so-called monstrous alliance, namely political interference in the administration, no matter what the rule of law said.[30] So it would be an act of transparency and justice if, in telling the story of the unified country we were to limit—with all the appropriate precautions—the term "Liberal Italy" to the fifteen years after 1861 or, better still, we were to agree to limit ourselves to defining it as the period of the government of the Right.

---

[29] State building, as we have already observed, rather than nation building. To quote Manlio Graziano (2010, p. 28), "at the beginning of the Italian adventure, the country's new leaders – the Destra – were preoccupied with building from nothing the structures of a new state with suddenly enlarged borders, and they had little time to abhor any ideological vacuum".

[30] Sabino Cassese (2014, p. 141) recalls some salient aspects of the prevalent discipline of relations between state and citizens right from the early years of unification: "the attribution of an imperative nature to administrative provisions, the option in favour of administrative self-protection (while in the Anglo-Saxon systems, it is necessary to apply to courts for enforcement), the slow creation of a special judge for citizen/state relationships (where in England these cases are heard by ordinary judges) are signs of the attribution to the public administration of a privileged position with respect to citizens". On the same line, Giorgio Rebuffa (2012, pp. 36–41) goes over the debates in the 1870s and 1880s on the subject of administrative justice and recalls the change impressed on it by Vittorio Emanuele Orlando, "with a view to subordinating the individual guarantees to the organisation of the constitutional powers and procedures... A proclamation of the supremacy of public interests, the extensions of the discretion of the administrative action, ended up imposing a vision of public law in which single subjective situations as such are guaranteed in so far as they are recognised by «objective» law, by the desire of the ordinary legislator" where "what defines citizens is not so much their belonging to a political community, as their position of liberty with respect to political power".

Certainly there were those—Francesco Ferrara among others, once again—who lavished their energies on putting individual initiative (and the creation of the relative enabling conditions) at the centre of the economic policy line of the time but, as Giampiero Carocci (1975, p. 42) underlined, diffidence remained however, and "was common to the majority of the political class both left and right [...], towards the most complete manifestations of capitalism for fear that the class struggle would be reawakened". A "caution, diffidence or open hostility towards the characteristics of what we today call «modern economic development»" (Toniolo, 1988, p. 113).[31] Caution and diffidence that, in the middle of the 1870s, were to take on not only an explicit but also a formal appearance.

Piero Bini (2021, pp. 45–58) accurately summed up the debate that, without sparing blows, took place in particular in 1874 between the supporters of classical economic liberalism[32] (gathered in the *Società Adamo Smith*—or "Adam Smith Society"—and around the review *L'Economista* or "The Economist") and the promoters of the historical school of economics of German origin (led by Luigi Luzzatti and the *Associazione per il progresso degli studi economici* or "Association for the progress of economic studies"). The debate focused in essence on the relationship between citizens and the state and as such it was crucial for the purposes of defining the systems of "values, beliefs and preferences" that would prevail in the future years and decades rather more than on the everyday debate on public intervention in the economy. Francesco Ferrara emerged isolated from the debate initially and then defeated. The *vincolisti* (or "restrictionists")—to quote Ferrara—were to triumph, Luigi Luzzatti was to assert himself as a protagonist of the Italian political scene, and the theme of the relationship between citizens and the state—the

---

[31] This point is expressed with great clarity by Giampiero Carocci (1975, p. 18): "the protagonists of the Risorgimento, apart from a few exceptions (the most important of whom was Cavour) were all things considered not very sensitive, though without rejecting it from their horizon to that irreplaceable dynamic and unifying element that is economic development".

[32] The term "liberalism" is used here and elsewhere in its proper sense (i.e. to indicate a theory of the limitation of power). We will distinguish it, when necessary, from the "liberal values" meaning by this the set of values that were imposed, in some way, with industrialisation, mass production and the emancipation of the productive classes and that are usually associated with market economies.

theme of Cavour's "sense of liberty"—would quickly be set aside if not indeed forgotten.[33]

Having definitively exhausted the governing experience of the Right, Italy was now ready for the next political phase which would culminate in the transformism of Agostino Depretis and would lead in the 1890s to a major financial crisis and to the collapse of the banking system during a period that was distinguished politically by the personality of Francesco Crispi. This phase was marked at European level by an expansion—both in intensity and in extension—of the presence of the state in the economy[34] which in the Italian case in particular took the form of public works (the "railway frenzies" as they said at the time) and, though to a lesser extent, of military spending (the policy of the "great armaments"), to the detriment—in a budget over a third of which was required to meet the charges for the public debt—of other items with a social content which in the best cases remained in stasis.[35] The increases in spending on public works and in defence spending—according to Agostino Magliani, mastermind of the budget policies between 1878 and 1888 (branded by Gianni Marongiu [2019, p. 38] as an "obfuscator of the real financial situation")—should

---

[33] Antonio De Viti De Marco (1930, p. 299) like and better than others summed up the sense of the cultural choice of those years: "our constitutionalists, instead of studying the history of the country in which the people kept up centuries-old struggles to conquer freedom, preferred to deduce them from the philosophical listings of German professors of public law who were paid to legitimise the absolutist regime under liberal formulae".

[34] Public spending by the State Administrations compared to GDP grew between 1870 and the first decade of the twentieth century, by 4–5 percentage points in France and Germany, by over 6 points in Austria and a little less than 3.5 in Great Britain and in Italy (Tanzi & Schuknecht, 2008, pp. 3–8), starting in this last case, as we have already seen, from higher levels than average. On the revenue side, the tax burden fluctuates in the same period around 15–16%, with more or less no change to the distance (between five and seven percentage points) from France and the UK (Tanzi & Schuknecht, 2008, pp. 51–55).

[35] Between the mid-1870s and the end of the first decade of the following century the share of public spending relating to the cost of servicing the debt, after hitting a maximum (38.4%) in 1879, recorded a constant reduction until it dropped below 20%. The resulting space, especially during the early years of the twentieth century, was partly absorbed by higher capital account expenses (which passed from circa 9% to 19% in the course of the period being discussed) and by the expenditure for personnel (up by about five percentage points to as high as about 27% in 1910). At the level of functional categories, the spending for education and culture rose from about 2% to 4% of the total, while defence spending, that reached 24% in 1889, never fell below 20% in the twenty years afterwards. Refer to Appendix D for the details.

have been "extraordinary, transient, exceptional". Obviously, it was not so: "the torrent of public spending [was] inflated [and] the spending for a whole generation was mortgaged [for public works and for] the enormous expense of permanent armies".[36] Quintino Sella's financial austerity policy was replaced by Magliani's "merry finance". And so, "between stop-gaps, retouches and contrivances"[37] the debt/GDP ratio soared to touch and exceed 120% during the 1890s, while remaining sustainable more-over thanks to a response of the primary surpluses—given the burden for servicing the debt—that was insufficient for returning to a balanced budget but still able to counterbalance the impact of an interest rate that tended to be higher than the output growth rate. Sustainability that was put to the test, moreover, in the second half of the 1880s when—Magliani *consule*—the fiscal effort required in order to guarantee sustainability of the debt, rendered even heavier by the growth of the debt itself, ended up by weakening to the point that it almost took Italian public debt to the threshold of unsustainability (Fig. 7.3, right panel, and Appendix D).[38] In what we termed the "Magliani area", i.e. the area beyond which adverse shocks capable of influencing the amount of the fiscal effort—for example, because the unwillingness of the political class to adopt this or that measure required to guarantee the primary surpluses envisaged—have a relatively high chance of bringing the public debt level over the unsustainability thresholds. An area, that on the basis of the evolution of the tax burden observed over the 160-year period, we could place in the negative territory (positive values in the indicator of sustainability corre-spond, in fact, to situations of acclaimed unsustainability) and in between zero and minus two per cent. That is in the area where the fiscal effort required for sustainability is barely below the actual one (sustainability therefore trembling at every whisper of the wind).

As has already been observed, the years of the so-called Historical Left (*Sinistra Storica*) were marked, from the point of view of political culture, by economic liberalism accompanied to a growing extent by such and so many adjectives as to finish by being drained of its deeper meaning and

---

[36] As Luigi Luzzatti said in 1884, quoted in Marongiu (2019, p. 37).

[37] As Sidney Sonnino said in 1888, quoted in Marongiu (2019, p. 79).

[38] It is interesting to note that from the viewpoint of the sustainability of the debt, the most critical moment is observable between 1885 and 1888, i.e. immediately before the banking crisis which was sneaking up at first and became self-evident in August 1889 (Toniolo, 2022a, pp. 114–117).

as a consequence ending up as being ineffective for laying the cultural foundations for stable and sustained growth.[39] The years in which with Agostino Depretis, first of all, "the ambivalent contrast between the liberal aspirations for potentially universal emancipation and the dubious restlessness as regards liberty that was not controlled by the centre" was reproposed and then, with "Francesco Crispi «authoritarian modernisation was imposed»: the state was responsible for the social and political backwardness, and while it took on the expectation of participation and democracy that this entailed, it extended and legalised both its competencies and its power" (Cammarano, 2011, pp. 78 and 110). These were the years in which the leader of Italian entrepreneurs, Alessandro Rossi, was to become the inspiration for a pronounced social, Catholic corporative solidarism, bearer of nationalistic demands and promoter of a concept of development that aimed at the colonial outlets much more than at export markets. Years in which—in 1878 first of all and then, more fully in 1887—Italy embraced the protectionist route, laying the foundations, according to Stefano Fenoaltea (2011), for the failure of post-unification Italy.[40]

In other words, the combination that made Italy what it was, what it still is and what it promises to be in the near future was taking form right from the years of the infancy of the new Kingdom: a combination that, to put it kindly, can be summed up as follows: on the one hand, a community without "ethics, spirit of research, entrepreneurial daring and civil passion", risk-averse and as a consequence open to dialogue and to compromise just to avoid the violence of change; and on the other—having quickly set aside Cavour's "governing with liberty"—a ruling class often divided and litigious but nevertheless united by the conviction that they had to mould the Italians and above all protect them from themselves, with the result that they magnified the features of

---

[39] On this point, see Piero Bini (2021, p. 57)—who does not fail to recall the judgement along the same lines, of Joseph A. Schumpeter—and, once again, Giampiero Carocci (1975, p. 19). The latter observed that "if being able to realise unification [...] of power and culture constitutes the moderates' glory, the pre-eminence of the culture to the detriment of the economy also had a serious negative aspect: the fact, that is, that the liberalism of the Risorgimento was not the ideology of a class but actually only of some bourgeois intellectuals or «bourgeoisified» aristocrats".

[40] For a summing-up of the debate on protectionism and its implications refer to Federico and Giannetti (1999, pp. 126–128).

their backwardness if such is possible.[41] Hence, therefore, from the stand-point of these pages, the laboured growth of the first thirty-five years of life of the unified state. Thirty-five years, as we have seen, marked—in terms of per capita product—by drops in position on all fronts (partic-ularly consistent compared to the United States but also anything but negligible with respect to the aggregate that we have called "Europe of 4", namely France, Germany, the Netherlands and Belgium). This was a period distinguished by a growth rate of total factor productivity above zero but more or less generally below the corresponding international performances (Broadberry et al., 2013, p. 216) and, in its last fifteen years, by a barely perceivable progression of Italy's patenting capacity.[42] And it was one in which, again in the last fifteen years, the first significant examples of bank and industry bailouts associated with happy-go-lucky management of public finances begin to appear, and not just in episodic terms, alongside the permanence of significant barriers to foreign trade (Gomellini, 2017), and a growing presence of the public operator asso-ciated with permeable and ambiguous state architecture (Cassese, 2014, pp. 24–31).

This is an overview that, among other things helps us to understand how this same 35-year period was instead, as recalled by Giovanni Vecchi (2017a), marked by significant results in terms of other metrics of well-being: from life expectancy to infant mortality, from the extension of literacy to improvement of sanitation, to limit ourselves to the most signif-icant example[43]; and by steps forward in the relationship between the

[41] As you can imagine, the less kindly (and, in a number of respect, frankly unfounded) version would brand the character of the Italians as tribal and clientelist if not indeed *mafioso*, would underline the preference of entrepreneurs for the broad corridors of the ministries rather than the narrow paths of the markets and, conversely, the irresistible tendency for all the Italian political cultures to identify the action of the state with the issuing of permits or licences, the protection of companies, professions or corporations, the protection of interests however they may have been constituted, and so on.

[42] The number of limited companies during the 35-year period in question passed from 379 in 1863 to 583 in 1896, with a quite limited annual growth rate and little over 1% (Assonime, 1981). Given the limited representativeness of the indicator, it is not possible, moreover, to infer anything about the dynamism of the Italian economy.

[43] The first 25 years of unification also saw a gradual reduction of phenomena of poverty (Amendola et al., 2017, pp. 358–363) and a barely perceptible reduction of the indicators of inequality (Amendola e Vecchi, 2017, pp. 310–316). All things considered and in the light of the more recent debate on the relationship between growth and

state and society. These may have been timid if you like but were significant: if before unity only 2% of the population had the right to vote, the number of voters rose in 1882 and then in 1912, respectively to 8% and to 23% of the population (Cassese, 2014, pp. 70–73). All dimensions for which the institutional infrastructure that the new Kingdom had been able to provide itself with was, more often than not, not just necessary but also sufficient to some extent.

Which was presumably not true—despite the conviction that "the problems of the under-developed areas could be solved by administrative unification, casting all the Italians into the same mould" (Cassese, 2014, p. 105)—for an indicator associated at times with those already mentioned: the gap between central/northern Italy and southern Italy. This gap grew significantly in the first decades after Unity (Brunetti et al., 2017, pp. 277–280) and information on its causes is still too tenuous to allow us to get beyond a generic indication of consistency between the pattern of that gap and the thesis proposed in these pages.[44]

Having left behind what Gino Luzzatto (1968, p. 176) called "the darkest years of the economy of the new Kingdom" (1889–1894), Italy apparently entered the "years of late industrialisation" under full sail (Toniolo, 2013, pp. 16–17), bringing together the impetus deriving from the favourable international context with a new season of institutional infrastructure provision. Already in 1893, a new institutional structure centred on the Bank of Italy had restored stability of the financial markets and monetary policy. But it was from 1900 that a broad spread of new institutions of high social value began to take form: in essence and also rather timidly the Italian welfare state was born (Rossi et al., 2017,

---

distribution indicators, this would seem to be compatible with limited growth such as that observed in the decades immediately after 1861.

[44] A snapshot of the Italian public administration in the first post-unification decades taken by Sabino Cassese (2014, p. 106) is illuminating from this standpoint: "Graduates from the developed north preferably headed towards the industries and economic activities rather than towards the public administrations. In the south, on the other hand, a petit bourgeoisie grew up hungry for jobs where the state was the only outlet. [...] A periphery, the less developed one, acquired a position where it could influence the centre. And contributed towards designing its organisation in accordance with its own culture, interwoven with idealism and cynicism, distrust in politics and of the search for guarantees of impartiality".

p. 422).[45] However hesitant and insufficient, the first signs of a growing competitiveness were recorded.[46] The presence of the public administration in the society made itself more visible (Melis, 2020, p. 603) just as the presence of the state in the economy became more manifest and not necessarily by means of a heavier tax burden but through an increase, however moderate, in public expenditure.[47] The trains of the state railways began to run on the nationalised railway lines. Life insurance was also nationalised. The Mezzogiorno saw the birth of policies of territorial development by means of special laws for Basilicata, for Calabria and for Naples.

The reading of that period that owes its name ("the Giolittian Era") to the presence on the political stage of Giovanni Giolitti is and remains controversial. In recent times we pass without a break from the already mentioned Giorgio Mori (1992), who speaks of it as the "real Italian economic miracle" to Emanuele Felice (2015, p. 142) who describes Giolittian Italy as "a power in expansion from all points of view" to Pierluigi Ciocca (2020, p. 137) who describes it as "an economic spring", to Stefano Fenoaltea (2011) who tends, on the other hand, to downplay the domestic components of Italy's performance during the period, underlining, rather, the dependence on the global economic recovery and indicating the elements of continuity of the decades between Unity and

---

[45] Sabino Cassese (2014, p. 107) is of the same view while Chiara Giorgi and Ilaria Pavan (2021) place the birth of the Italian welfare state immediately after the First World War. In effect, the obligatory pensions system was already established in the early 1860s for the public sector only. A national welfare fund for workers' invalidity and old age on a voluntary basis was established in 1898 on the other hand, after a debate lasting almost twenty years. But it is equally true that it was only in 1917 that the first explicit affirmation of direct state commitment was recorded (in this case for war orphans); (Cassese, 2014, p. 295).

[46] This can be traced, among other things, to the reduction of the size and incidence on import duties. A lot less—very probably—to the initiatives that led, in effect, to the replacement of private monopolies with public ones (railways, telephony, and life insurance).

[47] The tax burden dropped from about 16% during the early years of the century to circa 15% in the pre-war years, positioning itself, however, above the corresponding values of the main European countries or (foreseeably) the United States. During the same time span, Public Administration spending recorded an increase of about one percentage point, also in this case remaining well above the levels observed elsewhere in the Western world (Figs. 7.1, left panel, and 7.4, right panel, and Appendix D).

the First World War. The debated valuation of the Giolittian Era is, moreover, anything but a novelty and can be traced back to the 1920s and to the description that Benedetto Croce (1928, pp. 225–249) and Luigi Einaudi (1933, pp. 1–26) gave of it. In his *Storia d'Italia* ("History of Italy"), the former described Giolitti's Italy as a "fertile decade of works and hopes" and recalls the lively "spirit of enterprise", the "increasing daring and [the] associated detachment from the old preference for real estate, income from the state and state employment". The latter, much more prudently, instead photographed the two Italies that still cohabited in that Italy: that of the "great proprietors of the Mezzogiorno [and] of the great industrialists of the north", both dependent on commissions from the state, subsidies and duties and that of the "medium and little people" who "toiled to live in the fields overlooked by the big ones". From this cohabitation—or, rather, from this confrontation—originates, according to Einaudi, the "discontinuous" nature of growth, compromised by continuous public interferences that were intended, among other things, to protract—"with legislative provisions and aids from the issuing institutions"—crises whose solutions should have been found in market forces. The evidence provided in the previous pages suggests that on that occasion the economist—convinced of having before him "an Italy that was certainly different from the one dreamt of by Camillo di Cavour"—would have known how to read the Italian reality with greater acuity than the philosopher would have been able to do, probably influenced by his desire to celebrate the memory of that Italy that had then been swept away by the war and by fascism. Not that there were no timid signs of dynamism in the last five years of the nineteenth century and in the first decade of the twentieth[48] or that one must not recall the

---

[48] It is certainly true that the number of limited companies—no more than 400 from the beginning of the 1870s to the mid-1890s—doubled, or almost, in the first decade of the twentieth century (Assonime, 1981). But this regards of a smaller fraction of the joint stock companies and of a minuscule part of Italian companies from whose development it is frankly difficult if not impossible to infer anything at all regarding the country's "enterprise spirit". Luigi Einaudi (1933, p. 6) recalls that in 1903 the establishments (just over 15 thousand in 1876) numbered just over 110 thousand and would reach 243 thousand in 1911 (two thirds of them small and medium enterprises). Without prejudice to the obvious problems of comparability and bearing in mind that establishments are not firms, it is quite evident that, like the relative stasis of limited companies during the thirty years before 1903 was not reflected in the unquestionably more dynamic performance of the aggregate, in the decade after 1903 the progression of limited companies is not indicative of the aggregate trends.

prudent management—also from the distributive point of view[49]—of the public finances. And certainly, in the Giolittian decade the public debt/ GDP ratio was reduced by just less than 30 percentage points also thanks to the more consistent growth rates (in the presence of interest rates that were also falling) and some innovative ways of managing the debt. But in all these cases it was really a question of signs of the country's pre-existing limits rather than of "economic flourishing". The reality, as has already been observed, is that the growth rate of the gross domestic product per capita was up less than the corresponding figure observed for the aggregates, Europe "of 4" (EUR-4) and Europe "of 7" (EUR-7) by 0.3% and 0.1%, respectively, with Italy out-performing the United Kingdom (+1.0%). The same can be said of the total factor productivity that limped along behind the economic powers of continental Europe. The country's patenting capacity progressed at rhythms that were no different from those not particularly significant ones that had been recorded in the previous decades or the decade afterwards. As Emanuele Felice (2015, p. 158) himself is obliged to admit: "during that period the country revealed a low innovative capacity". After a brief stasis, the seductive call for bailouts began to be heard again.

Let it be clear, there is no desire with this to suggest that the Giolittian age did not bring elements of novelty—of vivacity—that were undoubtedly more evident than in the previous decades.[50] If compared to the previous forty years, the first decade of the century recorded average annual per capita GDP growth rates that were virtually double, but this is to be compared to a continental Europe (and not just) and a nascent technological power able, in the first decade of the century, to exhibit growth rates that were significantly higher than those recorded in the previous forty years. Timid openings, if you like, but insufficient nevertheless to modify the "fundamentals" of the country that Fulvio Cammarano (2011, pp. 296–297) efficaciously sums up as follows:

[49] It is hardly necessary to recall the inheritance tax transformed into a progressive levy (Marongiu, 2019, pp. 125–131).

[50] It is again Leandro Prados de la Escosura (2023) who reminds us that the important relative progress recorded by Italy in the field of contract enforcement (insofar as the concept of contract-intensive money represents it) extended up to the first decade of the twentieth century.

quite a few members of those popular classes who had grown up with solid rural roots or in lively but closed municipal identities, were becoming confident with the idea that well-being was associated with the experience of «movement»: school, emigration, railways, and holiday camps just to give a few examples of «new experiences», presented themselves as attractive symbols of movement, heralds of improvements in everyone's living conditions that were possible as well as fast and painless. This was a growth in expectation without an effective ability to profoundly influence the evolution of the national community, but capable of stimulating the acquisition, often opportunistic and superficial, of those essential rudiments of a shared public alphabet necessary for a «pass» towards modernity.

What emerges from the data is, in fact, that in the Giolittian era as in the four previous decades the Italian economy evolved, in the best of cases, as much as the context in which it found itself allowed it to. This lets us suppose that the economic policy decisions in the last decades of the nineteenth century, just as in the first decade of the twentieth, had little or no effect on the relative performance of the new Kingdom.[51]

Without prejudice to the reference to the international context, the hypothesis of relative continuity—or, if you prefer, of a discontinuity that is only apparent—emerges between the first post-unification decades and the years of Giuseppe Zanardelli and Giovanni Giolitti (possibly reinforced) from the review of the economic debate of the time carried out by Piero Bini (2021, pp. 123–159). Not as if in this case too there was an absence of more convinced voices favourable to a market economy and to its founding values—starting from the unequivocal Luigi Einaudi and Antonio De Viti de Marco and ending with a more wavering Maffeo Pantaleoni —but by this time they were "in the opposition" (Bini, 2021, p. 123), to the point of pushing Vilfredo Pareto to deem it to be impossible for "the values and beliefs" necessary for promoting and supporting a dynamic economy to survive in a country which seemed to have made

---

[51] It is impossible at this point not to quote Stefano Fenoaltea (2011, pp. 240–241): "The economic development of post-Unification Italy cannot be understood by examining Italy alone. Italy was already then part of a wider world characterised by the ready movement of goods, ideas, men and money; it develops as and to the extent that the mobile resources of that transnational economy chose to locate on Italian soil. [...] To a first approximation [...] after about 1870 the cyclical movements of the Italian economy do not seem to have been induced by changes in national policies. The effects of those policies are to be sought elsewhere, in the long-term rate of growth, in the significant but disappointingly limited development of the economy".

opportunism its rule of conduct (Bini, 2021, pp. 132–133). And it did so to the point, Giampiero Carocci (1975, p. 144) observed, of converting classical liberalism itself into pure and simple "privatism" and bursting out, for example, in entrepreneurial positions that have already been recalled regarding industrial bailouts: so much so as to induce Luigi Einaudi (1933, p. 24) to talk about "liberalism" as a "synonym for vague patriotic memories reserved for the last hour of commemorative banquets". It is of little use from this viewpoint to make distinctions between the ruling class of the Giolittian age and that of the previous decades (Felice, 2015, p. 148). Save the former and fail the latter. It is of little use, within the limits in which the former as much as the latter were, at best, victims of a conviction that we will see repeated several times in the country's history: the conviction that it was enough to provide the country with institutions that were deemed appropriate case by case to free its energies, as long as these latter did not take paths that were not expressly contemplated. This conviction was destined, though, to clash with the harsh reality of a country that, if we like, was anything but immobile in general but in which in the first years of the century those who were the most dynamic and readiest and willing to make the market their main field of action were still pretty far from being able and wanting to give the country a different cultural horizon.

To be convinced of this it is to none other than Benedetto Croce that we must go back, not to his economic-political summary but rather to his cultural analysis of the Giolittian age. Croce writes (1928, pp. 264–265):

> liberalism was then a practice and not already a living and intimate faith, a closed and fervid enthusiasm, an object of concern and meditation, something sacred to defend jealously with the first suggestion of threat to it [...]. When someone spoke of liberty, he would interrupt them with the observation that liberty existed, which everyone admitted, that ran no danger, and that it was important to revert to other more topical and urgent things, and perhaps to the harm done by too much liberty, to liberty as disorder and lack of discipline.

This was not unlike what had already happened, in contexts that were certainly different, in the previous forty years.[52] "The conclusions of *don*

---

[52] On the "scarce" impact of Giolittian politics on the behaviours and orientations of the country, see Carocci (1975, pp. 155–165).

Benedetto (1928, p. 265) were inevitable: the "tradition" [of liberty] in Italy was recent. Recent and had not penetrated deeply, [...] and the same recent tradition - Cavour's thought - had not been kept alive, nor were we in the habit of tracing back, from case to case, to those origins".[53]

There are reasons for thinking (Stone, 1985) that the 40 years before First World War were marked in the whole of continental Europe by a progressive dilution of liberal values—"ethics, spirit of research, entrepreneurial courage and civil passion"—that according to Umberto Cerroni (1999, p. 158) were already present in the Italians at the moment of unification at a lower level than elsewhere. But there are also elements for imagining that that cultural difference, far from reducing itself during the first decades of unity, had in some ways become greater. "Italy demonstrated the fragility of liberalism in an extreme degree" (Stone, 1985, p. 255).

When the war broke out, Luigi Einaudi also said, "the resistance encountered earlier to those who wanted to solve their own particular problem through the State collapsed, because of the exact vision of the sparsity of the available means" so that the road opened to "the enemies of the *res publica*" "for a disorderly and confused boarding of the ship that carried the public monies". And with it the doors into the *Ventennio* began to open. And of the fascism, that—in the height of the tempest of war—Alcide De Gasperi would describe as "as an almost atavistic mentality moreover, in which many ferments of the Risorgimento flourished again".[54]

---

[53] Sabino Cassese (2014, pp. 252–258) summarises and qualifies thus: "professions of liberalist faith abound the first forty years, but one can doubt that they [...] were always followed by the facts [...] Liberalism was prevalently verbal. But even in that way it did not fail to produce an effect, because the possibility was never considered of organising a state control board for the vast public hand. This diminished its weight".

[54] The words of Luigi Einaudi (1933, p. 25) and of Alcide De Gasperi (quoted in Craveri, 2006, p. 127) summarise certainly excessively a highly significant passage in Italy's history—the one regarding the origins of fascism—that would deserve much greater space, also in the light of the understandably very broad historiographic debate around the subject. A passage, moreover, that is not irrelevant for our purposes for which reference should be made in particular to the pages of Roberto Vivarelli (1981, pp. 163–344) that actually take their cue from Einaudi's words to point out the relationship between the "quality of liberalism" in the post-unification state—its fleeting nature, according to Benedetto Croce—and the events of the Great War. A relationship which, according to Silvio Lanaro (1979, p. 87)—who provides quite a different view from Vivarelli's and refers in particular to the figure of Francesco Saverio Nitti—can be recognised in the

From the "Sovereignty of the Spirits" to the "Rule of the Matter"

The story told in the previous chapters leaves no margins of doubt as regards the *Ventennio*.[55] Not one of the indicators of dynamism describes anything if not the (relative) immobility of Italian society and the economy between the two wars. In terms of per capita gross domestic product, the reversal is evident both with respect to continental Europe (approximated by the Europe "of 4") as well as to an enlarged aggregate that encompasses the whole Mediterranean region (Europe "of 7") and only the different impact of the Great Depression prevents the same to be told of the relative Italian performance compared to the United States. In terms of total factor productivity Italy visibly fails to stay abreast either with continental Europe or with the United States. Its relative patenting capacity is brusquely re-dimensioned and the indicators of dynamism mark time until they settle close to the minima in the history since Unification. The country—which already did not seem to possess "that psychological component which, nourished by a widespread faith in the possibility of progress, multiplies its energies to render human work full of hopes" (Vivarelli, 1981, p. 13)—stalled in an international context that, we should remember, was marked by the 1929 crisis and by the subsequent fragmentation of the international economic system. This immobility translated into inefficiency and lack of innovation and was marginally rocked by the brief experience—lasting three years (1922–1925)—of so-called liberal (or, more precisely, constitutional) fascism, associated with the name of Alberto de' Stefani. This immobility was

---

"*humus* of the Italy of Crispi and Giolitti: where [...] a well-rounded culture (dominant in the full sense of the term) seems to advance slowly and irresistibly towards the landing place of totalising conceptions of society and of the state". And which—without prejudice to the elements of obvious novelty present in the fascist *Ventennio*—recalls in turn what Rainer Maria Rilke wrote to Franz Kappus in the first years of the twentieth century: "the future enter us before it happens".

[55] On the events of the fascist *Ventennio* see, in particular, De Felice (1975), Toniolo (1980), Battilossi (1998), Federico and Giannetti (1999), Cassese (2014), Tarquini (2016), Gabbuti (2020), Melis (2020), and Marongiu (2020), as well, of course, as the Italian economic history texts already mentioned.

closely linked to the regime's autarchic decisions[56] and the progressive extension of its interventionist attitudes—both in the strictly economic field and in that of relations between the state and society (as witnessed by the structure of tax revenues, Fig. 7.5). One example that can stand for all (and more than others) is that of the controls introduced in the labour and goods market[57]—in a context in which the regime's orientations had easily made inroads into the culture of the Italians, giving rise to relatively widespread consent.[58] The interventionist attitudes translated, among other things, into a rising level of intermediation of the public sector—after the brief de' Stefani's parenthesis—expressed by increasing tax revenues and a growing expenditure to GDP ratio (even net of the military component). The former recorded an increase of about five percentage points between the start of the 1920s and the end of the 1930s (Fig. 7.1, left panel). This increase, moreover, was lower than those in the United Kingdom or France (Tanzi & Schuknecht, 2008, pp. 51–55). The latter allowed Italy to hold on to its record at international level in flows (Fig. 7.1, right panel) as well as in stocks. Tanzi and Schuknecht (2008, pp. 64–66) estimate that in the second half of the 1930s the public debt to GDP ratio in Italy was significantly higher than the corresponding ratio observed in France, Belgium, the Netherlands, Great Britain and the United States and, for obvious reasons, lower only than Germany.[59] Notwithstanding this, the trend in the cost of servicing the debt, net of the so-called growth dividend (negative right from the early years into the century) meant a relatively straightforward management of public debt during the *Ventennio*, also in the light of the sharp reduction in the public debt to GDP ratio following the Great Depression and in particular in

---

[56] To the extent necessary, we must not forget the reality in which Italy found itself in the 1930s (Gabbuti, 2020, p. 262). As has already been suggested previously, it is probably appropriate not to overlook the concrete ways with which the autarky manifested itself in the years between 1934 and 1942 and in specific sectors (Bertilorenzi et al., 2022).

[57] Recalled summarily in Federico and Giannetti (1999, pp. 132–135).

[58] The essential reference here is De Felice (1974, pp. 54–126).

[59] In terms of the breakdown of the expenditure at the State level, the twenty-year period between the First and Second World Wars is remarkable for the significant reduction of the interest expenditure occurring during the three de' Stefani's years, for the return of military spending in the second half of the 1930s right up to the levels of the final stage of First World War, for the highly significant spending in education and culture between the 1920s (circa 4% of total spending) and the middle of the 1930s (over 7%) and for social expenditures (from circa 5% to about 7% over the same timespan).

the 1930s, attributable, in particular, to the cancellation of debts to the United States and Great Britain that happened following the definition of the question of war reparations (Fig. 7.3, left panel).

It is interesting to note how the period between the two wars also coincides with a slowdown—if not indeed a reversal—of the country as regards the other metrics of well-being recalled earlier (Vecchi, 2017a). Between the end of the 1920s and the end of the 1930s the previously positive trend in the availability of calories for the Italians, and particularly for the less well-off, stalls or even goes into reverse. The positive trend in life expectancy at birth continues, though with a few signs of fatigue, just as an attenuation is recorded in the trends of the indicators of accumulation of human capital or of the distribution of resources.[60] And despite this—as we have seen—there was a significant increase in the levels of public spending for interventions with a social content (Rossi et al., 2017, p. 430). In one way this confirms that if the institutions are necessary but not sufficient this is even more so for public spending and, in another way, it highlights the nature—more evident than in other historical periods, but not so surprising, however—of the social policies of the *Ventennio*: before all other things, "instruments of consent [... and of] social control over vast swathes of the population" (Toniolo, 2022b, p. 156). Also recording growth—once again, not surprisingly—was the gap between the regions of the south and the islands and those of the north and centre.[61]

In this case too, recalling the economic debate helps to reconstruct the cultural climate of the period. Piero Bini (2021, pp. 172–190) recalls how the initial pursuit, and later achievement in 1925, of a balanced budget through a sharp reduction in public spending by Alberto de' Stefani "rocked the support of a significant part of public opinion, support that was genuine and spontaneous, during a phase in fascism that was not

[60] As regards inequality, the evidence available seems to point to a substantial stasis in the course of the 1920s (associated with a rise in the poverty indicators) followed, probably, by some increase up to the middle of the 1930s (Gabbuti, 2020, pp. 272–276) and Amendola e Vecchi (2017, pp. 310–316). Giacomo Gabbuti (2020, p. 287) summarises this trend as "a major reversal of the «benevolent» distributive dynamics of the liberal period".

[61] These are the years—not by chance—of the "second wave" of the "meridionalisation" of the public administration (Cassese, 2014, pp. 108–110).

yet characterised by the later (and not always genuine) mass approval"[62] support whose most eminent exponent (if not partly inspiration) was Maffeo Pantaleoni.[63] Initially this consensus would have been able to transform itself into something more profound and lasting if the circumstances (and in particular the management of the economic situation in the years 1924–1925) combined, above all, with a substantial diversity of views regarding the political prospects between de' Stefani himself and Mussolini, had not put an end to the brief season of constitutional fascism in July 1925,[64] opening the way for what Gianni Toniolo (2013, p. 27) defined as "the most sudden and complete 180-degree about-turn in the whole history of Italy", an about-turn, as we know, that took place under the banner of nationalism and corporatism. This was an about-turn of "increasingly restrictive protectionism all the way to the ridiculous confines of the autarky, [of an] obstinate over-valuation of the real exchange rate, [of an] increasingly interventionist approach to the allocation of resources" (Toniolo, 2013, p. 28), of an often only nominalist control of minor activities as long as they remained as such (Federico & Giannetti, 1999, p. 133). Only eight years after that July 1925—with the complicity of the Great Depression—Mussolini would officially declare the market economies to have been surpassed and classic liberalism with them (Bini, 2021, p. 214) and he opened or, more

---

[62] Within the limits of their reliability (discussed in Appendix B), the information on business demography before 1928 indicates an unquestionable entrepreneurial ferment in the three de' Stefani years.

[63] And the same can be said of Luigi Einaudi, Pasquale Jannaccone and Attilio Cabiati. And it can be said too of Umberto Ricci who also undertook one of the first spending review experiments recorded in the history since Unification. In that case the experiment was carried out with modest success.

[64] Piero Bini (2021, p. 185) quotes some parts of the letter of resignation sent by de' Stefani to Mussolini on January 5th, 1925 (and therefore two days after Mussolini's speech to Parliament in which fascism was constituted as an authoritarian regime). The atmosphere between the two had not been idyllic for some time. In the letter he essentially invited Mussolini to step down and submit to the judgement of the electorate. Piero Bini (2021, pp. 187–188) also recalls Mussolini's intolerance of the policy of curtailing spending. This intolerance manifested itself with expressions that could easily have been taken from the much more recent Italian debate on the so-called austerity policies: it was necessary "to prevent obtaining «a gasping balance» and being able to say «the clinic has triumphed but the patient is dead»" (the words in inverted commas inside the quotation from Piero Bini being attributable to Mussolini himself).

precisely, formally reopened the doors to a growing public presence in the economic system.

These doors, in truth, had never been closed but were thrown wide open, to say the least, as Mussolini demonstrated in Udine in September 1922. This was the Mussolini who at the same time as he was saying "enough with the railwayman state, the postman state ..." reminded himself and the Italians "not to say that the state stays small when emptied in this way. No! It remains a great thing because all the sovereignty of the spirits remains, while all the rule of matter is relinquished" (De Felice, 2004, p. 124). That spirits and matter could not be kept separate so easily is something that Alberto de' Stefani was soon to learn at his own expense and that his successors instead—from Giuseppe Volpi to Antonio Mosconi, from Guido Jung to Paolo Thaon di Revel, and to Giacomo Acerbo—would take for granted with various degrees of elegance.[65]

As more recent experience shows, declaring classical liberalism to be obsolete seems to be a virtually inevitable passage and a rite that is particularly dear to the autocrats of all times and latitudes. If it is possible to speak of a "parenthesis" in the unification adventure before the Second World War, perhaps this does not regard the *Ventennio* then, but—and only partially in truth—the three-year 1922–1925 period, with the prevalence before and afterwards of a body of values and beliefs that were to a great extent unchanged and, in essence, disinterested in the themes of growth (and the values underlying it: competition, individualism, cultural openness).[66]

---

[65] Cassese (2014, pp. 266–272) records the eloquent list of public businesses established or coordinated between 1923 and 1929.

[66] Gianni Toniolo (1980, pp. 43–58) tends to underline the common features of the economic policy of Alberto de' Stefani and the specific one of the governments led by Giovanni Giolitti. There is no doubt that from some viewpoints a few similarities can be seen. Commercial policy is a good example of this just as it is unquestionable that the fundamental reorganisation of the General Accounting Office by De' Stefani in 1923— a decision that laid the bases for an independent and effective control of the public expenditure process and of which Mussolini himself had the occasion to complain and, with him, many other Prime Ministers in more recent times too—rested on the works of many of his predecessors, including his master, Luigi Luzzatti, in particular. Just as, at least in part, the rescue policies constitute a good example. The Giolittian age is marked by the bailout of Società Bancaria Italiana first, and of the large iron and steel companies later. These interventions were promoted and favoured by the executive, approved by the Monetary Authority and carried out by means of the banking system. The same can be said, to a great extent but not completely, for the years 1922–1925; in the sense

But the elements of continuity between the *Ventennio* and the previous years (and later ones, as we will see) do not stop here. They also concern

that both the Ansaldo bailout and that of Banco di Roma (certainly not only approved but actively encouraged by the then head of the government), though imposed in 1922, were completed in 1923 and therefore after Alberto de' Stefani succeeded Vincenzo Tangorra at the Treasury Ministry in January 1923 and after the merger of the Ministries of Finance and of the Treasury. And they were completed—Gianni Toniolo observed (2022a, p. 373)—also thanks to the "incisive role" of the government and competent ministers. It is impossible however to ignore the accusation reported in Toniolo (2022a, p. 378)—addressed by de' Stefani himself to the Bank of Italy, that it had given in to political pressures, delaying more than necessary the problem posed by Banco di Roma (and therefore, presumably, forcing the government to intervene "incisively"). But the same cannot be said for the competition policies: the return to the market of the life insurance managed since 1912 in a monopoly by Istituto Nazionale delle Assicurazioni is due to de' Stefani and he is also responsible for the abolition of the rent freeze, the suppression of the monopolies for the sale of matches and coffee and for firm opposition to the privatisation of the electricity sector (quite a different attitude from the Giolittian one of replacing private monopolies with public ones). Conversely, the Giolittian age is marked by the "acquisition to the control of the administration of new provinces [and by the consequent assertion of] a model of assisted economy in which the capitalist development was grafted onto the bureaucratic structures" (Cassese, 2014. pp. 118–119). The flourishing of local public enterprises in the first years of the century contributes to clarifying the point. And evident elements of divergence are present in budget policies moreover. As has already been recognised, those in the first decade of the century were prudent. Those of the years 1922–1925 clearly targeted the goal of balancing the budget ("austerity policy" *ante litteram*, so to speak) and, as a consequence, the liberation of spaces earmarked for private enterprise. And it is not simply a case of differences of opinion. It is certainly true that between 1903 and 1913 the public debt to GDP ratio fell by about 30 percentage points (passing from 103 to 74%). This evolution is not so different from the one recorded between 1922 and 1925 (when it passed from 148 to 111%) also as a result of the restructuring or the foreign debt in 1925). But it is difficult to keep it quiet that in the first case the spending of the Public Administrations compared to GDP recorded a slight increase (from 17.6% to 18%) while there was a significant contraction of the burden of servicing the debt; whereas in the latter case the ratio passed from 32.1% to 17.7% in the space of three years and not just because of the contraction of the cost of servicing the debt and of spending on defence but also the general back-sliding of the state (and of its personnel) in all fields and especially in the field of interventions in the economic area (with the sole significant exception of spending for education and culture). Just as it is difficult not to recall the abolition, in 1922, of registered shares introduced by Giolitti himself in 1920. More in general, a reading of the aims of the tax system not just in distributive terms but mainly in terms of efficiency was actually due to Alberto de' Stefani who was also responsible, moreover, for the introduction of the first progressive personal income tax but also for the virtually complete abolition of the inheritance tax—(Marongiu, 2020, p. 20), a reading that it is hard to imagine Giovanni Giolitti agreeing with.

that which at face value appears as the event that marks out and distinguishes the *Ventennio*, namely the public disinvestment of the mixed bank in the years following the Great Depression. As is underlined in the pages dedicated to the "bailouts industry" in Appendix C, IRI was nothing more than a fine-tuned and magnified version of other public institutions that were already present in the Italian economy from the early years of the century: from the Consorzio Sovvenzioni Valori Industriali and the autonomous sections of the Istituto di Liquidazioni.[67] Of these, IRI shared the goal (stabilisation of the economic and financial system), the duration (temporary, on paper, and de facto indefinite), the tools (the provision of liquidity and, as a consequence, the control—more or less deliberate—of industrial companies and financial institutions) and the fathers (from Bonaldo Stringher to Donato Menichella, and to Alberto Beneduce). Above all, they shared the underlying idea: Italy and the Italians—given their structural limits—needed public instruments for stabilising the economic system: tools that would allow the ruling classes—well aware of those limits and, indeed, in truth, profoundly pessimistic regarding the ability of the people they were supposed to lead—to intervene promptly to prevent those same limits from having a negative influence on present and future collective well-being (and also, by the way, change the consolidated equilibriums). A "wet nurse", in short, to use Luigi Einaudi's figurative expression.

Giuseppe Berta (2016, p. 80) wrote it clearly:

> protagonists of the public economy, from the times of Mussolini and Beneduce onwards, from even earlier indeed, from when Francesco Saverio Nitti was Giolitti's minister, shared the conviction that Italian capitalism suffered from a chronic insufficiency. A deficit [...] that was affected by a spirit and a willingness to make a start that were not enough to infuse the Italian economy with the momentum it needed for its development [...] Italian capitalism needed the support of the state in order to develop. Otherwise, economic development would not have been produced and the space of

---

[67] It would not be so difficult then, as a general rule, to go even further back in time too and rediscover, though certainly in other more mediated forms, modalities of public intervention in the economy that are not then so different—and, to convince oneself of this it may be sufficient to read the pages dedicated by Luigi Einaudi (1933, pp. 403–409) to the events between the second half of the 1870s and the Great War—but it seems wise to explicitly take account of the caesura that occurred in 1893 at the moment of birth of the Bank of Italy.

capitalism itself would have ended up by contracting and declining, and imperilling the prospects for growth.

Which on the one hand is grist to the mill for the thesis put forward in these pages, namely the idea that for almost the whole of the country's history since Unification it is the Italians' culture that must be examined if we want to find the reasons for the absence of an autonomous capacity for growing the country. At the same time, we are forced to ask ourselves how was it ever possible for the Italians to make their own the values of a market economy in the presence of ruling classes who were at work daily to protect the Italians from themselves while keeping them, as consequence, in a condition of minority (which, moreover, they often accepted willingly)? And invested in a mission to which no one had called them (but from which, visibly, they did not have—and do not have yet—any intention of backing away). It is possible to mock the "bookish" liberalism of Francesco Ferrara, but his description remains an extraordinarily lucid one of the ideas that the ruling classes in unified Italy had of themselves and of their role, and that they would continue to have without interruption or almost so, up to the present day:

> For us we have leaders in the same way and for the same reasons that we have farmers, landlords, lawyers, etc.; governing is a job like lots of others; leaders are men in flesh and blood who assume, on their own or following express requests, the job of producing peace and justice, just as hunters produce game and tailors clothes. The concept from which the Authoritarian School starts off is radically different. In its social system it is supposed that, above the associated individuals, there is a body, an unknowable something unseen, unheard, impalpable, especially created, which knows when and how to raise and dominate the entire social order.

Seamlessly or almost so, because, if on the one hand the "nanny" attitude of the Italian ruling classes helps to understand why some basic characteristics of the Italians are so deep-rooted, on the other it provides, as we will see, some indication of why those same characteristics seem to have been suppressed in the years of the economic miracle.

"Faith in the Italian People"

But first thing first. As we have said, it is no small limit to have to dwell on the events of the 1930s without connecting them—in the sense outlined above—to the events of the preceding decades. It is a limit that induces us to concentrate on the specifics of the 1930s and that therefore prevents us from reading—as we would suggest—the events of unified Italy with absolute continuity up to the present day. Because, just as the paternalistic culture of the ruling classes did not actually originate in the 1930s but limited itself in the 1930s to dropping any remaining veils and appearing as such, that same culture crossed over into the republican era and continued to inform the post-war decades until our arrival at what only for convenience we call today the "second Republic".

The convention of the Azione Cattolica[68] graduates that would lead a few months later to the meeting in the Hermitage of Camaldoli which gave rise to the "code" of the same name—and which in turn was to prepare the ideal grounds for the season of the *Partecipazioni statali* (State holdings)—was held in January 1943 (Perrone, 1991, pp. 5–9). The fateful date of July 25th was still to come—and with it the collapse of the fascist regime—and so was September 8th (and the surrender of Italy to the Allied Forces), but already the intellectual foundations were being laid for the management of the economy, largely in continuity with that of the *Ventennio*. Instead of the muscular and folkloric paternalism of fascism—which had replaced the rapacious but not less pervasive paternalism of the Italy with plenty of side whiskers that was pleased to call itself liberal—it was now proposed (and in time) to put in place a double-breasted paternalism that was only formally different but no less aggressive.

On another front, Guglielmo Giannini—as early as December 1944—collected the testimony of the "humanist petit bourgeoisie" with the "ordinary man" movement. The former, who had played such a great part in the advent of fascism, was described as follows by Luigi Salvatorelli (1977, p. 14) in 1923:

> he ["the little humanist bourgeois"] depicts a fantasy world of abstract realism and ignores the effective values of the modern world; and when he comes into contact with it, in whatever way, he feels a mixture of moralistic

---

[68] A non-political lay organisation under the direct control of ecclesiastical hierarchies.

repulsion and intelligent and invidious covetousness for it. For him the capitalist is an exploiting shark, and the skilled worker a parvenu who is unjustly preferred in comparison with him ...

Twenty years later—and with a decisively less sophisticated prose—Guglielmo Giannini[69] was to describe his "crowd" as follows:

> we want to live quietly, we do not want to agitate ourselves permanently just as we did not want to live dangerously, ... What we ask for, we the «Crowd», we the great majority of the Community, we the masters of the Community and of the State, is for nobody to break our balls.

In this way one (highly) significant part of the country confirmed its reluctance to measure itself against modernity. It was not and would not be the last time.

In this context, as was soon evident, it was not quite so easy to get over IRI (granted for the sake of argument that it was realistic to imagine it). On the contrary there were plenty of reasons for not leaving it alone to carry out the public function of stabilising the economic system of which it was believed that Italy and the Italians, just for a change, always and however needed. With the establishment in 1956 the State Holdings Ministry, IRI would be backed up with ENI (already established in 1953) and in 1962 with EFIM which went on to further reinforce what we have called "the bailout industry" (see Appendix C). And when, in the 1970s, the ability of these bodies to "sort out" (of which "bailing out" constitutes a subset) whatever it was from time to time deemed necessary to sort out in Italy's shrinking "poor" capitalism, it was the turn of Enrico Cuccia's Mediobanca (founded in 1946 on the initiative of three banks controlled by IRI: Banca Commerciale Italiana, Credito Italiano and Banca di Roma) to step in. Finally, after the 2003 reform, Mediobanca's baton, in that specific function, would be taken by Cassa Depositi e Prestiti which still exercises it consciously and more or less actively depending on the government in office.

---

[69] The quotation that follows—contained in Lanaro (1988, p. 23)—is taken from Guglielmo Giannini's book, entitled simply "*Folla*" ("Crowd"). Again, it is difficult not to see in it the themes, already noted previously, of a musical hit such as "Mille lire al mese".

In this picture, the events of the period immediately after Second World War[70] would seem—and with every probability were—eccentric. If it is history what we are recounting how can we explain that sudden leap of "dynamism" observed in those magical fifteen years? To use the words of Pierluigi Ciocca (2020, p. 372), was it "antifascism, values of the Resistance, Republic, Constitution, democracy, opening to international stimuli and competition, progresses in public education, new forms of acculturation ..." that made Italy and the Italians something different from what they had been during the previous eighty years? Was it, as Gianni Toniolo (2013, p. 23) asked, the strategic decisions taken in the post-war years for the Italian economy based on extensive opening to foreign trade, accompanied by broad safeguards for domestic producers protected naturally from international competition and on an important role of the state as producer of goods and services?" Was it, with its brightness and darkness, that which Fabrizio Barca (1999, p. VIII) called "the compromise without reforms", a combination of "exemptions and subsidies for specific social groups [...] containment of wages [...] and, above all [...] considerable state intervention through the system of public bodies"?[71] Was it, finally, the extraordinary circumstance highlighted by Barry Eichengreen (2007) whereby the whole of Europe, in addition to its own mechanisms of a market economy, found itself at the "right" moment with the "right" set of rules and conventions, formal and informal, that were able to guarantee the necessary coordination

---

[70] For the events that followed the Second World War see, in particular, Baget Bozzo (1974), Barucci (1978), Battilossi (1998), Bottiglieri (1984), Crainz (2005), Cassese (2014), Federico (1999), Marongiu (2017), Melis (2020), and Mingardi (2021), as well, naturally, as the Italian economic history texts of already mentioned.

[71] We owe Paolo Di Martino and Michelangelo Vasta (2018) an interesting attempt to give empirical content to the thesis of the "compromise without reforms" using an information set that is unexplored in this respect (the sentences of the Italia supreme court, the *Corte di Cassazione*) to argue that in the years of so-called economic miracle, the competitiveness of small and medium-sized businesses was supported by an inefficient (or often disapplied or circumvented) legal infrastructure which also allowed the movement of resources from the businesses themselves to their ownership. However original, Di Martino and Vasta's attempt finds a limit in the observation that the institutional limits they underline can be found to a significant extent both before and after the years of the "miracle" so that it is difficult to associate those limits with the economic performances recorded by the country in those years.

of individual decisions?[72] Certainly yes, in part: many of the elements mentioned—some more, some less, really did contribute.[73] But it was, perhaps, also if not above all, an extraordinary circumstance: for the first

---

[72] If reference is made to the international institutions that marked the post-Second World War period, it is difficult not to see how much these made the difference. If, instead, attention is focused on the domestic institutions, then it is interesting to note how Barry Eichengreen (2007, p. 115) was in any case forced to consider it "more than a little difficult to understand how Italy could have grown as rapidly as it did", as in the Italian case much of the formal and informal architecture Eichengreen himself placed as the basis for European growth in the period after Second World War was absent. Moreover, it is striking—even if obviously, it is of purely indicative value—that when summarising the characteristic of that same architecture Eichengreen (2007, pp. 31–40) mentions Germany and Sweden four times, Austria three times, the Netherlands and Norway twice and Belgium, Denmark and Italy only once.

[73] Echoing Rolf Petri (2002) it would be necessary to ask ourselves if the "miracle" should be read not so much in terms of discontinuity but rather in terms of continuity. In his words (2002, p. 292), "remaining at the roots of the success obtained in the 1950s, however, were initiatives inspired by Nitti such as the support given to industrial development by a selectively protectionist commercial trade policy and, above all, the intervention targeting the formation of fresh industrial capital in the most technologically advanced sectors". Hence the confutation (2002, p. 358) "of the undying thesis of the liberalist rupture that supposedly occurred in 1947-1951 to the detriment of the economic policies inaugurated under fascism". This confutation that did not deny (2002, p. 358) "that the stimuli and conditionings should include the pressures of the market and of the competition [but underlined] the importance of the political desire to create, broaden and, for that purpose were deemed necessary, protect and regulate the market itself". Naturally, the scope of these pages is not to identify the limits of the previous theses. Others have done this authoritatively elsewhere (and, for all, refer to the brief review by Giovanni Federico; retrieved March 18, 2024, https://www.sissco.it/recensione-annale/rolf-petri-storia-eco nomica-ditalia-dalla-grande-guerra-al-miracolo-economico-2002/). Indeed, as has been noted repeatedly, the hypothesis of a relevant continuity between the decisions made in the 1930s and the events after Second World War has been underlined several times. Even if it should not be stretched beyond reasonable limits: you need a lot of imagination—to give just one example—to consider FIM (the Fund for financing the engineering industries, a key element of the "Italian bailout industry, Appendix C) to be a tool for "the guided allocation of resources", unless, of course, we give the expression a very peculiar meaning. But what is striking in Petri's account is the virtually total overlapping of one significant component—but nothing more than this—of Italian manufacturing and the entire production system. What we have been forced to suggest in the previous pages is that beyond the boundary fence of the strategic industries (to which the attention of this or that technocrat has probably been drawn) there was an entire world of companies operating in "non-strategic" sectors and of small or very small businesses which were born (and often died) during those years who were offered a chance to get into the market and the opportunity to stay there, often innovating in an atmosphere that if per se was not one of explicit support was, at least, one of benevolent disinterest, inspired, if not actually encouraged, by the highest State offices. It is that wave of widespread

time since unification Italy and the Italians found themselves having to measure themselves with a ruling class which at its top, like Cavour eighty years earlier and remembering the experience of the previous twenty years, accepted the invocation of Benedetto Croce (1944, p. 105) in August 1943—"liberty before all and above all"—and made liberty the alpha and omega of their own political action. And, for this reason, thought that Italy should be governed (in Francesco Ferrara's sense) and not protected from itself to the point of being left in a condition of minority that it had found and was still finding to be perfectly congenial, more-over—to an extent that was anything but negligible.[74] Much of the interventionist scaffolding of the fascist type was quickly dismantled. The opening of international trade (culminating in 1957 with the realisation of the European Common Market) made autarky a memory and allowed the country—albeit with reconstruction still in progress—to count on American financial support. Businesses were allowed to restructure and, if necessary, reduce the number of employees (also with recourse to social security nets). The chapter of worker control of company management (that had never really opened) closed definitively and with that "the reintegration of the proprietorial and entrepreneurial prerogatives was re-established in its entirety" (Craveri, 2006, p. 315). The activity of the small and medium enterprises was supported through the concession of soft loans[75]—it is undeniable—but, at the same time, the experience of the Consorzio Sovvenzioni Valori Industriali was brought to a conclusion, limiting rescue operations to the bare minimum.[76] The peremptory

---

entrepreneurship that, not by chance, escaped the attention of Rolf Petri (2002, pp. 328–336) who, when he tackles the theme of the company births and deaths, concentrates on the balance between entry and exit rates that—as has been observed—tells us little or nothing about the great "remixing" in progress during those years. And he does it—for the years between 1936 and 1951—starting from sources whose limited representativeness is highlighted by the information on company births and deaths provided previously.

[74] The pages of Barry Eichengreen (2007) are useful on this point. There are good reasons for thinking that "the rapid growth of the postwar golden age depended on more than just the free play of market forces" (2007, p. 4) but there are even better ones for supposing that without these latter—or rather without a rhetoric capable of giving them substance and "fuel" (if it is possible in this way to render the fact that "people changed their ideas about what is lovely in economic life" [McCloskey & Carden, 2020, p. 143])—the "golden age" would not have been such.

[75] Also, in order to tackle, towards the end of the 1940s, the credit crunch due to the about-turn in credit policies.

[76] Which, in essence, were limited to FIM as already mentioned.

demands for "plans and programs" were soon set aside[77] and the one for an extraordinary capital levy was soon forgotten.[78] After a sharp acceleration in the 1930s and early 1940s, the extension of the public administration (in terms of personnel and functions) came to a halt (Melis, 2020, p. 603).[79] The State Holdings Ministry largely remained a hollow shell. To a considerable extent—in homage to the principle of the continuity of the state, but not just for this reason—the institutional and administrative scaffolding remained unchanged.[80] And—pragmatically— the public enterprises were not done away with, but the stature of their management and their awareness of the risks inherent in the relationship between politics and public companies[81] suggested the maintenance of an arm's length approach and prevented degeneration.[82]

[77] With the sole exceptions of the Sinigaglia Plan for the iron and steel industry (1948) and the Fanfani Plan for housing (1949). It is interesting to note how, in explaining the reasons that played for an increase in Italian steel production, Oscar Sinigaglia was keen to clarify that "Finsider [is] in principle opposed to state aid" (Bottiglieri, 1984, p. 104), Finsider being the State holding in the iron and steel sector. And it is equally interesting to note how the State contributed no more than third of the volume of funding destined for the Fanfani Plan (Bottiglieri, 1984, p. 44).

[78] The reference is to the proposal for a proportional wealth tax made between 1947 and 1949 by a Commission established at the Finance Ministry. This was preceded in 1945 by the proposal made by the finance minister of the time, Scoccimarro, to change the currency and introduce a progressive wealth tax levy at the same time. This proposal was soon set aside—it is said—because of technical difficulties but, in reality opposed by Epicarmo Corbino, Alcide De Gasperi, Luigi Einaudi and Ezio Vanoni, among others, and promptly removed because of the political implications and economic consequences (Marongiu, 2017, p. 14). Instead, the early months of 1947 saw the implementation of an extraordinary property tax levy (split into two different components, a proportional one and a progressive one).

[79] In every sense. Even from the point of view of its composition. From this point of view, see among others the pages dedicated by Guido Melis (2020, pp. 410–419) to the theme of post-war purging.

[80] The decades-long delays in implementing the constitutional provisions on the one hand and, on the other, what Leopoldo Elia (1974, p. 465) called De Gasperi's "continuism" (*continuismo*) contributed to this result.

[81] These were risks which personalities like Luigi Sturzo had pointed out over time and fought against tirelessly.

[82] Giovanni Federico and Renato Giannetti (1999, p. 137) have described the operation of the public companies in the immediate post-war period as a combination of the entrepreneurial skills of the public managers and their ability to maintain close relations (but never of dependence) with the political world.

Just as there was no abandonment of the policy of strengthening the welfare state but maintaining the quota of the resources earmarked for education relatively unchanged while significantly increasing those in the health field balanced by a contraction in the welfare area (Rossi et al., 2017, pp. 429–435). The most radical proposals for extending the welfare state fell on deaf ears, moreover, up until the second half of the 1960s. Thanks to the wave of inflation immediately after the war, the public debt to GDP ratio fell to 25% in 1947. The consequent reduction—whether desired or suffered, is still not clear—in the burden of servicing the debt (around 1% of the product starting from the late 1940s) left some space for moderate growth in public spending (and in education in particular) in the presence of deficits that were fully compatible with today's Maastricht rules (with a few sporadic exceptions). Unlike what happened during the previous eighty to ninety years, Italy recorded a level of public spending and fiscal pressure that was lower than that of the other Western countries, with the sole exception of the United States (Tanzi & Schuknecht, 2008, pp. 3–8 and 51–55).

In more detail, having touched 25.4% of the product, the debt of the Public Administrations recorded a marginal increase (27.4%) up to 1964. Spending by the public administrations passed from 20% to a little more than 28% in the same period and was more than counterbalanced by significantly higher fiscal pressure (from circa 14% in 1947 to 28% in 1964).[83] In other words, even though the fifteen post-war years recorded unprecedented (falling) levels in interest rates net of the "growth dividend", and therefore despite the fact that the prevailing conditions at the time allowed "generous" budget policies, policy in that period nevertheless went in the direction of strict management of the public budget. Indeed it was stricter than the one that rightly went down in history during the first fifteen years of unity to the point that it guaranteed sustainability levels that were never recorded (neither before nor after) in the country's unified adventure (Fig. 7.3, right panel), confirming the fact that the underlying aim was not just to "reassure the markets" but also and especially to leave as much space as possible to the initiative of the Italians, present and future.

Significant trends were recorded inside the aggregates of expenditure and revenue during the 15-year (1947–1964) period. A considerable

---

[83] Refer to Appendix D for the details.

increase in the capital account spending at State level up to the middle of the 1950s was followed from that moment by an increase in expenditure for personnel that was compensated by a contraction of other current spending. In functional terms, spending for education and culture took the lion's share, tripling over the fifteen years. This trend was compensated for by a significant reduction in the weight of interventions in the economic field (as well as by an obvious reduction in the share of expenditure for defence).

On the revenue front, the 15 post-war years stand out, in particular, for the share without precedents (and without "subsequents") of income and property taxes compared to total tax and fiscal revenues, not far off 20% and 10–14%, respectively, up to the early 1960s (Fig. 7.4). This is a very rough and approximate indicator of the degree of progressiveness of the system but also an element that reveals the scale of the incentives to entrepreneurship and innovation which—deliberately to various degrees—it was desired to have in the system.

The intervention in the Mezzogiorno was channelled, through the Cassa del Mezzogiorno, into civil and communication infrastructures only, and contributed towards closing the gap between the south and centre-north of the country for the first and only time in the history since Unification.[84] The country rediscovered currency, monetary and banking stability that it had not enjoyed for some time, also thanks to a different banking supervisory discipline.[85] There was no shortage of reforms,[86] but they amounted to very little compared to the real, great reform from

---

[84] Count Cavour had already indicated before what use it would be for the Mezzogiorno: "Anybody can govern with a state of siege, I will govern them [author's note: the southerners] with liberty and will demonstrate what ten years of liberty can do in these lovely places"—quoted in Ciocca (2020, p. 82). That he could not have said a truer word is shown not by the 15 post-war years but rather by the eighty years that preceded it and the sixty years that came afterwards. Years which, of course, have not experienced a state of siege but which, equally certainly, have experienced a suffocating dependency culture and an unbearable paternalism.

[85] The lira was recognised as a star currency in 1960.

[86] We could mention, between the second half of the 1940s and the first half of the 1950s, not only the land reform (with a quite questionable outcome moreover), but also the first important signs of the tax reform (with the introduction of the single, annual obligatory income and of corporation tax statement, on the one hand, and with the assertion of good faith and trust in relations between the revenue service and the taxpayer on the other) not to mention the first significant overhaul of parliamentary rules.

those years: not only was political freedom restored to the Italians but also the economic freedom and the spaces for enjoying it in.

It should be remembered with Gianni Baget Bozzo (1974) and Bruno Bottiglieri (1984) that it was not a linear event as the above lines might suggest. On the contrary. In the middle of the 1940s it was the daily emergencies that set the rhythms of the days, and it was the myriad needs of the reconstruction that dictated the line: as the protagonists of those years recall, it was necessary to guarantee supplies, ensure that refugees had a roof over their heads, that the returning veterans were properly welcomed and that the urgencies that came one after the other without respite were remedied (Barucci, 1978, pp. 98–105). The turning point did not come, therefore, before 1947 "with a proper change in the conception and management of our economic policy. [With] its delivery into the hands of illustrious exponents of liberal economic thought" (Barucci, 1978, p. 45). And it was a turning point that was not reached without difficulty[87] and that Barucci (1978, pp. 140–141) maintains was the result of various factors:

"the prestige and the ability of the protagonists, [their] insistence on reproposing the same recipe on every occasion, a favourable cultural and academic tradition, the weakness of the proposed alternatives."[88] And last but not least the fact that at the moment of the Liberation the economists of the liberal school "brought a bill of exchange for collection that had been kept in the drawer for many years and signed repeatedly during fascism, of which they had criticised every attitude of a restrictive nature."

The change of direction was then consolidated in the 1948–1949 biennium, unquestionably weakened by the growing leadership difficulties of Alcide De Gasperi that followed but not undermined even by the programming desires of the so-called Vanoni Scheme (1954) that, undoubtedly, anticipated some of the themes that would be brought to

---

[87] Materialised in the government's activities but not—and this is not irrelevant—in the drafting of the Republican Constitution.

[88] Piero Barucci (1978, p. 19)—certainly not a sympathiser of "liberalist integralism"—summarised the causes of this "weakness" as follows: "[the] abstraction of many alternative proposals, [the] trap – always evoked – of the «revolution-restoration» antinomy, the perennial «ransom» of the economic situation, [the] chaotic screaming of those who believed that they had carried by hand the historical occasion for who knows what social palingenesis".

the attention of the Italians a few years later with variations that, as we will see, would decree the end of an extraordinary fifteen-year period.

Though their cultural backgrounds were not marginally different, the two personalities who would leave their mark on the decade between the middle of the 1940s and the middle of the 1950s—Alcide De Gasperi and Luigi Einaudi—were both profoundly convinced that there would be no reconstruction unless full trust was placed on the spirit of initiative and on the desire for redemption of the Italians (in their capacity, in particular, as savers and entrepreneurs; small and medium ones especially),[89] and unless both the former—the spirit of initiative—and the latter—the desire for redemption—could express themselves freely, also—but certainly not only—for the market and in the market.[90] Entrepreneurship and industriousness were not only have guided by them but actively urged—think of Luigi Einaudi author of *Il Buongoverno* ("Good government") and of *Lo scrittoio del presidente* ("The president's desk"). "The resurrection is not in others; it is in us", was how Luigi Einaudi concluded his first "Final considerations" as Governor of the Bank of Italy on 29 March 1946 (Banca d'Italia, 1946, p. 161).[91] So that the phrase with which Alcide

[89] Andrea Colli (2002, pp. 44 and 48) acutely observes that "supporting an industrialization model centred on small and medium-sized enterprises was [...] a sort of lock pick, a pretext for affirming the need to alleviate state pervasiveness that fascism had brought, between bank bailouts and «IRIsations», at the highest degree, logically concluding a parable that had begun over fifty years earlier". He adds appropriately moreover that, "the contingent defence of small business [was also based] on the awareness [...] that many of the interested parties [...] had about the weight that smaller companies had within the national economy".

[90] As far as Luigi Einaudi is concerned, there should be no need for quotations to support his conviction regarding the impossibility of separating economic freedoms from political ones. Not so, perhaps, for Alcide De Gasperi of whom it is therefore appropriate to recall some of his considerations regarding "problems of the restoration and renewal of the Country [...] There does not appear to be a Catholic/non-Catholic split, but distinction between progressive-conservative supporters of radical solutions [...] or defenders of economic freedom" (where the "progressives-conservatives" were the political adversaries of the statesman from Trento) (Barucci, 1978, p. 60).

[91] The "Final considerations" were notable for a phrase that obviously no one remotely imagined uttering even after the 2008 financial crisis, after the sovereign debt crisis in 2011 or after the pandemic emergency in 2020: "... it is important for the Italians to know how to look reality in the eye: the national income, which is the sole source of private incomes and of public revenues, has shrunk. [...] As the national income is a total of which the incomes of individuals are the parts, it is absolutely necessary to resign ourselves to wages, salaries, profits and in general to real incomes that are lower than before; [...] We have to continue to tighten our belts whether we want to or not.

De Gasperi commented on the electoral victory on the afternoon of April 19th, 1948—"I feel only pride: that of having had faith in the Italian people" was in reality to be the keystone of the next decade—rather than a celebration of that specific event.

It is hardly necessary to observe that it is not just a question of personal convictions or political considerations—though these were certainly there of course—but also of realistic assessments of the state of the economy and of Italian society. In the recollections of Guido Carli (quoted in Craveri, 2006, p. 289):

> the state structure had been destroyed and would have required reorganisation in times that were not brief; economic restructuring could not wait for the reconstitution of the state; the only tool to leverage was the potential of the initiative and fervour of the individuals. In this way the system would ensure the psychological premises of enterprise, i.e., the guarantee of an ample space of freedom, dismissal of political hypotheses that overwhelmed the market economy, and the rejection of centralised social and planning policies.[92]

Where the expression "psychological premises of enterprise" encapsulates the climate of those years.

Just as it is necessary to underline how, in soliciting the "spirit of initiative" and the "will for redemption" of the Italians, Alcide De Gasperi and Luigi Einaudi were certainly helped by the cultural influence exercised in those years by the United States. Mario Cannella and Matteo

---

This is the substance of the economic plan that Italy must follow today, spontaneously or obligatorily, for its reconstruction. Reconstruction is synonymous with renunciation, with saving". A sentence that clarifies, without any possibility of equivocation, that—unlike many of his predecessors and successors—Luigi Einaudi thought of the Italians as a population of adults.

[92] It is interesting to note that the conviction that it was "not possible to rebuild Italy on the sole basis of the industriousness of the working classes and against private initiative" was also shared by what, from 1947, was to become the main opposition party, the Italian Communist Party, whose central committee recognised "the only exit from the grave situation [also lay in leaving] a lot of freedom to private initiative" (Barucci, 1978, p. 81). And it is similarly interesting to note that in the decades that followed, in situations that were fortunately not identical but similar in many ways (e.g. the persisting inefficiencies of the Public Administration), the idea of leveraging the dynamism of individuals very rarely dawned on the minds of the Italian ruling classes (both of government and opposition). There would be many examples. The Mezzogiorno is perhaps the most obvious, but it certainly is not the only one.

Magnaricotte (2023) have recently documented in detail the significant presence of American movies in Italy in the 1950s and 1960s. A presence that followed the closure towards international cinema desired by fascism and which leveraged on the widespread presence of cinemas in all Italian regions and the country's tradition in the field of dubbing. A presence suitable for conveying the idea of the American way of life and the values underlying it and, associated with the message that came from the highest authorities of the Republic, capable of making inroads into the imagination of Italians. Here it is impossible not to remember Nando Mericoni, played by Alberto Sordi in "An American in Rome" (1954) or even Renato Carosone who sings *Tu vuò fà l'americano* ("You'd like to be an American", 1956).

Italy finally started breathing after eighty years. And as it breathed it grew in more than economic terms too. Once again it is Giovanni Vecchi (2017a) who reminds us of the progresses recorded during those fifteen years in nutrition, health and education. In terms of participation, because of access to the ballot box—as from 1945—by women aged at least twenty-one.[93] Unfortunately, the available evidence does not permit any firm conclusion to be reached regarding the implications in terms of equality of the tumultuous process launched with the reconstruction. We know—and it should not surprise us—that the phenomena of economic and social marginalisation were significant at the beginning of 1950s. In the Mezzogiorno in particular, but we cannot but imagine—without moreover availing of any precise evidence—that a straight descending line unites the inequality and poverty data for the late 1940s and the same information recorded in the early 1960s (Amendola & Vecchi, 2017, pp. 313–316; Amendola et al., 2017, pp. 358–363).[94] And we know even less in statistical terms about the social mobility of those years. From this point of view, the prose of a writer like Guido Piovene (2017, pp. 148 and 826) comes to our aid, who in his *Viaggio in Italia* ("A journey

---

[93] Just as it is again Leandro Prados de la Escosura (2023) who underlines the brilliant recovery that took place in relative terms between the mid-1940s and the early 1960s in the field of personal protection and property rights.

[94] Andrea Brandolini (1999, p. 222) is lapidary on this point: "it appears that income inequality in the early 1970s [...] was not much different from two decades earlier, if some change occurred in the period, it was probably towards equality". Giuliana Freschi's (2023) assessments relating to occupational mobility in Italy in the years 1950–1970 go in this same direction, from which it is possible to extract the indication of a growing equality of opportunities for the cohorts born between the 1930s and 1960s.

in Italy") describes Italian society in the 1950s with eloquent adjectives: the "most mobile, most fluid and most destructive of Europe". A society characterised by "continuous rotation: those who rise and become bosses, those who return to being workers". Or even the pen of a thoroughbred journalist like Giorgio Bocca (2018, p. 31) who, in *Miracolo all'italiana* ("Miracle, the Italian way"), tells of peasants who became artisans and of artisans who became industrialists in a flash. Certainly, as it breathed Italy accumulated imbalances that sooner or later would present the bill. In order to "improve [their] situation"[95] they added, without hesitation, wage work to their own business, which was carried out, often and willingly at home, financed by friends and relatives.[96] And they got rich—Giorgio Bocca underlines it again—without thinking about opening some bookshop.[97] But Italy breathed. It breathed in lungfuls as it had never done for decades, to say the least. At all levels. "It boiled with energies that found expression in an entrepreneurship that [was] dimensionally insignificant, but vital, creative, irrepressible" (Colli, 2002, p. 38). And there is no need to recall what that implies in terms of creativity, productivity[98] and, finally, per capita income: we have already done so in the

[95] The quotation is taken from Colli (2002, p. 225) who, in turn, cites a report from the municipal police of Lecco dated October 1953.

[96] The cases collected by Andrea Colli (2002, pp. 252–277) best depict the interior of the "factory" after the Second World War.

[97] "Making money, to make money, to make money: if there are other perspectives, I apologize, I have not seen them. Fifty-seven thousand inhabitants, twenty-five thousand workers, millionaire side by side, not a single bookshop". This is the now famous incipit of *Miracolo all'italiana* (published in 1960 [Bocca, 2018, p. 31]) which continues as follows: "Let's say that reading is not reconciled with running and here, under the fog that exhales from Ticino, is a continuous and frantic run. Ravenous tribes come from the Veneto provinces and from Calabria: on the meadows [...] stand, in the usual disorder, shacks, houses and condominiums [...]. Now even the labourers of Lomellina are urbanizing in this Vigevano where the peasants can become cobblers and cobblers can become industrialists in the space of a few weeks".

[98] That total factor productivity grew at rhythms never known before in the immediate post-war period is backed by the figures—as we have seen. That it was not just a question of innovation of big business but also, to a significant extent, of grass root innovation à la Phelps is suggested, among other things, by the interesting and little-known story of the *Centri Nazionali della Produttività* (National Productivity Centres). National Productivity Centres were launched in 11 of the 16 Marshall Plan beneficiary countries in the early 1950s in the framework of the redefinition of the goals of American international aid policy, in order to introduce American work methods and management techniques to Europe. The results of the experience of the Centres, moreover, was quite variegated

previous chapters. For once, for one stage, the wingman was leading the race. It did not last long. We would soon return to political leaders dedicated to thanking—on the day of the victory—the Italians for having had faith in them, who "would have thought of us" unfailingly.

THE AGE OF THE "UNDIVIDED PEARS"

Alcide De Gasperi left the stage in 1953. Luigi Einaudi two years later. With them Italy lost, respectively, the political mastermind and the economic and institutional director[99] of what Piero Craveri (2006, pp. 311–319) called the "liberalist compromise", an economic model that was obligatorily mixed—because this was its inheritance from the past—operating within and in full compliance with strict rules specific to a market economy and supported by relatively widespread shared values and embodied by the highest officeholders of the state. The decisions taken in the years immediately after Second World War and, as a consequence, the impetus impressed on the Italian economy and society remained unaltered to some extent and still produced their effects for a decade, thus permitting the Italian catch-up to bear unhoped-for and better fruit than what a pure and simple catch-up phenomenon might have justified.[100] The Italian per capita GDP—amounting to just less than 50% of the corresponding US figure—would touch and exceed circa 60% in the 1960s. From that moment onwards the rhythm of the pursuit was to slacken initially and then to stop completely starting from the 1980s. And the same could be said of total factor productivity or the country's patenting activity. The performance of the "turnover" rate, which reached even higher values (by Italian standards) until the middle of the 1960s and declined from that moment onwards until it touched historic minimums

when not actually questionable. In the Italian case it clashed, in particular, with resistance from the leadership of the association of industrialists. See Sapelli (1989) on the new industrial bourgeoisie in post-war Italy.

[99] After Einaudi assumed the Presidency of the Republic in 1947, it was then Giuseppe Pella who personified the economic policy line—though with some distinctions (which, moreover, Einaudi did not fail to mention by sending Pella himself notes on the various economic issues [Bottiglieri, 1984, p. 65]). Giuseppe Pella would then replace Alcide De Gasperi as Prime Minister between 1953 and 1954, to become Deputy Prime Minister between 1957 and 1960, and then assume more secluded positions starting from the early 1960s.

[100] As Toniolo also wrote (2013, p. 32).

starting from the 1980s, would have clearly indicated the return of the country to the "normality" of its first eighty years.[101]

Confirming its recurrent (karstic) nature, the continuity elements in Italian society—its cultural fundamentals, if we can say so, that had never disappeared from the scene—did not take long to re-emerge forcefully in the middle of the 1960s. Not (as is often thought) to remedy the imbalances—social, productive, urbanistic and so on that had continued to grow in the immediate post-war period, as is indeed evident because of the simple fact that, as we have seen, many of those imbalances were extended over time and are effectively still with us. Or at least not only for this reason. But rather to leverage those imbalances and turn the tables. In the new political and institutional structures that emerged after the war it was the spirit of Camaldoli, present in the ruling classes as well as in the country and never dulled,[102] that channelled those elements of

---

[101] On the thirty years prior to the Maastricht Treaty and the birth of the European Union, see Franco (1993), Barca and Trento (1997), Federico (1999), Crainz (2005), Crafts and Magnani (2013), Cassese (2014), Marongiu (2017), and Melis (2020), as well, naturally, as the texts of Italian economic history already mentioned.

[102] Illuminating from this standpoint is how Piero Craveri (2006, p. 134) summarised the political debate of the early 1940s in the Catholic world before the birth of the *Democrazia Cristiana* (the Christian Democracy party) and especially of the positions of Alcide De Gasperi and of Franco Rodano. As is the comparison between the above-mentioned document of the Azione Cattolica graduates and the articles of a programmatic nature by De Gasperi that appeared in the newspaper, *Il Popolo* between November 1943 and January 1944 (and recalled in Craveri, 2006, pp. 131–134). And, again, as is the debate inside *Democrazia Cristiana* during the second De Gasperi government (13 July 1946–2 February 1947). The debate saw Giuseppe Dossetti and Giuseppe Lazzati opposing Alcide De Gasperi, giving rise to a "generational and ideological fracture [...] that was destined to clash with the politics of De Gasperi, or indeed constitute itself as a culture of internal opposition to the Catholic political world and, at a later moment, enter a process of osmosis with the communist culture, while in the secularised world of the struggle for power, transforming itself into the form of practice politically oriented towards the so-called «occupation of power»" (Craveri, 2006, p. 270). Just as also illuminating is, then, the role played by Giuseppe Dossetti and Giorgio La Pira—quite often in agreement with the leadership of the main party on the left—in the constitutional debate and the distance between the ideological and programmatic drafting of the first part of the Constitution that derived from it and the political vision of Alcide De Gasperi (Craveri, 2006, pp. 338–344 but also Mingardi, 2021). Also illuminating, finally, are a pair of further episodes that were perhaps not of the first order of magnitude, but which cannot be completely overlooked. The first related to an observation contained in the speech that Alcide De Gasperi gave at the third national congress of Democrazia Cristiana held in Venice in June 1949: "There was a phrase lately in the speech by Dossetti which

continuity and allowed them to prevail again.[103] Despite their obvious success, the decisions taken immediately after the war were quickly set aside in the middle of the 1960s. According to Alberto Mingardi (2021), only the presence of non-repeatable circumstances had, for a brief period, allowed those decisions, which being of course fruit of extraordinary circumstances (and—we would add—in partial contrast with the country's way of life), never became founding values of the newly established Republic. This did happen, on the other hand, during those same years in

irritated me a little. Perhaps I did not understand properly. The subject was jobs. [...] after a period in which the membership card was everything and ability very little, today the country is entitled to know that according to our system it is not the party card that decides when positions requiring ability are concerned; and our members must know that along with the party card, intended as a conception of life, it is also necessary to add competence" (retrieved March 18, 2024, http://www.dellarepubblica.it/congressi-dc/iii-venezia-2-6-giugno-1949). The second, on the other hand, regards the delegate law on the control of wages and salaries (1950) that De Gasperi intended as an exceptional tool to limit to emergency war situations; Dossetti, however, was among the main authors seeing in it as an effective interventionist tool (Craveri, 2006, p. 461). Giuseppe Dossetti would leave politics in 1952. The spirit of Camaldoli would soon find other (and undoubtedly politically more equipped) interpreters in the persons in particular of Amintore Fanfani and Aldo Moro. It is not irrelevant to underline that the first obtained his university chair in 1936 and the second began his academic career in 1940, and therefore in both cases almost in the middle of the fascist era. Fanfani's marked sympathies for fascism are well-known as well as his attempt to see corporatism as the point of contact between Catholic social doctrine and the authoritarian state and his confidence in the state's role in the economy. Less known but equally relevant are Aldo Moro's relations with fascism which are explicit in his lectures of 1941 and 1942 (and collected in the volume entitled *Lo Stato* ("The State")). Let it be clear, the adherence of both Amintore Fanfani and Aldo Moro to the values that informed the Italian Republic after 25 April 1945 are not in question, but the cultural climate in which both the former and the latter (and, to a very large extent the generation that took over *Democrazia Cristiana* towards the early 1960s) were formed should not be forgotten when one re-reads the sequence of events which in the mid-1960s put an end to the choices that had given rise to the "economic miracle" and allows us to wonder what the common ground on which to base ever closer alliances between the relative majority party and the main opposition parties could possibly be. The relevance of the "generational issue" did not escape an attentive observer like Alcide De Gasperi who already at the height of the Second World War noted: "I am convinced that fascism is a congenital mentality of the young generation" (Formigoni et al., 2023, p. 23).

[103] In any case, to say it in the words of Pietro Scoppola, "the party of the Catholics found itself playing a role that was not its own [...] it found itself carrying out the pre-eminent role of offering the mass base [...] to a new phase in the hegemony of the capitalist bourgeoisie" (quotes in Barucci [1978, p. 18]). When things are like that it is hard for a "miracle" to last very long. On the "irresistible metamorphosis of Democrazia Cristiana" see Craveri (2006, pp. 407–439 and 463–466).

the German Republic. So began a thirty-year period marked by a gradual and inexorable return and in great style of Einaudi's "wet nursing".

Being indulgent we could agree with Giangiacomo Nardozzi (2003, p. 262): the ruling classes that took the place of the De Gasperis and of the Einaudis did not understand that "if that particular development model that had mobilised the best energies of the country had not been strengthened the same success that had already been achieved would have turned out to be ephemeral".[104] But it would do wrong to those ruling classes to adhere to this thesis and reduce everything to a mere "failure to understand". It seems quite plausible to imagine that "that development model that had mobilised the best of the country's energies" was simply incompatible with the culture of those ruling classes in which, after a brief parenthesis, the most widespread interventionist and profoundly paternalist component became prevalent again and, when well-being had been achieved, turned to be unwilling to listen to an important but very probably a minority part of society. In fact, in the mid-1960s "a «year zero» attitude prevailed towards the choices that had informed the previous fifteen years" (Bottiglieri, 1984, p. 328). The very brief season of "entrepreneurial and productive" capitalism was to be and remain a parenthesis in over a century and a half of "assisted capitalism".[105] The outcome was inevitable (Nardozzi, 2003, p. 266):

> in «assisted capitalism» the managerial enterprise of the State Holdings changed its function, subjected to the devastating effect of political control, and private companies once again found opportunities for deviating from competitive comparison. The Italian economy entered a new phase of old dependence on the protectionisms whose elimination had constituted the backbone of the project conceived and implemented after the war.

[104] The same defect of "understanding" is mentioned in the writings of Guido Carli (1996, p. 165).

[105] The words between inverted commas in this last sentence come from Guido Carli (1977). It is interesting to note how in summarising a conversation that took place in the midst of the political crisis of 1964 with the then Governor of the Bank of Italy, the then President of the Republic, Antonio Segni, reports the following description by Carli of the Prime Minister (then outgoing and, within a few days, returning), Aldo Moro: "… he is outside the liberal system: he is a paternalist" (Segni, 2016, p. 262).

After the "schemes" and plans of the 1950s,[106] which regularly remained
on paper (and without thereby provoking, in truth, any particular trauma)
and the nationalisation in 1962 of the electricity industry, came political
decisions of a programming nature on quite different levels of compul-
soriness,[107] which, according to Guido Carli (1996, p. 131), revealed
"the trend among the «popular» forces towards consociationalism" and
the failure of which would only be registered when it was too late. In the
words of a witness above all suspicion (Ciocca, 2020, p. 264):

> there were reversals in the public enterprise contribution to competition.
> The public enterprises were required to shoulder improper responsibil-
> ities and burdens that were not consistent with efficient management.
> They were counted among the tools of political economy even in the
> attempt at programming the economy. The departure from the stage of
> personalities who had run it from the early post-war period contributed
> to stripping innovative gloss from state-owned companies in more than
> one case [and] ratified the subordination to which the government parties
> intended to constrain the public administrators [...]. The state-owned
> companies connected with and became increasingly mixed up with poli-
> tics, the government parties and public finance both through the ministry
> specifically designated in 1956 and directly.

The connecting rods and pistons of the bailout industry started running
again—as we have seen—with greater and greater force. At this point they
were driven not only by the considerations of a systemic nature (whether
they were true or not case by case) that had been prevalent up to Second

---

[106] In particular, the so-called Vanoni Scheme (1954) or even the supplementary note
to the General Report on the Economic Situation of the Country in 1962, presented to
Parliament in 1962.

[107] Rather than to the law establishing the Ministry of State Holdings, the reference
is to the National Economic Program for the 1966–1970 five-year period approved by
Parliament in July 1967 and, above all, to the various sectoral programs (Cassese, 2014,
pp. 233–234). Remaining at the preliminary stage, however, was the later 1973–1977
Second National Program Project (which was followed by the associated Report on planning). The National Economic Program for the five-year period 1966–1970 was preceded
in 1964 by the so-called Giolitti Plan, the contents of which were at the centre of the
government crisis of June 1964, due to their financial and constitutional profiles (see, in
this regard, the documentation deriving from the Antonio Segni Archive reported in Segni
[2021]). Once the crisis was over, the Giolitti Plan was then replaced by the Pieraccini
Plan which formed the basis of the National Economic Program for the five-year period
1966–1970.

World War, but also by the idea attributable to Pasquale Saraceno—one of the authors of the Camaldoli Code that we have already encountered—of the "improper burdens": "the spending [of the state controlled companies] earmarked for goals of a general nature, that did not produce balance sheet profits [...] or spending that did not generate development but simple conservation to be implemented by supporting employment or by rescuing bankrupt industrial companies" (Perrone, 1991, p. 12). Years later one of the protagonists of those years—Guido Carli (1996, p. 151)—commented:

> ... preference was given to the birth of assisted entrepreneurship that [...] would have been unable to stand up to international competition [...]. I did not imagine then that the forces that were able to impose the creation of sham employment would have become stronger and stronger, imposing on the parties, blackmailed by the electorate, to force the state to shoulder the burden of managing businesses that were devastated or born dead, propagating across the years the cancer that has reached our own time.

It was only European constraints that would slow down those rods and pistons—from the early 1980s[108]—and do so which greater clarity from the beginning of the nineties, without, moreover, stopping them as we have seen. In this way, a feature that had been present in the Italian economy right from the last decade of the nineteenth century re-emerged. While only apparently contingent on and dictated by circumstances, this feature was, in reality, the expression of a clear interventionist desire. During the decades after Second World War, the public industrial sectors elsewhere in Europe would also reach dimensions that were not really so different from those observed in Italy. But—as we have already cautioned—the Italian case stood out because of a continuity over time that was unknown in other parts of Western Europe.

For about thirty years the deficits of the Public Administrations were close to an annual average of 8% and higher than 3% in primary terms (again as an annual average; Appendix D). These deficits were favoured,

---

[108] Membership of the European Monetary System dates from 1979. The so-called divorce between the Treasury Ministry and the Bank of Italy occurred in 1981. The Maastricht Treaty was signed in 1992 and the Single European Market was established in 1993. The agreement between the Foreign Minister, Beniamino Andreatta and the Vice-President of the European Commission, Karel van Miert, aimed at reducing the indebtedness of state companies and privatising their subsidiaries, dates from 1993.

in 1966, by the decision of the Constitutional Court to deem laws without the necessary financial cover to be compliant with the Constitution, contrary to what authoritative constituent fathers thought that they had established by means of article 81.[109] They were also to a significant extent intended to fund the higher current spending[110] that was linked, but not exclusively, to the social reforms at the time, in particular in the fields of pensions, health and welfare.[111] What was redistributed was not what work had created and was creating but what it was taken for granted that "plans and programs" could and should create in the future.[112] It

[109] Article 81 of the Constitution approved by the Constituent Assembly in 1947 envisaged that "new taxes and new expenses cannot be approved by the law approving the budget. Any other law that entails new or greater expenditure must indicate the means for meeting it". In a letter in 1955 to the Treasury Minister, Pella, Luigi Einaudi—the President of the Republic—listed the reasons leading to interpreting the reading of article 81 as a clear indication of the need to achieve a balanced budget (retrieved March 18, 2024, https://www.luigieinaudi.it/doc/lettera-del-presidente-della-repubblica-einaudi-al-ministro-del-tesoro-pella/). Twenty years after the approval of the Constitution and a little over ten years from the above-mentioned letter, the Constitutional Court decided, instead, that a "bookkeeping" significance should not be attributed to the above articles but instead a "substantial" one, translatable not into an "automatic balancing of accounts, but prospective achievement of the balance between revenue and spending" where, according to the Court, it was also possible to include debt issuance among the hedging instruments (retrieved March 18, 2024, https://www.cortecostituzionale.it/actionSchedaPronuncia.do?anno=1966&numero=1). With which the intentions of the authors of the constitution were bypassed.

[110] In terms of the composition of the spending of the State Administrations, the almost 30-year 1964–1992 period recorded charges for interest that overall passed from circa 4% to 26% of total spending, to the detriment of the other current expenses but above all the capital account ones. In functional terms, the burden of expenditure on justice, public order, education and culture was halved while spending on interventions in the social field increased considerably. On the revenue front, there were no precedents for the increase recorded between the second half of the 1960s and the early nineties, by the share of income and property taxes out of total tax revenues. Circa thirty percentage points (starting from just less than 30%), and over twenty-five recorded in the decade between 1973 and 1982. Refer to Appendix D for the details.

[111] The reform of civil invalidity benefits dates from 1966 followed in 1968 by the reform of the procedures for calculating pension benefits and in 1969 by the introduction of social pensions for those aged over sixty with no income, and in 1978 the reform that introduced a universal health service.

[112] For the evolution of public spending between the 1960s and 1980s, see the painstaking work of Daniele Franco (1993) who also analyses the trends in specific spending chapters (education, health, welfare and assistance) in detail and distinguishes between two different moments: the period up to the middle of the 1970s in which the increased spending seems to be linked to structural causes (e.g. demography or production

was not and would not be the last time. The "burning" dilation of the public administration (in terms of personnel and functions) that occurred between the 1960s and 1970s is not surprising therefore (Melis, 2020, p. 603). Nor is it surprising that between 1964 and 1992 the debt of the General Government leapt from just less than about 30% of the product to over 100% and that the charges for interest grew by more than ten times compared to the 1% or almost in the middle of the 1960s. It is no wonder that the fiscal pressure almost doubled from about 28% to 45% in the same period of time, not unlike what happened to primary expenditures, with a macroscopic increase in the quota of income and property taxes out of total tax revenues.[113] In other words, it is not surprising that for about thirty years the country had got into debt above all in order to pay the interest bearing on the debt it had contracted previously. In August 1970, recalling a well-known anecdote in the columns of *Corriere della Sera*, Ennio Flaiano was to observe caustically that with the disappearance of the De Gasperis, the Einaudis, the Vanonis and the Pellas the poor but sober and dignified Italy of the 1940s also disappeared. The age of the "undivided pears" had begun.[114]

---

costs) and the subsequent period (up to 1990) in which the reasons for the growth are largely discretionary (and fruit, more than anything else, of the nature of the decision-making processes). In other words, if the tumultuous growth of the 15-year post-war period had led to imbalances that it was attempted to remedy through public spending (and debt) these could have been fixed already in the middle of the 1970s. To the actions already mentioned we should add the establishment of the Ordinary Statute Regions because of their significant consequences for public finances in a framework in which responsibilities were attributed to them but without any corresponding attribution of resources of their own. With all the related consequences for the evolution of public finances.

[113] Inflation was not extraneous to this result, of course. Between the early 1970s and the early 1980s, it hovered between 10 and 20%, provoking increased tax yields that were not the consequence of changes in the rates. This result was also a consequence of the configuration assumed by the tax system after the far-reaching reform launched and implemented between 1971 and 1973 centred among other things on personal taxation of a highly progressive nature and substantially limited since then to income from employment, from pensions and some income from self-employment.

[114] The reference is to an anecdote that was the subject of an article by Ennio Flaiano on *Corriere della Sera* dated August 18, 1979, which told the story of a dinner in the early 1950s with Einaudi, then President of the Republic, and several intellectuals (including Flaiano himself) in the rooms of the Quirinale Palace. When the fruit was served, seeing the size of the lovely pears to the surprise of those present, Einaudi asked his fellow diners if anyone wanted to share one of them with him.

In comparative terms, after a brief post-war parenthesis, Italy was back in the lead but in the wrong terms. In terms of public spending, the country, which in the early 1970s recorded levels in the General Government spending to GDP ratio below those of France, Germany and the UK and higher than those of the United States, in 1990 was three percentage points away from France, eight from Germany, thirteen from the UK and a little over twenty from the United States (Tanzi & Schuknecht, 2008, pp. 18–20). In terms of fiscal burden, in this case too, the 1990 figure was above the corresponding figure for the UK and the United States, and not marginally, while only remaining behind France (Tanzi & Schuknecht, 2008, pp. 51–55). The fiscal effort that was intended to guarantee the sustainability of the debt progressively lost impetus but without any appreciable immediate consequences however, thanks to an interest rate on public debt that was even lower than the growth rate (Fig. 7.3, left panel). However rough the indicator shown in Fig. 7.4 may be, the degree of progressivity of the system more than doubled in fifteen years.

The process of closing the gap between the regions of the south and islands and those of the centre and north ground to a halt. From that moment onwards, Italy would be back once again asking itself what the reasons were for a gap that was deep-rooted and tending increasingly towards the maxima recorded in the years straddling Second World War.[115]

The out-of-control performance of public finance would then be attributed to the imperative need to maintain social cohesion. It is possible that things were just like that even if Daniele Franco (1993, p. 205), when writing of the spending plans that were intended to attenuate situations of social conflict, is quite explicit in this regard. "Such interventions nevertheless explain a very modest part of the hasty spending" between 1960 and 1990. But we should not exclude the possibility that hidden behind a noble motive was the inability of a ruling class to guarantee even a minimum discipline of public finances and its tendency to take the easiest path every time: that of debt. This might seem to be an ungenerous judgement of a ruling class that found itself having to tackle that social phenomenon of extraordinary gravity that was the wave of terrorism

---

[115] And scholars of the public administration would continue to observe its continuous "meridionalisation" and, with it, the stability of its fundamental values: "State employment as a remedy for unemployment, peace of mind" (Cassese, 2014, p. 133).

that swept through Italy from the early 1970s and was only extinguished definitively thirty years later. But as such counterfactual experiments are pretty useless, it is impossible not to ask ourselves if the cracks that appeared in Italian society during those years and which lasted so long—and terrorism is only one aspect—were not the product rather than the cause of an attitude that was shared by Italian society and by a ruling class which found its most evident expression in the recourse to indebtedness. In this case too, Italy had to wait at least a couple of decades however to glimpse a different route.

Once again it is Giovanni Vecchi (2017a) who reminds us of what happened during those thirty years regarding the different scale of well-being and point out the unquestionable progresses that continued to be recorded in several fields—though at more limited rhythms than in the previous decades:—in the field of health and, notably, in life expectancy at birth;—in the education field;—in that of the inequality of income and of poverty (that had experienced the greatest reduction in the history of unification during the decade after the early 1970s). Confirming once again the fact that if new and different institutions (and, it goes without saying, the associated resources) can contribute to significant progresses in the non-economic dimensions of well-being, it does not follow at all that they are sufficient for guaranteeing the dynamism of an economy. Indeed, in laying the bases for future imbalances, they can create the conditions that lead to the annulment over time of these same progresses.

So, did the 1960s and 1970s constitute a lost opportunity? Could things have gone differently, in other words? To be more precise, could planning have been different from what it was? The question, obviously, is not odd and, indeed, is of particular prominence from the viewpoint in these pages. Pierluigi Ciocca (2020, p. 271) attributed the planning failure to a "total shortage of human and material resources". It is not clear, however, in what sense one can attribute to the aforesaid shortage of resources the failure "to keep the programming exercise along the narrow ridge that separates the inefficiency of the interventions from their antinomy with the market economy". Fabrizio Barca and Sandro Trento (1997) have spoken, instead, of "betrayal of the mission" of the state holdings and pointed to the desire to make the state holdings a tool of economic policy as the starting point of the degeneration in the thirty years that followed. Giovanni Federico (1999, p. 331) has recalled the limits imposed on an inefficient public administration by a political class that was afraid to touch vested interests while being well aware of its own

at the same time. But both in the first case as well as in the second and third cases, we are forced to believe that the ruling classes of the time (and with them a large number of Italians) were pursuing goals that differed from those that were achieved in practice. In other words, that neither one nor the others knew what they were doing. This is something that is anything but obvious from a reading of the abundant documentation on the subject (and that would not do justice to the calibre in both positive and negative terms of some of the personalities of the period). Everything lets it be supposed, on the contrary, that it was not a question of a missed opportunity but of a deliberate and conscious (and, obviously, completely legitimate) about-turn compared with the choices made in the years immediately after the war, an about-turn that was anything but instinctive or sudden but which, on the contrary, came from afar. Meditated when the woollen *orbace* fabric was still fashionable, it had been ready for a long time and was finally realised also because it was solidly rooted in the culture of a significant part of Italian society and was accepted immediately and supported by those who were supposed to lead that society, favoured by the vacuum following the deaths of figures like Luigi Einaudi and Alcide De Gasperi and the absence of appropriate successors.[116] It was fully compliant, moreover, with the international climate and with the culture that was prevalent among the ruling classes[117] while reflecting the deep and never appeased humours of the Italians. It was a film that had already been seen—if we can put it like this—and which would be shown again. Much with the same results.[118]

[116] After Attilio Piccioni left the stage in 1954 because of legal proceedings involving his son, ten years later Antonio Segni was forced to leave the Presidency for health reasons.

[117] At the turn of the 1940s and 1950s, John Maynard Keynes' ideas made inroads in the financial, entrepreneurial and trade union worlds and spread in both opposition and majority political circles. Giorgio La Pira (1950)—already member of Parliament but not yet mayor of Florence—went so far as to declare that Keynes's "new economy" was—so to speak—logically Christian, and to establish a parallel between the return of putting talents to work in the homonymous parable and the theory of the multiplier. Dying in 1946, John Maynard Keynes just managed to dodge Giorgio La Pira's daring connections.

[118] Aside from the failures and degenerations that undeniably marked it, the inadequacy (or, better still, the irrationality) of the programming strategy prevailing in Italy from the second half of the 1960s emerges in great detail from the pages of Barry Eichenhgreen (2007).

In thirty years, the wingman sadly returned to the group. He would progressively have to struggle more and more to stay in it. The country would soon be handed the bill for those thirty years in which:

> society's animal instincts were unleashed [...] battling strenuously against the acceptance of the principles of the market economy, the constraints that opening borders imposed and imposes, of being part of international division of labour and of a common market in Europe. External protectionism was replaced by a rather more robust and pervasive domestic variety that could count on extremely vast «transversal» political consent that cut right across the majority and opposition and prevented the introduction into our political culture and our legislation of the principles of free enterprise, competition and the market economy. (Carli, 1996, p. 259)

"SERIOUS CONCERN"

Thirty years after those years of the early 1960s the Treaty of the European Union, better known since as the Maastricht Treaty, came into force. The Italian ruling classes who had always thought that they had to protect the Italians from themselves and behaved as a consequence, found themselves having to face a weird situation: having to ask Europe to protect them (and with them, the whole country) from themselves. As Guido Carli would say a few years later (1996, p. 406), as one of the signatories of the Maastricht Treaty:

> I informed my action with the idea that for our country the presence of an international legal constraint would have a positive function for the effects of restoring healthy public finances, deeming pessimistically that without this obligation it was unlikely that our political class would change its ways.

With the Maastricht Treaty the foundations were laid not only for a semblance of discipline in public finances but also, if not above all, for the disappearance of the public enterprises created between the two wars or immediately afterwards. INA was privatised between 1992 and 1996. EFIM and IRI (or what remained of them) were put into liquidation in 1992 and 2000, respectively. The public banks were privatised between 1992 and 1994, iron and steel in 1995, telecommunications in 1997, and the motorways in 1999. The goal of entry into the common currency area—already prefigured in the Treaty, arduously pursued and, finally, achieved towards the end of the nineties—brought with it a series of impressive structural reforms. Already near the end of 1990, Italy finally provided itself with an Authority for Competition and the Market and, in between the months marked by the 1992 currency crisis and 2020, Alberto Saravalle and Carlo Stagnaro (2021, pp. 236–239) counted all of five reforms of the Public Administration, ten and five reforming interventions in civil justice and competition respectively, more than ten overall in employment and welfare and the same number regarding taxation. And the list cannot be deemed to be exhaustive.

It should be recognised that in some cases the times for implementing those reforms, the widespread resistance and attempts—often crowned by success—to drain them of any content (the 1995 pension reform being a prime example) undermined the reformer's goal in whole or in part. In other cases, the quality of the reforming intention was inadequate for the challenges to tackle, or it was even such as to exacerbate the problems that it was to help to solve (and here the textbook example is that of the procedures to spend the funds earmarked for the Mezzogiorno). In still more cases, the reforms were pure and simple *flatus vocis* (the so-called municipalised companies come to mind) or were followed by real counter-reforms that were able to turn the clock back in history (the most interesting example of this regards the "theory and practice" of the Independent Authorities).[119] But it would be inexact and ungenerous not to recognise the great strides forwards made in the nineties from very many different standpoints, including the interventions relating to the labour market (within the limits in which they survived), those regarding the operation of the markets (liberalisations) with particular reference to the financial markets, those relating to relations between the citizen and the public administration (simplifications) or the presence of the state in the economy.[120] And the list is anything but exhaustive. However, aside from

---

[119] Not by chance, therefore, the quantitative indications due to Leandro Prados de la Escosura (2023) signal moderate relative progress between the second half of the 1990s and 2020 both in the field of the protection of personal rights and property rights and in that of market regulation. However, it should be acknowledged that we are dealing with progress of a far lesser magnitude than that observed, for example, in the first thirty-five years of the new Kingdom's life.

[120] Even if it is hard not to recall that at the beginning of the 2010s the state portfolio—despite the privatisations in the 1990s ranged and still ranges from transport (Ferrovie dello Stato, Anas) to electricity (Terna, GSE) and telecommunications networks (Open Fiber), from petroleum (ENI) to gas (Italgas) and from electricity (ENEL) and

"reform accounting", important as that may be, it was a drastic remedy that ought to have given us institutions that were up to the challenges. Or would it?

Results: on annual average, about one point less in the per capita GDP and between half a point and a point down in total factor productivity growth vis-a-vis any benchmark (Europe "or 4" or Europe "of 7", United States or Great Britain), a patenting activity that was relatively stagnating or even declining, net negative turnover rates and rapidly falling gross turnovers of businesses, systematic re-proposing of bailout and rescue interventions for industrial and financial enterprises.

And extraordinarily resilient public finances, with all their disturbing basic trends. It is certainly true that there was a conspicuous drop in the public debt to GDP ratio (about twenty percentage points) between 1994 and the early years of the current century. But it is equally true that the result of the 1990s was much more than rendered entirely futile in the last fifteen years (even ignoring the pandemic emergency). The point is, that faced with interest rates on the public debt—net of the smaller and smaller "growth dividend"—that had turned positive starting from the 1990s, what can be observed is a fiscal effort intended to guarantee the sustainability of the debt that was always less intense not only between the 1960s and 1990s but also in the last thirty years, so that the Italian public debt sustainability indicator has been positioned in more recent years—starting from the second decade of the present century, to be precise—at levels that were even more worrying than those experienced in the 1880s, in the so-called Magliani area. Those were years during which Gianni Marongiu (2019, p. 49) accused Agostino Magliani of being unable to do anything other than "minimise the problem [of the public finances] to the point of denying them". We might as well today re-baptise the "Magliani area" after any one of the many economy ministers who followed one another

electronics (STM) to the media (RAI), to finance (AmCo formerly SGA) to insurance (PosteVita, Sace, Simest), to ships (Fincantieri) to defence, to aerospace and security (Leonardo), from postal and banking services (Poste) to air (ENAV) and airport navigation services (Naples, Bologna, Turin, Alghero, Milan), from tourism (TH Resort, Rocco Forte) to real estate (EUR, Manifattura Tabacchi), from mechanical engineering (Valvitalia) to plant engineering (Ansaldo Energia). This was a portfolio to which the holdings of regional and local bodies must be added and that shortly before the pandemic absorbed a significant part of the stock exchange capitalisation of the time. But, notwithstanding this, too insubstantial and inadequate so as not to try to strengthen it with selected and well-motivated interventions as listed in the Appendix to Rossi (2024).

since the 2010s. Carlo Bastasin has recalled[121] the events of the night between March 24 and 25, 1997 that led to Italy's participation in the single European currency. This participation was extremely close to being thwarted by the expression "serious concern", with reference to Italy's economic prospects, that appeared (before being replaced by the blander "continuous concern") in the report of the European Monetary Institute containing the selection of countries admitted. Whether "serious" or "continuous", it was an unquestionably justified concern.

In comparative terms too, the performance of Italian public finances leaves no room for great interpretations. General Government spending amounts to 55% of GDP today (2021) as it was in 1992 (after reaching a minimum only just above 46% in 2000). About four percentage points above European Union levels that reduced its public spending to product ratio by about three points over the same time period. The fiscal burden today is close to 48% (three points higher than the 1992 figure), just less than two percentage points above the values in the EU where it only rose by a few tenths.[122] The volume of resources intermediated by the public sector (revenues and expenditures) exceeds the value of the product. And it is certainly no coincidence that in 2011—replying, apparently to a European indication regarding the introduction of the principle of a balanced budget in the regulations, not necessarily constitutional, of the member states—the Italian parliament rewrote article 81 of the Constitution actually completing the demolition work launched by the Constitutional Court in 1966.[123] From that date, both in the rainy days and in the sunshine ones the country has only ever experienced deficits (on average only marginally lower than those recorded during the previous twenty years). Just as it had done in all the previous one hundred and sixty years of its life.[124]

---

[121] Retrieved March 18, 2024, https://www.repubblica.it/economia/2021/12/30/news/la_notte_dell_euro_cosi_vent_anni_fa_l_italia_salvo_se_stessa_e_scrisse_il_suo_futuro-331924064/.

[122] The source for the data regarding the European Union is the AMECO database of the European Commission (retrieved March 18, 2024, https://economy-finance.ec.europa.eu/economic-research-and-databases/economic-databases/ameco-database_en).

[123] On this point see Rossi (2018, pp. 7–15 and 147–149).

[124] The reference is to the deficits of the General Government and not to those of the Central Government.

And, finally, it is again Giovanni Vecchi (2017a) who reminds us that in the last thirty years very variegated results have materialised in more generically social terms too. Here and there evidence of malnutrition persists at some levels—certainly marginal—of the population and there was no suggestion of closure of the gap between Italy and other countries in terms of the quantity and the quality of the education and training system. Towering over everything is a process of divergence between central-southern Italy and the south which has intensified and been consolidated in the last thirty years. The progress recorded in the distribution of income in the 1970s and 1980s—the intrinsic fragility of which has already been observed—has largely been undone.

Without a doubt the decades between the early nineties and today have been marked by a financial crisis of the first magnitude and by a global pandemic event. And therefore, a little understanding is due. But the reality is what it is. And interrogates us silently. We can—with Carlo Bastasin and Gianni Toniolo (2023, pp. 103–126)—speak of another "lost opportunity" as if, regularly, the Italian ones had always and in every case been "wrong turns". It can be argued as done by Gianni Toniolo (2013, p. 41) and Emanuele Felice (2015, pp. 307–308)—that in the last thirty years Italy has been unable to adapt—mainly because of the nature of its institutions—to the changes that have marked them: from the technological innovations to the opening of the international markets, from the acceleration of the process of European integration, to the redefinition of the geopolitical structures.[125] Like Pierluigi Ciocca (2020, pp. 384–390) we can complain about the limits of the European institutional structures. Or, we can go further and point out, like Nicholas Crafts and Marco Magnani (2013, pp. 140–144)—the limits imposed by the "divided" nature of Italian society or the negative consequences of the "distributive coalitions". In this case too, there is no desire to deny that each of these arguments contains a grain of truth, but it is difficult not to think that there is something more. Were the dozens of reforms not intended to overcome the limits of our institutions? Is it ever possible

---

[125] In this regard it is obligatory to mention the work of Barry Eichengreen (1996) who, as regards the 1950s to 1980s of the last century designs the life cycle of institutional structures that were able to guarantee European post-war growth but—if one can put it like this—were victims of their own success. It is hardly necessary to observe that these interpretations are not necessarily alternatives to the one proposed in these pages whose basic message is fundamentally one: institutional structures favourable to growth are necessary but, unfortunately, not sufficient.

that they were all, literally all, badly designed and applied even worse? Is it so difficult to see something deeper and more resistant in this story? The consistent refusal by one part of the country to measure itself with the constituent elements of a market economy: the attempt, the undertaking, the risk of failure. A refusal that was explicit and noisy at times and, in other cases, dark and deaf (Nesi, 2019). A refusal that was visibly present during the decades between the two wars (and even before), reinforced and consolidated in the thirty years between the second half of the 1960s and the early 1990s and which re-emerged forcefully at the beginning of the current century, also in response to the reforming hyper-activism of the 1990s. A refusal which, on its own—whatever the institutions—was able to prevent and did prevent the country from adapting to the changes in course.[126] This rejection was photographed recently by opinion polls which make it possible—with due care—to compare the attitude of the Italians, of their neighbours and of the Anglo-Saxons with the values that usually underlie market economies.[127] Or—if taken with a pinch of salt—by the indices of economic freedom that consistently rank Italy after its main Western counterparts.[128]

[126] To put it in the words of Alberto Saravalle and Carlo Stagnaro (2021, p. 225), the reforms "did not work because we did not want them".

[127] Among them, the 2012 Report of the Pew Research Center (retrieved, March 18, 2024, https://www.pewresearch.org/wp-content/uploads/sites/2/2012/07/Pew-Global-Attitudes-Project-Economic-Conditions-Report-FINAL-July-12-2012.pdf). These results are obviously influenced by the unquestionably extraordinary events in 2008–2011 and then again in 2020. This having been said, only France would seem to take a more negative view than Italy of the values and implications of the market economy. Similar results—even if not directly comparable unfortunately—are contained in Zitelmann (2020). It is interesting to note how—according to the Pew Research surveys—the distances between Italy and the other European countries would have fallen, if not actually been cancelled, during the first years of the century, i.e. at the moment of entry into the euro.

[128] Apart from Prados de la Escosura (2023), the obvious reference is the Economic Freedom of the Heritage Foundation (retrieved 18 March, 2024, https://www.heritage.org/index/).

This refusal made Italy into the country of Bartleby[129] and in the years closer to us this translated into the rejection, at times even violent, of infrastructural works, whether they were for railways, or roadworks or power supplies and so on. It expressed itself in the negation of science. It revealed itself in the rediscovery of protectionism. It manifested itself in the vilification of entrepreneurial activity and was exalted in the production in increasingly new and baroque normative and regulatory obstacles to the same. It manifested itself in the idea that budget constraint was an option and not already a reality, often an unpleasant one. It translated itself into the conviction that the Italians did not have the resources to overcome the difficulties on their own—a conviction which, finally, found once again a political expression able to translate it into choices and decisions that might condition the life of the Italians for a long time. A refusal that found an immediate counterpart in the policy of "bonus schemes"[130] and that is in the choice made by all governments of the current century to provide subsidies allowing access to a tax reduction, aimed at this or that economic category or even this or that social typology. Let's be clear, there is no reference here to fiscal expenses which constitute an integral part of the tax structure and which, consequently, should be evaluated from this perspective. And, quite clearly, fiscal expenditures are to be found, more or less in every country. But it is impossible not to remember that in 2020 Italy recorded a "garden bonus" and a "grand-parents bonus", and in 2022 an "electric scooter bonus" and a "household appliance bonus".[131] All instances that exemplify, as one could not better,

[129] Bartleby is the protagonist of the famous Herman Melville story entitled *Bartleby the Scrivener: A Story of Wall Street*, published in several instalments in *Putnam's Magazine* in 1853. Employed as a clerk in a law firm, Bartleby—described by Melville as "pallidly neat, pitiably respectable, incurably forlorn"—stuck strictly to his duties and replied "I would prefer not to" whenever he was asked to carry out other tasks and, in the end, would stop any activity with the same justification.

[130] According to the Cambridge Dictionary, a bonus is "an extra amount of money that is given to you as a present or reward for good work". It is impossible not to notice the closeness between the terms bonus and tip or gratuity (*regalia* in Italian, again for the Cambridge Dictionary: "to give someone who has provided you with a service an extra amount of money to thank them").

[131] In the survey carried out during 2023, 740 bonuses were listed (with an increase of more than 20% compared to what was observed in the 2010s) capable of negatively impacting tax revenue by more than 6% of GDP, certainly an underestimate, in light of the disruptive impact of the building bonuses introduced from 2020. (Ministero dell'Economia e delle Finanze, 2023).

the profoundly distorted relationship between the Italian ruling classes and the citizens. It had already happened a few times before and therefore it was more than possible that it would happen again given that the events of the 1990s had, among other things, contributed to brutally and thoughtlessly resetting the memory of the Italian ruling classes.

Gianni Toniolo (2013, p. 40) has observed that "it is not possible to trace parallels between the years 1992–2011 and the period of divergence after 1861". This is true, but doing so is nevertheless instructive. The two periods, in fact, share one significant aspect more than others: the conviction that growth travels, first of all, through adequate institutional structures and that therefore the high road for growth is that of the reforms. And from this viewpoint both periods confirm the idea that the institutions are of course necessary but not sufficient: they are impotent, in other words, if they do not rest on a culture of growth. As they confirm the idea that assigning some thaumaturgical virtue to reforms is—in the absence of an adequate cultural background—the sure recipe for generating disillusionment and detachment when the reforms, by themselves, prove incapable of affecting the medium–long-term prospects.

In addition to this assertion is a further observation that marks a far from minor difference between the first thirty-five years and the final thirty years of the unified state's life. And which is equally instructive. If in the years immediately after Unification, the ruling classes identified themselves with the institutional architecture of the new Kingdom and with their reforms, the same cannot be said for the years straddling the twenty and the twenty-first centuries: years in which reforms appeared and were often deliberately presented as coming from a no-better-specified "elsewhere" that was imposed but never really wanted. As being necessary for putting the Italians on the right path and force them to accept a modernity towards which they displayed reluctance day after day. But they were never really accepted by the ruling classes that drafted them, to the point that a few years later it was not rare to find the authors of the reforms among the critics of the same. The detachment and hostility of a significant part of public opinion towards the ultimate aim of the reforms was—as we have attempted to suggest—present for some time. For a long time. And deeply rooted. Once again—as is often the case—the Italian ruling class took on the task of doing everything possible to reinforce that detachment and consolidate that rejection.

References

Amendola, N., Salsano, F., & Vecchi, G. (2017). Poverty. In G. Vecchi, *Measuring Wellbeing. A History of Italian Living Standards* (pp. 333–372). Oxford University Press.

Amendola, N., & Vecchi, G. (2017). Inequality. In G. Vecchi, *Measuring Wellbeing. A History of Italian Living Standards* (pp. 293–332). Oxford University Press.

Assonime. (1981). *Statistiche sulle Società Italiane per azioni* (Vol. 26). Associazione fra le Società Italiane per Azioni.

Baget Bozzo, G. (1974). *Il partito cristiano al potere. La Dc di De Gasperi e di Dossetti 1945/1954*. Vallecchi.

Banca d'Italia. (1946). *Assemblea Generale Ordinaria dei Partecipanti tenuta in Roma il giorno 29 marzo 1946*. Banca d'Italia.

Banti, A. M. (1996). *Storia della borghesia italiana. L'età liberale*. Donzelli.

Barca, F. (1999). *Il capitalismo italiano. Storia di un compromesso senza riforme*. Donzelli.

Barca, F., & Trento, S. (1997). La parabola delle partecipazioni statali: Una missione tradita. In F. Barca (Ed.), *Storia del capitalismo Italiano* (pp. 186–263). Donzelli.

Barucci, P. (1978). *Ricostruzione, pianificazione, Mezzogiorno. La politica economica in Italia dal 1943 al 1955*. Il Mulino.

Bastasin, C., & Toniolo, G. (2023). *The Rise and Fall of the Italian Economy*. Cambridge University Press.

Battilossi, S. (1998). Annali. In P. Ciocca & G. Toniolo (Eds.), *Storia economica d'Italia* (Vol. 2). Laterza.

Berselli, A. (1997). *Il governo della Destra. Italia legale e Italia reale dopo l'Unità*. Il Mulino.

Berta, G. (2016). *Che fine ha fatto il capitalismo italiano?* Il Mulino.

Bertilorenzi, M., Cerretano, V., & Perugini, M. (2022). Between Constraints and Opportunities: Big Italian Business and Autarky. *Rivista di Storia Economica/Italian Review of Economic History, 38*(3), 303–336.

Bini, P. (2021). *Scienza economica e potere. Gli economisti e la politica economica dall'Unità d'Italia alla crisi dell'euro*. Rubettino.

Bocca, G. (2018). *Miracolo all'italiana*. Feltrinelli.

Bottiglieri, B. (1984). *La politica economica dell'Italia centrista (1948–1958)*. Bollati Boringhieri.

Brandolini, A. (1999). The Distribution of Personal Income in Post-War Italy: Source Description, Data Quality, and the Time Pattern of Income Inequality. *Giornale degli Economisti e Annali di Economia, 58*(2), 183–239.

Broadberry, S. N., Giordano, C., & Zollino, F. (2013). Productivity. In G. Toniolo (Ed.), *The Oxford Handbook of the Italian Economy Since Unification* (pp. 187–226). Oxford University Press.

Brunetti, A., Felice., E., & Vecchi, G. (2017). Income. In G. Vecchi, *Measuring Wellbeing. A History of Italian Living Standards* (pp. 255–292). Oxford University Press.

Cammarano, F. (2011). *Storia dell'Italia liberale*. Laterza.

Cannella, M., & Magnaricotte, M. (2023). *Electoral Effects of U.S. Soft Power: Evidence from Hollywood Movies in Cold War Italy*. Retrieved March 18, 2024, https://drive.google.com/file/d/1nHLCYIylOHhUs0-mK7r6v0Hsqga7RzY3/view

Carli, G. (1977). *Intervista sul capitalismo italiano*. Laterza.

Carli, G. (1996). *Cinquant'anni di vita italiana*. Laterza.

Carocci, G. (1975). *Storia d'Italia dall'Unità ad oggi*. Feltrinelli.

Cassese, S. (2014). *Governare gli italiani. Storia dello Stato*. Il Mulino.

Cerroni, U. (1999). Dinamica politica e modernizzazione in Italia. Tendenze e discrasie prima dell'Unità. In P. Ciocca e G. Toniolo (Eds.), *Storia economica d'Italia* (Vol. 1, pp. 119–158). Laterza.

Ciocca, P. (2020). *Ricchi per sempre? Una storia economica d'Italia (1796–2020)*. Bollati Boringhieri.

Clague, C., Keefer, P., Knack, S., & Olson, M. (1999). Contract-Intensive Money: Contract Enforcement, Property Rights, and Economic Performance. *Journal of Economic Growth, 4*, 185–211.

Colli, A. (2002). *I volti di Proteo: storia della piccola impresa in Italia nel Novecento*. Bollati Boringhieri.

Crafts, N., & Magnani, M. (2013). The Golden Age and the Second Globalization in Italy. In G. Toniolo (Ed.), *The Oxford Handbook of the Italian Economy since Unification* (pp. 69–107). Oxford University Press.

Crainz, G. (2005). *Storia del miracolo italiano*. Donzelli Editore.

Craveri, P. (2006). *De Gasperi*. Il Mulino.

Croce, B. (1928). *Storia d'Italia dal 1871 al 1915*. Laterza.

Croce, B. (1944). *Per la nuova vita dell'Italia. Scritti e discorsi, 1943–1944*. Riccardo Ricciardi Editore.

De Felice, R. (1974). *Mussolini il duce I. Gli anni del consenso 1929 – 1936*. Einaudi.

De Felice, R. (1975). *Intervista sul fascismo*. Laterza.

De Felice, R. (2004). *Autobiografia del fascismo. Antologia di testi fascisti (1919–1945)*. Einaudi.

De Viti De Marco, A. (1930). *Un trentennio di lotte politiche*. Collezione Meridionale Editrice.

Di Martino, P., & Vasta, M. (2018). Reassessing the Italian «Economic Miracle»: Law, Firms' Governance and Management, 1950–1973. *Business History Review, 92*(2), 281–306.

Eichengreen, B. (1996). Institutions and Economic Growth: Europe After World War II. In N. Crafts & G. Toniolo (Eds.), *Economic Growth in Europe Since 1945* (pp. 38–72). Cambridge University Press.

Eichengreen, B. (2007). *The European Economy Since 1945. Coordinated Capitalism and Beyond*. Princeton University Press.

Einaudi, L. (1933). *La condotta economica e gli effetti sociali della guerra italiana*. Laterza.

Elia, L. (1974). De Gasperi e Dossetti. *Nuova Antologia, 109*, 464–468.

Federico, G. (1999). Harmful or Irrelevant? Italian Industrial Policy, 1945–1973. In H. Miyajima, T. Kikkawa, & T. Hikino (Eds.), *Policies for Competitiveness* (pp. 309–335). Oxford University Press.

Federico, G., & Giannetti, R. (1999). Italy: Stalling and Surpassing. In J. Foreman-Peck & G. Federico (Eds.), *European Industrial Policy. The Twentieth-Century Experience* (pp. 124–151). Oxford University Press.

Felice, E. (2015). *Ascesa e declino, Storia economica d'Italia*. Il Mulino.

Fenoaltea, S. (2011). *The Reinterpretation of Italian Economic History*. Cambridge University Press.

Formigoni, G., Pombeni, P., & Vecchio, G. (2023). *Storia della democrazia Cristiana*. Il Mulino.

Franco, D. (1993). *L'espansione della spesa pubblica in Italia*. Il Mulino.

Freschi, G. (2023). A Social Elevator? Occupational Mobility in Italy, 1950–1970. *Rivista di Storia Economica/Italian Economic History Review, 39*(2), 131–161.

Gabbuti, G. (2020). «When We Were Worse Off». The Economy, Living Standards and Inequality in Fascist Italy. *Rivista di Storia Economica/Italian Economic History Review, 36*(3), 253–298.

Gabrielli, P. (2011). *Anni di novità e di grandi cose. Il boom economico fra tradizione e cambiamento*. Il Mulino.

Giorgi, C., & Pavan, I. (2021). *Storia dello Stato sociale in Italia*. Il Mulino.

Gomellini, M. (2017). La concorrenza internazionale. In A. Gigliobianco e G. Toniolo (Eds.), *Concorrenza, mercato e crescita in Italia: il lungo periodo* (pp. 235–268). Marsilio.

Graziano, M. (2010). *The Failure of Italian Nationhood*. Palgrave Macmillan.

Lanaro, S. (1979). *Nazione e lavoro. Saggio sulla cultura borghese in Italia, 1870–1925*. Marsilio.

Lanaro, S. (1988). *L'Italia nuova. Identità e sviluppo 1861–1988*. Einaudi.

La Pira, G. (1950). L'attesa della povera gente. *Cronache Sociali, 1*, 2–6.

Luzzatto, G. (1968). *L'economia italiana dal 1861 al 1914*. Einaudi.

Marongiu, G. (1995). *Storia del fisco in Italia. La politica fiscale della Destra storica (1861–1876)*. Einaudi.

Marongiu, G. (2017). *Una storia fiscale dell'Italia repubblicana*. Giappichelli.

Marongiu, G. (2019). *La politica fiscale dell'Italia liberale. (1861–1922).* Giappichelli.

Marongiu, G. (2020). *Il fisco e il fascismo.* Giappichelli.

McCloskey, D. N., & Carden, A. (2020). *Leave Me Alone and I'll Make You Rich.* The University of Chicago Press.

Melis, G. (2020). *Storia dell'amministrazione italiana.* Il Mulino.

Mingardi, A. (2021). Why Italy's Season of Economic Liberalism Did Not Last. *The Independent Review, 25,* 593–616.

Ministero dell'Economia e delle Finanze. (2023). *Rapporto annuale sulle spese fiscali 2023.* Ministero dell'Economia e delle Finanze.

Mori, G. (1992). L'economia italiana dagli anni Ottanta alla Prima guerra mondiale. In G. Mori (Ed.), *Storia dell'industria elettrica in Italia. Le origini, 1882–1914* (pp. 1–106). Laterza.

Nardozzi, G. (2003). Il miracolo economico. In P. Ciocca e G. Toniolo (Eds.), *Storia economica d'Italia* (Vol. 3, pp. 213–268). Laterza.

Nesi, E. (2019). *Storia della mia gente.* Bompiani.

Oriani, A. (1939). *La lotta politica in Italia.* Cappelli.

Patriarca, S. (2010). *Italianità. La costruzione del carattere nazionale.* Laterza.

Pedone, A. (1967). Il bilancio dello Stato e lo sviluppo economico italiano, 1861–1963. *Rassegna Economica, 31*(2), 285–341.

Perrone, N. (1991). *Il dissesto programmato. Le partecipazioni statali nel Sistema di consenso democristiano.* Edizioni Dedalo.

Petri, R. (2002). *Storia economica d'Italia. Dalla Grande Guerra al miracolo economico (1918–1963).* Il Mulino.

Piovene, G. (2017). *Viaggio in Italia.* Mondadori.

Prados de la Escosura, L. (2023). Economic Freedom in Retrospect, *European Historical Economics Society WP 236.* Retrieved March 18, 2024, https://ehes.org/wp/EHES_236.pdf

Rebuffa, G. (2012). Cittadino? Quale cittadino? In N. Rossi (Ed.), *Sudditi. Un programma per i prossimi 50 anni* (pp. 33–43). IBL Libri.

Romanelli, R. (1991). Le radici storiche del localismo italiano. *Il Mulino, 4,* 711–720.

Rossi, M., Vecchi, G., & Latino, L. (2017). Vulnerability. In G. Vecchi, *Measuring Wellbeing. A History of Italian Living Standards* (pp. 415–453). Oxford University Press.

Rossi, N. (2018). *Flat tax. Aliquota unica e minimo vitale per un fisco semplice ed equo.* Marsilio.

Rossi, N. (2024). Italian Bailouts, 1861–2021, *Rivista di Storia Economica / Italian Review of Economic History, 40*(1), forthcoming.

Salvatorelli, L. (1977). *Nazionalfascismo.* Einaudi.

Sapelli, G. (1989). *L'Italia inafferrabile. Conflitti, sviluppo, dissociazione dagli anni Cinquanta a oggi.* Marsilio.

Saravalle, A., & Stagnaro, C. (2021). *Molte riforme per nulla. Una controstoria economica della seconda repubblica*. Marsilio.

Segni, A. (2016). *Diario, 1956–1964*. Il Mulino.

Segni, M. (2021). *Il colpo di stato del 1964*. Rubettino.

Stone, N. (1985). *Europe Transformed 1878–1919*. Fontana Press.

Tanzi, V. (2012). *Centocinquant'anni di finanza pubblica in Italia*. IBL Libri.

Tanzi, V. (2018). *Italica*. Schena Editore.

Tanzi, V., & Schuknecht, L. (2008). *Public Spending in the 20th Century: A Global Perspective*. Cambridge University Press.

Tarquini, A. (2016). *Storia della cultura fascista*. Il Mulino.

Tedoldi, L. (2018). *Storia dello Stato italiano. Dall'Unità al XXI secolo*. Laterza.

Tomatis, J. (2021). *Storia culturale della canzone italiana*. Feltrinelli.

Toniolo, G. (1980). *L'economia dell'Italia fascista*. Laterza.

Toniolo, G. (1988). *Storia economica dell'Italia liberale*. Il Mulino.

Toniolo, G. (2013). An Overview of Italy's Economic Growth. In G. Toniolo (Ed.), *The Oxford Handbook of the Italian Economy Since Unification* (pp. 3–36). Oxford University Press.

Toniolo, G. (2022a). *Storia della Banca d'Italia* (Vol. I). Il Mulino.

Toniolo, G. (2022b). La solidarietà sociale. In G. Amato (Ed.), *La democrazia nel XXI secolo. Riflessioni sui temi di Alfredo Reichlin* (pp. 135–162). Treccani.

Toniolo, G., Conte, L., & Vecchi, G. (2003). Monetary Union, Institutions and Financial Market Integration: Italy, 1862–1905. *Explorations in Economic History, 40*, 443–461.

Vecchi, G. (2017a). *Measuring Wellbeing. A History of Italian Living Standards*. Oxford University Press.

Vecchi, G. (2017b). Introduction. In G. Vecchi, *Measuring Wellbeing. A History of Italian Living Standards* (pp. 1–10). Oxford University Press.

Vivarelli, R. (1981). *Il fallimento del liberalismo. Studi sulle origini del fascismo*. Il Mulino.

Zitelmann, R. (2020). *The Rich in Public Opinion. What We Think When We Think About Wealth*. Cato Institute.

CHAPTER 9

Epilogue

If we were at the closing address—as we are—it could only sound like this: the system of beliefs, of values, of preferences that—in its various incarnations—permeated Italian society throughout the unified adventure was not, is not and—very probably—will not be capable in the near future of generating and sustaining autonomous growth processes. Italy was, is still and very probably will remain for a long time a "follower" country whose economic fortunes will depend greatly on the technological leader of the moment. And it is illusory to think that it will be the material resources or institutional architectures that will save Italy from this destiny. These are and certainly will be necessary but have not been, are not and will not be sufficient. Filling the tank of your car with petrol (or recharging the batteries if you prefer), reducing its weight or installing a new electronic control unit or air-less tyres (for the latter you have to wait until 2027), will never be sufficient for letting us move speedily and efficiently if the idea itself of movement is not present in the mind of the driver and of the passengers; just as it was not—except for a brief fifteen-year period—and still is not today.

In a trial such as the one we are holding in these pages, there is not, nor could there ever be a "smoking gun", a hard and objectively verifiable proof of what we have just affirmed. We believe however that there are clues that cannot be ignored that the above assertion is worthy of

© The Author(s), under exclusive license to Springer Nature
Switzerland AG 2024
N. Rossi, *Reframing Italian Economic History, 1861–2021*, Palgrave
Studies in Economic History,
https://doi.org/10.1007/978-3-031-67271-2_9

being taken seriously into consideration. How "grave, precise and concordant"—as the Italian criminal code (art. 192, p. 2) requires—these clues are, is a question that it is up to the reader to decide. But the consequences of those clues should, however, be carefully considered for the implications they may have.

Fabrizio Galimberti and Luca Paolazzi (1998) have been comparing Italy to the bumblebee for more than twenty years now.

> It should not even be able to lift itself off the ground. It's chunky. Its wings are small. Bumblebees, aeronautical engineers tell us, were not born to fly. And yet, they are able to fly fast and very high, making a racket. The Italian economy is like a bumblebee. With no raw materials and with few advanced industries. Widespread social conflict. Weak and unstable governments. Recent unification that is still not properly digested. And yet Italy became one of the World's seven major industrial powers.

Unfortunately, however, bumblebees (*xylocopa violacea*) of the kind described by Galimberti and Paolazzi (1998) simply do not exist. Do not exist in general and certainly not in economics.[1] And, in fact, it is worth repeating that the story told in the preceding pages is not one of success. On the contrary, it is the story of a country that, to use a typically Italian expression, we could describe as being "without infamy and without praise". And not just because of the shortage of raw materials, the poor social cohesions, the inadequate institutions. But because, all things considered—behind the rhetoric—it was conscious and content to be so.

The first to be aware of this weakness are the Italians themselves. The term—or to put it more appropriately—the epithet "Italietta" or "Little Italy" has a history as long as our unification adventure. It was first used by Enrico Corradini's nationalists who labelled Italy this way in *Il Regno* ("The Kingdom") in the first decade of the last century, the one that Maurizio Maraviglia defined as "demo-liberal, moderate and slipper-wearing". Then the fascists came along and used it to contrast the post-*Risorgimento* nation to "their" muscular Italy that was reaching out towards "inexorable destinies". Almost fifty years later, in the summer of 1974, it was Italo Calvino who mocked Pier Paolo Pasolini from the columns of a national daily for what he defined as his "lament for the

---

[1] The idea that bumblebees' flight is impossible goes back to the 1930s of the last century. Since then, science has proven that bumblebees can and do fly in style.

peasant ... and paleo-capitalist Italietta", provoking the piqued reaction: "Italietta is petit-bourgeois, fascist and Christian democrat; it is provincial and on the margins of history ... Do you want me to regret all of this?". A few decades later in 2007 it would be Silvio Berlusconi who defined Italietta as the Italy of Romano Prodi, provincial—according to him—in its anti-American compulsions. And a little more than ten years afterwards at the height of the pandemic, it will be Nicola Zingaretti—then secretary of the largest party in the Italian left—who invited the country to "think big", and not to choose to keep on being the Italietta that is unable to do of anything other than just get by. And even later again, at the peak of the crisis triggered by the Russia-Ukraine conflict, it was the turn of an important government exponent from the ranks of the centre-right—the minister, Renato Brunetta—to recall, with evident contempt, "the unreliable Italietta of past times." And try and google the term "Italietta" along with the most relevant names of the current Italian political landscape: you will be surprised by the results. Italietta, then, but which, exactly?

Right and left, monarchists and republicans, northerners and southerners, short and tall, fat and thin, they have all used the term "Italietta". We've all used it. Yes, all of us! To indicate the "other" Italy. The one that "we" don't like. The one that differs from the one "we" would like. The one that's a thousand miles from the one that "we" would be able to propose to build in a more or less distant future. Us, all of us: right and left, parliamentarians and presidentialists, northerners and southerners, tall and short, fat and thin.

All of which suggests that in reality Italietta is not an "other" Italy but is "this Italy" whose qualities (or what we consider to be such) "we" limit ourselves individually to considering to be our own, and whose limitations (or what we consider to be such) we attribute to others, all of which leads us to the conclusion that Italietta is nothing other than what we have in front of our eyes: what there is. What accompanied us in the past, recent or remote: what there was. What we will very probably see in the years to come. What—without surprises—there will be. What Alessandro Manzoni already glimpsed clearly in the early years of the nineteenth century: "And always deploring your mistakes and faults/Always regretted and never changed".[2] What Sabino Cassese (2014, p. 327) describes as characterised by "a deep, underground life, that continues whatever the interruptions,

[2] The verses quoted are the last two lines of a 1802 sonnet addressed to Francesco Lomonaco (https://www.alessandromanzoni.org/opere/35).

presenting recurrent characteristics." In short, in just a few extraordinary words: the star of "a cold story".

This is the story that we have attempted to describe in the preceding pages, with all the appropriate approximations; the story of an Italy limited to a great extent in its ambitions, typically suspicious of change, often adverse to risk, and hostile to growth and to it consequences. One in which, certainly, there is no shortage of cases of excellence but, equally certainly, where they very rarely made any real difference: an Italy that was also able to obtain significant results but only and exclusively by profiting—in a manner that was not entirely passive—from the experiences of others. It was a victim of itself, of its cultural habits and of the attitude of its ruling classes who, convinced of the limits of the Italians and in order to defend them from themselves, invariably collaborated with their paternalism and with their interventionist aspirations to ensure that they would continue to look with reluctance on the changes imposed by modernity. As we have sought to point out, it was not always so. In the fifteen to twenty years immediately after Second World War a different ruling class, one that was prepared to give credit to that part of Italy that wanted to embrace modernity—in the most varied and, if you like, disorderly ways—created the premises for what not coincidentally we call the "economic miracle". It was an event without precedents and one that would not be repeated, and the Italians would remember it, of course, as a miracle but whose main inspirations would never have found a place—such as in Germany, for example—in the Pantheon of the Italians (Mingardi, 2021). Unlike what happened following the *Wirtschaftswunder* (Mesini, 2023), Italy's post-war economic success was not to be a source of legitimisation and a constituent element of the identity of the Republic that we consider—with a use of the words that is not at all coincidental but actually revealing—to be founded on the "Resistance" and not also on the "Reconstruction". On political freedom and not on economic freedom.

The limits of a "wingman" model of growth have emerged with clarity in recent decades. Lovers of "minute by minute" performance point out that between 2021 and 2023 important signs of recovery that appear to be equal to if not greater than that recorded elsewhere have been recorded in the Italian economy. Time will tell if this is just a flash in the pan or a real turnaround, if the wingman is back at the front of the race. We hope so but allow ourselves to seriously doubt it. Temporary deviations from decades-long trends have often materialised in the past but actually never left any great trace over time.

And these decades have been characterised in the United States as well—insofar as we can understand from the information available—as in much of Europe by significant degrowth in economic dynamism. Such degrowth could only but be reflected in an Italy in which the dynamism levels were already significantly lower than those prevalent elsewhere. In both components of Fig. 4.4—and therefore both in the graph on the left that illustrates the relationship between the growth rate of the total factor productivity and the indicator of the economic dynamism, and in the graph on the right that refers instead to the relationship between patenting activity and economic dynamism—Italy is located below the linear interpolant in correspondence, therefore, with levels of dynamism, patenting activity performance and total factor productivity growth rates that are lower than those recorded in most of the countries considered. Stated in other terms, the slowdown in the economic dynamism in progress in much of the developed world—and, as we have seen, at least partly attributable to demographic trends and to more pronounced ageing processes in Italy than elsewhere—translated, in the absence of an autonomous capacity for growth, into a complete stasis in the Italian case.

All this suggests prudence. At all latitudes. Like the US, the European countries should start debating the issue of economic dynamism and deal with trends in business demography with the sense of urgency underlying the debate on the twin transitions (decarbonisation and digitalisation) or the perspective of a common European defence.[3] Unless one believes—and this writer certainly does not believe it—that the twin transitions (and not just them) can only walk on the legs of the state. In this respect, they would do better looking at the Italian economy— as in Oscar Wilde's "The Picture of Dorian Gray"—to understand what happens when dynamism is not the first and foremost issue of an economy.

And Italy should do so with its past with even greater commitment. Given the many and often radical uncertainties of the moment, given the obligations that the country has accumulated over time and particularly in recent years, and given the challenges that more recent events have posed for Italy and for Italy in Europe, it becomes impossible today to avoid a simple question: will Italietta be enough for us? Is there enough

---

[3] In this respect a recent lecture of Isabel Schnabel, member of the Executive Board of the ECB, represents a significant departure from the standard narrative (retrieved March 18, 2024, https://www.ecb.europa.eu/press/key/date/2024/html/ecb.sp2402 16~df6f8d9c31.en.html).

for us in the Italietta that places a sepia image of the "seventh industrial power" on the shelf but then nearly always opts for the provincial? Is there enough for us in the Italietta that has lacked any autonomous capacity for growth, not for decades but perhaps always—with the sole exception of the twenty years after Second World War? We think not. "This" Italy— the Italietta of the last century and a half—will not be enough. And that could cost us very dearly. And not just from a mere economic point of view. Convincing ourselves of it will be the first step towards trying to avoid the rocks looming in the distance.

In fact, getting into the essence of things, the theme that is the subject of these pages is, in the first place, the autonomy of a society. Economies and societies without an autonomous capacity for growth can undoubt-edly achieve more than appreciable economic performances—as happened in Italy—but only and exclusively by exploiting the ability of others to shift the frontiers of their productive possibilities forward day after day. When these are in hiding or even completely absent, dependent societies like Italy's slow down first of all and then come to a stop altogether. Then when they are faced with tackling a very significant public debt, their vulnerability is magnified, and their dependence accentuated even further. As doubts remain about the sustainability of that debt, the lack of dynamism also ends up significantly contributing to the stalemate that often seems to characterise the supranational organisations of which the countries we are talking about are part of (in our case the European Union).

We have attempted to suggest how things have not always gone like that in the Italian case. During the fifteen or twenty years after the Second World War, for the reasons described, Italy experienced a season of "inno-vism" *à la* McCloskey or, if we prefer, grassroot innovation *à la* Phelps, one that was short-lived however: a season that exhausted Italy's catch-up process in its entirety. Before and after that we regularly fooled ourselves that we could make ends meet when, in reality, if and when we managed to, it happened because the world gave us (sold us) the tools to do so.

A part of the ruling class as well as some segments of Italian society have been realising that the matter of the country's autonomy is on the agenda. But this has happened without attempting to understand the genesis or being able to see its causes and ended up, as a consequence, by expressing it superficially (often, unfortunately, in a slovenly manner too), indicating solutions that were capable of deepening it rather that solving it. Another part, hastily convinced that the problem was unsolvable, imagined that they could mitigate the consequences thanks to closer and closer links with Europe. Both the former and the latter shared a hope: that it was possible to overcome the difficulty without paying the price, that it was possible to get around the fundamental cultural problem by saddling others with the inevitable burden of the change. It is quite evident that this was a vain hope, and it is highly probable, if not really certain—as we have indicated in the previous lines—that it is a fantasy that can be cultivated even less in the future.

Let it be clear, there is no doctor who ordered us to turn up our sleeves, take on risks, grasp opportunities, set more ambitious goals for ourselves and accept change. We need not necessarily think that the king of Brobdingnag—"a prince of much gravity and austere countenance"—was right in saying:

> ... that whoever could make two ears of corn, or two blades of grass, to grow upon a spot of ground where only one grew before, would deserve better of mankind, and do more essential service to his country, than the whole race of politicians put together

as reported by Jonathan Swift in his *Gulliver's Travels* (1909, pp. 102 and 134).

On the contrary—although this writer does not agree with it at all or desire it—aspiring to a protected environment, considering positively the fact that someone will think and act for us, and tending to prefer the status quo, can be perfectly legitimate choices for every society. But the really important thing to remember about these decisions, always and in every way, is the price: a price that is often impalpable in the short term but in reality, stead heavy to the point of becoming unbearable in the medium and long term. And this is true today and will be true in the years to come even to a greater extent than it was, perhaps, in the past.

To use the words of Gianni Toniolo, every book, even a history one, is written with the future in mind. And these pages are no different. They spring, in fact, from a desire to understand what we can expect. And from the conviction, matured over the years, that the answer does not lie (or not only) in our own time.

REFERENCES

Cassese, S. (2014). *Governare gli italiani. Storia dello Stato.* Il Mulino.

Galimberti, F., & Paolazzi, L. (1998). *Il volo del calabrone. Breve storia dell'economia italiana nel Novecento.* Le Monnier.

Mesini, L. (2023). *Stato forte ed economia ordinata. Storia dell'ordoliberalismo (1929–1950).* Il Mulino.

Mingardi, A. (2021). Why Italy's Season of Economic Liberalism Did Not Last. *The Independent Review, 25,* 593–616.

Swift, J. (1909). *Gulliver's Travels into Several Remote Nations of the World.* Cassel & Co.

Appendices

Appendix A: Innovators and Imitators

Daron Acemoglu et al. (2006) are the originators of a stylised representation of the growth process centred, among other things, on the co-presence of entrepreneurs with different capacities and attitudes:— for example, some of them innovators and other imitators (these latter limiting themselves to the adoption of processes or products located on the technological frontier and already adopted elsewhere in the world). While reference should be made to the aforementioned work itself for the details, what is highlighted here is that, letting q_{it} denote the average productivity of country i at time t, the average productivity growth rate of the system can be represented—in the aforesaid simplified economy—as follows (Aghion et al., 2014):

$$q_{it} - q_{it-1} = \delta_{it}^{IN}(\gamma - 1)q_{it-1} + \delta_{it}^{IM}\left(q_t^* - q_{it-1}\right) \qquad \text{(A.1)}$$

from which:

$$(q_{it} - q_{it-1})/q_{it-1} = \delta_{it}^{IN}(\gamma - 1) + \delta_{it}^{IM}(q_t^*/q_{it-1} - 1) \qquad \text{(A.2)}$$

In (Eq. A.2), average productivity growth rate turns out to be a function of the distance of country i from the technological frontier as represented by the average productivity of the technological leader of the moment

N. Rossi, *Reframing Italian Economic History, 1861–2021*, Palgrave Studies in Economic History, https://doi.org/10.1007/978-3-031-67271-2

(q_t^*). As soon as the technological gap is filled $(q_t^* = q_{it-1})$ and the technological frontier has plateaued, the average productivity growth of country i depends exclusively on its capacity for innovation and therefore on the fraction of business sectors engaged in innovating activities $(\delta_{it}^{IN}$; with δ_{it}^{IM} on the other hand indicating the fraction of business sectors engaged in adopting imported technologies) and on the productivity growth rate originating from innovation activity $(\gamma > 1)$ which we will suppose, for simplicity, to be invariant with respect both to time and to space (i.e. independent from the specific country in which innovation takes place).

Equation A.2 can be traced back to a Schumpeterian model of endogenous growth in which technological innovations (a) are the source of growth, (b) derive from entrepreneurial choices that are motivated in turn, by expectations of monopoly rents and (c) substitute the previous technologies, giving rise to creative destruction phenomena. Philippe Aghion et al. (2014) have analysed the Schumpeterian model of growth underlying (Eq. A.2) in detail and pointed out its multiple implications, for example, in terms of structure of the markets, of business demography or of policy. In the first case, to show the non-linear relationship between competition and innovation activities. In the second case to highlight the paths of the new businesses and to clarify that innovation activity is not attributable solely to them. In the third case, in order to suggest the adoption of policies that are capable of stimulating passive innovation (imitation) until the distance from the frontier is, in some sense, appreciable and of policies for innovation in the strict sense at the moment in which the frontier has been reached or is sufficiently close. Important for our purposes, in particular, is the fact that the same Schumpeterian growth model without too much trouble allows for the presence of different contexts relating, for example, to the dominant political or cultural conditions in which a specific economic activity takes place. Philippe Aghion et al. (2014, pp. 542–547) consider, for example, the case of contexts that are more or less democratic, that resemble situations of greater or lesser freedom of entry into the market by new businesses. However, what in their case is the political environment could, without much difficulty, be read as a relating to the body of beliefs, values and habits—the cultural stance, in other words—that can influence the system's rate of innovation and, as a consequence, its prospects for growth. And this, obviously, shows all the more how close the country is to the frontier (and, as a consequence, it is forced to leverage its innovative capacities) but is not irrelevant even when the frontier is far off. All of this, in turn, does not imply that the estimate of the parameters of (Eq. A.2) can throw light in an unequivocal manner on the role of the cultural aspects (compared, for example, to those of the institutional factors) but does not rule out that the former can play a role. It will be the task of other information to help us to understand their importance.

The estimate of the parameters δ_{it}^{IN} and δ_{it}^{IM}—which in theory could be allowed to vary in both time and space—would make it possible, for a given γ, to assess the relative weight in a given economy and at every point in time of the fraction of innovative entrepreneurs compared to the fraction of imitator entrepreneurs and therefore, implicitly, the degree of dynamism of an economy. It is legitimate to presume that the latter can be present however (and presumably prevail) in the follower economies and that, conversely, in the leader economy or economies the rhythm will be dictated virtually exclusively by the former.

Starting from the information set on which Table 3.1 is based—superimposable to a very great extent on the one used by Bojilov (2020)—and therefore for the period 1890–2021, we can first of all estimate the parameters of (Eq. A.2) under the hypothesis, undoubtedly restrictive on such a vast time span, that parameters δ_{it}^{IN} and δ_{it}^{IM} can vary from country to country but not over time (save of course testing the hypothesis itself at a later moment):

$$(q_{it} - q_{it-1})/q_{it-1} = \delta_i^{IN}(\gamma - 1) + \delta_i^{IM}\left(q_t^*/q_{it-1} - 1\right) + u_{it} \qquad \text{(A.3)}$$

In (Eq. A.3) for the zero mean error term (u_{it}) it will be assumed that

$$E(u_{it}u_{js}) = \sigma_{ij} \quad (t = s),$$
$$= 0 \quad (t \neq s) \qquad \text{(A.4)}$$

and that, therefore, the residuals are correlated in space (but not in time) and that, as a consequence, it would be possible for technological shocks that are not necessarily channelled by the proximity indicator with respect to the technological frontier to hit several countries at the same time. We expect, of course, the product $\delta_{it}^{IN}(\gamma - 1)$ to be positive and, for plausible values of γ, to be between zero and the long-term productivity growth rate in the technological leader country. We expect, in turn, δ_i^{IM} to be positive (and, presumably less than one). In theory, nothing prevents the sum of the two parameters of interest (δ_i^{IN} and δ_i^{IM}) from being greater than one (it being possible for spontaneous innovation and passive innovation to coexist side by side inside the same business sector).

Estimating $\delta_i^{IN}(\gamma - 1)$ and δ_i^{IM} requires, however, that the criteria for identifying the technological frontier be defined beforehand and, as a consequence, the technological leader as well. Given that the sample—for the details of which refer to Bergeaud et al. (2016)—covers the twentieth century entirely, and the nineteenth and twenty-first centuries only marginally, it comes completely naturally to imagine that this role be attributed to the United States. If this hypothesis were to be correct, we would expect, first of all, the parameter δ_i^{IM} in the case of the United States not to be far off zero when referred to potential technological leaders other than the US (e.g. the UK, France, Germany and Japan) and the data appear to confirm this. A simple test on the linear restrictions that rule out the presence of indicators of distance from the frontier calculated for countries other than the United States (Great Britain, Germany, France and Japan) in the estimate of (Eq. A.3) for the United States (shown in Table A.1) makes it possible, in fact, to accept the hypothesis that they are equal to zero and suggests that reference should be made exclusively to the United States when constructing the indicator of the distance from the frontier.

The system of equations (A.3)–(A.4) is a system of seemingly unrelated regression equations (SURE) for which the OLS (Ordinary Least Squares) estimator is known to be unbiased but inefficient. As a consequence, the estimates provided in Table A.1 are based on a GLS (generalised least squares) estimator. Table A.1 reports the results for the European countries that make up the aggregate that we have called Europe of 7 (EUR-7) and for the United Kingdom and Japan, as well as—as a reminder—for the United States. It is important to underline that there are quite a few outliers in the sample in correspondence with the First and Second World Wars, and with several domestic war events as well as with the two global financial crises that occurred during the twentieth and at the start of the twenty-first centuries. As a consequence, some specific dummies take account of the 1914–1918 and 1939–1946[1]

---

[1] In the case of Belgium, there was a clear leap in the series in 1920, such as to determine an increase in TFP close to 60% and which is difficult to attribute to the Antwerp Olympics held in the summer of the same year or to the return of the Eupen and Malmédy cantons to Belgium occurred in 1919. In the case of Greece account was taken of the appendix to the Second World War due to the civil war that followed it

Table A.1 Estimates of the system (Eq. A.3)–(Eq. A.4) under the hypothesis of time invariant parameters $\delta_i^{IN}(\gamma - 1)$ and δ_{it}^{IM} (1891–2021; GLS; standards errors in parentheses)

Country	$\delta_i^{IN}(\gamma - 1)$	δ_i^{IM}	R^2	DW^*	$CuSum^{**}$
Belgium	0.005 (0.003)	0.085 (0.010)	0.93	1.33	1.67
France	0.002 (0.005)	0.059 (0.008)	0.77	2.01	1.22
Greece	−0.004 (0.010)	0.035 (0.012)	0.65	1.92	0.75
Germany	0.017 (0.003)	0.073 (0.008)	0.85	1.94	1.78
Italy	−0.001 (0.003)	0.096 (0.010)	0.81	1.51	1.38
The Netherlands	0.023 (0.003)	0.079 (0.020)	0.85	1.61	1.65
Portugal	−0.004 (0.007)	0.032 (0.010)	0.30	2.15	0.64
United Kingdom	0.013 (0.002)	0.023 (0.008)	0.42	1.97	0.73
Spain	0.012 (0.003)	0.028 (0.008)	0.51	1.75	1.23
Japan	−0.010 (0.006)	0.042 (0.007)	0.74	2.40	0.73
*United States******	*0.15 (0.003)*	*−*******	*0.41*	*2.67*	*0.62*

Note (*) computed on the basis of the residuals deriving from the OLS estimates (in the specific case unbiased but inefficient); (**) computed on the basis of the residuals deriving from the OLS estimates (number of observations: 131); (***) OLS; (*** *) the hypothesis that the parameters relating to the proximity indicators (with respect to United Kingdom, France, Germany or Japan) are jointly zero is not refuted by the data ($F(4, 113) = 1.03$)

wartime events and of the 1929 and 2008 crises[2]: for the sake of simplicity their coefficients, even when significantly different from zero, are not

(1946–1949). In the case of Spain, the choice of neutrality during WWI prevented the same from having significant consequences for the country's economy while the same is not true of WWII. Significant consequences were also triggered by the civil war that started in 1936 and ended in 1939 so that, in the Spanish case, the dummies also take account of this aspect. Furthermore, what has been said about Spain in the Second World War also applies to Portugal, while the role Portugal played in the Spanish Civil War also suggested the extension to it of the treatment applied for Spain. In the case of Japan there were significant impacts on TFP growth rate from the Sino-Japanese conflict at the end of the nineteenth century (1894) but not from the Russo-Japanese one in the early twentieth century (1904–1905). Finally, the impact of the pandemic, in 2020, seems evident only in some countries, that is Italy, the Netherlands and the United Kingdom.

[2] In the first case the impact of the Great Depression manifested itself to various extents from country to country between 1930 and 1931. In the second case, only in the year 2009 and not in all the countries.

recorded in Table A.1.[3] Last but not least, the simplified representation of the economy underlying (Eq. A.3) rests on the hypothesis that there were no obstacles to the technological transfer other than those implicit in the incentives structure prevailing at any given moment in the economy itself. This is certainly not true in the Italian case and in the middle of the 1930s, a period that was marked by provisions of the League of Nations, (Toniolo, 1980, pp. 269–299). The so-called "unfair sanctions" were adopted—as we know—around the end of 1935 and then suspended in the course of 1936. In this case too, a specific dummy (regarding 1936) takes account of the phenomenon.

Dummies undoubtedly play an important part of the work, but still it is difficult not to consider interesting the explanatory ability of an indisputably over-simplified representation of the reality such as the one described by (Eq. A.3). At the same time, the Breusch and Pagan test of the hypothesis $\sigma_{ij} = 0 (\forall i \neq j)$ hints at a non-zero correlation coefficients for some residuals belonging to different countries for given $t(\chi^2(45) = 188.6)$ which, in turn, confirms the appropriateness of the GSL estimator. A deeper analysis suggests that non-zero correlation coefficients (although small: between 0.3 and 0.4) can be observed for contiguous countries (France and Italy, France and Belgium, Belgium and the Netherlands or Spain and Portugal) or for ones notoriously linked by historical relationships (UK and Portugal) indicating technological links of some importance but of a local nature.[4] Last but not least, in the estimate of (Eq. A.3) for countries other than the United States, the hypothesis of endogeneity of the proximity index (with respect to the US) may be

---

[3] The estimates in Table A.1 were preceded by the customary valuation of the order of integration of the variables in (Eq. A.3). The TFP growth rates appear to be I(0), beyond every reasonable doubt and in all the countries considered (whether a deterministic trend is present or not). The same cannot be said for the index measuring the distance of individual countries from the technological frontier for which, instead, the evidence goes, to a large extent, in the opposite direction. In principle, the joint presence of a stationary dependent variable and of a non-stationary regressor—this would seem to be the case with Italy, for example—should be read as an outright indicator of misspecification (and this because it cannot be hypothesised that a variable I(0) reflects the non-stationary evolutions of variables I(1)). As we will see below the source of the incorrect specification will be identified in the time-variability of the model's parameters.

[4] Reference is made in the text only to the significant correlation coefficients after Šidàk's correction.

refuted in the seemingly unrelated regressions system as a whole (on the basis of the test of Durbin, Wu and Hausman: $F(10, 1139)$: 1.04).

The usual test of the stability of the coefficients based on the cumulative sum of the squares of the residuals (computed from the unbiased OLS estimates) would make it possible—with the usual levels of confidence— not to reject the hypothesis of $\delta_{it}^{IN}(\gamma - 1)$ and δ_{it}^{IM} being time-invariant.[5] At the same time, the known reduced power of the tests based on the cumulative sum of the square of the residuals as well as the visual inspection of the performance of the same magnitude leaves more than a doubt regarding the stability of the coefficients of the system (Eq. A.3)– (Eq. A.4). And this, in particular, is true in some cases including, for example, Italy as well as Belgium, Germany and the Netherlands. There are reasons, as we know, to presume that the propensity for innovation (and therefore the fraction of business sectors engaged in the innovation activity) is the expression of the capacity and willingness of the country to generate spontaneous innovation and of the presence of a series of enabling factors including institutional ones. These elements are all susceptible to variations of various degree of importance over time and, as we have seen, likely to be present at least in some of the countries analysed. Nor can we exclude that it is the terms $(\gamma - 1)$ and δ_{it}^{IM} that vary over time (perhaps like or more than in space).[6]

To start with, some preliminary evidence in this respect was derived from the rolling estimate of (Eq. A.3) and from the consequent rolling estimates of the parameters $\delta_{it}^{IN}(\gamma - 1)$ and δ_{it}^{IM}.[7] These estimates quite

---

[5] The coefficient stability test could also have greater meaning than the one just recalled in the sense of indicating not only the variability of the coefficients with time but also a more general misspecification of (Eq. A.3) for the specific individual countries. From this standpoint the overall result appears quite comforting.

[6] Taking seriously the hypothesis of a time-varying $(\gamma - 1)$ term, the average annual productivity growth rate $(\gamma - 1)$ has been approximated by the trend component of the TFP growth rate of the technological leader $(\gamma^* - 1)$ as derived from the application of the Hodrick-Prescott filter. The contribution of the term specified in this way appears significantly different from zero only in the case of the Netherlands, leaving the message contained in the estimates practically unchanged compared to what has been discussed in the text. In particular, in the case of Italy, the estimate of the parameter δ_t^{IN} is never significantly different from zero.

[7] For clarity, the estimates in question derive from samples smaller (40 observations) than the full sample (131 observations), the start date of which runs from the first date available (1891) onwards, up to the point at which the ending date is that of the last available observation (2021). It is hardly necessary to point out that letting some

clearly indicated how the source of variability is virtually entirely contained in the term $\delta_{it}^{IN}(\gamma - 1)$, the quota of imitating enterprises (δ_{it}^{IM}) being relatively time-invariant. Since $\delta_{it}^{IN}(\gamma - 1)$ appears in more than one case to change not only in space but, however gradually, also in time, a supplementary investigation was deemed appropriate—for some if not all the countries considered—allowing (Eq. A.3) to be rewritten as follows:

$$(q_{it} - q_{it-1})/q_{it-1} = \beta_{0i} + \beta_{1it} + \delta_i^{IM}(q_t^*/q_{it-1} - 1) + u_{it} \qquad (A.5)$$

(where $\beta_{0i} + \beta_{1it} = \delta_i^{IN}(\gamma - 1)$), letting the time-varying parameter β_{1it} be described by a simple AR(1) process:

$$\beta_{1it} = \rho_i \beta_{1it-1} + \epsilon_{it} \qquad (A.6)$$

and where, swapping efficiency with simplicity, we will hypothesise that the error terms are normally distributed with mean zero and variances σ^u and σ^ε with $E(u_{it}u_{js}) = 0$ ($\forall t \neq s$ and $\forall i \neq j$), $E(\varepsilon_{it}\varepsilon_{js}) = 0$ ($\forall t \neq s$ and $\forall i \neq j$) and $E(\varepsilon_{it}u_{js}) = 0$ ($\forall t, s$ and $\forall i, j$).

The representation (Eq. A.5)–(Eq. A.6) is well-known as the state-space representation (Eq. A.5) being the observation equation and (Eq. A.6) being the state equation). Estimates of the parameter β_{1it} are usually—but not necessarily—arrived at through the so-called Kalman filter whose recursive application requires knowledge of the initial values of the latent variable and of the variances of the error terms in (Eq. A.5) and (Eq. A.6). The latter usually end up being ML (maximum likelihood) estimates (over the full entire sample).

Before passing to the estimates, it is useful to underline one important point. The nature of the Kalman filter is fully recursive and we would expect ML estimates over the full sample (allowing the recursive calculation of the expected value of the state variable) to be the same as the least squares estimates. It would be a legitimate expectation if two further hypotheses—implicit in the state-space representation—were effectively tenable: the linearity of the representation itself and the normality of

---

parameters change continuously through time is obviously to be preferred with respect to the more usual introduction of dummy variables intended to shift the values of individual coefficients upwards or downwards at a given point in time. Apart from being inevitably arbitrary, structural breaks uneasily catch parameters (presumably) varying gradually over time. It is fairly evident that the bent for innovation does not emerge in the space of a single night, nor does it evaporate all of a sudden.

Table A.2 Estimate of the parameters of the system (Eq. A.5)–(Eq. A.6) under the hypothesis of time-invariant δ_{it}^{IM} (1891–2021; QML; standards errors in parentheses)

Country	β_{0i}	δ_i^{IM}	ρ_i	ΔAIC^*	ΔBIC^*
Belgium	−0.017 (0.011)	0.210 (0.016)	0.946 (0.030)	−71.43	−62.80
France	−0.004 (0.010)	0.070 (0.017)	0.925 (0.067)	−0.09	8.54
Germany	0.017 (0.011)	0.090 (0.029)	0.986 (0.033)	−0.98	7.65
Italy	−0.010 (0.011)	0.126 (0.041)	0.940 (0.030)	−15.54	−6.92
The Netherlands	0.044 (0.035)	0.509 (0.115)	0.976 (0.020)	−70.41	−61.79
United Kingdom	0.013 (0.002)	0.019 (0.008)	0.847 (0.089)	4.00	9.75
Spain	0.011 (0.005)	0.028 (0.017)	0.881 (0.094)	1.75	10.38

Note (*) the columns respectively indicate the differences between the Akaike (or the Schwartz) information criterion based on the estimates given in Table A.2 and the corresponding criterion based on the OLS estimates

residuals. Were it not so, we would have to expect significant differences between the two estimates but the differences themselves would constitute quite evident indications of misspecification of the basic relationships not only and not so much in the sense of a temporal variability of a given parameter but very probably also in the sense of the presence of non-linearity in the relationships themselves (given also the fact that the QML estimator used in Table A.2—which shows, in fact, the results of the estimate of the system (Eq. A.5)–(Eq. A.6)—does not rest on the normality hypothesis).

The estimation of the parameters of state-space models (being the outcome of an optimisation process and so inevitably conditioned to a specific initial parameter set) is notoriously demanding and often affected by convergence problems. In our case this theme seems to pose itself, in particular, in the case of Greece while in the case of Portugal and Japan—as already suggested by the test for parameter stability shown in Table A.1—the parameter $\delta_{it}^{IN}(\gamma - 1)$ seems to deviate randomly over time with respect to a constant. For all the other cases (Belgium, France, Germany, Italy, the Netherlands, United Kingdom and Spain), Table A.2 shows the estimates of the parameters of the state-space representation (Eq. A.5)–(Eq. A.6). Notice that—with the eye-catching exception of

Belgium and, above all, the Netherlands—all δ_{it}^{IM} are found to be reasonably close to the corresponding OLS estimates. In all cases the parameter ρ_i is found to be close to one and significantly different from zero while the two most common criteria for model comparison confirm what has already been hypothesised regarding the prevalence of the state-space representation (notably, in the cases of Belgium, Germany, Italy and the Netherlands, that is in the case where parameter instability was rather clearly detected).

REFERENCES

Acemoglu, D., Aghion, P., & Zilibotti, F. (2006). Distance to Frontier, Selection, and Economic Growth. *Journal of the European Economic Association, 4*(1), 37–74.

Aghion, P., Akcigit, U., & Howitt, P. (2014). What Do We Learn from Schumpeterian Growth Theory? In P. Aghion & S. Durlauf (Eds.), *Handbook of Economic Growth* (Vol. 2, pp. 515–563). Elsevier.

Bergeaud, A., Cette, G., & Lecat, R. (2016). Productivity Trends in Advanced Countries Between 1890 and 2012. *Review of Income and Wealth, 62*(3), 420–444.

Bojilov, R. (2020). Sources of Indigenous Innovation and Channels of Its Transmission Across Countries. In E. Phelps, R. Bojilov, H.Teck Hoon, & G. Zoega, *Dynamism* (pp. 48–67). Harvard University Press.

Toniolo, G. (1980). *L'economia dell'Italia fascista*. Laterza.

APPENDIX B: BUSINESS DEMOGRAPHY[8]

The Chambers of Commerce Registers

Firm entry and exit rates discussed in Chapter 3 are based on the records of the *Camere di Commercio, Industria, Artigianato e Agricoltura* (Chambers of Commerce, Industry, Crafts and Agriculture, CCIAA) and in particular on the contents of the so-called *Registro delle Imprese* (Business Register; retrieved March 18, 2024, www.registroimprese.it). Already envisaged by the 1942 Civil Code (art. 2188), the Business Register was concretely implemented by Act 580 of 29 December 1993, and became operational with presidential decree D.P.R. n. 581/1995. Firms with head offices in Italy are obliged to register in the Business Register. The

---

[8] With Stefano Chianese (Household Budget Survey, Rome Tor Vergata University).

Register collects information concerning the legal form, the economic activity sector and the head office in Italian territory, as well as all the deeds concerning the company business. The Register constitutes the primary source of certification of the firms' articles of association. It is kept by the CCIAAs located in (almost) all the Italian Provinces and is regularly updated.

The *Registro delle Società* (Company Register), originally kept in the Court Clerks' Offices, and the *Registro delle Ditte* (Firm Register) lodged in the Chambers of Commerce flowed into the Business Register. Before 1942 the two registers, of the Companies and of the Firms, constituted the two founding systems of registration of the State's commercial records system. The first—the Company Register—was envisaged by the 1882 Code of Commerce (that had replaced the 1865 Code of Commerce with which the provisions of the Code of Commerce of the Kingdom of Sardinia were extended to the territory of unified Italy). The second on the other hand—the Firm Register—was established by Act n. 121 of 20 March 1910 on the reorganisation of the Chambers of Commerce. The Firm Register was supposed to represent an organic and complete system of legal publicity of all the commercial businesses (other than the very small ones) carried out as sole-trader ones or not. No obligation was imposed on agricultural business either as their publicity was indirectly guaranteed by the transcriptions in the property registries of the lands of the farming businesses.

The information contained in the Business Register regarding the birth and death of the enterprises are available online—generally accompanied by a press release that comments on their performance over time— at quarterly intervals in the Movimprese records starting from the 1st quarter of 1995 (retrieved March 18, 2024, https://www.infocamere. it/movimprese) and are updated regularly by the IT company of the CCIAAs (*InfoCamere*) which is entrusted with the computerised management of the CCIAA system. The same information is also available, again from the Movimprese records, on paper support and at half-yearly intervals for the years 1982–1994, while as regards the earlier periods it is necessary to refer to the paper registers (in the case of both Firms and Companies) that can be sourced—in whole or in part—in the historical archives of the CCIAA and recalled in the *Guida agli archivi storici delle Camere di Commercio Italiane* ("A Guide to the Historical Archives of the Italian Chambers of Commerce", 1996).

The 1982–2021 Archive

The Movimprese archive aggregates the elementary information by province, business sector (with reference from time to time to the most recent Ateco classification), legal form of the company (joint stock company, partnership, sole proprietorship and other forms) and by type of information (stocks such as registered businesses, flows such as active, enrolled or ceased businesses and finally variations, that is changes in the existing set of information). As is obvious, a multi-decade reconstruction of the information on the deaths and births of companies makes it necessary to carefully tackle a series of problems linked, in particular, to the consistency of the information itself over time. In fact, some of the indicators contextually use flow and stock information which makes the consistency of the data even more important. The most significant problems tackled for this purpose are briefly reviewed in what follows and thoroughly discussed in Rossi (2024, Appendix B).[9]

Let us start with the territorial scope of the available information. Over time, the Chamber system had quite a few ups and downs. Shortly after unification Act n. 680 of 6 July 1862 defined a unitary structure for the Chambers of Commerce, extending them over the entire newborn Kingdom of Italy, ratifying their electivity and financial autonomy and limiting government interference to the approval of the financial statements and the winding up of the Chambers themselves. On that date 26 Chamber of commerce were counted. At a distance of about half a century—with Act n. 121 of 20 March 1910—the Chambers assumed the name of Chambers of Commerce, Industry, Crafts and Agriculture, saw their attributions extended but, above all, were given the ability to carry out the certification activity completely thanks to the listing obligation on the firms in their districts, which until then had been optional. 77 Chambers of Commerce and Industry were counted on the date of the reform.

The 1910 reform prepared the ground for the transformation of the Chambers into public bodies which formally became operational with the royal decree law n. 750 of 8 May 1924 (the so-called Corbino act). The next step—due to Act n. 731 of 18 April 1926, was the complete

---

[9] Among these is the discrepancy between the number of companies listed in the quarterly and annual databases and the cessations mentioned in the press releases. Below we will refer in any case to the information contained in the databases.

integration of the chamber system into the state system by means of the suppression of the Chamber of Commerce and Industry and the establishment of the Provincial Councils of the Economy (from 1931, Provincial Councils of the Corporative Economy and, from 1937, the Provincial Councils of the Corporations) in all the provinces of the Kingdom (which took the number of Chamber organisation present to more than 80). Following the liberation of Italy, D.LG.LGT. n. 315 of 21 September 1944 then suppressed the Provincial Councils of Corporations and replaced them in every province with the Chamber of Commerce, Industry and Agriculture (with the functions and powers of the suppressed Councils). Later—with Act n. 792 of 26 September 1966, the name of the Chambers was extended to include Crafts as is still the case today.

Following restructuring with Act n. 580 of 29 December 1993, the Chambers became "autonomous bodies under public law" generally with registered offices in every provincial capital. They were entrusted with regulating access to and the carrying out of economic activities by means of the management of the registers, as well as a series of promotional activities. Following the reform of Title V of the Constitution, lawmakers returned to the subject with Legislative Decree n. 23 of 15 February 2010—taking a further step in the direction already begun in 1993, defining the Chambers as public bodies provided with functional autonomy and expressly recalling the subsidiarity principle laid down in art. 118 of the Constitution. Unlike what happened in the past, it was laid down on that occasion that the establishment of new Chambers did not follow the establishment of new Provinces but only became possible where there was an adequate entrepreneurial fabric (and provided that the economic-financial equilibrium of the body be guaranteed). The decision to intervene on the breakdown of the Chamber system was fully expressed, finally, just a few years later with Leg. Decree n. 219 of 25 November 2016, and the consequent redetermination of the territorial divisions, with the establishment of new Chambers of Commerce and with the suppression of those interested by the unification and rationalisation process. As a result, the number of Chambers fell from 105 to 60 following voluntary mergers or on the orders of the Ministry for Economic Development.

As can be seen, over time, the changes made to the responsibilities and funding procedures and to the very nature of the Chambers were joined by changes—not always negligible—to the territories of reference of the various authorities, often superimposed on which was the establishment or, much more rarely, the suppression of provincial bodies. To be precise, the, 1982–2017 period saw the creation (with establishment of the CCIAA at the same time) of some new 8 provinces. At the level of the single provinces, the events mentioned are a source of distortions in the information contained in the Company Registers that are by no means minor because with the establishment of a new province the enterprises already registered in the Chamber of Commerce of the "mother province" were cancelled from it before being registered again in the Chamber of Commerce of "the child province". And this, as can be guessed, can considerably influence the birth and death rate of each individual province in the year of establishment (even if it has no effects at regional level or even less so at the national one). Such problems, therefore, are not relevant for the purposes of this work whose level of aggregation is such that they have no influence.

Let us now revert to the sector of economic activity accounted for by the available information set. The information available starting from 1982 is aggregated with reference to the different ATECO classifications that are prevalent from time to time. For the purposes of the present work, a 16-sector aggregation scheme was devised, intended to guarantee a reasonable homogeneity in the observations, constructed while maintaining the validity of the ATECO 2007 classification as the point of reference. At the selected level of aggregation, the correspondence between the items in the various ATECO classifications is reasonably high but some aggregations have been necessary. In particular, the new aggregation scheme envisages a single item referring to the supplies of energy and water while these two elements are separate in ATECO 2007. Another significant difference regards the "Post and telecommunications" item that, to preserve the maximum degree of homogeneity with the ATECO 2007 classification, has been placed inside the "Information" item and not just in the specific "Telecommunications" one. Finally, the last substantial aggregation regards a series of items that can be referred to "Services to the person, to families and companies" that have been aggregated in a single category defined as Other Services.

Unfortunately, for the years 1982–1984, the quality of the information does not permit a sectoral aggregation at the above level of detail and makes it necessary to pass from the previously mentioned 16 sectors to just 8 macro-sectors identifiable as follows with reference to ATECO 2007: Agriculture (A), Manufacturing (B + C), Supplies (D +

E), Building (F), Commerce (G), Transport (H), Finance (K), and Other services (I + J + M + N + P + Q + L + O + R + S + T + U). As we will see below, moreover, the problems present in the 1982–1984 triennium are such as to advise against its use.

It should be observed, finally, that as for the years prior to 1982, the elementary data being available, the single pieces of information have been attributed to the individual macro-sectors, making reference to the activity indicated at the moment of registration of the enterprise.

We finally revert to the nature of the information provided by the available data. The body of information just described is—as has been said—anything but problem-free from other points of view too. Beginning with the simplest, during the entire 1982–1990 period the aggregated information between types of businesses does not correspond to the information relating to the individual items. In particular, no information is provided on the so-called Other forms type. This makes it impossible to perform a time-based comparison (at least for the 1982–1990 period) of the information broken down according to legal form, but does not affect the comparison over time at aggregated level.

In the years after 1990, the relationship between flows and stock turns out not to be always exactly verified and therefore the stock for the period $t - 1$, calculated starting from the information available in year t, does not necessarily coincide with the stock observed in year $t - 1$. On average in the 1991–2021 period—a period for which this type of comparison is possible—there are annual discrepancies amounting to about 0.02% and attributable to the fact that if the registrations and cancellations only record the opening or effective closure of new businesses, the registrations also reflect other types of variations (e.g. changes of activity or legal nature). However, the scale of these discrepancies is not such as to prevent the reconstruction of the stocks of businesses registered for the years before 1991 too, starting from the flows for the individual years and from the opening stock.

In a significant number of cases, on the other hand, we found ourselves looking at an information set clearly affected by errors, distorted for a number of reasons or, more simply, by missing data. Belonging to the first category is the case in the 1995–1996 biennium of the information relating only to sole traders in the province of Perugia that show registrations and cessations higher than the stock of registrations at the end of the same year. In this case, the *Warnings* relating to the same year speak of "distortions deriving from putting the records online".

To the second category belongs what can be considered to be the main problem in the dataset under discussion. This is linked to the consequences of the succession over time of regulatory provisions, some of which already recalled above, which in some cases led to changes in the reference population—extending, for example, the number of business types subject to the compulsory registration—and thereby giving rise to discontinuities so that the temporal series may not always be fully legible.

This is what happened, for example, following implementation of art. 8 of the aforesaid Act n. 580 of 29 December 1993 (that established the Company Registry Office which, already in operation from 19 February 1996 became fully operational from 27 January 1997). Among the other novelties at legal level, the rule mentioned envisaged mandatory registration for all those who exercise businesses activities, including some who had previously been exempt such as simple companies, small business operators, farm business operators and farmers. From the quantitative point of view, the scale of the regulatory innovation appears to be very significant. At the same time, it seems quite circumscribed in that it refers virtually entirely to sole traders in the "Agriculture, forestry and fishing". Since, as already discussed, for the sake of international comparison we will focus on enterprises other than sole proprietorship, we will be able to by-pass the problem to a very large extent.

Finally, in the period 1982–1991 information gaps are recorded for some provinces and/or regions.[10] Overall, the integrations of the information base required by the problems just mentioned refer to a relatively limited share of the information available in the nineties and in much of the second half of the 1980s but quite significant starting from 1986 backwards. Out of an annual total of 27 thousand elementary observations (i.e. referring to all provinces, to all sectors, to all legal forms and to all registration types), the share of observations subject to correction and/or integration would amount in the 1992–1997 period to little more than 1.5% (with an incidence in terms of overall registrations of 20%). This would rise to slightly more than 3% (about 21% in terms of registrations) up to 1988 and then pass 6% in 1987 (22% in registration terms) and rise further in the five-year period to over 21% in 1982 (43% in terms of registrations). Starting from 1986 the list of missing provinces includes significant ones: Naples in Southern Italy, Rome in

---

[10] A detailed list is provided by Rossi (2024, Appendix B).

Central Italy and Milan in Northern Italy. It therefore appeared reasonable—rather than proceed with the outright exclusion of the affected provinces, sectors or types (thereby preventing meaningful time comparisons)—to proceed, instead, by using attribution techniques but limiting the attribution activity to the 1987–1997 period.

At the same time, completely neglecting all the information relating to the 1982–1986 five-year period (for much of which, as we have seen, there is also a problem of consistency of the sectoral classifications) would certainly be an inefficient solution. In fact, it is a five-year period in which information is available for over 70% of the provinces, the trend for which, if examined in the 1987–2021 period, presents a very high degree of correlation with the overall trend for the individual territorial divisions or of Italy as a whole.[11] In the text, therefore, the data for the whole period (1983–2021) is considered but readers should take account of the fact that, while the data relating to the 1987–2021 period are the data drawn from the Movimprese records, integrated and/or corrected as follows, the data for the 1983–1986 five-year period—when used and usable—are instead estimates based on the partial information available for the same five-year period.[12]

Given the above, the three types of problems mentioned above were tackled in a methodologically uniform manner starting from the bottom, i.e. first of all tackling the theme of integrating the sample in the case of information gaps or of correcting it if the information was affected by errors at individual province level or at that of the individual production sector and proceeding then to tackle any discontinuities induced by normative innovations. In all cases of missing or corrupt information, the attribution or correction of the elementary information was obtained applying a deterministic version of the "hot deck" method, i.e. attributing to the missing or distorted information the value inferable from similar or "kindred" elementary information units.

---

[11] To be precise, whatever indicator is employed, the degree of correlation oscillates at territorial level between 0.81 for Central Italy and 0.99 for North-east Italy, while, at the production sector level, it passes from 0.87 for services to 0.94 for industry.

[12] The statement refers to the aggregate. The information is sometimes simply unusable at individual province level. In the case of Turin, the data are available right from 1983 and therefore the problem does not arise. But in the case of Milan and of Rome, the relevant information is only available respectively from 1985 and from 1986 and this because during the "launch" stage of the Movimprese archive the registration of new businesses tends to reflect the existing stocks of the same.

Finally, but no less important is the fact that it is only since 1991 that the registered companies (i.e. those present in the records and which have not ceased, whether active or not) are distinguished from the active companies (i.e. registered and carrying out activities and for which no ongoing winding-up procedures are recorded). Before that date—and therefore from 1982 to 1990—the information on paper distinguishes between the companies, registered and operating (i.e. presumably active), the number of businesses registered being easily calculable recursively, moreover (given that the companies registered at the end of a given year are given by the sum of the new registrations less the cessations in the same year plus the businesses registered at the end of the previous year). The distinction between registered and active (or operational) enterprises on the other hand is not available for the information deducible from the historical archives, so that in the reconstruction of the company birth/ death information starting from 1910 and up until 1981, the only option for us was to refer to the simplest distinction between registered, listed and ceased.

The degree of approximation implicit in the decision to focus on the registered (more than on the active) business can be assessed by referring to the period in which both the registered and the active companies are recorded (i.e. to the years 1991–2021). Overall, in this period, the activity rates (active enterprises/registered enterprises) tend to reveal variations that are limited over time but not in space or between business sectors. On aggregate, in the period mentioned, the activity rates vary, in fact, between 84 and 89%, settling on average close to 86%, with a barely perceptible downward trend. Until 2007 the activity rates in central Italy tend to fall below the corresponding rates for northern Italy even by 10 percentage points, aligning themselves with the latter in the decade afterwards. Not dissimilar are the activity rates at sectoral level, with values close to 99% in agriculture and not far off 88% in industry in the average for the period.[13]

---

[13] For clarity, the database that is regularly updated by the OECD (retrieved March 18, 2024, https://www.oecd-ilibrary.org/industry-and-services/entrepreneurship-at-a-gla nce_22266941) makes reference, for example, to the active enterprises but covers a timespan that is much more limited than the one referred to in this Appendix. Published starting from 2011, *Entrepreneurship at a Glance* contains a broad range of information on entrepreneurial dynamism but only dating from 2005. The ASIA statistical register on which ISTAT bases its own observations on business demographics (retrieved March

In reality, the apparent variability in the rates virtually entirely derives from a single category: the so-called Unclassified activities that show extremely low activity rates, amounting on average to little over 11% during the 1991–2020 period. In quantitative terms, the "Unclassified activities" play a role that is anything but marginal. With reference to the 1991–2021, they represent on average about 6% of the companies registered but only less than 1% of the active companies and are, as a consequence, responsible to a great extent for the level and evolution of the activity rate at aggregate level. If reference is made to the most recent *Guida all'utilizzo di ATECO* ("Ateco User Guide", 2016),[14] the non-classification of some activities at the moment of registration derives from the difficulty in tracing from the content of the registration itself to one of the activity sectors identified by ATECO codes. This in turn stems from the presence of quite a lot of cases in which an enterprise is established "in the dark", i.e. before the sector of activities of interest is identified. It should be noted that the growth of the phenomenon up to the middle of the first decade of the century seems in some way to be connected to the growing presence of immigrant enterprises. On aggregate, when the "Unclassified activities" are removed, the activity rates appear to oscillate around 90% without any particular trend. At territorial level, the territorial division that is particularly interested by the phenomenon of the "Unclassified activities" seems to be Central Italy starting from the nineties. Net of the component under discussion, the activity rates of the central macro-region from the start of the current century are not, then, so different from those of other divisions.

The elementary information for the period 1987–2021 according to province, production sector and legal form of the enterprise—integrated and/or corrected as just described, in order to allow reading over time—is freely accessible (and downloadable in Excel form, by single year and in homogeneous form) in https://dinamismo.brunoleoni.com/ (retrieved March 18, 2024).

18, 2024, https://www.istat.it/it/archivio/219823) also make reference to the active companies but does not cover the years before 1996.

[14] https://ebiblio.istat.it/digibib/Metodi%20e%20norme/Guida%20utilizzo%20nuova%20ateco%202007.pdf (retrieved March 18, 2024).

The Historical Archives (1911–1981)

In general, it would be possible to extend the information available starting from 1982, having recourse to the CCIAA Historical Archives and in particular to the Firm Register (in existence as from 1911) and Company Registers (present since unification). A database with these characteristics would of course constitute a source of information of great importance and permit, among other things, very precise reconstructions at territorial level of the country's entrepreneurial demography too.

This would be a very ambitious objective but, unfortunately, far from easily achievable in many ways. As can clearly be seen from the aforesaid "Guide to the historical archives of the Italian Chambers of Commerce" (1996), in quite a few cases the historical archives of the Chambers include gaps and shortcomings that can be attributable to natural events (earthquakes, floods, fires, ...) or human ones (wars) or, more banally, human carelessness. If, therefore, the reconstruction of the information universe simply appears impossible, it is certainly possible however to select a sample among the 105 Italian provinces that is hopefully a significant one and capable of leading to reasonably reliable conclusions. As an initial approximation, therefore, attention was concentrated on 10 provincial capitals (Turin, Milan, Venice, Bologna, Florence, Ancona, Rome, Naples, Bari and Palermo) that were presumably capable of reliably representing the main enterprise birth/death trends over the entire Italian territory (without prejudice, however, to the fact that the peculiar nature of Italian entrepreneurship—widespread and often anything but confined to the large metropolitan areas—would also impose a broadening of the investigation beyond the first sample). Following an initial investigation, the examination then concentrated only on the Historical Archives of the CCIAAs of Ancona, Milan, Rome and Turin.

The basic objective—it is well to reiterate it—is not therefore to perform a complete census but rather the construction of a sample that is representative of the underlying population, and capable of offering a reliable indication as regards the main dynamics of enterprise birth-deaths. From this standpoint it is appropriate to keep the following in mind. With reference to the period, 1987–2021, and to the main indicators of enterprise births and deaths (birth rate, death rate, net turnover and gross turnover) the correlations between the sample composed of the four three provinces of Ancona, Milan, Rome and Turin and the national aggregate are rather high and oscillate between 91% (births) and 71% (deaths). What is even more important is that there does not seem to be evidence of particularly high variations in the same correlations over time.

Both the Firm Register and the Company Register contain a much broader range of information than the one needed to compute business birth and death rates. However, the quantitative dimension makes it impossible to register all the data contained in the registers. On their own the Firm Registers of Ancona, Milan, Turin and Rome, for the 1911–1981 period contain about two million registrations. For the purposes of the research here and given the budget constraint, it was therefore decided to reduce the information to consider to a minimum in order to streamline the data collection procedure, restricting the field exclusively to information of use for backdating the series already available or reconstructed for the 1983–2021 period. The data collected, therefore are as follows: registration number, year of registration and of establishment, company type, activity carried out and year of cessation.

This said, it is possible to examine the content of the four Archives that are the subject of investigation whose records were digitalised and analysed between 2016 and 2022 (including a two-years stop because of the pandemic emergency). The historical archive of the Chamber of Commerce of Ancona ("Guide to the historical archives of the Chambers of Commerce", 1996, pp. 7–8) preserves both the Register of Firms and the Register of Companies (with deficiencies linked to war events). At the instigation of the Aristide Merloni Foundation and thanks to the kind and effective collaboration of the head of the Archive, an agreement was defined to obtain the photographic digitisation of the Company Register and free access to all the material relating to the Company Register. The digitisation of the registers and the subsequent transcription of the information were started in autumn 2021 and completed in summer 2023. It was possible to reconstruct the main indicators of business births and deaths for the period 1925–1972.

The Historical Archive of the CCIAA of Milan ("Guide to the historical archives of the Chambers of Commerce", 1996, pp. 73–77) conserves both the Firm Register and the Company Register (with gaps that can be linked to wartime or natural events). It proved possible to reconstruct—between the last week of 2017 and the autumn 2022—both entry and exit indicators for the years 1911–1972. It should be noted that from the standpoint of territorial jurisdiction, up until act no. 731 of

18 April 1926, the Milan Chamber cohabited with the Lodi Chamber (even though the corresponding province had already been suppressed in 1859).

The Historical Archive of the CCIAA of Rome ("Guide to the historical archives of the Chambers of Commerce", 1996, pp. 100–105) conserves both the Company Register and the Firm Register (with gaps that can be linked to both natural and wartime events). The Historical Archive does not include—because of a flood—the Firm Register for the years between 1925 and 1947. What's more, even though summaries for those same years are available in secondary registers they did not make it possible to reconstruct the main trends. It was possible therefore to reconstruct the main business entry and exit indicators for the 1911–1924 and 1948–1960 periods. From the standpoint of territorial jurisdiction, up until Act n. 731 of 18 April 1926, the Rome Chamber was responsible for the districts of Rome, Frosinone, Velletri and Viterbo and cohabited with the Chamber of Civitavecchia that was responsible for the district of that name. In 1923, the Chamber's jurisdiction was extended to include Rieti but in the years between 1927 and 1934 the concrete implementation of Act n. 731 of 18 April 1926 led to the establishment of the Provincial Councils of the Economy in all the provinces of Lazio and, as a consequence, reduced the competence of the Rome Chamber exclusively to the province of that name.

The Historical Archive of the CCIAA of Turin ("Guide to the historical archives of the Chambers of Commerce", 1996, pp. 115–117) conserves both the Firm Register and the Company Register (with gaps that can be linked to natural and wartime events). It proved possible to reconstruct the main company birth and death indicators for the 1911–1980 period. From the standpoint of territorial jurisdictions, until 1899 the Turin Chamber remained responsible for the provinces of Turin and Novara (also corresponding to the present-day provinces of Aosta and Vercelli). Starting from 1899, with the establishment of the Chamber of Novara, the Turin Chamber's competence was reduced accordingly. Following Act n. 731 of 18 April 1926, the districts of Biella and Vercelli were brought back under the Turin Chamber. The competence of the Turin Chamber was reduced in 1945, moreover, following the establishment of the province of Aosta and the associated Provincial Council of the Economy.

Common to three of the above four information sets is the discontinuity implied by the regulatory intervention in 1926 (with Act n. 731 of

18 April 1926) which—as has already been recalled—led to the suppression of the Chambers of Commerce and Industry and the establishment of the Provincial Councils of the Economy in all the provinces of the Kingdom. The latter were charged with recording the reports of the establishment and cessation of undertakings, excluding the agricultural businesses which were subject to farm income tax only, and reiterated its obligatory nature (art. 28). Compared to Act n. 76 of 20 March 1910, the new provisions entailed, moreover, several significant innovations. As we have already observed, first of all the territorial areas of competence of the single Chambers were revised. Then (art. 28) the deadline by which entrepreneurs were required to report the establishment was revised and shortened (from the 60 days of the 1910 rules to 15 days under the new rules) and the fine envisaged in the event of omission or late registration was reviewed accordingly (art. 31): from 5 to 200 lire of 1910 (between 20 and 820 euro circa today) to 20 to 800 lire in 1926 (between 15 and 610 euro circa today). Finally, a new and significant provision envisaged (art. 30) that "in every written contract entered into in the interest of a firm and in every deed, letter, publication or announcement that refers to it a clear indication [should] be given" both of the Chamber of reference and of the number of registration, on pain of a fine of 500 lire (about 380 euros today).

It is legitimate to presume that the combined mentioned provisions and the *ex officio* registrations by the Chambers in the event of failure to report by the firms had led to an anomalous increase of new registrations in the first year of application of the law (and—it cannot be excluded—also in the preceding two years given that the law in question was preceded by royal decree law n. 750 of 8 May 1924, promptly replaced by the 1926 act). This entails several orders of problems from the viewpoint of retrospective reconstruction of the data which, after careful examination, were deemed to be hardly solvable since the regulatory 1924–1926 changes were in fact such as to transform an obligation without sanctions into a binding rule as regards reporting the establishment, modification or cessation of the firm, thereby as a consequence rendering the previous information unreliable. This solution—while undoubtedly implied a considerable loss of information—appeared more reliable so that we will refer in the text to the information available only starting from the year 1928.

In all the cases—Ancona, Milan, Rome and Turin—two additional questions arise, moreover. Firstly, unlike what apparently happens in the case of Ancona, up until 1920 (in the case of Milan), 1924 (in the case of Rome)[15] and 1938 (in the case of Turin) the data on cessations indicate a visibly reduced volume of them. Secondly, the years 1951 and 1961 (1953 e 1963 in the case of Ancona) are characterised by average volumes of registrations and, conversely, instead by implausibly high volumes of cancellations. The two phenomena mentioned—low volume of cessations right up through 1938 and the abnormal volume of cancellations in 1951 (1953 for Ancona) and, to a different extent, in 1961 (1963 for Ancona)—turned out to be linked to a large extent.

We know that on the occasion of the III General Census of Industry and Commerce (1951), just as on the occasion of the IV Census (1961), not only were the "local units" counted (the facility, the factory, the mill, the workshop, the establishment ...) as had been done until then, but also the firm themselves (made up, at times, of several local units). This, in turn, entailed a review of the Firm Registers and the cessation ex officio of "untraced" or "ceased" undertakings for which no cessation notice had been filed. In the case of Turin, for example, cessations can be observed in 1951 relating to 3590 firms (established between 1870 and 1951 and in the form of partnerships or joint stock companies or in "other forms"). Given the average volume of annual cessations observed in the early 1950s (between 500 and 900), it is quite clear that a great majority of the cessations observed in 1951 regards cancellations *ex officio* of firms that had de facto ceased without being recorded as such in the Chamber records; the cessation was then recorded in 1951, giving rise to the abnormal volume of cancellations mentioned above. The same can be said for 1961 in which 1253 cessations can be observed compared to a volume of cessations in the contiguous years close to 800 units. It can be noted fairly immediately that, if the cessation of the mentioned firms—occurring formally between 1951 and 1961—had been notified correctly at the moment of effective cessation, we would not observe the zero volume of cessations observed in the years 1911–1938 and, very probably we would observe a higher volume of cessations in the years 1939–1960. In the case of Milan, on the other hand, 12,737 cessations were observed in 1951 (compared to a volume of cessations in the contiguous years close on average to 700 units) while those present in 1961 were 26,637 (compared to contiguous years characterised by a maximum of 3 thousand cessations per year). In

---

[15] It should be remembered that in the case of Rome, the information is missing for the 1925–1947 period.

this case too—even more so than in the case of Turin—it is evident that the Firm Register attributes to the years 1951 and 1961 cessations that had occurred in reality in the previous years. In the case of Rome, on the other hand, the phenomenon is much less evident: the cessations observed in 1951 numbered 236 (compared to a volume of cessations in the contiguous years close to 150 units on average).[16] In this case, the discrepancy between the substantial figure for the cessation of the activity and the formal data of the same essentially appears to be marginal.

Finally, in the case of Ancona, the cancellations observed in 1953 are 329 and 300 those present in 1963 (on average double compared to those recorded in the contiguous years) which confirms the hypothesis that the data for 1953 and 1963 contain cancellations which should have intervened previously. And it should not be surprising that in the case of Ancona reference is made to 1953 and 1963 rather than to 1951 and 1961: the operations relating to the two censuses in fact continued well beyond the date of the censuses themselves (the publication of the 1951 Census actually occurred in 1955).

Estimating the volumes of cessations "in excess" observed in the year 1951 or 1961 (1953 or 1963 for Ancona) and, above all, attributing it to the receding years, is possible only if we have more detailed information or information from different sources available, as in fact happens. Referring to Rossi (2024, Appendix B) for a detailed account of the modalities employed for estimating the "excess" cessations and distributing them in the previous years, it is appropriate to underline that the corrections just mentioned all implied fewer cessations in the 1947–1964 period and, as a consequence, lower exit rates and, gross and net turnovers and, conversely, higher exit rates and gross and net turnovers in the 1930s and early 1940s. In other terms, for the purposes of the arguments being put forward in this text, they fully express the prudential attitude recalled on several occasions.

Having in this way reconstructed the flows of registrations and cessations and, in a recursive manner, the stocks of registrations, an initial check is possible by comparing this last magnitude to the stocks as reconstructed on the basis of the Movimprese records starting from 1982. Unfortunately this comparison is only possible in the cases of Ancona, Milan and Turin in which the historical reconstruction stops, in 1972

---

[16] As has already been noted, in the case of Rome the elementary information does not go beyond 1960.

(Milan) and in 1980 (Ancona and Turin) and the reconstruction based on the Movimprese records starts in 1983 (Ancona and Turin) or 1984 (Milan) and it turns out to be an encouraging comparison as the figure regarding the stock of non-sole traders—about 8 thousand in 1980 in Ancona, about 122 thousand in 1972 in the case of Milan and 50 thousand in 1980 in the case of Turin appear highly compatible with the corresponding figures observed for the province of Ancona and Turin in 1983 and for the province of Milan in 1984 (10 thousand, 160 thousand and 53 thousand respectively) and with average net flows observed in the period. In the case of Rome, on the other hand, the distance between the last observation deriving from the historical archives (1960) and the first deductible from the Movimprese records (1986) frankly makes any comparison adventurous.

The elementary information for the available periods since 1927 according to province, production sector and legal form of the enterprise—integrated and/or corrected as just described, in order to allow reading over time—is freely accessible (and downloadable in Excel form, by single year and in homogeneous form) in https://dinamismo.brunol eoni.com/ (retrieved March 18, 2024).

Demography and Entrepreneurship

The interpretative framework of the relationships between demographic trends and entrepreneurial propensity proposed by James Liang et al. (2018) constitutes a useful starting point for a quantitative assessment of the impact of aging processes on business demography in countries, such as Italy, where demographic trends have been and promise to be more intense than elsewhere. Its main implication can be summarised in the negative relationship that we would expect to observe between the propensity towards entrepreneurship (defined as the ratio between new businesses—other than sole proprietorships and non-classified companies—per 100,000 inhabitants of working age and therefore between 15 and 64 years) and an indicator of the aging process that we will identify with the share of the over-64-year-old population out of the total:

$$n^j = f(q, d^j) \quad (f'_q \gtrless 0, f'_d < 0) \tag{B.1}$$

where n^j indicates the entrepreneurship rate (i.e. the propensity to set up—and therefore to register—firms other than sole proprietorships and not belonging to the "Unclassified activities" in the j-th macro-region), q indicates the indicator of the cyclical trend of economic activity in the country as a whole (specifically the relative distance between the gross domestic product observed in year t and its potential level) and d^j is, on the other hand, an indicator of the aging process of the population (as above) in the j-th macro-region where $j = 1$ identifies north-western Italy, $j = 2$ north-eastern Italy, $j = 3$ central Italy, $j = 4$ southern Italy and island and, finally, $j = 0$ Italy as a whole. The sign of the impact of cyclical conditions on the entrepreneurship rate is not obvious, as there are good reasons to hypothesise both a cyclical behaviour of the entrepreneurship rate as well as an anti-cyclical behaviour. In the light of the properties of the time series involved, it seems reasonable to consider (Eq. B.1) as a representation of the prevailing long-term relationship between the entrepreneurial propensity and the aging process, therefore allowing the short-term dynamics to be captured by an extended version of (Eq. B.1) incorporating an error correction mechanism:

$$\Delta \ln n_t^j = \alpha_0^j + \alpha_1^j \Delta \ln d_t^j + \alpha_2^j \ln\left(n_{t-1}^j\right)$$
$$+ \alpha_3^j d_{t-1}^j + \alpha_4^j \Delta q_t^j + \alpha_5^j q_{t-1}^j + \varepsilon_t^j \tag{B.2}$$

In (Eq. B.2), ε_t^j is an error term with zero mean and constant variance for all j and, for given j, with zero covariance for $t \neq s$. Table 2.1 reports the OLS estimates of the parameters of (Eq. B.2) for $j = 0,...,4$.

The impact of the economic cycle on the creation of new businesses is mostly zero or only very moderately anti-cyclical. The impact of the population aging process on the formation of new businesses, mostly nil in the short term, is instead significant, negative—as expected—and quantitatively very significant in all macro-regions. If measured through the elasticity of the propensity for entrepreneurship with respect to the share of the over-64-year-old population—which in the cited literature measures the obstacles posed by the aging process to the formation of human capital that can be spent in entrepreneurial terms—it is clearly more pronounced in north-western and central Italy and less in north-eastern Italy and very close to the national average in southern and insular Italy (Table B.1).

Table B.1 Estimates of the parameters of (Eq. B.2) (OLS, 1984–2021)

	α_0	α_1^j	α_2^j	α_3^j	α_{40}^j	α_{41}^j	R^2	DW	$\epsilon_{n,d}$
Italy	0.80	0.97	−0.35	−0.53	0.00	−0.01	0.26	2.25	−1.50
	(0.37)	(2.87)	(0.13)	(0.23)	(0.01)	(0.01)			
Macro-regions:									
– Nort-west	0.44	−0.04	−0.29	−0.66	0.02	−0.00	0.30	2.30	−2.26
	(0.38)	(3.04)	(0.11)	(0.31)	(0.01)	(0.01)			
– North-east	1.09	−1.48	−0.36	−0.44	0.02	−0.02	0.49	2.12	1.24
	(0.38)	(2.84)	(0.12)	(0.23)	(0.01)	(0.01)			
– Centre	1.17	4.65	−0.44	−0.59	−0.00	−0.03	0.32	2.29	1.34
	(0.56)	(4.54)	(0.13)	(0.29)	(0.02)	(0.02)			
– South and Islands	1.07	4.74	−0.54	−0.68	−0.03	−0.01	0.32	1.93	1.26
	(0.47)	(4.04)	(0.16)	(0.28)	(0.02)	(0.02)			

Note Standard errors in parenthesis

Creative Destruction and Growth

The quantitative information reconstructed as in the previous pages—along with the information relating to the growth of total factor productivity referred to in Appendix A—are, finally, at the base of the exercise aimed at ascertaining the causality links *à la* Granger (1969) briefly discussed in the text.

For the definition of causality in Granger's sense it is useful to refer to the words of Clive Granger himself (1980, p. 334): "A (time series) variable A causes B, if the probability of B conditional on its own past history and the past history of A (beside the set of the available information) does not equal the probability of B conditional on its own past history alone", provided that (Granger, 1988, p. 200) "possible causation is not considered for any arbitrarily selected group of variables, but only for variables for which the researcher has some prior belief that causation is, in some sense, likely".

The limits of causality *à la Granger* are known and concern, for example, the impact of elements such as frequency of the data or the non-linearity of the relationships analysed or the presence of other determinants that are extraneous though to the set of information that is the subject of analysis or, finally, to the impact of expectations. So that it appears more appropriate to speak, rather than of causality, of "incremental foreseeability" or even—more simply—of "precedence" and assess the results, whatever they are, with the necessary prudence and a healthy dose of detachment.

Given all the above, in the case in question, verifying the existence of links of causality in the specified sense implies estimating the parameters of a multivariate autoregressive process of the order p—VAR(p)—of the type:

$$\hat{q}_t = \alpha_{10} + \sum_{i=1}^{p} \beta_{1i}\hat{q}_{t-i} + \sum_{i=1}^{p} \gamma_{1i}d_{t-i}^{AN} + \sum_{i=1}^{p} \delta_{1i}d_{t-i}^{MI} + \sum_{i=1}^{p} \eta_{1i}d_{t-i}^{TO}$$

$$+ \sum_{i=1}^{p} \theta_{1i}d_{t-i}^{RM} + \varphi_{10}\left(q_t^*/q_{it-1} - 1\right) + \varepsilon_{1t} \tag{B.3}$$

$$d_t^{AN} = \alpha_{20} + \sum_{i=1}^{p} \beta_{2i}\hat{q}_{t-i} + \sum_{i=1}^{p} \gamma_{2i}d_{t-i}^{AN} + \sum_{i=1}^{p} \delta_{2i}d_{t-i}^{MI} + \sum_{i=1}^{p} \eta_{2i}d_{t-i}^{TO}$$

$$+ \sum_{i=1}^{p} \theta_{2i}d_{t-i}^{RM} + \varphi_{20}\left(q_t^*/q_{it-1} - 1\right) + \varepsilon_{2t} \tag{B.4}$$

$$d_t^{MI} = \alpha_{30} + \sum_{i=1}^{p} \beta_{3i}\hat{q}_{t-i} + \sum_{i=1}^{p} \gamma_{3i}d_{t-i}^{AN} + \sum_{i=1}^{p} \delta_{3i}d_{t-i}^{MI} + \sum_{i=1}^{p} \eta_{3i}d_{t-i}^{TO}$$

$$+ \sum_{i=1}^{p} \theta_{3i}d_{t-i}^{RM} + \varphi_{30}\left(q_t^*/q_{it-1} - 1\right) + \varepsilon_{3t} \tag{B.5}$$

$$d_t^{RM} = \alpha_{40} + \sum_{i=1}^{p} \beta_{4i}\hat{q}_{t-i} + \sum_{i=1}^{p} \gamma_{4i}d_{t-i}^{AN} + \sum_{i=1}^{p} \delta_{4i}d_{t-i}^{MI} + \sum_{i=1}^{p} \eta_{4i}d_{t-i}^{TO}$$

$$+ \sum_{i=1}^{p} \theta_{4i}d_{t-i}^{RM} + \varphi_{40}\left(q_t^*/q_{it-1} - 1\right) + \varepsilon_{4t} \tag{B.6}$$

$$d_t^{TO} = \alpha_{50} + \sum_{i=1}^{p} \beta_{5i}\hat{q}_{t-i} + \sum_{i=1}^{p} \gamma_{5i}d_{t-i}^{AN} + \sum_{i=1}^{p} \delta_{5i}d_{t-i}^{MI} + \sum_{i=1}^{p} \eta_{5i}d_{t-i}^{TO}$$

$$+ \sum_{i=1}^{p} \theta_{5i}d_{t-i}^{RM} + \varphi_{50}\left(q_t^*/q_{it-1} - 1\right) + \varepsilon_{5t} \tag{B.7}$$

where $\hat{q}_t$ denotes the growth rate of the total factor productivity and $d_t^{AN}, d_t^{MI}, d_t^{RM}, d_t^{TO}$ represent indices of creative destruction (the gross turnover or the so-called churn rate) at time t, respectively for Ancona, Milan, Rome and Turin and, as above, q_t^* represents the average productivity of the technological leader of the moment. In the (Eq. B.3)–(Eq. B.7) system, ε_t is a multivariate *white noise* term with mean zero and is such as to exclude the correlation between every element of the process and the past history of the entire process but not the correlation between contemporary elements of the process. Furthermore, p is the order of the VAR(p) and is determined with the help of the information criteria of current use (Akaike, Schwartz, Hannan and Quinn).

It can be noted that in the light of the fact that information regarding the creative destruction processes is available for different periods in the different provinces (Ancona: 1928–1980 and 1983–2021, Milan: 1928–1972 and 1984–2021, Rome: 1948–1960 and 1986–2021, Turin: 1928–1980 e 1982–2021), it was decided—as already previously—to keep the information itself distinct without, in other words trying to infer the evolution of the creative destruction process at national level from the separate provincial information sets.

In the VAR(p) just described, verifying or not verifying the mono- or bi-directional causality links *à la* Granger is the equivalent of verifying the hypothesis that each of the variables of interest depends only and exclusively on its own past history (and therefore that the dynamics of the creative destruction indices are irrelevant for the purposes of forecasting the growth rates of the TFP and vice-versa). Table B.2 shows the results of the OLS estimate of the system (Eq. B.3)–(Eq. B.7). The results refer to the sample composed from the years 1950–1960 and 1988–2021. Eliminating the observations for the province of Rome, it would theoretically have been possible to extend the sample backwards but at the same time, given the role played by the creative destruction indicator for the province of Rome in the estimate of the system (Eq. B.3)–(Eq. B.7), the causality test would have been invalid as it would have been conditioned to an incomplete set of information. Evident signs of misspecification are not apparent from Table B.2. The linear restrictions on the parameters $\beta, \gamma, \delta, \eta e \theta$ in which the hypothesis of absence of Granger-causality expresses itself appear to be clearly rejected as long as the links between indicators of creative destruction and growth rate of the TFP are investigated. In the opposite sense the evidence is not completely absent but would seem to be limited only to the ratio between the growth rate of the TFP and creative destruction processes in the province of Ancona.

Table B.2 OLS estimate of the parameters of (Eq. B.3)–(Eq. B.7)

Number of observations: 45 (1950–1960, 1988–2021)

α_{10}	−0.006	(0.011)	γ_{32}	−0.258	(0.141)	η_{32}	−0.040 (0.106)
α_{20}	0.015	(0.011)	γ_{41}	0.095	(0.347)	η_{41}	0.521 (0.305)
α_{30}	0.042*	(0.010)	γ_{42}	−0.023	(0.310)	η_{42}	−0.023 (0.233)
α_{40}	−0.005	(0.023)	γ_{51}	0.102	(0.149)	η_{51}	0.192 (0.131)
α_{50}	0.025*	(0.010)	γ_{52}	0.144	(0.133)	η_{52}	−0.011 (0.100)
β_{11}	0.116	(0.149)	δ_{11}	−0.171	(0.219)	θ_{11}	0.415* (0.170)
β_{12}	−0.192	(0.176)	δ_{12}	−0.084	(0.211)	θ_{12}	0.006 (0.148)
β_{21}	−0.367*	(0.139)	δ_{21}	0.070	(0.204)	θ_{21}	0.297* (0.159)
β_{22}	0.172	(0.164)	δ_{22}	−0.352*	(0.197)	θ_{22}	0.153 (0.138)
β_{31}	0.142	(0.137)	δ_{31}	0.270	(0.200)	θ_{31}	0.056 (0.156)
β_{32}	0.077	(0.161)	δ_{32}	0.044	(0.193)	θ_{32}	−0.053 (0.136)
β_{41}	0.572*	(0.302)	δ_{41}	0.182	(0.442)	θ_{41}	−0.131 (0.344)
β_{42}	0.007	(0.355)	δ_{42}	0.321	(0.427)	θ_{42}	0.026 (0.299)
β_{51}	−0.038	(0.129)	δ_{51}	0.179	(0.190)	θ_{51}	0.608* (0.148)
β_{52}	0.343*	(0.152)	δ_{52}	−0.426*	(0.183)	θ_{52}	−0.257* (0.128)
γ_{11}	−0.085	(0.172)	η_{11}	0.378*	(0.151)	φ_{10}	−0.006 (0.022)
γ_{12}	0.131	(0.154)	η_{12}	−0.482*	(0.115)	φ_{20}	0.029 (0.021)
γ_{21}	0.534*	(0.160)	η_{21}	0.165	(0.141)	φ_{30}	0.040* (0.021)
γ_{22}	−0.290*	(0.143)	η_{22}	0.101	(0.108)	φ_{40}	0.033 (0.046)
γ_{31}	0.081	(0.157)	η_{31}	0.098	(0.138)	φ_{50}	0.047* (0.020)

R^2 (Eq. B.3): 0.77 – R^2 (Eq. B.4): 0.95 – R^2 (Eq. B.5): 0.59
– R^2 (Eq. B.6): 0.79 – R^2 (Eq. B.7): 0.96
LM (1): $\chi^2(25) = 28.37$ – LM (2): $\chi^2(25) = 19.48$
JB: $\chi^2(10) = 20.81$
Stationarity: checked
Causality test *à la* Granger:

$d_{t-i}^{AN} \rightarrow \hat{q}_t (\forall i)$	$F(2,32) = 0.73$	$d_{t-i}^{RM} \rightarrow d_t^{MI} (\forall i)$	$F(2,32) = 0.51$
$d_{t-i}^{MI} \rightarrow \hat{q}_t\ (\forall i)$	$F(2,32) = 1.70$	$d_{t-i}^{TO} \rightarrow d_t^{MI} (\forall i)$	$F(2,32) = 0.21$
$d_{t-i}^{RM} \rightarrow \hat{q}_t (\forall i)$	$F(2,32) = 18.11$		
$d_{t-i}^{TO} \rightarrow \hat{q}_t (\forall i)$	$F(2,32) = 7.14$	$\hat{q}_{t-i} \rightarrow d_t^{RM} (\forall i)$	$F(2,32) = 3.68$
$\Sigma d_{t-i}^k \rightarrow \hat{q}_t (\forall i, k)$	$F(8,32) = 29.31$	$d_{t-i}^{AN} \rightarrow d_t^{RM} (\forall i)$	$F(2,32) = 0.08$
		$d_{t-i}^{MI} \rightarrow d_t^{RM} (\forall i)$	$F(2,32) = 1.65$
$\hat{q}_{t-i} \rightarrow d_t^{AN} (\forall i)$	$F(2,32) = 7.42$	$d_{t-i}^{TO} \rightarrow d_t^{RM} (\forall i)$	$F(2,32) = 0.15$

(continued)

Table B.2   (continued)

Number of observations: 45 (1950–1960, 1988–2021)

$d_{t-i}^{MI} \rightarrow d_t^{AN}\,(\forall i)$	F(2,32) = 3.92		
$d_{t-i}^{RM} \rightarrow d_t^{AN}\,(\forall i)$	F(2,32) = 3.85	$\hat{q}_{t-i} \rightarrow d_t^{TO}\,(\forall i)$	F(2,32) = 5.07
$d_{t-i}^{TO} \rightarrow d_t^{AN}\,(\forall i)$	F(2,32) = 7.52	$d_{t-i}^{AN} \rightarrow d_t^{TO}\,(\forall i)$	F(2,32) = 3.16
		$d_{t-i}^{MI} \rightarrow d_t^{TO}\,(\forall i)$	F(2,32) = 5.65
$\hat{q}_{t-i} \rightarrow d_t^{MI}\,(\forall i)$	F(2,32) = 1.48	$d_{t-i}^{RM} \rightarrow d_t^{TO}\,(\forall i)$	F(2,32) = 2.47
$d_{t-i}^{AN} \rightarrow d_t^{MI}\,(\forall i)$	F(2,32) = 3.57		

Notes Alongside the estimate of the parameters, in parenthesis, standard errors (corrected for the sample size); LM (1), test for first order residual autocorrelation; LM (2) test for second order residual autocorrelation; JB, Bera and Jaque test for the normality of the residuals; as regards the stationarity, this is considered to have been verified when this is considered to have been verified when the eigenvalues of the so-called "*companion matrix*" are below one in absolute value; in the bottom part of the Table, the arrow indicates the direction of the causality *à la* Granger subject to verification; Finally: $i = 1, 2$ and $k = $ AN, MI, RM, TO; to remember: it is not possible for all the variable involved to reject the hypothesis that they are I(0) processes

REFERENCES

Granger, C. W. J. (1969). Investigating Causal Relations by Econometric Models and Cross-Spectral Methods. *Econometrica, 37*(3), 424–438.

Granger, C. W. J. (1980). Testing for Causality. A Personal Viewpoint. *Journal of Economic Dynamics and Control, 2*(1), 329–352.

Granger, C. W. J. (1988). Some Recent Developments in a Concept of Causality. *Journal of Econometrics, 39*(1–2), 199–211.

Liang, J., Wang, H., & Lazear, E. P. (2018). Demographics and Entrepreneurship. *Journal of Political Economy, 126*(S1), 140–196.

Rossi, N. (2024). *Un miracolo non fa il santo. La distruzione creatrice nella società italiana, 1861–2021.* IBL Libri.

Appendix C: Bailouts

The Italian Bailout Industry

The story of the Italian bailout industry formally began—as we have seen—with the Consorzio per le Sovvenzioni sui Valori Industriali (CSVI), operational from February 1915, whose capital was underwritten by the Bank of Italy and by two other Issuing Institutions (Banco di Napoli and Banco di Sicilia), as well as by other minor credit institutions. This Consortium was allowed to pay advances of industrial securities and discount industrial bills of exchange, drawing on its own capital and, should this have been insufficient, discounting the financial instruments mentioned c/o the main Issuing Institutions. As recalled by Ernesto Cianci, it was envisaged that the Consortium—established in order to provide the economic system with "special provisions"[17] at the moment in which the need might arise—was "exceptional and transient" (Cianci, 1977, p. 16). Whatever the intentions of its authors were and also thanks to the climate determined by the events of the war,[18] with the Consortium bailouts became part of the country's material constitution. And stayed there up to now (with all due respect—it should be added—to the European rules on State aid). In the late winter of 1922, the CSVI deemed it appropriate to create a Special Autonomous Section of the CSVI itself. For all intents and purposes, a new and additional tool enabled—to a considerably greater extent than that envisaged for CSVI itself—rediscounting c/o the Issuing Institutions.

---

[17] Gianni Toniolo (1993, pp. 17–18) underlines how it was necessary in the years following WWI "to invent ad hoc instruments that would allow the Bank of Italy to indirectly discount bills that it would not have been able to discount if presented directly. Hence the Special Autonomous Section, the Institute of Liquidations (IL) ...".

[18] Luigi Einaudi (1933, p. 407) observed how it was specifically this climate that provided "an abstract justification to what was, in reality, a state guarantee to private economic enterprises of success or salvation in the event of loss". This climate did not fail, evidently, also to influence CSVI's father, Bonaldo Stringher, then Director General of the Bank of Italy, who was convinced that the industrial securities market "abandoned on its own without effective support, could get into serious danger" (Cianci, 1977, p. 15) and put the banking system at risk as a consequence. Ernesto Cianci (1977, p. 64) adds that, in Stringher's intentions, CSVI's experience should have concluded with the liquidation of the assets of the same (something that would then be met with widespread resistance). And there is no need to evoke the name of Mary Shelley (the renowned author of *Frankenstein or The Modern Prometheus*) to observe that CSVI would not be the first case of an organism that got out of its creator's control.

In November 1926 the Special Autonomous Section was suppressed and its asset arrangements were taken over by the Istituto di Liquidazioni (IL), also created for the occasion and obviously of a transitory nature. Provided with legal personality, IL was entrusted with the liquidation of its assets as well as with their management; but if, just for a change, in the intentions of its fathers—the Finance Minister, Volpi, and the Director General of the Bank of Italy, Stringher—its primary function was supposed to be that of liquidator, the secondary function—the managerial one—was to be the winner over time, also in virtue of the circumstances and—Cianci notes—"because of the resistance of the trade unions and local interests" (Cianci, 1977, p. 61). To an extent not appeared evident at the time, state holdings came into being with IL. In 1933, one of the two Sections into which IL had been divided—the Industrial Disinvestments Branch (the other being the Industrial Loans Branch)—was taken over by the Istituto per la Ricostruzione Industriale (IRI), established that same year for openly time-limited purposes (the disinvestment of the assets that constituted its capital). The veil of pretence would fall definitively in 1937 with the transformation of IRI (from 1936 significantly limited to the sole Industrial Disinvestments Branch) into a permanent entity.[19]

And if the grandchild—IRI—had become permanent, the grandfather—CSVI—could certainly be no less.[20] In fact, downstream from a new capital injection in 1936, CSVI—prorogued until the end of 1950—was transformed into an autonomous section of Istituto Mobiliare Italiano (IMI, established in 1931) with the explicit task—Alberto Caracciolo (1992, pp. 68–69) recalls—to facilitate "with its special operations, the performance of the most important State contracts" and with the implicit mandate to perform a "social function, of intervention in difficult liquidity

[19] It is very probably true that in the first post-war period "it was not thought that the State could manage manufacturing businesses directly" (Toniolo, 1978, p. 290). But it is frankly difficult to think that it was not clear to the ruling class at the time that the mere establishment of similar organisms would have created the basis for the permanence of the same.

[20] The close relationship of kinship between CSVI (and, in particular, between its Special Autonomous Branch) and IRI was already recognised in the immediate post-war period by Pasquale Saraceno (1956).

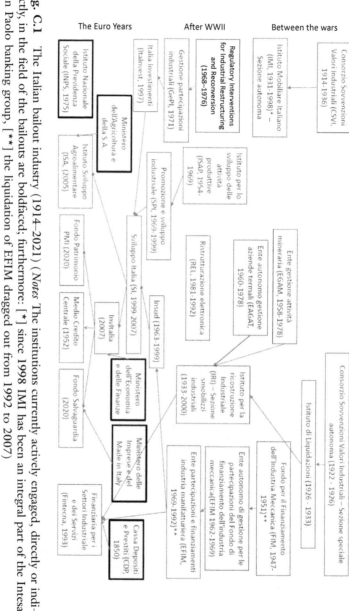

Fig. C.1 The Italian bailout industry (1914–2021) (*Notes* The institutions currently actively engaged, directly or indirectly, in the field of the bailouts are boldfaced; furthermore: [*] since 1998 IMI has been an integral part of the Intesa San Paolo banking group, [**] the liquidation of EFIM dragged out from 1992 to 2007)

and employment situations".[21] CSVI was then wound up in 1959[22] but certainly not because of the completion of the rescue policies. 1947, in fact, saw the establishment of the Fondo per il Finanziamento dell'Industria Meccanica (FIM) whose purpose, among others, was to subscribe

[21] What then the "special operations" were is explained by Alberto Caracciolo (1992, pp. 68–69): "emergency and speedy public expenditure (and some would say sometimes unscrupulous) to support the more dynamic industrial sectors and those more accustomed to settling the company accounts with State aid". State expenditure funded by increases in the currency in circulation as can be seen clearly from the concern clearly manifested by the Issuing Institution regarding "the effects such a position [Author's note: the CSVI's disinvestments] has on the currency in circulation" (Caracciolo, 1992, doc. 51). It must be pointed out however that the "special operations"—which comprise the almost totality of the advances and loans in the years marked by the war—then shrank rapidly starting from 1946 and were almost completely exhausted in the span of four years. At the moment of approval of the accounts for the year 1948, the then chairman of CSVI, Donato Menichella, was able to note with satisfaction that the special operations "were by now in liquidation and without losses for the Consortium" (ASBI, CSVI, files, n. 2, doc. 1), as the State had presumably honoured its commitments. It should be noted, moreover, that this result was achieved also because in some cases (notably in the case of the Caproni group) the State's intervention permitted the resolution of a situation that otherwise would have had far from negligible consequences for CSVI too.

[22] Alberto Caracciolo (1992, pp. 68–75) summarises the fate of CSVI after its integration into IMI and underlines the political pressures that marked its operation. Political and social pressures that are easily unearthed in the documentation that is still available regarding the many funding dossiers. It should also be underlined that the initiatives of CSVI went well beyond supporting businesses and also concerned, for example, land reclamations in Apulia and Campania, in the Agro Pontino and in the Ferrara area, or the funding of public works (including the precincts for the 1942 World Fair). Obviously, for the purposes of this Appendix (and therefore of Figs. 6.1 and 6.2) these interventions cannot reasonably be described as rescue operations. On the other hand, as regards funding other than the cases mentioned (namely the so-called ordinary operations) the fragmentary nature of the documentation unfortunately only rarely makes it possible to accurately, operation by operation, reconstruct both the procedure for awarding the funding and the times and procedures for the repayments. In the Annex and for the years for which the annual accounts are available, reference was therefore made to two specific balance sheet items: the losses "on distressed bills and the "allocations to the credit devaluation fund" [ASBI, CSVI, dossiers, n. 2 and registers, nos. 1–32]. It should be pointed out, however, that the sums in question are marginal in any case and compatible with the observation contained in the Report on the accounts for the 1948 financial year according to which the unsecured loans amounted in the year mentioned to around 8.5% '[ASBI, CSVI, files, n. 2].

to or guarantee capital increases and facilitate the disinvestment of holdings by companies in the engineering sector.[23] Francesca Fauri (2007, pp. 201–202) recalls that, in the first report on the activities of FIM, the Committee that determined its strategic objectives (its management being entrusted to IMI) did not fail to point out that it had taken account of "situations of particular urgency ... (so as not to jeopardise) irreparably the existence of firms that could probably be recovered".[24] As it is easy to imagine, the Committee's working hypothesis turned out to be extremely optimistic. As observed by Francesca Fauri (2010, p. 123) in reality FIM "had been given an impossible mission: funding bankrupt companies as well, knowing that their return to health in the short term would be difficult, but that leaving thousands of workers without jobs would have been unacceptable". FIM was put into liquidation in 1951 (after running the risk of being taken over by CSVI) but its mission obviously was not. The holdings in the FIM portfolio (when not in in compulsory liquidation) would be transferred to IRI or, to a generally prevalent extent, to an autonomous management agency for the holdings of FIM (Ente autonomo di gestione per le partecipazioni del Fondo di finanziamento dell'industria meccanica) established in 1962 and in 1969 renamed Ente partecipazioni e finanziamento industria manifatturiera (EFIM). The latter—initially established to manage the State's holdings in the engineering industry, and manufacturing—later ignominiously ceased operations in 1992 with the launch of the liquidation procedure. Not before allowing the EFIM liquidator, Alberto Predieri, to caustically report—how can we put it?—the imaginative nature of

[23] The establishment of the Fund was preceded by a series of significant state loans to the engineering industry (Fauri, 2007, pp. 197–199) which are overlooked in this context as they cannot necessarily be depicted as rescue operations.

[24] Not by chance, a member of the Committee (Ernesto Rossi, who resigned only three months after the appointment of the Committee) could not avoid reporting in writing to the Prime Minister of the time that "the Committee sees itself obliged to distribute billions to pay the wages of workers and prevent or postpone the bankruptcy of engineering companies that were already insolvent, as it has been continuously subjected to pressures of all kinds from ministers and prefects... FIM destroys much more wealth than what would be destroyed if the same sums that were given as wages to the workers were given as benefits to the unemployed ... It tends to transform companies that can no longer be restored to health into State companies" (quoted in Fauri, 2007. p. 202). Evidently, the appointment of experts from outside the civil service as members of the Committee—backed by Luigi Einaudi, then Governor of the Bank of Italy (Fauri, 2007, p. 200)—was not enough to prevent undue interferences.

the EFIM balance sheets.[25] In 2007 (after a liquidation process that lasted fifteen years) the residual capital of EFIM, along with the voluminous package of outstanding litigations, was transferred to Finanziaria per i Settori Industriale e dei Servizi (Fintecna) established in 1993—and controlled today by Cassa Depositi e Prestiti (CDP)—with the task of rationalising, restructuring and disposing of the controlled companies in liquidation deriving among others from IRI and EFIM, these latter via Ligestra, a finance company.[26]

Before that date—in 1978—Ente Gestione Attività Minerarie (EGAM) had also halted its activities after having being established in 1958 for the purpose of managing all Italy's mining production but being operational only from 1971. Its holdings portfolio was split between IRI and Ente Nazionale Idrocarburi (ENI). Also put into liquidation in 1978 was Ente Autonomo per la Gestione delle Aziende Termali (EAGAT), established in 1960 with the task of managing "in a cost-effective manner" the State holding in the spa industry after these activities had, in 1978, assigned to EFIM for fiduciary administration, as mentioned and transferred by it in 1995 to IRI.

The seed planted in 1914 did not fail, moreover, to produce new fruits without interruption. 1954 saw the establishment of Istituto per lo Sviluppo delle Attività Produttive (ISAP) transformed in 1970 into Promozione e Sviluppo Industriale (SPI) whose mission was discretely identified with the creation and internationalisation of small and medium businesses. In between the 1960s and the 1970s, the climate did change, though, significantly. Towards the end of the 1950s, IRI's top management made clear that IRI was ready to face "social costs" in order to guarantee employment levels in specific areas of the country, in spite of all sound economic principles (Bottiglieri, 1984, pp. 305–306). In 1961, a set of rules defining instruments for supporting enterprises engaged in restructuring and reconversion paths (a euphemism for indicating situations of objective economic and financial hardship) took form. In practice these rules only became fully operational between 1968 and 1976 and

[25] In fact, Predieri stated—in terms that would today be considered as inappropriate—that only a fool could believe in the truthfulness of the EFIM balance sheets and their accounting criteria.

[26] One of the firms that appears in the portfolio of the latter, among others, was Nuova Breda Fucine, a distant echo of one of the rescues carried out by FIM in the 1940s.

opened the road in 1971 for the birth of Società per le Gestioni e Parte-cipazioni Industriali (GePI). GePi, established in order to facilitate the restoration to health of companies in difficulty, on the basis of specific reconversion plans, and then sell them, gradually ended up limiting itself to maintaining the employment levels in the presence of industrial crises of a transitory nature. After becoming Italia Investimenti (ItaInvest) in 1997, in 1999 it flowed with SPI into a single national agency for business development and attracting investments, Sviluppo Italia. This was entrusted, among other things, with the task of coordinating, reordering and controlling the activities for promoting industrial development and employment.[27] And 1981 saw the birth of Ristrutturazione elettronica (REL) dedicated to restructuring and recovering Italian companies that operated in the consumer electronics sector, then liquidated a decade later. And again, in those fateful early 1980s came the entry into the "bailouts industry" of Cassa Depositi e Prestiti (CDP) which since then has maintained its active presence and its "sense of duty"—if we can call it so—in that sector.

A specific social safety net—a wage supplementation scheme pending the employment relationship—was then established in 1968 for workers in companies experiencing production difficulties or undergoing restructuring processes—the Cassa Integrazione Guadagni Straordinaria (CIGS) that was intended to replace or integrate the wages of the workers themselves. Salvatore Lo Bello looked in detail at its evolution through time and its characteristics and observed that it was "unique among those European countries that also envisage wage supplementation systems". His conclusions are worth quoting in full:

> ... for companies that receive CIGS treatments the probability of closure of their economic activity within a year is almost 12% compared to 10% for the totality of companies (...). After three years, about 40% of companies in which the CIGS had been made use of were no longer in business. (Furthermore) the companies availing of the CIGS undergo more marked drops in employment, equivalent on average to about 30% within one year. (...) We can conclude that (...) most applications of the CIGS are therefore for the benefit of workers whose jobs are more often than not destined to

[27] Flowing into Sviluppo Italia came SPI, ItaInvest, Insud (an offshoot of EFIM established 1963, whose holding in the tourism sector it took over), Ribs (the financial holdings company for the agricultural sector) and Finagra (dedicated to the promotion of the same sector). The expected passage of ENISud into Sviluppo Italia never materialised.

be abolished. In addition to not having the desired effect on the continuity of the economic activity of the businesses involved, it is possible that the interventions also delay the process for reallocating the workers in more productive enterprises. (Lo Bello, 2021, p. 20)

It is hardly necessary to observe that, though funded by the workers and employers, the management of the CIGS repeatedly recorded shortfalls which were covered of course from the public purse.[28]

Alongside new instruments, bailout policy continues to recall the lessons from the past. So therefore, in the banking field, came the discovery of the way of doing things of the decades before both the First and the Second World Wars. In the industrial field, on the other hand, in 1979 first, again in 1999 and yet again in 2003, an organic legal framework was passed to deal with major business crises inspired by the principle of company reorganisation and recovery rather than liquidation and fair creditor satisfaction. This discipline was also intended, in its more recent versions, to respect the guidelines of European rules on State aid but also, from 2003, to transfer the job of appointing the liquidator from the courts (that until them had also been responsible for discovering the causes of the insolvency) to the politicians, namely to the then Ministry for Economic Development (currently Ministry of Enterprises), releasing the latter from the need to ascertain the causes of the disruption and identify the prospects for rebalancing the company accounts.[29] It is hardly necessary to observe how at the end of August 2021 there were 132 enterprise groups under extraordinary administration comprising a total of 357 firms; of these 59 closed, 51 were insolvent and 3 (yes, just 3) returned to health. In only 13 cases out of 132 the groups had continued in business after the first three years of extraordinary administration, for the most part having started the liquidation stage right from the third or fourth year. These liquidation stages virtually always tended and tend to last decades, during which time, alongside any other supports for recovery paths, CIGS often contributed to crystallising jobs in companies in a

[28] In addition to the CIGS, use has often been made in rescue operations of early retirement schemes in order to facilitate restructuring of the businesses in difficulty. Unlike the CIGS, in this case identifying the cost to the taxpayer in the events that can be described as bailouts is not immediate. For this reason, it appears prudent to skip this specific instrument.

[29] The reference is to known provisions, respectively such as the "Prodi" act, the "Prodi-bis" act and the "Marzano" act.

precarious state without—as we have seen—benefitting their return to health.

Nor must we imagine moreover that the aforesaid rationalisation operation carried out in 1999 through the establishment of Sviluppo Italia could in some way represent a real about-turn or, if those were the intentions, the results were once again quite different. Yet again, everything was resolved in new packaging that allowed a new face to be put on procedures that had been very well tried.[30] The experiment was repeated in 2007 when, without a lack of fantasy, Sviluppo Italia would become a national agency for attracting investments and business development (Invitalia).[31] The latter, wholly controlled by the Ministry of the Economy and Finance, was asked to manage, disinvest or liquidate the non-strategic holdings, in this way qualifying what in precedence had been an often unconditional mission. And Invitalia did so through its subsidiary Invitalia Partecipazioni which—at the moment in which Fintecna started to complete the disinvestment of the EFIM inheritance—became the main heir to a tradition that was by now over a century old: that of bailouts.

---

[30] When instead even renewing the packaging did not reveal itself to be unbearable. See, for example, the case of RIBS, the financial firm of the Ministry of Agriculture, which in 1999 flowed into Sviluppo Italia and left it then in 2005 to return to the Ministry of Agriculture with the name, Istituto Sviluppo Agroalimentare (ISA, which in 2015 flowed into the Istituto di Servizi per il Mercato Agricolo Alimentare).

[31] Invitalia is the controlling entity of MedioCredito Centrale banking group, Infratel Italia, and Italia Turismo, as well as of the holdings contained in Invitalia Partecipazioni. Established in 2013, Italia Turismo is the proprietor of eight tourist villages in southern Italy which had already belonged to Insud. From the year of its establishment, it never closed a single year in profit, piling up total losses of about 50 million euros. The procedure for divesting all the shares in Italia Turismo, launched in 2018, did not produce results of any kind and is still open. Confirming a trend that was over a century old, the assets of Italia Turismo (indirectly subordinate to the Ministry of the Economy) are currently being transferred to the I3-Sviluppo Italia fund, managed by Investimenti Immobiliari Italiani (Invimit), which belong to the Economy Ministry. Invitalia Partecipazioni was supposed, instead, to "disinvest shares in non-strategic companies and invest in key sectors". At the end of 2019 Invitalia Partecipazioni was the parent of three subsidiaries (one of them in liquidation) and had investments in thirty of which twelve were bankrupt, nine in liquidation and two under extraordinary administration. On the date of its last available annual returns, it recorded overall losses close to 10 million euros. In the last five years no more than two disinvestment operations have been recorded for holdings in the portfolio with an overall recovery of the balance sheet values. It is difficult not to think that in this case too—as in the case of FIM—the fundamental goal is to "transform companies that are beyond recovery into State enterprises" (see Note 24 above).

But the field of bailouts, as we have seen, is one in which tradition and innovation walk hand in hand (Fig. C.1). This is evidenced by the return, on the one hand, to situations already seen in the past. The direct presence of the Ministry of the Economy and Finance in the banking field (following the bailout of Monte dei Paschi di Siena) or the birth of a new public banking group (composed of Medio Credito Centrale [MCC],[32] Banca Popolare di Bari and Banca Popolare di Orvieto) which obviously never fails to come to mind every time a creak in the world of credit is heard of. On the other hand, it is witnessed by the fantasy with which it was thought that the serious consequences of the pandemic crisis could be tackled with the addition of new pavilions to what had been defined as "a State sanatorium"[33] but which, more correctly perhaps, should have been defined as a "a State hospital for the chronically ill". We are talking on the one hand of the so-called Fondo Patrimonio PMI, with a financial budget for the year 2021 as high as one billion euros. It was supposed to subscribe to bonds and debt securities that were newly issued by small and medium enterprises, with the express provision that it was not expected to assess their credit worthiness, something that recalls without mincing words the establishing provisions of various intervention tools designed between the two wars, and of Fondo 4R, whose shares were subscribed by CDP (and by other institutional investors) in 2016, in order to "support companies in temporary crisis situations but with solid industrial foundations". The very same expression, it should be admitted, that had been used more than once in the past. And, on the other hand, mention should be made of the considerable and always concerning volume of guarantees

---

[32] MCC was established in 1952 as a public body for long- and medium-term funding of regional credit bodies for small and medium enterprises. Privatised in 1999, it was purchased by Poste Italiane and later sold in 2017 to Invitalia to become, in the course of the years that followed, the operational branch for public intervention in the banking sector.

[33] The term was coined by the industrialist Alberto Pirelli (quoted by Ernesto Cianci, 1977, p. 270).

given by the State via MCC or SACE[34] to bank loans[35]; or, further, the variously named intervention procedures aimed at companies that differ in terms of size or in business sectors that had been hit by the pandemic events[36]; or, again, interventions of a fiscal nature aimed at attenuating, at the taxpayer's expense, the costs arising out of bailout operations in the banking sector.[37] These were interventions, whose fallout on taxpayers has not yet been calculated and which, as a consequence, play no role in Figs. 6.1 and 6.2 (or in the Appendix to Rossi, 2024) just as—it should be emphasised—happens to proceeds arising from disinvestment operations resulting from some of the rescue operations of the last two decades which are yet to materialise.

[34] Established in 1977 as a special section of the Istituto Nazionale delle Assicurazioni (INA) in charge of the insurance cover of export credits and transformed in 1989 into Istituto per i Servizi Assicurativi del Commercio Estero, SACE, along with Medio Credito Centrale (MCC), starting from 2020, guarantees loans (counter-guaranteed by the State) granted to enterprises hit by the pandemic.

[35] At the end of the first 2022 half year, the guarantees provided by MCC through the guarantee fund for the SMEs or by SACE, amounted to just under 300 billion euros (retrieved March 18, 2024, https://www.bancaditalia.it/media/comunicati/documenti/2022-02/cs_task_force_06072022.pdf). If we accept the reliability of the recent assessment regarding the exposure of small and medium Italian enterprises to risks of a financial nature and the consequent appraisal of the exposed enterprises (around 13%; Confindustria-Cerved, 2022, p. 18) it is immediate to conclude that it is possible in the near future for there to be additional costs for the State balance sheet of the order of several tens of billions of euros.

[36] In 2020 alone, there were four decrees on the theme of "reliefs" while, in the two years 2021–2022 there were three "support" decrees and four "aid" ones. And the list is certainly incomplete.

[37] The reference here is to the possibility of transforming the deferred tax assets (or DTA, deriving, e.g., from value adjustments made by banks to receivables from customers and reducing taxable income in a given period of time in the future) into tax credits on the occasion of aggregation operations (for a fee). This possibility allowed, Banca Popolare dell'Emilia-Romagna to take over Banca Carige in 2022 in an operation that also involved Fondo Interbancario di Tutela dei Depositi. As a consequence, it would have been irrelevant for our purposes if it were not for the transformation at the same time of about 400 million euros into deferred tax assets. This transformation clearly involved the Italian taxpayer (within the limits in which one is convinced—and it is frankly difficult not to be so—that the condition of the shaky banks was unlikely to have allowed the deferred tax assets at that time to have found the future taxable incomes necessary for absorbing them). However, a quantification of the implications of the rules in question is extremely complex, as it not only regards the small number of operations on a grand scale but also lots of smaller-scale operations during the course of the last two years.

The Sample

The basic information underlying Figs. 6.1 and 6.2 in the text is provided in the Appendix to Rossi (2024) where a brief description is provided for every bailout-related event along with an estimate of its scale in addition to a note with the relevant bibliographical or archival references. It should be recalled that the list only includes bank or industrial bailouts which, directly or indirectly, could be traced to the Authorities of the time (with the exclusion, therefore, of bailout operations carried out inside the private sector as well, obviously, as government support for businesses for reasons other than their survival).[38] The list therefore excludes operations between private parties that did not imply or do not imply direct or indirect charges for the taxpayer. As far as the subject of government support for businesses is concerned, on the other hand, it is appropriate to point out how the boundaries between the latter and bailout operations are not always clearly defined or definable. In the absence of further information, the content of any relevant legislative measures holds sway (which, by the way, led to the inclusion in the final list of public fundings provided for the operation of the wage supplementation scheme called Cassa Integrazione Guadagni Straordinaria [CIGS]). As has already been pointed out, finally, the estimated magnitude of the intervention takes account, as far as possible, of any proceeds deriving, for example, from the disinvestments resulting from the intervention itself. These are reported, when present and available, in footnotes and, obviously, are not given in cases in which the disinvestments have not yet occurred.

It is appropriate to recall that the list that follows is unavoidably incomplete. Above all, it is legitimate to presume that quite a few smaller-scale

---

[38] To give just a few examples of the former case, think of the bailout of Società Metallurgica Tardy e Benech by Banca Nazionale nel Regno in 1890, the 1964 Montecatini rescue operation arranged by Mediobanca and carried out by Edison or the takeover of the Pesaro company, Berloni, by the Taiwanese holding HCG in 2013 or, more recently, the intervention in 2015 of the Fondo Nazionale di Risoluzione (the national resolution fund backed by all banks operating in Italy) on the occasion of the crisis of four Central Italy banks (Banca delle Marche, Banca Popolare dell'Etruria e del Lazio, Cassa di Risparmio di Ferrara and Cassa di Risparmio di Chieti) or, finally, of the entirely private rescue of the Pernigotti confectionery industry in 2019. As far as the latter case is concerned see, for example, the intervention of FSI (Fondo Strategico Italiano) in Trevi, a company specialised in special foundations and land consolidation, which took place in 2014, before (and not after) the financial instability that kicked off in 2015 and led to further interventions by the public shareholder. In itself, then, the operation did not take the form of a bailout but, rather, it showed that it was not appropriate for the State to do jobs that others probably do better (and above all with their own resources).

rescue operations whose essential elements are not completely known, or which did not grab the attention of the media, do not appear.[39] It is to be hoped, in this regard, that the future research will fill the likely gaps (as well as update a list that seems not to experience interruptions). On the other hand, the list deliberately ignores bailouts of entities, that were often anything but minor, "hidden"—in the 1960s, 1970s and 1980s—in the folds of the State holdings system because they were parts of it.[40] It was decided, in other words, to explicitly consider only bailouts by the public sector of entities that were wholly or partly private, ignoring those in which the public sector played the role of both the rescued entity and of the saviour. And therefore, for example, account was taken of the rescues of Officine del Pignone (1954) or of Lanerossi (1962) by Eni but no account was taken, for example, of the bailout of ItalTrade (previously Fime Trading) by the public agency for Southern Italy named Agenzia per la promozione dello sviluppo del Mezzogiorno in 1989.[41] In those

---

[39] As an example take the bailout of the Cotonificio Valle Susa (a textile company) arranged in 1964 by Mediobanca—an institution owned then by publicly owned banks—which then took part with a 20% stake in the Esercizi Tessili Italiani Vallesusa, the bailing-out vehicle, which only five years later and without having made investments of any significance went on to sell the assets of the bailed-out company and liquidate it. Unfortunately, it proved difficult to define with any precision all the economic aspects of the whole operation. When drawing up the list of the bailout operations, recourse was had, among other things, to the historical archives of two leading Italian newspapers: *Il Corriere della Sera* and *Il Sole 24 Ore*.

[40] Actually, during the thirty years from the 1960s to the nineties, the illiquidity or insolvency of companies belonging to the State holdings system were resolved inside the system itself (through periodical increases in capital allocations, externalisation of costs or even loans provided by public banks), which obviously again makes it very difficult to take account of them appropriately.

[41] In this case too, the line of separation is not always so obvious and there are plenty of borderline cases, the UNIDAL story being a memorable one. Between 1974 and 1976 both Motta and Alemagna (historic Milanese confectionery businesses) recorded heavy and escalating losses that induced SME (Società Meridionale Finanziaria, formerly Società Meridionale di Elettricità)—which owned the majority stake in the first case and a holding amounting to 50% of the capital in the second—to merge them together in UNIDAL (Unione Industrie Dolciarie e Alimentari) and launch a far-reaching restructuring plan that envisaged the redundancies of about four thousand workers among other things. Given the resolute stance of the State Holdings Ministry (*Ministero delle Partecipazioni Statali*) against any downsizing of the workforce, being UNIDAL a "company belonging to the State holdings system", SME had no option other than to provide further funding to UNIDAL in order to guarantee its survival, calling for a resolution to wind up the business, writing down its own holding in UNIDAL and eventually approving a capital

cases in which both situations exist side by side—Alitalia being one such case, for example, and ILVA another—it was decided to take account of them explicitly.

The practical consequences of what has just been said are, however, less significant that what might be imagined. In fact, in the case of public bodies explicitly charged with bailout operations (i.e. Gepi or EFIM) account was taken of the scale of the public funding allocated to them (also in the light of the results that emerged on the occasion of the insolvency procedures that the same were heading towards). It was decided not to extend this option to public bodies such as IRI, ENI or ENEL, protagonists, in specific cases, of bailout operations but whose activities certainly could not be attributed to this aspect alone.

Finally, note should be taken of the comments in the text regarding the bailout interventions that came on the heels of the 2020 pandemic. As already pointed out, in far from a few cases, they took forms that make quantification quite problematic even when this is potentially important. Think, for example, of the aforementioned guarantees provided, directly or indirectly, by the State on a now very considerable volume of bank loans or even of the above-mentioned incentives of a fiscal nature included in the bailout operations for credit institutions. Both the former and the latter being burdens which, prudentially, are not recorded in the list that follows and which could counterbalance any proceeds which has not yet materialised as a consequence of the bailout operations in recent years.

That said, between 1861 and 2021 it has been possible to record slightly less than 260 distinct bailout-related events. The essential features of the sample reconstructed in this way are shown in Table C.1, while—as already said—details on the individual events are provided in the Appendix to Rossi (2024).

---

increase as a consequence. The main private shareholder, Bastogi, did not participate in the capital increase and later sold its residual holding to third parties, thereby leading to the definitive entry of SME into the public sphere. Lucio Sicca (1987) described the entire matter in detail, underlining moreover how the private presence—albeit a minority one—had, since 1978, contributed to defending SME "from the pressures coming from the outside (and in particular from the political and trade union worlds) aimed at burdening the public operator with social demands that were not very compatible with the economic criteria of business management" (Sicca, 1987, p. 76). SME was therefore a "public operator" in which, however, the presence of the private holding contributed to preventing behaviour similar to what would then happen after 1978. Despite this, the fact that the bailout was completed with the intervention of IRI in 1982, after years of more heavy losses, suggested that the case be considered as one inside the public sector.

Table C.1 Bailout-related events and costs

	All sectors	Financial sector	Non-financial sectors
No. of events recorded:			
- 1861–2021	257	67	190
- 1861–1918	18	12	6
- 1919–1946	61	43	18
- 1947–1964	22	–	22
- 1965–1991	104	8	96
- 1992–2021	52	4	48
Average no. of events per year:			
- 1861–2021	1.61	0.42	1.19
- 1861–1918	0.32	0.21	0.11
- 1919–1946	2.26	1.59	0.67
- 1947–1964	1.29	0.00	1.29
- 1965–1991	3.15	0.24	2.91
- 1992–2021	2.36	0.18	2.18
Sectoral composition (%):			
- Agriculture	0.5	–	0.6
- Mining industry	13.6	–	16.4
- Building Industry	13.3	–	16.1
- Manufacturing industry	37.5	–	45.3
- Services	35.1	–	42.5
- of which: Financial services	17.3	100.0	–
- Transport services	5.2	–	6.2
Geographical composition (%):			
- Northern and central Italy	30.2	71.6	13.6
- Southern Italy and Islands	5.0	9.5	3.3
- Italy	64.7	18.9	83.1
Stranded costs (ml. € 2020; average per event):			
- 1861–2021	478.3	675.2	408.2
- 1861–1918	142.3	169.2	88.5
- 1919–1946	182.1	253.0	12.6
- 1947–1964	62.3	n.a	65.3
- 1965–1998	684.9	1,590.2	609.5
- 1999–2021	686.9	4,900.1	335.6
Stranded costs (% of GDP; average per year):			
- 1861–2021	0.17	0.29	0.11
- 1861–1918	0.28	0.36	0.13
- 1919–1946	0.18	0.34	0.02
- 1947–1964	0.06	n.a	0.06
- 1965–1998	0.21	0.14	0.24
- 1999–2021	0.09	0.30	0.05

Notes (i) The sectoral composition was calculated with reference to all the sectors involved in the single bailout-related event on a total which consequently exceeds the total number of events; (ii) the geographical composition takes into account the presence of events whose potential audience was (or is) the entire national territory

Sources For bailout-related events, costs and proceeds, Table C.2; for GDP figures, Baffigi (2015, pp. 178–184)

References

Baffigi, A. (2015). *Il PIL per la storia d'Italia. Istruzioni per l'uso.* Marsilio.

Bottiglieri, B. (1984). *La politica economica dell'Italia centrista (1948–1958).* Bollati Boringhieri.

Caracciolo, A. (1992). *La Banca d'Italia tra l'autarchia e la guerra.* Laterza.

Cianci, E. (1977). *Nascita dello Stato imprenditore in Italia.* Mursia.

Confindustria-Cerved. (2022). *Rapporto regionale PMI 2022.* Confindustria.

Einaudi, L. (1933). *La condotta economica e gli effetti sociali della guerra italiana.* Laterza.

Fauri, F. (2007). La strada scabrosa del risanamento economico delle aziende: la missione impossibile del FIM. *Imprese e Storia, 36*(2), 193–217.

Fauri, F. (2010). *Il Piano Marshall e l'Italia.* Il Mulino.

Lo Bello, S. (2021). La CIG: evoluzione storica, caratteristiche e limiti. *Banca d'Italia Quaderni di Economia e Finanza 602.*

Rossi, N. (2024). Italian Bailouts, 1861–2021. *Rivista di Storia Economica/ Italian Review of Economic History 40*(1), 77–102.

Saraceno, P. (1956). Origini, ordinamenti e attività svolta. In Ministero dell'Industria e del Commercio (Ed.), *L'Istituto per la Ricostruzione Industriale* (Vol. III). UTET.

Sicca, L. (1987). *Strategia d'impresa. La formazione di un Gruppo italiano: la SME.* Etas Libri.

Toniolo, G. (1978). Crisi economica e smobilizzo delle banche miste (1930–34). In G. Toniolo (Ed.), *Industria e banca nella grande crisi 1929–34* (pp. 284–352). Etas Libri.

Toniolo, G. (1993). Il profilo economico. In G. Guarino & G. Toniolo (Eds.), *La Banca d'Italia e il sistema bancario, 1919–1936* (pp. 5–101). Laterza.

Appendix D: Public Finances

The Statistical Sources

References to public finance trends (as, in particular, in Chapter 7) required a reconstruction of various public accounts items for the years 1861-2021. The essential elements of this reconstruction are provided below. It can be noted that limiting ourselves to Central Government aggregate (i.e. the institutional units making up the central government plus those non-profit institutions that are controlled and mainly financed by central government) the reconstruction would have been relatively straightforward. Extending the analysis to the General Government aggregate—and therefore to the sum of three distinct sectors: (i) the Central Government, (ii) the Local Governments (Regions, Provinces,

Municipalities, Universities, Chambers of Commerce, and Local Health Authorities), and (iii) the Social Security Funds controlled by the above units—entails tackling quite a few additional difficulties as indicated below. Given the inevitable degree of approximation implicit in the reconstruction of the public finance items for the General Government aggregate (at the very least for the first century of unification), it was deemed appropriate to make reference both to this aggregate and to the Central Government only (or, as we will see, to the State Administrations only).[42] Finally, it should be remembered that between 1884 and 1964 the financial years closed on 30 June. The annual figure in this period was obtained as the simple average of two contiguous ones.

As regards public debt—both when it refers to the Central Government sector or when its takes the General Government aggregate into consideration instead—it is not necessary to do anything more than extend to 2021 the reconstruction made by Francese and Pace (2008, Table 2), regarding the period 1861–2007, having recourse to the information contained in *Finanza pubblica: fabbisogno e debito* (retrieved March 18, 2024, https://www.bancaditalia.it/pubblicazioni/finanza-pubblica/index.html). Not provided in Francese and Pace (2008) is the information relating to the part of the sovereign debt placed abroad, courteously provided separately by Maura Francese and Angelo Pace for the whole period considered.

As regards revenues, if we limit ourselves to the State Administrations (that represent the totality, or almost, of the Central Government, the difference being given, for example, by the National Council of Economy and Labour or CNEL) or by the independent Authorities reference can be made to the reconstruction contained in Ragioneria

---

[42] The problem, obviously, is not a new one. For example, Silvana Bartoletto et al. (2014, pp. 319–320) make explicit reference to the State Administrations. Fabrizio Balassone et al. (2011), on the other hand, seem to consider the State Administrations in the period prior to the Second World War and the General Government aggregate for the period afterwards, in the same way as Carlo Bastasin et al. (2019) seem to do implicitly. The first option obviously ignores the information contained in the trends in the local finance and social security funds. The latter introduces a discontinuity on a scale that is presumably not insignificant. For these reasons, it seemed appropriate to reconstruct distinctly and in a manner as temporally homogeneous possible the two aggregates—the Central Government and the General Government—underlining any differences if and when possible or necessary.

Generale dello Stato (1969: Vol. II, Table 5), for the period 1862–1967, updating it in homogeneous terms having recourse to the *General Statements of the State Administration* (Budget accounts) (retrieved March 18, 2024, https://www.rgs.mef.gov.it/VERSIONE-I/archivio/index.html).[43] If, on the other hand, reference is made to the General Government aggregate, the starting point is given by the information in Istat (2011, Table 12.17) for the period 1980-2009, integrable backwards, for the years 1958–1979, with the information contained in the *Relazione Generale sulla Situazione Economica del Paese* (Treasury Ministry, various years), for the same aggregate, and updatable to 2021 by having recourse to the Istat database (retrieved March 18, 2024, http://dati.istat.it/#). For the years before 1959, without prejudice to what has been said previously regarding the revenues of the Central Government (which we identify, by and large, with the State Administrations), it becomes necessary to integrate the aforesaid reconstructions with the information regarding two specific sectors: Local Governments and the Social Security Funds. As we will see, such integration is possible only in part. Information is actually available in Brosio and Marchese (1986, Tav.7A) regarding the revenues of the local bodies (i.e. special status regions, ordinary regions, provinces and municipalities, thereby excluding the universities, chambers of commerce and the local health authorities), for the years 1866–1980 (with the proviso that the information is limited to tax revenues only). The same source also shows the revenues from contributions to the pension and welfare bodies for the same period. It was therefore decided to approximate the revenues of the General Government aggregate for the period 1862–1957, adding the tax revenue of the local bodies and the social contributions of the pension and welfare bodies deduced by Brosio and Marchese (1986: Table 7A) to the aforesaid figure.[44] In the years in which the figure contained in the *Relazione Generale sulla Situazione Economica del Paese* for the Public Administrations and the reconstruction relating to the years before 1958 are superimposed (1958–1980), an over-estimate close to about 0.3% can be noted (compared to an under-estimate close to 40% that would be

---

[43] The first case refers to taxes "paid up" and the second to "final" receipts. That is the magnitudes of importance for the purposes of calculating net indebtedness (or credits).

[44] The operation required estimation of the values absent from Brosio and Marchese (1986, Table 7A) for the years 1862–1865 starting from the values contained in the table itself.

recorded if in the same years due account were not taken within the limits of the possible of the Local Governments and of the Social Security Funds). Finally, it was decided to ignore the gaps in the series observed in 1980 and in 1995 as they were on a relatively small scale.

In addition to the total revenues, reference is also made in the text to their composition and to the trends of some specific taxes. For this purpose, as far as tax revenues are concerned, use was made of the information provided in Ragioneria Generale dello Stato (1969, Vol. III, Table 12), for the period 1862–1967, updatable in homogeneous terms having recourse to the *General Statements of the State Administration* (Budget accounts; as above).

As far as the expenditure of the State Administrations is concerned, on the other hand, the starting point remains the reconstruction contained in Ragioneria Generale dello Stato (1969, Vol. II, Table 5), updated to 2009 in Ragioneria Generale dello Stato (2011) and further updatable in homogeneous terms having recourse to the *General Statements of the State Administration* (Budget accounts, as above) for the years that followed. The passage to the General Government is possible by maintaining as the starting point—as was already the case for revenues—the information in Istat (2011, Table 12.17) for the period 1980–2009 and in the General Government consolidated accounts along with, for the years 1958–1979, with the information contained in the *Relazione Generale sulla Situazione Economica del Paese* (Treasury Ministry [various years]), and updatable to 2021 by having recourse to the Istat database (as above). For the years before 1959, the data for Central Government expenditures (or, more precisely, for the State Administrations expenditures) referred to above was integrated with those of the Local Governments and Social Security Funds, as well as those on transfers between Public Administrations, in order to avoid manifest duplications. As regards transfers from the State Sector and directed to Local Governments and Social Security Funds the latter can be deduced for the years 1862–1958 from the reconstruction by the Ragioneria Generale dello Stato (1969, Vol. IV, Table 5).[45] As regards the spending of the Local Governments and Social Security Funds, reference was made to the reconstruction of the spending of the Local Governments and Social Security Funds in Brosio

---

[45] And they are updatable—though with some difficulty—by examining the General Statements of the State Administration for the years considered (as above).

and Marchese (1986, Table 1A), net of transfers.[46] It becomes possible in this way to make an approximation of the Public Administrations aggregate accepting an over-estimate in the overlap years, 1958-1980, close to 3% (compared to a discrepancy, on the opposite sign obviously, of more than 50% observed between the spending of the State Administrations and the spending of the General Government). Just as in the case of the revenues, it was decided to ignore the gaps in the series observed in 1980 and in 1995 as they were on a relatively small scale.

In addition to the total spending, reference is also made in the text to their composition and to the trend for some specific items. For this purpose, as regards the State Administrations, use was made of the information provided in Ragioneria Generale dello Stato (1969, Vol. II, Table 5), updated to 2009 as in in Ragioneria Generale dello Stato (2011) and further updatable in homogeneous terms having recourse to the *General Statements of the State Administration* (Budget accounts; as above) for the subsequent years that contain the desired level of detail.

It should be noted that, for the entire 1862–2021 period, though very high, the degree of correlation between the magnitudes referring to the Central Government only and those relating to General Government aggregate is such as to suggest that, within the limits of reliability of the information used, the different information content of the two aggregates does merit separate analysis.

Convergence and Sustainability

The well-known breakdown of the temporal evolution of the public debt/ GDP ratio reads as follows:

$$\Delta b_t = \left[\frac{r_t - g_t}{1 + g_t} \right] b_{t-1} + d_t + e_t \tag{D.1}$$

where b_t is the public debt/GDP ratio at the end of the period t, d_t is the ratio between the primary deficit (non-interest expenditures minus revenues) and GDP in period t, r_t is the interest rate at time t, g_t is the GDP growth rate at time t (and r_t just as g_t both are expressed in real or nominal terms). Finally, e_t indicates a residual term that reflects,

---

[46] In this case too, the operation required estimation of the values absent from Brosio and Marchese (1986, Table 1A) for the years 1862–1865 starting from the values contained in the table itself.

for example, any acquisition or transfer of assets or the impacts of the valuation of the same.

Letting $e_t = 0$, from (Eq. D.1) the convergence condition of the public debt corresponding to the case in which the change over time of the public debt/GDP ratio is null (and therefore $\Delta b_t = 0$) may be derived:

$$\left[\frac{r_t - g_t}{1 + g_t}\right] b_{t-1} = -d_t \qquad (D.2)$$

and, so, for the public debt/GDP ratio to remain unchanged it is necessary, if the interest rate exceeds the growth rate and therefore if the term in brackets is positive), that the primary surplus ($-d_t$, and therefore the excess of revenues over non-interest expenditures) is such as to compensate the growth of the public debt/GDP ratio that otherwise would arise as a result of what we call the snowball effect (when the charges for servicing the debt are not compensated in turn by the expansion of the economy).

Letting (a) the nominal cost for servicing the public debt be approximated with the ratio between the interest expenditure of the Central Government and the corresponding debt stock at the start of the specific period, and (b) the inflation rate be proxied by the rate of growth of the GDP deflator, the quantity:

$$I_t = \left[\frac{r_t - g_t}{1 + g_t}\right] b_{t-1} + d_t \qquad (D.3)$$

turns out, on average (over the 1862–2021 period), to be close to zero both in the case of the State Administrations (+0.8%) and in that of the General Government (−0.6%).

If an exception is made for the years marked by the events of the two world wars, the convergence indicator oscillates around zero to a limited extent: a little above zero, in the decades prior to First World War and during the decades that followed Second World War and a little below zero in the years of the phase leading up to joining the single currency or adopting it, with the obvious exception of the biennium of the pandemic emergency.

Condition (Eq. D.3) tells us little or nothing about the sustainability of specific levels of the public debt/GDP ratio but by underlining the relationship between public debt and the primary surplus or deficit it indicates the path to us for reaching more accurate conclusions. In fact, any level of debt becomes sustainable if the primary deficit response is such as to guarantee stabilisation. If, in fact, we hypothesise for simplicity a response function of the public operator linear in b_{t-1}

$$d_t = \delta_0 + \delta_1 b_{t-1} + u_t \tag{D.4}$$

(with $\delta_1 < 0$ and u_t represents, among other things, the cyclical component of the primary deficit), (Eq. D.1) can be rewritten as follows

$$\Delta b_t = \left[\frac{r_t - g_t}{1 + g_t} + \delta_1 \right] b_{t-1} + \delta_0 + u_t \tag{D.5}$$

and, as long as the term in square brackets (an indicator of sustainability) is negative, the public debt/GDP ratio would converge at a given level (positive or negative, as a function of the value assumed by the intercept) (Bohn, 1998). From this viewpoint, the attention shifts from the level of the public debt/product ratio to the speed of adjustment of the primary surplus or deficit compared to the public debt. This is not to imply that the response to the primary surplus implicit in (Eq. D.4) is always and in any case achievable. The levels of the public debt/GDP ratio could be so high as to render the adjustment implicit in (Eq. D.4) impracticable (politically, e.g.) and the response of the financial markets could contribute to rendering the previous limit more stringent, and for these reasons the condition implicit in (Eq. D.5) has been qualified as a condition of sustainability in the weak sense (Gosh et al., 2013).

Silvana Bartoletto, Bruno Chiarini and Elisabetta Marzano (2014), among others,[47] have provided an estimate of the parameters of an "enriched" version of (Eq. D.4)[48] for the period, 1862–2012, from which

---

[47] Also see Ricciuti (2008), Piergallini and Postigliola (2013), Di Iorio and Fachin (2021). In all the cases mentioned—though in the presence of different analytical methodologies and with reference to different periods—the evidence would seem to confirm the hypothesis of sustainability of the fiscal policy, though with a caveat of some importance. For a broad-ranging review of the literature in question see the work of Cristina Checherita-Westphal and Vaclav Zdarek (2017) from which evidence emerges that is consistent to a considerable extent with the fiscal sustainability hypothesis in the sense described in the text.

[48] Compared to the elementary response function described by (iv) the fiscal rule used by Bartoletto et al. (2014), recalling Barro (1979), permits a gradual adjustment compared to the steady state (represented by (Eq. D.4)) and takes account of extraordinary events (captured by the spending for defence).

they derive—in the case of the Central Government—a relatively positive conclusion regarding the sustainability of the Italian public debt in the one hundred and sixty years since Unification, while some doubt remains in fact as regards the period between the two wars. There would be no reason, therefore, for returning to the subject were it not for the unavoidably arbitrary nature of the temporal breakdown of the sample,[49] on the one hand while, on the other, the availability of information regarding the General Government aggregate (in addition to that of the Central Government) induces us to believe that a supplementary investigation might not be completely futile. The latter point is worth emphasising as today, General Government constitutes the main aggregate of interest from the standpoint of the European fiscal responsibility rules but it is still legitimate to imagine that—even in the light of the Italian institutional make-up—the response in terms of the primary deficit compared to the dynamic of the debt may be attributable to the State Administration rather more than to the Local Governments and Social Security Funds.

The inevitable starting point is an analysis of the properties of the historical time series of the public debt/GDP ratio and of the primary GDP deficit in the two different configurations: Central and General Government (Table D.1). This analysis confirms what has already been observed by Bohn [1998] for the United States and noted for Italy, for example, by Bartoletto et al. (2014) and that is, whatever the institutional sector of reference, the presence of a unit root in the historical series of the public debt/GDP ratio but not in the ratio between the primary surplus or deficit and GDP.

Which implies (Bohn 1998) the need to go beyond the simple fiscal rule described in (Eq. D.4) to take account of further determinants of the budget policy along with the possibility for the parameter δ_1 to be anything but constant over time, the fiscal effort implicit in the parameter

---

[49] The periodisation in Bartoletto et al. (2014) rests on considerations of a historical nature: inside the entire 160-year period, the gold standard years (1862–1913) were followed by the two wars (1914–1945), then by the Bretton Woods years (1945–1971) and finally by the more recent decades (1971–2012). This periodisation is well-known but also not necessarily relevant in the case in question, especially because it is based on the temporal dynamic of the debt/output dynamic, i.e. the dynamic of the actual subject of the analysis. It is interesting to note, in this regard, that the aforesaid periodisation does not correspond with the one apparently contained in the data, as Bartoletto et al. (2014, p. 309) themselves point out.

Table D.1   Unit root test (1862–2021)

	ADF test	McKinnon p-value	Notes
State administrations			
b_t	−1.989	0.607	H_0: random walk with or without drift
Δb_t	−7.876	0.000	H_0: random walk with or without drift
d_t	−3.867	0.014	H_0: random walk with or without drift
Public administrations			
b_t	−1.964	0.621	H_0: random walk with or without drift
Δb_t	−8.016	0.000	H_0: random walk with or without drift
d_t	−3.995	0.009	H_0: random walk with or without drift

δ_1 being, for example, a function of the level of the public debt/GDP ratio.

In particular, in (Eq. D.4) it should be possible to distinguish between the primary surplus or deficit that would arise in the absence of the need (but also desire and possibility) to put in place a "fiscal effort" capable of bringing public debt onto a sustainability path and the "fiscal effort" itself.[50] In (Eq. D.4) the latter element should be enclosed in the term $\delta_1 b_{t-1}$ where the dynamics of the "current" primary surplus or deficit should be summarised in the term u_t (as well as in the constant term). We will suppose, therefore, that the parameter δ_1—that, for a given public debt, measures the intensity of the "fiscal effort" and that, as can be inferred from (Eq. D.5), is crucial for the purposes of sustainability— could vary linearly in time reflecting the evolution of the public debt/ GDP ratio (thereby introducing a significant non-linearity in (Eq. D.4)). In line with the literature on the subject, we will suppose, moreover, that the "current" primary surplus or deficit could reflect the deviations from the public spending trend (g_t, attributable to events other that the war or pandemic ones such as, for example, the financial crises of 1929

---

[50] The two aspects of the phenomenon are not independent, moreover, as long as primary deficits that are the consequence of extraordinary events can render the "fiscal effort" requested in a given situation even more burdensome if not unsustainable.

and of 2008-2011 or also lower-scale war events), the cyclical trends in the economy $(y_t e \Delta y_t)^{51}$ and the evolution of the inflation rate in the previous year $(\pi_{t-1}$, by virtue of the indexing rules for some spending items or on the income side, of the effects of fiscal drag). We will suppose, furthermore, that the events on a global scale—both as regards wars and pandemics—could be captured by a series of specific dummies (regarding the years 1915-1918, 1940-1945 and 2020). We will take account of the presence of a fiscal responsibility rule regarding the overall deficit of the Public Administrations starting from 1992 (i.e. the signature of the Maastricht Treaty) by means of shifting the intercept of (Eq. D.4) and therefore by means of a dummy with value 1 in the period 1992-2021 and zero otherwise (m_t).[52] We will suppose, finally, that the adjustment of the primary deficit could be done gradually, introducing into (Eq. D.4) the delayed dependent variable:

$$d_t = (\delta_{00} + \delta_{01} m_t) + \delta_{1t} \ b_{t-1} + \delta_2 \ g_t + \delta_3 \ y_t$$
$$+ \ \delta_4 \ \Delta y_t + \delta_5 \ \pi_{t-1} \ + \ \delta_6 d_{t-1} \ + \ u_t \qquad (D.6)$$

where

$$\delta_{1t} = \delta_{10} + \delta_{11} b_{t-1} \qquad (D.7)$$

and $u_t \sim N(0, \sigma^2)$, , $\text{cov}(u_{t-s}, u_{t-k}) = 0$ $(t \neq s)$.

The OLS estimate of the parameters of (Eq. D.6) and of (Eq. D.7) is given in Table D.2.Being reasonably possible to argue that the cyclical trend of the economy can in turn be fruit of budget policy decisions,

---

[51] In particular, the transitory component of public spending (g_t) and the cyclical indicator (y_t) were approximated by the ratio of the observed value and the trend component of the specific variable derivable from the application of the Hodrick and Prescott filter. The variation of the cyclical indicator of the economy (Δy_t) also appears in (Eq. D.6) and presumably captures the changing behaviour of specific income and spending items not only in the various cyclical phases but also on the basis of the different intensity of the same.

[52] It could be observed that with the Maastricht Treaty also came the introduction of a target regarding the stock of existing debt (60% of GdP) while the Stability and Growth Pact (1997) was intended to indicate the paths towards approaching that goal. The sparsely binding nature both of the target and of the procedures for achieving it suggested that attention be concentrated on the rule regarding the flow rather than on that regarding the stock.

Table D.2 also lists the corresponding IV estimates.[53] In the light of the exogeneity tests, all the comments that follow will make reference to these last estimates even if the substantial uniformity of the estimates should be emphasised. In the first place, as we would have expected, the European fiscal responsibility rules contributed to reducing the primary deficits or increasing the primary surpluses of the General Government by 1% starting from 1992. As was foreseeable given that the focus of those rules was on the General Government aggregate, the effect is not visible in the case of the Central Government. As expected, the component of the primary deficit not linked to the "fiscal effort" concept is positively affected by the presence of public spending of a transitory nature (linked, for example, to events such as the two financial crises that marked the early decades of the twentieth and twenty-first centuries or to wartime adventures undertaken towards the end of the nineteenth century or between the two wars). Independently from the aggregate of reference, higher inflation rates lead with a year's delay to rising primary deficits reflecting the impact on the spending components more than on the revenues. Both in the case of the Central Government and in that of the General Government, levels of activity higher than the underlying trends means that greater primary deficits are more than compensated by the spending decisions taken in the presence of a positive economic scenario. Moreover, in like for like conditions, accelerating economic activity levels lead to more evident reductions of primary deficits in the case of the General Government aggregate where social security contributions are concentrated (and, conversely, the welfare measures in the case of slowdowns in the economic activity).

Over the long term, the measurement of the fiscal policy response to debt variations ($\delta_{1t}/(1 - \delta_6)$), amounts on average to -0.126 for the Central Government aggregate and to -0.083 for the General Government one.[54] In other words, on completion of the adjustment, a variation

---

[53] It is appropriate to point out the stationary nature of all the regressors present in (Eq. D.6) other than the public debt/GDP ratio. It is also important to point out the presence of a unit root both in the public debt/GDP ratio and in its square (a point on which the attention of Di Iorio and Fachin (2021) is concentrated).

[54] Values compatible with those in Bartoletto et al. (2014, p. 311) whose variability between periods is very high, passing from zero in the years between the two wars to -0.35 in the twenty-five-year period after the Second World War. An excessive interval perhaps: fiscal effort values above -0.10 are not recorded in any of the works in question except in Bohn (1998, p. 952) who records -0.05 in the case of the United States

Table D.2 Estimate of the system parameters (Eq. D.4)–(Eq. D.6) (OLS and IV, 1862–2021)

Dependent variables: d_t	OLS Central government	General government	IV Central government	General government
constant	−0.159 (0.035)	−0.174 (0.030)	−0.194 (0.042)	−0.230 (0.038)
m_t	−0.003 (0.004)	−0.009 (0.003)	−0.002 (0.004)	−0.009 (0.003)
b_{t-1}	−0.073 (0.020)	−0.055 (0.018)	−0.077 (0.020)	−0.062 (0.019)
b_{t-1}^2	0.035 (0.012)	0.028 (0.011)	0.036 (0.012)	0.031 (0.011)
g_t	0.045 (0.011)	0.050 (0.012)	0.048 (0.011)	0.056 (0.013)
y_t	0.143 (0.034)	0.149 (0.030)	0.177 (0.041)	0.203 (0.039)
Δy_t	−0.106 (0.047)	−0.165 (0.042)		
π_{t-1}	0.044 (0.015)	0.048 (0.014)	0.044 (0.015)	0.052 (0.014)
d_{t-1}	0.648 (0.045)	0.625 (0.042)	0.630 (0.044)	0.583 (0.043)
R^2	0.944	0.958	0.941	0.951
DW			1.786	1.626
Breusch-Godfrey (χ^2 (1))	1.588	5.719		
Breusch-Godfrey (χ^2 (2))	2.032	6.630		
Breusch-Pagan (χ^2 (1))	0.550	0.739		
Durbin (χ^2 (1))			4.476	13.706
Wu-Hausman (F(1,139))			4.027	13.112

Notes (i) standard errors in brackets; (ii) the Breusch and Godfrey tests check the hypothesis of the absence of an autocorrelation of the first and second order respectively, (iii) the Breusch and Pagan test checks the hypothesis of a normally distributed error term with zero mean and constant variance; (iv) the Durbin test and the Wu-Hausman test check the hypothesis of the exogeneity of the regressors that are considered to be endogenous; (v) dummy variables refer to the years 1915–1918, 1940–1945 and 2020

in the public debt/GDP ratio of ten percentage points leads to a little over one percentage point reduction of the primary deficit or increase on the primary surplus in the first case and to just less than one percentage point in the second (about a third of which in the first year). However, the scale of the fiscal policy response is not independent from the level of the public debt/GDP ratio: an increase of the latter leads, in fact, to an increase in the "fiscal effort" in the way represented by the parameter δ_{1t}. This is an interesting example of what we usually call fiscal fatigue. The last of these aspects, in turn, means that the "fiscal effort" is variable in the period and not in accordance with periodisation defined more or less arbitrarily.

Figures D.1 and 7.3 show the performance trend, in the 160-years period, of the sustainability indicator (I_t^*) and of its two components: the evolution of the interest rate net of the growth rate and the measure of the fiscal effort (($\delta_{1t}/(1-\delta_6)$)), both in the case of the Central Government and in the case of the General Government

$$I_t^* = \left[\frac{r_t - g_t}{1 + g_t} + \delta_{1t}/(1 - \delta_6) \right] \qquad \text{(D.8)}$$

Some observations can be made immediately. Italy's public finances followed a sustainability path both in the case of the Central Government and in the case of the General Government over the entire 160-year period. The sustainability factor is negative in fact, without exceptions, over the entire timespan considered. Various factors contribute to this result to different extents and in different periods. During the years from the end of the nineteenth century to the end of the twentieth century, the growth rates (frequently of an exclusively nominal character) would have been more than sufficient for guaranteeing the sustainability of the public debt. Their impact is magnified, moreover, during the years immediately after the Second World War by a fiscal policy inspired by fiscal rigour and discipline. Before and after that period, in the presence of interest rates that were positive net of the growth rates, it is the "fiscal effort" that guarantees that the sustainability indicator assumes negative values. In the passage from the Central Government to General Government

(1916–1995); see, for example, Checcherita-Westphal and Zdarek (2017, p. 10) whose estimates do not exceed -0.10 for the period 1970–2013 and with reference to the euro area. It is legitimate to presume that such high values are the consequence of of the periodisation adopted.

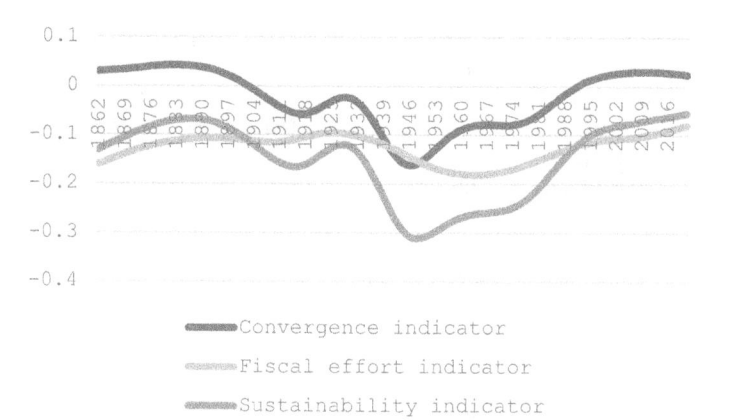

Fig. D.1 Sustainability indicator, interest rate less the growth rate and scale of the fiscal effort over the long term (Central Government, trend components, 1862–2021)

the "fiscal effort" partly fails and, especially at the end of the period, the sustainability indicator perilously approaches zero.

REFERENCES

Balassone, F., Francese, M., & Pace, A. (2011). Public Debt and Economic Growth: Italy's First 150 Years. In G. Toniolo (Ed.), *The Oxford Handbook of the Italian Economy Since Unification* (pp. 516–532). Oxford University Press.

Barro, R. (1979). On the Determination of the Public Debt. *Journal of Political Economy, 87*(5), 940–971.

Bartoletto, S., Chiarini, B., & Marzano, E. (2014). The Sustainability of Fiscal Policy in Italy (1861-2012). *Economia Politica* 31(3), 301–324.

Bastasin, C., Mischitelli, M., & Toniolo, G. (2019). Living with High Public Debt, Italy 1861–2018. *LUISS School of European Political Economy WP 11.* Retrieved March 18, 2024, https://leap.luiss.it/wp-content/uploads/2022/09/WP11.19-Living-with-high-public-debt-Bastasin.Mischitelli.Toniolo-WP.pdf

Bohn, H. (1998). The Behavior of U.S. Public Debt and Deficits. *The Quarterly Journal of Economics, 113*(3), 949–963.

Brosio, G., & Marchese, C. (1986). *Il potere di spendere.* Einaudi.

Checcherita-Westphal, C., & Zdarek, V. (2017). Fiscal Reaction Function and Fiscal Fatigue: Evidence for the Euro Area. *European Central Bank Working Paper Series 2036.*

Confalonieri, A. (1975). *Banca e industria in Italia 1894–1906* (Vol. II). Banca Commerciale Italia.

Di Iorio, F., & Fachin, S. (2021). Fiscal Reaction Functions for the Advanced Economies Revisited. *Empirical Economics, 62*(6), 2865–2891.

Diamond, A. (2006). Schumpeter's Creative Destruction: A Review of the Evidence. *The Journal of Private Enterprise, 22*(1), 120–146.

Francese, M., & Pace, A. (2008). Il debito pubblico italiano dall'Unità a oggi. Una ricostruzione della serie storica. *Banca d'Italia Questioni di Economia e Finanza 31.*

Gosh, A., Kim, J., Mendoza, E., Ostry, J., & Quereshi, M. (2013). Fiscal Fatigue, Fiscal Space and Debt Sustainability in Advanced Economies. *Economic Journal, 123*(566), F4–F30.

Istat. (2011). *L'Italia in 150 anni. Sommario di statistiche storiche 1861–2010.* Istat.

Piergallini, A., & Postigliola, M. (2013). Non-linear Budgetary Policies: Evidence from 150 Years of Italian Public Finance. *Economics Letters, 121*(3), 495–498.

Ragioneria Generale dello Stato. (1969). *Il bilancio dello Stato italiano dal 1862 al 1967.* Ragioneria Generale dello Stato.

Ragioneria Generale dello Stato. (2011). *La spesa dello Stato dall'Unità d'Italia.* Ragioneria Generale dello Stato.

Ricciuti, R. (2008). The Quest for a Fiscal Rule: Italy, 1861–1998. *Cliometrica, 2*(3), 259–274.

INDEX

Printed in the USA
CPSIA information can be obtained
at www.ICGtesting.com
CBHW050834211024
16148CB00007B/477